Franklin County Tennessee

COUNTY COURT MINUTES VOLUME 2

1832–1837

WPA RECORDS

Heritage Books
2025

HERITAGE BOOKS

AN IMPRINT OF HERITAGE BOOKS, INC.

Books, CDs, and more—Worldwide

For our listing of thousands of titles see our website
at
www.HeritageBooks.com

A Facsimile Reprint
Published 2025 by
HERITAGE BOOKS, INC.
Publishing Division
5810 Ruatan Street
Berwyn Heights, MD 20740

Nashville, Tennessee
The Tennessee Historical Records Survey
November 1940

International Standard Book Number
Paperbound: 978-0-7884-8858-0

The Historical Records Survey Program

> Sargent B. Child, Director
> Madison Bratton, State Supervisor

Research and Records Section

> Harvey E. Becknell, Director
> Milton W. Blanton, Regional Supervisor
> T. Marshall Jones, State Supervisor

Division of Professional and Service Projects

> Florence Kerr, Assistant Commissioner
> Blanche M. Ralston, Chief Regional Supervisor
> Betty Hunt Luck, State Director

WORK PROJECTS ADMINISTRATION

> Howard O. Hunter, Acting Commissioner
> Malcolm J. Miller, Regional Director
> Harry S. Berry, State Administrator

May Term 1834

(p-336) At a Court of Please and Quarter Sessions begun and held for
Franklin County in the Town of Winchester on the fourth Monday of May
in the year of our Lord one thousand eight hundred & thirty-four and on
the 26th day of said month and of the Independence of the United States
the 58th.   Present a legal number of the acting Justices of the Peace
for Franklin County.

On motion of John Holder it is ordered by the Court that Adam S.
Caperton, Benjamin Elliott, Peter Sells, Randolph Champion & James M.
Chiles be appointed a Jury of view to view and turn the road that runs
through his land of third class and that they view and turn the same
with the most convience and as little as may be to the prejudice of
individuals and make report to the next term of this Court.

Ordered by the Court that John Dougherty be appointed Overseer of
the same part of the road that Benjamin Powell was formerly Overseer and
that he keep the same in good repair according to law and that he have
the same hands that worked under the former Overseer.   Rescinded.

Ordered by the Court that Samuel Austill be appointed Overseer of
the road from Joseph Willis's to Bradley's Creek on the Shelby road and
that he keep the same in good repair according to law & that he have the
hands that worked under the former Overseer.

Ordered by the Court that John Beard be appointed Overseer of the
road from the Pond Spring road to Bradleys Creek on the Shelby road and
that he keep the same in good repair according to law and that he have
the same hands that worked under the former Overseer.

Ordered by the Court that David Willis be appointed overseer of
the road from Joseph Willis to Sims Kellys it being the road leading
from said Willis' to Haris Bridge and that he keep the same in good
repair according to law and that he have the same hands that worked
under the former Overseer.

(p-337)   Ordered by the Court that William Johnson be appointed Overseer
of the road from David Bells to the county line in room of James Cox and
William Larkin & Davis Bell give a list of hands and that he keep the
same in good repair according to law.

Ordered by the Court that Robert Campbell be appointed Overseer of
the road from Campbells to where it strikes the stage road at Salem and
that he keep the same in good repair according to law and that he have

the same hands that worked under the former Overseer.

Ordered by the Court that John B. Wilkinson be appointed Overseer of the road from Cross's Creek to the mouth of Rush's Creek and that he keep the same in good repair according to law and that Meredith Catchings give a list of hands.

Ordered by the Court that William Francis be appointed overseer of the milk sick fence in Bigams Cove in room and stead of William Thurman Joseph Francis and that he keep the same in good repair according to la w and that he have the same hands that worked under the former Overseer.

Ordered by the Court that Elisha Copeland be appointed Overseer in the room of William Greenlee and that he keep the same in good repair according to law and that he have the same hands that worked under the former Overseer.

Ordered by the Court that Nat Finch be appointed Overseer of the road of Second Class in room and stead of John Upton and that he keep the same in good repair according to law and that he have the same hands that worked under the former Overseer.

A deed of Conveyance from William Cook to Jesse Wagner for four hundred and ninety-seven acres of land lying in the county of Franklin was brought into Open Court and proved by David Prator one of the subscribing witnesses thereto and ordered by the Court to be certified.

(p-338)   Ordered by the Court that Henry Garner be allowed the sum of three dollars for a wolf scalp ~~the wolf under the age of~~ out of the monies of the Treasury of West Tennessee not otherwise appropriated. Isd.

Ordered by the Court that Amos Garner be allowed the sum of three dollars for a wolf scalp out of any monies in the Treasurer of Middle Tennessee not otherwise appropriated. Isd.

~~Ordered by the Court that William Raines be allowed the sum of three dollars forty-three and three fourths cents.~~

Present Samuel Norwood, John Dougherty, James Kelly, William Crownover, David Bell, James Keith, Saml. Bradshaw, William Simmons, Andrew Campbell, M. W. Howell, Richmond P. Harris, Meredith Catchings, John W. Holder, George W. Thompson, Littleton G. Simpson, Andrew Mann, James Howard & William Lasater.

Esquires, It is ordered by the Court that William Raines be allowed the sum of three dollars and forty-three & three-fourths cents for keeping James a slave of James Triggs in jail and that the county Trustee pay the same the ayes & noes having been taken, were unanimous:

Ordered by the Court that Richmond P. Harris Col Stramler & Littleton G. Simpson be appointed to settle with Joseph Smith Guardian & make return to next Court.

Present Samuel Norwood John Dougherty, James Kelly, William

Crownover, David Bell, James Keith, Saml. Bradshaw, William Simmons, Andrew Campbell, Marshall, W. Howell, Richmond P. Harris, Meredith Catchings, John W. Holder, George W. Thompson, Littleton G. Simpson, Andrew Mann, James Howard, & William Lasater, Esquires, Ordered by the Court that James Underwood Woodard be allowed the sum of fifty dollars for her support one year to be appropriated by Reuben Stramler and that the Clerk issue certificates to the County Trustee Quarterly to pay the same.. The ayes & Noes, having been taken were unanimous in favor of the allowance, Isd. Isd.

Ordered by the Court that John Orear be appointed Overseer of the road from where it leaves the stage road to where it intersects the same and that he keep the same in good repair according to law and that he have the same hands that worked under the former Overseer.

(p-339) Present Samuel Norwood, John Dougherty, James Kelley, William Crowinover, David Bell, James Keith, Samuel Bradshaw, William Simmons, Andrew Campbell, Marshall W. Howell, Richmond P. Harris, Meredith Catching, John W. Holder, & George W. Thompson, Ordered by the Court that Tabby Moore wife of John Moore be allowed the sum of fifty dollars for her support for one year and that the same be appropreated by Alaxander R. Patton and the clerk issue certificates to the County Trustee Quarterly for the same, the ayes & noes having been taken the Court were in favor of the allowance. Ayes 12 Noes 2. Isd. 2

Present the foregoing mentioned Justices Ordered by the Court that William Hardcastle be allowed the sum of thirty dollars for his support for one year to be appropriated by George W. Thompson and that the Clerk issue certificates Quarterly to the County Trustee for the same the Ayes & noes having been taken were unanimous in favor of the allowance. Isd 2 Isd. 3. Isd 4.

Present the foregoing Justices. Ordered by the Court that Willie B. Wagner be allowed the sum of twelve dollars & fifty cents for a Record Book also the sum of one dollar for a blank bought for the County Clerk's office and that the County Trustee pay the same the Ayes & noes having been taken were unanimous in favor of the allowance.

This day came on an election for the purpose of electing a constable in the bounds of Captain Sargeants Company and on counting out the votes it was found that Benjamin Franklin was duly and constitutionally elected constable for two years in the bounds of said Company --who entered into bond according to law and was qualified accordingly.

This day came on an election for the purpose of electing a constable in the bounds of Captain Martains Company and on Counting out the votes it was found that Robert S. Sharp was duly & Constitutionally elected constable for the two ensuing years in the bounds of said Company---who entered into bond according to law and was qualified accordingly.

Ordered by the court that David O. Anderson, John Sylor & George Mosely be appointed commissioners of the School Land at the mouth of Beans Creek who entered into bond with William Simmons & George Hudspeth their securities according to law.

(p-340) ~~On petition of Wilson Hudson, David Prator, L. G. Woodward, John Roleman~~

Ordered by the Court that Reuben Stramler, Jesse Waggoner, David Prator, Jacob Waggoner & James Parks be appointed a Jury of view to lay off the road, ~~running by Jesse Wagners~~ to the most convenience of travlers and as little to the prejudice of individuals as may be from Manns ford road to the Fayettesville road running by Jesse Waggoners then running by Jacob Waggoners Mill then to intersect the Fayettesville road at Jonathan Horton Smith Shop and make due return to the next Term of this Court.

Ordered by the Court that next Monday be set apart for the purpose of Transacting County business.

The last will and testament of John Bratton deceased late of Franklin County was this day brought into Open Court and proved by the oaths of Samuel Corn & James J. Harrell subscribing witnesses thereto.

It appearing to the satisfaction of the Court that Jacob Vanzant late of this County died intestate and Polly Vanzant widow & relict of said deceased came into open Court and applied for letters of administration on the estate of said decd. It is therefore ordered by the Court that she have letters accordingly who entered into bond with Richard C. Holder & James Robinson her securities in the sum of forty-two thousand dollars according to law and was qualified accordingly.

On motion it is ordered by the Court that John Staples, George Staples and Richard C. Holder be appointed commissioners to lay off to the widow Vanzant one year support out of the estate of Jacob Vanzant and make due return to the next Term of this Court.

(p-341) The Commissioners appointed to settle with Sasanah Haws Administratrix of the estate of Harrison decd ~~and make due return to the next term of this Court~~ was recd by the Court and ordered to be made a part of the record.

An inventory of the estate of E. L. Beckley decd. was this day returned was this day returned into open Court was received by the Court and ordered to be made a part of the record.

This day James E. Davis came into Open Court and was qualified as deputy Clerk in and for the County of Franklin agreeably to law.

JAMES LEWIS)
  agst)
THOMAS ANDERSON) This day came the Defendant into upen Court and saith he cannot gainsay the plaintiffs action against him and confesses Judgment for the sum of eighty two dollars and fifty cents debt besides costs. It is therefore considered by the Court that the plaintiff recover against the defendant his debt confessed as afresaid and also his costs by him about his suit in this behalf expended and the said defendant in Mercy &.

Ordered by the Court that William Little, Thomas D. White, &
William Little, Thomas D. White & William C. Handly commissioners to settle
Robert Taylor administrator of Joshua Taylor deceased and make their report
to the next Term of this Court.

An Inventory of David Hickerson decd was this returned into Open
Court which was received and ordered to be made a part of the record.

Ordered by the Court that the following persons be appointed
Alexander E. Patton on the head of the river, John Hickerson Stone
Fort, William C. Handly for the lower end of the County Willey W. Harris
on Rock Creek, Elijah D. Robins on the river, James Kelly Crow Creek,
James Robinson Winchester, be appointed School Commissioners to meet
and organize a board of Managers to take charge of the school funds for
Franklin County.

(p-342)   Ordered by the Court that Alexander A. Myers John Byrom &
Laben Jones be appointed common school commissioners for the Rock Creek
tract of school land.

The last will and testament Michael Bowlin decd late of the County
of Franklin was this day produced in Open Court and the execution thereof
proven by the oaths of J. A. Rutherford, Richard Charles & C.B.Sawyer
subscribing witnesses thereto and ordered to be made a part of the record.

The last will and Testament and also the codicle thereof of
Ann Wilkinson decd late of the County of Franklin was this day produced
in Open Court & the will proven by the oaths of Thos. Wright & John
Hickerson the witnesses thereto and the codicle was proven in part by
the oath of Thomas Wright one of the subscribing witnesses thereto in
order to be certified.

This day Joseph Smith executor of the last will & Testament of
Martin Adams this day came into Open Court and entered into Bond with
Robert Smith & Littleton G. Smith Simpson his securities in the sum of
five hundred dollars according to law and was qualified accordingly.

The amount of sales of Joseph Blake decd was this day returned into
Open Court and received by the Court and ordered to be made apart of the
record.

A Power of attorney from Calvin H. Robbards to Alfred E. Hanner was
duly proven in Open Court by the oaths of George Hudspeth and Cornelius
Homan subscribing witness thereto and also a certificate signed by
Barshaba Robbard was duly proven in Open Court by the oaths of George
Hudspeth & Cornelius Homan subscriging witnesses thereto and ordered to
be certified.

A deed of conveyance from Andew Hines & James Erwin attorney in fact
for A.A. Erwin Junior was duly proven in Open Court by the oaths of
William H. Murray, John Hickerson and Thomas Powers (p-343)   subscribing witnesses thereto to be the act and deed of the said Andrew Hyms &
James Erwin Jnr. attorney in fact as aforesaid upon the day that it bears

date and ordered to be registered. Let it be registered.

The return of Anderson L. Goodman Guardian for the heirs of Henry Goodman decd, was this day returned into Open Court and ordered to be recorded.

John Perkins & Thomas Carson and applicant for a pension under an act of congress passed on the 7th day of June 1832 came into Open Court and filed his declaration and made oath to the same in conformity to said act and the Court being satisfied to the truth of said declaration whereupon it is ordered by the Court ~~to be certified~~ to be certified to the war department.

Ordered by the Court that Michael A. Watt, Michael Tipps, Solomon Timbough Joseph Bradin, William Marshall, Wilson Hudson, Lemuel Brandon & John Berger be appointed commissioners to view and lay off a road from Zachariah H. Murrell and that they view and turn the same to the most convience of Travellers and as little as may be to the prejudice of Individuals and make report to the next Term of this Court.

Court adjourned until ~~court in course~~ tomorrow morning 9 o'clock.
                                    James Robinson
                                    James Keith
                                    William Simmons

Tuesday May the twenty seventh one thousand eight hundred and thirty-four Court met according to adjournment.
Present. JAMES ROBINSON   )
          JAMES KEITH &   )   Esquirs Justices of the peace for
          M.W. HOWELL   )   Franklin County.

Proclamation being made the sheriff of Franklin County made return pf the States writ of venire facias to the Court that he had summoned the following persons being all good and lawful men of said County of Franklin to attend and serve as Jurors at the present term of this Court which persons so summoned and returned as aforesaid had been nominated for that purpose by the Justices, (p-344) of this said Court of pleas and quarter sessions of said County of Franklin at its last session a list of whom was delivered to the said Sheriff of Franklin County by the Clerk of this said Court, to wit, Nelson Carter, Willie J. Hines, William Simmons, Dudley Johnson, Daniel Martin Senr. Littleton Faris, Benjamin Decherd. William Buchanan, John Staples, Absalom Faris Senr. Larson Rowe, John Buckern, Dyer Moore, John Frame, James Woods, Micager L. Gallaspie, Edmond P. Lee, William Orear, Mark Hutchins, Isaac Vanzant, Thomas J. Laster, Samuel Norwood, Joseph Holder & William Faris of whom the follow, ing this day attended, to wit. William Simmons, Dudley Johnson, Daniel Martin, Senr. Littleton Faris, Benjamin Decherd, William Buchanan John Staples, Absalom Faris Senr. Benjamin Wear, Larson Rowe, John Buckner, Dyer Moore, James Woods, John Frame, Micager L. ~~Gallaspie Edmond P. Lee~~ William Orear, Mark Hutchins, Isaac Vanzant, Thomas L. Lasater, Samuel Norwood, Joseph Holder & William Faris, out of whom the following persons all being good and lawful men of said County of Franklin were elected empaneled sworn & charged a grand jury of inquest for the body of the

County of Franklin aforesaid, towit, John Buckner, Daniel Martin Sr.
John Staples, James Woods, Joseph Holder, Benjamin Wear, Littleton,Faris,
Absalom Faris Sr. Benjamin Decherd, Mark Hutchins, William Buchanan,
Isaac Vanzant & John Frame out of whom Benjamin Decherd was appointed by
the Court foreman of said Grand Jury of inquest, who after receiving their
charge from Erwin J. Frierson the Attorney General retired to consider of
presentments.

MARK HUTCHINS ADMR &   )
            vs   )   This day came the parties by
ROBINSON & DARDIS   )
their attorney and on motion it is ordered that the plaintiff have leave
to take the deposition of Jesse Duncan at the Counting room of
Hutchins & Pryor in Winchester on 28th day of May 1834 to be read
de bene isse on the trial of this cause.

        This day, the Court appointed Elijah D. Robbins coroner of
Franklin County for the next ensuing two years.

        This day came on an election for Sheriff of Franklin County and
on counting out the votes it was found that Thomas Finch was duly and
constitutionally elected (p-345)   Sheriff in and for the County of
Franklin for the next two ensuing years, who was thereupon qualified
according to law.

        This day Robert H. Oliver & Cornelius Homan appeared in Open Court
and were duly qualified deputy Sheriff for Franklin County.

        This day Stewart Cowan, William H. Murray, John W. Holder,&
Charles Duncan Esquires, appeared in Open Court and tendered their
resignations as Justices of the peace in & for Franklin County which
resignations were received by the Court.

        This day the grand Jury returned into Open Court and returned a bill
of indictment against Madison Goodman & Benjamin Morris for an affray
a true bill. Also a bill of Indictment against John W. Carpenter &
Jordon Morris for an affray a true bill. Also a bill of Indictment
against Thomas Burrows & Wilson Morris for an affray a true bill. Also
a bill of Indictment against John Anderson for an affray a true Bill.
Also a bill of Indictment against Rowland Morris, Madison Goodman,
Wm. B. Willis, Benjamin J. Jaceway for an affray a true bill against all
the defendants except Rowland Morris & Not a true Bill against him.

        Ordered by the Court that William H. Murry & Thomas Wright be appoint-
ed to take the privy examination of Mary Adams and to report to the next
Term of this Court according to the act of assembly passed in the year 1833.

        Ordered by the Court that James Robinson, John Goodwin & Mark
Hutchins be appointed commissioners to settle with James Sharp administrator of the estate of David R. Slater deceased and report to the next Term
of this Court.

        This day Edmond Russell Clerk of the Court of Pleas and Quarter
Sessions of Franklin County tendered his resignation as Clerk aforesaid

in the words & figures following towit, to the worshipful County Court of Franklin County the undersigned resigns his commission as Clerk of Franklin County Court this 27th day of May 1834.

E. Russell, Clerk
of Franklin County Court

which resignation was received by the Court and ordered to be spread upon the record.

(p-346)   This day came on an election for Clerk of the Court of Pleas & Quarter Sessions for Franklin County to fill the vacancy occasioned by the resignation of Edmond Russell late Clerk of said Court (one hour having been given for candidates to come forward and enroll their names) whereupon on counting out the votes it was found that Willie B. Wagner was duly and constitutionally elected clerk of the Court of Pleas and Quarter Sessions and for the County of Franklin who was thereupon qualified according to law.

Ordered by the Court that the following receipts be recorded, towit, Nashville Inn 1st day of May 1834. Received of Thomas Finch Sheriff of Franklin County four hundred and forty four dollars & forty-five cents being the one-half of the State tax in said County for the year 1833 which he is bound to pay to the Treasurer of his district agreeably to the Clerks return for said year 1833. Also has produced the Trustees receipt for the Counties portion for said year.

Thos Crutcher
Treasurer

$444.45
Trustees Alsd.

Recd. Winchester 21st May, 1834 of Thomas Finch Sheriff and Collector of the State & County tax for the year 1833 for Franklin County twelve hundred and fifty-five dollars and fourteen cents being the amount of the county poor & Jurors taxes on property not listed after deducting his commission for collecting as per Clerks returns.

Benjamin Decherd
County Trustee

Received Winchester 28th April 1834 of Thomas Finch Sheriff and collector of the State & County tax for Franklin County for the year one thousand eight hundred and thirty-three four hundred and forty-three dollars & sixty-three cents one-half of the State tax after deducting his commissions on the same.

Benjamin Decherd
County Trustee for
Franklin County.

140.56\frac{1}{4}$
Received of Thomas Finch Sheriff and collector of the public taxes in and for the County of Franklin and State of Tennessee for the year 1833 one hundred & forty dollars fifty-six & a quarter cents it being the full amount of the taxes arising on school land for said year 1833 after deducting eight dollars and ninety-seven cents his commissions on the same May the 16th 1834.

Signed duplicate   James Sharp
                        Bank Agt. for
                        Franklin County.

(p-347)   HIRAM CARSON   )
               vs   )   Whereas there was issued by Stewart Cowan
          ANDREW WEBSTER   )
an acting Justice of the peace for Franklin County on the 21st day of
April 1834 an execution in favor of the plaintiff against the defendant
for the sum of twenty-one dollars & twenty-five cents and costs of suit,
which execution was returned to the present Term of this Court with the
following endorsement thereon, towit, came to hand the same day issued;
no personal property found executed by levy on two hundred acres of land,
being a part of the Calwell bridge old tract being on the North side of
the road leading from Winchester to Senterville on each side of Elk river
joining the land of William G. Given & Benjamin J. Jackaway as the
property of Andrew Webster at the instance of Hiram Carson by James Oliver
cst. April 24th 1824, and on motion of the plaintiff it is ordered by the
Court that said land be condemned to be sold to satisfy the debt aforesaid and that an order of sale issue to the Sheriff of Franklin County
to sell the same according to law.

ROBERSON BAKER to the use of R. H. OLIVER)
        AGAINST   )
ANDREW WEBSTER   )   Whereas
there was issued on the 5th day of April 1834 by Marshall W. Howell an
acting Justice of the peace for Franklin County an execution in favor of
the plaintiff against the defendant for the sum of five dollars and costs
of suit which execution was returned to the present Term of this Court
with the following levy thereon endorsed, towit no personal property
found, executed by levy on two hundred acres of land being a part of the
Calwell Bridge old tract being on the North side of the road leading from
Winchester to Centersville on each side of Elk River ajoining the land
of Wm. G. Guinn and Benj. J. Jackaway as the property of Andrew Webster
at the Inst of Roberson Baker to the use of R. H. Oliver
May 1, 1834   By James Oliver Cst.
And on the motion of the plaintiff it is ordered by the Court that said
land be condemned to be sold to satisfy the debt and costs aforesaid and
that an order of sale issue to the Sheriff of Franklin County to sell
the same according to law.

(p-348)   ROBERT H. OLIVER)
            against   )   Whereas there was issued by Marshall
          ANDREW WEBSTER   )   W. Howell, an acting
Justice of the peace for Franklin County on the 21st day of April 1834
an execution in favor of the plaintiff against the defendant for the sum
of twenty-five dollars and costs of suit which execution was returned
to the present Term of this Court with the following levy thereon endorsed
towit, no personal property found executed by levy on two hundred acres
of land being a part of the Colwell Bridge old tract being on the North
side of the road leading from Winchester to Centerville on each side of
Elk River joining the land of Wm. G. Guinn, Benj. J. Jacaway as the
property of Andrew Webster at the Inst of R. H. Oliver

By James Oliver Cst
April 25th 1834

And on motion of the plaintiff it is ordered by the Court that said land be condemned to be sold to satisfy the debt & costs aforesaid and that an order of sale issue to the Sheriff of Franklin County to sell the same according to law.

ROBT. H. OLIVER)
  against) Whereas there as issued by Marshall W. Howell
ANDREW WEBSTER)

an acting Justice of the peace for Franklin County on the 21st day of May 1834 an execution in favor of the plaintiff against the defendant for the sum of twenty-five dollars & costs of suit which execution was returned to the present Term of this Court with the following levy thereon endorsed, towit, no personal property found executed by levy on two hundred acres of land being a part of the Coldwell Bridge old tract being on the north side of the road leading from Winchester to Centerville on each side of Elk River joining the land of Wm. G. Guinn & Benj. J. Jacaway as the property of Andrew Webster at the Inst of R. H. Oliver
May 21st 1834   By Jas. Oliver Cst.

And on motion of the plaintiff it is ordered by the Court that said land be condemned to be sold to satisfy the debt & costs aforesaid and that an order of sale issue to the Sheriff of Franklin County to sell the same according to law.

ROBERT S. SHARP)
  Against) Whereas there was issued by John Oliver an acting
JEREMIAH SMITH &) Justice of the peace for Franklin County on the
JAMES H. MOSELY)

10th day of April 1834 and execution in favor of the plaintiff against the defendant for the sum of twenty eight dollars and fifty-five cents & costs of suit which execution was returned to the present Term of this Court with the following levy thereon endorsed, towit, no personal property found. I have levied this alias Fi Fa on one tract or (p-349) parcel of land containing three hundred acres as the property of Jeremiah Smith & boundas follows on the South by Cumberland mountain and on the West by the land of James Petty and on the north by the Bridge tract of land and on the east by the lands of James Murphy and Joseph Bradshaw.
April 11th 1834   R. H. Oliver D.S.

And on motion of the plaintiff it is ordered by the Court that said land be condemned to be sold to satisfy the debt & costs afore said and that an order of sale issue to the Sheriff of Franklin County to seel the same according to law.

ZACHARIAH H. MURRELL)   Motion
  against)
ALEXANDER T. MCDOWELL) On motion of the said

plaintiff by his attorney and it appearing to the Court that on the 28th day of August 1833 William Street assignee & C recovered against Zachariah H. Murrell & Micaiah Warren in an action of debt by him prosecuted in the Court a judgment for four hundred & eighty-four dollars & sixty-four cents debt and damages and also the costs of suit eight dollars

and seventy-seven & one-half cents as will more fully appear by the record
of said former suit which Judgement is founded upon the following note,
towit, $446. On the 28th day of December next we promise to pay
Micaiah Warren or order four hundred and sixty-six dollars for value
received witness our hands & seas this 4th day of June 1832

Alexr. T. McDowell (Seal)
Z. H. Murrell (Seal)

And also the following assignments for value received I assign the
within note and quarantee the payment to Wm. Street waiving demand and
notice. - June 4th 1832

Micaiah Warren

Whereupon came a Jury of good and lawful men towit, William Simmons,
Dudley Johnson, Daniel Martin Senr. Littleton Faris, Benjamin Decherd
William Buchanan, John Staples, Absalom Faris Senr. Benjamin Wear,
John Buckner, James Woods, & Micager L. Gillespie who being elected
tried and sworn well and truly to try whether said Murrell executed
said note as the security only of the said Alexander T. McDowell upon
their oaths do say that the said Murrell did execute said note as the
security only of the said Alexander T. McDowell. It further appears to
the Court that said judgment & costs have been satisfied by the said
Zachariah H. Murrell. Whereupon it is considered by the Court that the
plaintiff recover against the defendant five hundred & fifteen dollars &
fifty-nine cents that being the amount of the judgment & costs aforesaid
and interest on the same up to this time and also the costs of this
motion in this behalf expended and the said defendant in Mercy &.

(p-350) This day Erwin J. Frierson Esq. the Attorney General called
upon the Clerk of this Court for his execution Docket for the purpose
of making motions against the Sheriff in conformity with the act of
assembly passed the 16th day of November 1833 entitled an act better to
provide for the collection of the State & County revenue, whereupon it
is ordered by the Court, with the assent of the Atto Genl. that said
motions be continued until tomorrow.

A Deed of Trust from Benjamin J. Jacaway to Elisha Copeland for the
land and personal property therein named was duly acknowledged in Open
Court by Elisha Copeland the Trustee therein named to be his act and
deed. Whereupon it is ordered by the Court to be certified.

A Deed of conveyance from James Standley by his attorney R. E.
Standley to Benjamin J. Jacaway for one hundred and sixty-two acres of
land lying in Franklin was duly proven in Open Court by the oaths of
James Wilkinson & William Wilkinson subscribing witnesses thereto to be
the act and deed of the said E. R. Standley Attorney as aforesaid on the
day it bears date whereupon it is ordered to be certified for registration
Let it be registered.

A plat and certificate of survey from John Upton to William Faris
for two hundred and fifty acres of land was duly acknowledged in Open
Court by the said John Upton to be his act and deed whereupon it is ordered to be certified.

Court adjourned until tomorrow morning.

nine o'clock.

James Robinson, M. W. Howell
James Keith

Wednesday May the twenty-eighth one thousand eight hundred and thirty-four. Court met according to adjournment.

Present - James Robinson   )
         M. W. Howell   )   Esquires
         James Keith   )   Justices of the peace for Franklin County.

JAMES GILLASPIE)   Plaintiff
     Vs   )
WM. M. FINCH   )   Defendant

On motion of the parties by their attorneys it is ordered by the Court that this suit be dismissed and each party assumes one-half the cost. It is therefore considered by the (p-351) Court that the plaintiff recover against the defendant his part of the costs about said suit in t'is behalf expended. And it is also considered by the Court that the defendant recover against the Plaintiff his part of the costs by him about said suit in this behalf expended and the said parties in mercy &.

DENIS B. MUSE &   )
KINDRED H. MUSE   )
     Vs   )   On motion of the plaintiffs by their attorneys
TURNER B. HENDLEY)   it is ordered by the Court that this suit be
dismissed and the plaintiffs assumes the costs. It is therefore considered by the Court that the defendant recover against the Plaintiffs his costs by him about his defence in this behalf expended and the said plaintiffs a mersed &.

MILTON MCQUEAN ASHE & C   )   Plaintiff   )
     Vs   )   )
CHAS. J. GILLASPIE, FANNIE)   )   Debt
GALLASPIE, R. C. HOLDER   )   Defendants   )
BENJAMIN POWELL & THOS. S. LOGAN)   )

This day came the parties by their attorneys and thereupon came a Jury, to wit, DudleyJohnson, Thomas J. Laciter, Micigah L. Gillaspie, Lawson Rowe, William Orear, Samuel Norwood, William Simmons, William Faris Dyer Moore, Abraham Kirkendall, John D. Stovall & John Armstrong who being elected tried and sworn the truth to speak upon the issue joined, upon their oaths do say, they find the issue in favor of the plaintiff and assess his damage to four dollars and fifty-five cents besides costs. It is therefore considered by the Court that the plaintiff recover against the defendants, one hundred and ninety five dollars the debt in the declaration mentioned together with his damages aforesaid in form aforesaid assessed and also his costs by him about his suit in this behalf expended and the said defendant in mercy &.

SAMUEL HOPPER ASSEE & C)
     Vs   )
DAVID C. HUTCHINSON &   )
WILLIAM H. MURRAY   )   On motion of the defendants by their attorney

it is ordered by the Court that this cause be continued until the next term of this Court as on their affidavit.

A transfer of a plat and certificate of survey from John Upton to William Faris for his interest in two hundred and fifty acres of land in Franklin County was duly acknowledged in Open Court by the said John Upton to be his act and deed. Whereupon it is ordered by the Court to be certified.

A deed of conveyance from John Goodwin to Robert Dougan, Robert Z. Hawkins, Wiley Denson, Charles Faris, William Stuart & John D. Terrel trustees of the Methodist Episcopal Church for a lot of land adjoining the town of Winchester was duly acknowledged in Open Court by the said John Goodwin to be his act and deed. Whereupon it is ordered by the Court to be certified for registration. Let it be registered.

A deed of conveyance from John Simmons to John R. Patrick for one lot of land in Salem Franklin County Tennessee was duly proven in Open Court by the oath of George Simmonds one of the subscribing witnesses thereto to be the act and deed of the said John Simmonds upon the day it bears date and it was also proven by him that he saw Reuben Simmonds sign the same as a witness who is now dead. Whereupon it is ordered by the Court to be certified for registration. Let it be registered.

This day Thomas Finch who was heretofore on yesterday elected Sheriff of Franklin County came into Court and entered into bond with James Sharp, William Orear Senr, James Robinson & Hopkins L Turney his securities according to law.

This day Willie B. Wagner who was heretofore on yesterday elected Clerk of Franklin County Court came into Court and entered into bond with Solomon Wagner, Dyer Moore & Portland J. Curle his securities according to law.

On petition of Ralph Crabb for leave to keep an ordinary at his house in Franklin County. It is therefore ordered by the Court that he have license for the Term of one year who entered into bond with Stephen Adams his Security according to law and was qualified accordingly.

A Power of Attorney from Calvin H. Roberts to Alfred E. Hanner and also a certificate of Barshaba Roberts was duly proven in Open Court by the oaths of George Hudspeth & Cornelius Homan subscribing witnesses thereto to be the act and deed of the said Calvin H. Roberts and Barshaba Roberts. Whereupon it is ordered to be certified.

(p-352)   JOHN M. BENNETT assu & c   )   Debt
                    against   ) This day came the parties
          MICAH TAUL, MATHEW L. DIXON   ) by their attorneys and
          PORTLAND J. CURLE & JOHN J. HAYTER) thereupon came a Jury,
towit, Dudley Johnson, Thomas J. Lasater, Micagah L. Gillaspie, Larson Rowe, William Orear, Samuel Norwood, William Simmons, William Faris, Dyer Moore, Abraham Keykendall, John D. Stovall & John Armstrong who being elected tried and sworn the truth to speak upon the issue joined

upon their oaths do say they find the issue in favor of the plaintiff and assess his damages to thirteen dollars & ninety three cents besides costs. It is therefore considered by the Court that the plaintiff recover against the defendent one hundred and thirteen dollars the debt in the Declaration mentioned together with his damages aforesaid in form aforesaid assessed and also his costs by him about said suit in this behalf expended and the said defendants in Mercy &.

THOMAS M. PRYOR & CO.)   Debt·
 against   )
HAYDEN ARNOLD   ) This day came the parties by their attornies and thereupon came a Jury, towit, Dudley Johnson, Thomas J. Lasater, Micajah L. Gillaspie, Larson Rowe, William Orear, Samuel Norwood, William Simmons, William Faris, Dyer Moore, Abraham Key Kendall, John D. Stovall & John Armstrong, who being elected tried and sworn the truth to speak upon the issue joined upon their oaths do say they find the issue in favor of the plaintiff and assess their damages to nine hundred and sixteen dollars besides costs. It is therefore considered by the Court that the plaintiffs recover against the defendant his damages aforesaid in form aforesaid assessed and also their costs by them about said suit in this behalf expended and the said defendant in Mercy &.

JOHN R. PATRICK & CO.) On motion of the defendants by their
 Against   ) attorney this cause is continued until
JAMES ARMSTRONG   ) the next Term of this Court as on their
CHARLES J. GILLASPIE &) affidavit.
JONATHAN SPYKER   )

HUDSON ALLEN   )
 vs   )
JAMES RUSSEY   ) On motion of the defendant by his attorney this cause is continued until the next term of this Court on his affidavit and a commission is awarded him to take the deposition of Elijah Campbell before any one Justice of the peace for Madison County Alabama to be read in evidence on the trial of the above cause by his giving the plaintiff 10 days notice of the time & place of taking said deposition.

(p-353) JOSEPH HINKLE)
    against   )
    KINDRED. H. MUSE) On motion of the defendant by his attorney this cause is continued until the next Term of this Court on his affidavit by his paying the costs. It is therefore considered by the Court that the plaintiff recover against the defendant his costs by him about said suit in this behalf expended and the said defendant in Mercy &. And on motion of the parties by their attorneys a general order is awarded them to take depositions to be read in evidence on the trial of the above cause by the adverse party giving the other term days notice of the time and place of taking said depositions.

JOHN W. PEARSON   )   Case
   against   )
CORNELIUS HOWAN   ) This day came the parties by their attornies and
thereupon came a Jury, towit, Dudley Johnson, Thomas J. Lasater,
Micajah L. Gillsspie, Larson Rowe, Samuel Norwood, William Faris,
Abraham Keykendall, John D. Stovall John Armstrong, Henry Emerson,
Andrew Webster, & Samuel Davis who being elected tried and sworn the
truth to speak upon the issue joined who after retiring to consult of
their verdict afterwards returned into open Court and declared they could
not agree and by the consent of the parties and with the assent of the
court Dudley Johnson, one of the Jurors aforesiad is withdrawn and the
rest of the Jury from rendering their verdict are discharged and cause
continued for a new trial to be had thereon at the next erm of this Court.

From information and it appearing to the satisfaction of the Court
that Edmond Russell of Franklin County is insane. It is therefore ordered
by the Court that a writ issued directed to the Sheriff of said County
to summon a Jury of twelve free holders to ascertain by inquisition
the alledged lunacy aforesaid and also such lands and chattels as the
said Edmond Russell shall hold or possess and to make return of their
proceedings to the next Term of this Court.

R. R. PRICE &   )   Attachment
JOHN CAIN   )
    vs   ) This day came the plaintiffs by their attorney and
RUTHY WHITNEY
dismissed their suit and not further prosecuting it is ordered that this
suit be dismissed and the plaintiffs assume the costs. It is therefore
considered by the Courr that the defendant go hence without day & recover
against the plaintiffs her costs by her about her defence in this behalf
expended and the said plaintiffs in Mercy &.

(p-354)
    This day the Trustees of Carmick, Academy came into Court and
executed their bond to the Chairman of Franklin County Court according
to the provisions of the act of assembly entitled an act to make distribution of the academy funds amongst the academies of this State passed
5th of January 1830 which bond was received and approved of by the Court.

Court adjourned until tomorrow morning nine o'clock.
                      James Robinson
                      M.W. Howell
                      James Keith

Thursday May 29th one thousand eight hundred and thirty four, Court
met according to adjournment.
Present - James Robinson   )
        James Keith &   )   Esquires Justices of the peace for
        M.W. Howell   )   Franklin County.

THE STATE OF TENNESSEE)   Indictment for an affray
    against   )
JOHN G. BOSTICK   )   This day came the attorney General who

prosecutes for the State on this behalf as well as the defendant in his proper person and the said defendant having heard said Indictment read says he is therefore not quilty & puts himself upon the Country and the attorney General doth the like and thereupon came a Jury, towit, Dudley Johnson, Thomas J. Lasater, Larson Rowe, Samuel Norwood, William Simmons William Faris Stephen Elliott, Henry Emerson, William Emerson, Daniel Martin Senr. Littleton Faris & Isaac Vanzant who being elected, tried and sworn the truth of and upon the premises to speak upon their oaths do say they find the defendant not quilty in manner & form as shared in the bill of Indictment. It is therefore considered by the Court that the defendant go hence without day.

THE STATE OF TENNESSEE   )   Indictment for gaming
   against   )
JAMES RUSSELL   )   This day came the Attorney General who prosecutes for the State on this behalf as well as the defendant in his proper person and the said defendant having heard said Indictment read says he is thereof not quilty and puts himself upon the country and the attorney General doth the like and thereupon came a Jury, towit, William Orear, John Staples, Joseph Holder, Benhamin Wear, Absalem Faris John Frame, John Buckner, John H. Lee, Micajah L. Gillaspie, Elijah D. Hammons, James Gillaspie & Henry Runnels (p-355) who being elected tried & sworn the truth of and upon the premises to speak upon their oaths do say they find the defendant quilty in manner & form as charged in the bill of Indictment. It is therefore considered by the Court that the defendant for such his offence be find the sum of five dollars and pay the costs of this prosecution and remain in custody of the Sheriff till paid or Security given for the same whereupon John Russell came into Court and acknowledged himself security for the fine and costs in this case & that a Fi Fa issue against him for the same.

A deed of conveyance from Richard Sharp to James H. Estill for twenty acres of land lying in Franklin County was duly acknowledged in open Court by the said Richard Sharp to be his act and deed Whereupon it is ordered by the Court to be certified for registration. Let it be registered.

THE STATE OF TENNESSEE   )
   Against   )   Indictment for an Assult & Battery.
PORTLAND J. CURLE &   )
CLAIBORN HERBERT   ) This day came the Attorney General who prosecutes for the State on this behalf as well as the defendants in their proper person and the said defendants having heard said indictment read say they are thereof not guilty and put themselves upon the Country and the attorney General Doth the like and thereupon came a Jury, towit, Dudley Johnson, Samuel Norwood, Larson Rowe, William Simmons, Solomon Hogue John Herndon Bailey Ragan, William Emerson, William M. Finch, Abraham Keykendall, Alexander Emnes & Henry C. Garner, who being elected, tried and sworn the truth of an upon the premises to speak upon their oaths do say they find the defendants guilty of the first & second Count as charged in the bill of Indictment.

William B. Thompson a witness for the State against John Hughes, William McCoy & Charles Woods for unlawful gaming at the house of

Henry Runnels in Winchester sworn & sent before the grand Jury.

William B. Thompson a witness for the State of Tennessee against John Hughs and others for unlawful gaming at the hous of Henry Runnel in Winchester sworn and sent before the grand Jury.

Court adjourned until tomorrow morning nine o'clock.

James Robinson
M. W. Howell,
James Keith

(p-356)   Friday May the thirtieth one thousand eight hundred and thirty four Court met according to adjournment.
Present   James Robinson   )   Esquires
          M. W. Howell   )   Justices of the peace for Franklin County.
          James Keith   )

THOMAS N. HOLT   )   Debt
   Against   )
JOHN FARIS   )   This day came the parties by their attorneys and thereupon came a Jury, towit, Dudley Johnson, Thomas J. Lasater, Larson Rowe, Samuel Norwood, William Faris, Dyer Moore, William Orear, Senr. Micajah L. Gillaspie, William Simmons, Andrew Webster, George Miller, & James Gillaspie who being elected tried & sworn the truth to speak upon the issue joined upon their oaths do say they find the issue in favor of the plaintiff and assess his damages to one dollar and seventy-four cents besides costs. It is therefore considered by the Court that the plaintiff recover against the defendant sixty-nine dollars & sixty-five cents the balance of the debt in the declaration mentioned together with his damages afpresaid in form aforesaid assessed and also his costs by him about his suit in this behalf expended and the said Dependant in Mercy &.

JOHN TURNER   )   Debt
   against   )
HENRY RUNNELS   )   This day came the parties by their attorneys and therefore came a Jury, towit, Dudley Johnson, Thomas J. Lasater, Larson Rowe, Samuel Norwood, William Faris, Dyer Moore, William Orear Senr. Micajah L. Gillaspie, William Simmons, Andrew Webster, George Miller & James Gillaspie who being elected tried and sworn the truth to speak upon the issue joined upon their oaths do say they find the issue in favor of the plaintiff and assess his damage to four dollars & sixty-two cents besides costs. It is therefore considered by the Court that the plaintiff recover against the defendant fifty-five dollars the debt in the declaration mentioned together with his damages aforesaid in form aforesaid assessed and also his costs by him about said suit in this behalf expended and the said defendant in Mercy &.

THOMAS M. PRYOR & CO.   )   Debt
      Against   )
GEORGE W. RICHARDSON   )
HAYDEN ARNOLD & JAMES L BRYANT)   This day came the parties by their attorneys and thereupon came a Jury, towit, Dudley Johnson, Thomas Lasater,

Larson Rowe, Samuel Norwood, William Faris, Dyer, Moore, William Orear, Senr., Micajah L. Gillaspie, William Simmons, Andrew Webster, George Miller & James Gillaspie who being elected tried and sworn the truth to speak upon their oaths do say they find the issue in favor of the plaintiffs andassess their damages to twenty-two dollars (p-357) and fifty cents besides costs. It is therefore considered by the Court that the plaintiff recover against the Defendants nine hundred dollars the debt in the Declaration mentioned together with his damages aforesaid in form aforesaid assessed and also his costs by him about said suit in this behalf expended and the said defendant in Mercy &.

JONATHAN SPYKER, assu & C   )   Debt
      Against   )
ALEXR. L. BAKER   )
I. H. ARNOLD & ROBERT S. SHARP) This day came the parties by their attorneys and thereupon came a Jury, towit, Dudley Johnson, Thomas J. Lasater, Larson Rowe, Samuel Norwood, William Faris, Dyer Moore, William Orear, Senr. Micajah L. Gillaspie, William Simmons, Andrew Webster, George Miller & James Gillaspie who being elected, tried and sworn the truth to speak upon the issue joined upon their oaths do say they find the issue in favor of the plaintiff and assess his damages to three dollars thirty seven & one half cents besides costs. It is therefore considered by the Court that the plaintiff recover against the defendant one hundred and thirty five dollars the debt in the Declaration mentioned together with his damages aforesaid in form aforesaid assessed and also his costs by him about said suit in this behalf expended and the said defendant in Mercy &.

JOHN J. HAYTER assu & C   )   Debt
      Against   )
HAYDEN ARNOLD   )
JOSEPH DUNCAN &   )
PORTLAND J. CURLE   ) This day came the parties by their attorneys and thereupon came a Jury, towit, Dudley Johnson, Thomas J. Lasater, Larson, Rowe, Samuel Norwood, William Faris, Dyer Moore, William Orear Senr. Micajah L. Gillaspie, William Simmons, Andrew Webster, George Miller & James Gillaspie who being elected tried and sworn the truth to spead upon the issue joined upon their oaths do say they find the issue in favor of the plaintiff and assess his damages to four dollars & twenty five cents besides costs. It is therefore considered by the Court that the plaintiff recover against the defendants one hundred and twenty six dollars the debt in the Declaration mentioned together with his damages aforesaid in form aforesaid assessed and also his costs by him about said suit in this behalf expended and the said defendant in Mercy &.

SAMUEL WIGGIN   )   Debt
      Against   )
JOHN P. WIGGIN   ) This day came the parties by their attorneys and thereupon came a Jury, towit, Dudley Johnson, Thomas J. Lasater, Larson Rowe, Samuel Norwood, Wm. Faris, Dyer Moore, William Orear, Senr. Micajah L. Gillaspie, William Simmons, Andrew Webster, George Miller & James Gillaspie (p-358) who being elected ried and sworn the truth the truth to speak upon the issue joined upon their oaths do say they find the issue in favor of the plaintiff and assess his damages to nine hundred

hundred and seventy-five dollars & thirty-four cents besides costs. It
is therefore considered by the Court that the plaintiff recover against
the defendant eleven hundred forty-three dollars the debt in the declaration mentioned together with his damages aforesaid in form aforesaid
assessed and also his costs by him about said suit in this behalf expended
and the said defendant in Mercy &.

RICHARD B. MOORE   )   Covenant
  Against   )
KINDRED B. MUSE &   )
EDWIN EANS   )   This day came the parties by their attorneys
and thereupon came a Jury, towit, Dudley Johnson, Thomas J. Lasater,
Larson Rowe, Samuel Norwood, William Faris, Dyer, Moore, William Orear
Senr. Miojah L Gillaspie, William Simmons, Andrew Webster, George Miller
& James Gillaspie who being elected tried and sworn the truth to speak
upon to speak upon the issue joined upon their oaths do say they find
the issue in favor of the plaintiff and assess his damages to one hundred
and thirteen dollars & twelve cents besides costs. It is therefore considered by the Court that the plaintiff recover against the defendant
his damages aforesaid in form aforesaid assessed and also his costs by
him about said suit in this behalf expended and the said defendant in
Mercy &.

JOHNSON & RAYBURN   )   Debt
  Against   )
UBERTO DESAIX EZELL   )   This day came the parties by their attorneys
and thereupon came a Jury, towit, Dudley Johnson, Thomas J. Lasater
Larson Rowe, Samuel Norwood, William Faris, Dyer Moore, William Orear,Senr.
Micajah L. Gillaspie, William Simmons, Andrew Webster, George Miller,
& James Gillaspie who being elected tried and sworn the truth to speak
upon the issue joined upon their oaths do say they find the issue in
favor of the plaintiffs and assess their damages to ten dollars and
thirty-one cents besides costs. It is therefore considered by the Court
that the plaintiffs recover against the defendant one hundred and seventy-
six dollars and three cents the debt in the declaration mentioned together
with his damages aforesaid in form aforesaid assessed and also their costs
by them about said suit in this behalf expended and the said defendant
in Mercy &.

JAMES LEWIS   )
  Against   )
THOMAS ANDERSON   )   On motion of the defendant by his attorney
     It is ordered by the Court that this execution be stayed in this
case according to the agreement filed in the papers of said suit.

(p-359)   EDWARD & CHARLES TRABUE   )   Debt
             Against   )
           WILLIAM P. CAMPBELL   )
           GEORGE W. RICHARDSON   )
           HAYDEN ARNOLD & JAMES H. ARNOLD)   This day came the parties
of their attornies and thereupon came a Jury, towit, Dudley Johnson,
Thomas J. Lasater, Larson Rowe, Samuel Norwood, William Faris, Dyer Moore
William Orear, Senr. Micajah L. Gillaspie, Wm. Simmons, Andrew Webster

George Miller & James Gillaspie who being elected tried and sworn the truth to speak upon the issue joined upon their oaths do say they find the issue in favor of the plaintiffs and assess their damages to fifty-eight dollars and ninety-seven cents besides costs. It is therefore considered by the court that the plaintiffs recover against the defendants eight hundred and thirty-two dollars and eighty-six cents the debt in the Declaration mentioned together with their damages aforesaid in form aforesaid assessed and also their costs by them about said suit in this behalf expended and the said defendants in Mercy &.

EDWARD & CHARLES TRABUE)   Debt
 Against)
HAYDEN ARNOLD JAMES H. ARNOLD)
& A. F. WILLIS)   This day came the parties by their attorneys and thereupon came a Jury, towit, Dudley Johnson, Thomas J. Lasater, Larson Rowe, Samuel Norwood, William Faris, Dyer Moore, William Orear, Senr. Micajah L. Gillaspie, William Simmons, Andrew Webster, George Miller & James Gillaspie who being elected tried and sworn the truth to speak upon the issue joined upon their oaths do say they find the issue in favor of the plaintiffs and assess their damages to twenty seven dollars besides costs. It is therefore considered by the Court that the plaintiffs recover against the defendants nine-hundred and seventeen dollars and thirty four cents the debt in the declaration mentioned together with their damages aforesaid in form aforesaid assessed and also their costs by them about said suit in this behalf expended and the said defendant in Mercy &.

JOSEPH MILLER assu & C.)
 Against)
GEORGE W. RICHARDSON)
HAYDEN ARNOLD &)
WILLIAM OREAR JR.) This day came the parties by their attorneys and thereupon came a Jury, towit, Dudley Johnson, Thomas J. Lasater, Larson Rowe, Samuel Norwood, William Faris, Dyer Moore, William Orear Senr. Micajah L. Gillaspie, William Simmons, Andrew Webster, George Miller & James Gillaspie who being elected tried and sworn the truth to speak upon the issue joined upon their oaths do say they find the issue in favor of the plaintiff and assess his damages to seven dollars and eighty-three cents besides (p-360) costs. It is therefore considered by the Court that the plaintiff recover against the defendant one hundred and twenty dollars and fifty cents the debt in the declaration mentioned together with his damages aforesaid in form aforesaid assessed and also his costs by him about said suit in this behalf expended and the said defendant in Mercy &.

WILLIAM STREET assignee & C)   Debt
 to the use of Joseph Miller)
  against)
GEO. W. RICHARDSON, HAYDEN ARNOLD,)
ROBERT. S. SHARP & WILLIAM REEVES) This day came the parties by their attorneys and thereupon came a Jury, towit, Dudley Johnson, Thomas J. Lasater, Larson Rowe, Samuel Norwood, William Faris, Dyer Moore, William Orear, Senr., Micajah L. Gillaspie William Simmons, Andrew Webster,

George Miller & James Gillaspie who being elected tried and sworn the truth to speak upon the issue joined upon their oaths do say they find the issue in favor of the plaintiff and assess his damages to three dollars & seventy-seven cents, besides costs. It is therefore considered by the Court that the plaintiff recover against the defendant one hundred and fifty dollars the debt in the declaration mentioned together with his damages aforesaid in form aforesaid assessed and also his costs by him about said suit in this behalf expended and the said defendant in Mercy &.

WILLIAM STREET assu & C)   Debt
  to the use of JOSEPH MILLER)
    against)
WILLIAM B. WILLIS & HAYDEN ARNOLD) This day came the parties by their attorneys and thereupon came a Jury, towit, Dudley Johnson, Thomas J. Lasater, Larson Rowe, Samuel Norwood, William Faris, Dyer Moore William Orear, Senr. Micajah L. Gillaspie, William Simmons, Andrew Webster, George Miller & James Gillaspie who being elected, tried and sworn the truth to speak upon the issue joined upon their oaths do say they find the issue in favor of the plaintiff and assess his damage to two dollars & seventy cents besides costs. It is therefore considered by the Court that the plaintiff recover against the defendant one hundred and sixty dollars the debt in the declaration mentioned together with his damages aforesaid in form aforesaid assessed and also his costs by him about said suit in this behalf expended and the said defendant in Mercy &.

JAMES BRIGHT ADMR & C)   Debt
  Against)
HAYDON ARNOLD &)
GEO. W. RICHARDSON) This day came the parties by their attorneys and thereupon came a Jury, towit, Dudley Johnson, Thomas J. Lasater Samuel Norwood, William Faris, Dyer Moore, William Orear Senr. Micajah L. Gillaspie, William Simmons, Andrew Webster, George Miller & James Gillaspie (p-361) who being elected tried and sworn the truth to speak upon the issue joined upon their oaths do say they find the issue in favor of the plaintiff and assess his damages to four dollars & forty three cents besides costs it is the therefore considered by the Court that the plaintiff recover against the defendant one hundred and thirty one dollars the debt in the declaration mentioned together with his damages aforesaid in form aforesaid assessed and also his costs by him about said suit in this behalf expended and the said defendant in Mercy&.

JAMES BURROWS to the)   Debt.
  use of JOHN WINTON)
    against)
THOMAS KING senr.) This day came the parties by their attornies and thereupon came a Jury, towit, Dudley Johnson, Thomas J. Lasater, Larson Rowe, Samuel Norwood, William Faris, Dyer Moore, William Orear, Senr. Micajah L. Gillaspie, William Simmons, Andrew Webster, George Miller & James Gillaspie who being elected tried and sworn the truth to speak upon the issue joined upon their oaths do say they find the issue in favor of the plaintiff and assess his damages to three dollars & sixty cents besides costs. It is therefore considered by the Court that the plaintiff

recover against the defendant one hundred and fifty dollars the balance
of the debt in the Declaration mentioned together with his damages
aforesaid in form aforesaid assessed and also his costs by him about
said suit in this behalf expended and the said defendant in Mercy &.

LARKIN & LIPSCOMB   )   Debt
  Against   )
HARDMAN PURYEAR   ) This day came the plaintiffs by their attorney
& having filed their Declaration and the defendant being solemnly called
came not but made default. It is therefore considered by the Court that
the plaintiffs recover against the Defendant one hundred and eight dollars
& fifty six cents the debt in the Declaration mentioned together with the
further sum of twenty two dollars and three cents interest thereon at the
rate of six per cent per annum and also their costs by them about said
suit in this behalf expended and the said defendant in Mercy &.

LARKIN & LIPSCOMB   )   Debt
  against   )
HARDMAN PURYEAR   ) This day came the plaintiffs by their attorney
& having filed their Declaration and the defendant being solemnly called
came not but made default. It is therefore considered by the Court that
the plaintiffs recover against the Defendant seventy-five dollars and
fifty-nine cents the debt in the Declaration mentioned together with
the further sum of ten dollars and fifty cents interest thereon at the
rate of six per cent per annum and also their costs by them about said
suit in this behalf expended and the said defendant in Mercy &.

(p-362)   HENRY C GARNER & wife   )
    against   )
    MARY WILLIAMS & others   ) On motion of the parties by their
attorneys this cause is continued until the next term of this Court
by consent.

This day the Grand Jury came into Open Court and returned a ~~bill~~
of ~~indictment~~ presentment against William McCoy & John Hughes for gaming
also a presentment against Merrell Embry for gaming, also a presentment
Gainum Scroggins for gaming, also a presentment against Charles Wood for
gaming.

This day Benjamin Decherd County Trustee made his report to the
Court of all monies which have come into his hands since the last
settlement and likewise the amount paid out by him for the use of said
County and on what account it was paid out and was qualified thereto
according to law which report was received and ordered to be filed.

This day the Codicil to the will of Ann Williams was produced in
Court and duly proved by the oath of Samuel Murray a subscribing witness
thereto it having been heretofore proven by Thomas Wright the other
subscribing witness thereto whereupon it is ordered by the Court to be
recorded.

THE STATE OF TENNESSEE   )
    against   )
JOHN G. BOSTICK   ) This day came the defendant into Open Court

and filed his affidavit and thereupon moved the Court to set aside the
forfeiture heretofore taken against him at the last term of this Court
for failing to attend in pursuance to his recognizance to answer a charge
of the State against him for an affray and on argument thereon had. It
is considered by the Court that said forfeiture be set aside on the
payment of the costs.

THE STATE OF TENNESSEE   )   Sci Fa
    Against   )
JOHN G BOSTICK   )   This day came the parties by their attornies
and the plaintiffs demurer to the defendants pleas being argued and fully
understood. It is considered by the Court that said demurer be over ruled
It is therefore considered by the Court that the defendant go hence without day and recover against the plaintiff his costs by him about his
defence in this behalf expended and the said plaintiff amersed & c from
which judgment & opinion of the Court the attorney General prayed an appeal
in the nature of a writ of error to the next circuit Court to be held for
this County which was granted.

THE STATE OF TENNESSEE   )
    Against   )
PORTLAND J. CURLE   )   This day again came the attorney General who
& CLAIBORNE HUBBERT
prosecutes for the State and the defendants also being present moved the
Court for a judgment against the defendants. It is therefore considered
by the Court. (p-365) that the defendants for such their offense be
fined one cent each and pay the costs of this prosecution.

ABRAHAM KIRKENDALL   )   Debt
    Against   )
JOSHUA YOWELL &   )
ALLEN YOWELL   )   This day came the parties by their attorneys
and the plaintiffs demurer to the defendants first, second & third pleas
being argued, and by the Court fully understood it is therefore considered
by the Court that the defendant go hence without day and recover against
the plaintiff their costs by them about their defence in this behalf
expended and the said plaintiff in Mercy &. From which judgment & opinion
of the Court the plaintiff prayed an appeal in the nature of a writ of
error to the next circuit Court to be held for this County. Bond & security
given and the appeal granted.

    Court adjourned until tomorrow morning nine o'clock.
          James Robinson
          M. W. Howell
          Geo. W. Thompson

Saturday May the 31st one thousand eight hundred and thirty four. Court
met according to adjournment.
Present.   James Robinson   )   Esquires, Justices of the peace
         Geo. W. Thompson   )   for Franklin County.
         M. W. Howell   )

A deed of Trust from Joseph H. Bradford to Jonathan Spyker for the real & personal property therein named for the benefit of Susan Ann & Maria Catharine Bradford was duly proven in Open Court by the oaths of John Goodwin & George W. Thompson subscribing witnesses thereto to be the act and deed of the said Joseph H. Bradford on the 31st day of May 1834 whereupon it is ordered by the Court to be certified for registration let it be registered.

DENNIS B. MUSE   )   Case
 Against   )
PORTLAND J. CURLE   ) This day came the parties by their attornies came a Jury, towit, Benjamin Dechard, Mark Hutchins, Hayden Arnold, Alexander E. Patton, Joseph Willis, Robert Cowan, Elisha Meredith, Wm. Strother, George Smith, Richard Faris, Richard B. Moore & Daniel Martin Jr. who being elected tried and sworn the truth to speak upon the issue joined upon their oaths do say they find the issue in favor of the plaintiff and assess (p-364) his damages to fifty-eight dollars & eighteen & three-fourth cents besides costs. It is therefore considered by the Court that the plaintiff recover against the defendant his damages aforesaid in form aforesaid assessed and also his costs by him about his suit in this behalf expended and the said defendant in Mercy &. from which judgment the defendant prayed an appeal to the next Circuit Court to be held for Franklin County.

THOMAS N. HOLT   )
 Against   )
JOHN FARIS   ) This day came the defendant by his attorney and prayed an appeal from the Judgment of the Court of Pleas & Quarter Sessions heretofore at this Term rendered against him to the Next Circuit Court to be held for Franklin County bond a security given & the appeal granted.

ISAAC REED   )   Case of Burwell Thompsons last will.
Against   )
GEO. W. THOMPSON & others) This day came again the parties by their attorneys and the matters in dispute between them having by mutal consent been referred to the obitrament and final determination of Sims Kelly who in conformity thereto made the following award, towit, "By virtue of an agreement entered into between Geo. W. Thompson John Mcgowan, David Mcgowan and Margarett Thompson for herself and as guardian for Melinda Thompson and Samuel Thompson under date of the 1st January 1834 referring to the undersigned all matters in dispute between them relative to the estate of Burwell Thompson Decd. and the will of said Decedent. I have on the 28th day of February 1834 taken the matter into consideration and after hearing the whole case have come to the following opinion and decision thereupon and do award accordingly, towit, that the paper purporting to be the will of said Decedent be disregarded and held for nought and that the estate of which said decedent died ceased and possessed, be divided equally between the parties share and share alike that is to say said Margarett, the widow of said decedent, one share, to Matilda Thompson one share, Samuel Thompson one share, Geo. W. Thompson one share, George Mcgowan and Polly his wife one share, and David Mcgowan and Sally his wife one share, given under my hand and seal this day and year aforesaid   Sims Kelly (Seal)
And the parties having the pursuance of said award agreed to a division

of theslaves belonging to said estate and having further agreed to a
division to be made by Stewart Cowan Esq. which is in the following words
and figures, towit: " We the parties have this day met together and agreed
on the following terms and have agreed that Stewart Cowan Esq. be appointed to settle and liquidate all of the accounts of the estate of Burwell
Thompson deceased and to seal all the property belonging to said estate
and pay to each heir their equal share, agreeable to a division made by
Sims Kelly Esq. having date the 28th day of February 1834. Agreeable
to a bond, (p-365)   entered into between the parties, on the first day
of January 1834 and we the legatees have taken the following property
towit? Margaret Thompson, widow, for herself, one negro
named Jim at $600.00
& as guardian of Samuel Thompson
one negro man named Davidt   600.00
& as guardain of Malinda Thompson
one negro woman named Prishad   525.00
& Geo. W. Thompson for himself
one negro man named Jerry   600.00
& also for the share of John Mcgowan
one negro woman named Jenny   450.00
& David Mcgowan for himself
one negro man named Tim   600.00
This done at Caldwells bridge on the 12th day of March 1834, given
under our hands and seals in the presence of us & c

William McClelland   Geo. W. Thompson (Seal)
Sims Kelly   John Mcgowan
                                          David Mcgowan
                                          Margaret Thompson
                                          for myself and Guardian for
                                          Samuel & Malinda Thompson

In conformity of all which by consent of the parties it is ordered that
said paper writing purporting to be the last will and testament of
Burwell Thompson deceased be set aside and held for nought, as though
the said Decedent had died intestate. And it is further ordered by the
Court, by consent of parties, that each party pay an equal portion of
the costs, to be paid out of the estate.

      Administration of the Estate of Burwell Thompson decd is granted to
Stewart Cowan Esq. by consent of the widow and next of kin of said
decedent who made oath and entered into bond with Geo. W. Thompson his
security in the penalty of five hundred dollars consideration as the law
directs.

      Stewart Cowan Esq. who was authorized by the widow and distributees
of Burwell Thompson deceased to seth and divide the Estate of the said
Decedent made a return of property sold by him which was ordered to be
recorded.

JOSIAH MUSE   )
   Against   )
ANDREW BYERS   ) This day came the plaintiff by his attorney and dismissed his suit & not further prosecuting. It is ordered that this suit
be dismissed. It is therefore considered by the Court that the defendant
go hence without day and recover against the plaintiff his costs by him
about his defence in this behalf expended and the said plaintiff in Mercy &.

ALFRED DEAN assu & c   )   Debt
 Against   )
HAYDEN ARNOLD   ) This day came the plaintiff by his attorney
,and having filed his declaration and the Defendant being solemnly called
came not, but made default. It is (p-366)   therefore considered by the
Court that the plaintiff recover against the Defendant one hundred Dollars
the debt in the declaration mentioned together with the further sum of
eight dollars and fifty cents interest thereon at the rate of six per cent
annum and also his costs by him about his suit in this behalf expended and
the said defendant in Mercy &.

        Court adjourned until Monday morning nine o'clock.
                                    James Robinson
                                    M. W. Howell
                                    James Keith

        Monday morning 2nd June one thousand eight hundred & thirty four,
Court met according to adjournment. Present a legal number of the acting
Justices of Franklin County.

        Ordered by the Court that Larson Rowe be appointed overseer of the
same part of the road that Lemuel Brandon was appointed for at the last
term of this Court and that he keep the same in good repair according to
law & that he have the same hands that worked under the former overseer.

        Ordered by the Court that Thomas Finch be allowed the sum of one
dollar & forty six cents the tax on 230 acres warranted land 450 acres
school land overcharged to William Faris for the year 1833 also four
dollars & forty seven cents on property twice listed for said year 1833
& that the County Trustee pay him the same.

        Present George Gray, Samuel Norwood, James Keith, James Robinson,
Marshall W. Howell, Andrew Campbell, James F. Green Meredith Catchings,
Asa D. Oakley, Zachariah H. Murrell, Thomas Wright and John Dougherty Esqrs.
Ordered by the Court that Thomas Finch Sheriff of Franklin County be
allowed the sum of fifty dollars for his Eseficio Services for the year
ending at the present term of this Court and that the County Trustee pay
him the same which was unanimously made by said Justices.

        Present George Gray, Samuel Norwood, James Keith James Robinson,
Marshall W. Howell, Andrew Campbell, James F. Green, Meredith Cathings,
Asa D. Oakley, Zachariah H. Murrell, Thomas Wright & John Dougherty Esqrs.
Ordered by the Court that Thomas Finch Sheriff be allowed the sum of six
dollars for wood furnished for the Court house & that the County Trustee
pay the same which was unanimously made by said above named Justices.
(p 367)
JOHN TURNER   )
 Against   )
HENRY RUNNELS   ) This day came the defendant by his attorney &
prayed an appeal from the Judgment of the Court of Pleas and Quarter
Sessions heretofore at this Term rendered against him to the next Circuit
Court to be held for Franklin County bond and security given & the appeal
granted.

Ordered by the Court that Thomas Finch & Thomas Howard be appointed commissioners to lay off to the widow of Alexander S. Acklin deceased one years support out of the Estate of said deceased & make report of their proceedings to the next Term of this Court.

Ordered by the Court that the following persons be appointed Jurors to the next County Court towit: Thomas Cunningham, Edom Holder, John W. Holder, Charles Duncan, John Handley, John Russell, Chapman McDaniel, James Morris, Thomas Williamson, James Robinson Senr. William Dirwin Milton McQueen, Green Brazleton, Barnaby Burrow, Archibald Hatchett, Amos Horton, Geo. Box, William Corn, William Gibson, Thomas S. Logan, John S. Morton, John Anderson, Meredith Kitchen, Thomas Howard, Jesse Runnels & Porter Keith.
And it is further ordered that John G. Brazleton & James Campbell constables be appointed officers to attend at the next Court and the Sheriff is hereby ordered to summons them to appear accordingly.

Ordered by the Court that Thomas Finch have the railing around the Court house repaired so as to keep out stock of all kinds and present his account to the next Term of this Court.

Ordered by the Court that James Howard, James B. Stovall & John Oliver be appointed commissioners to settle with William G. Guinn Administrator of the Estate of Nathaniel Wilder Deceased & Make due return of their proceedings to the next Term of this Court.

Ordered by the Court that Benjamin Walker be appointed overseer of the road from the mouth of Rush Creek to Hugh Montgomerys and that he keep the same in good repair according to law and that Meredith Catchings Esqr. divide the hands between him & John Wilkinson Jr.

Ordered by the Court that James Campbell, William N. Taylor & Willie B. Wagner be allowed the sum of one dollar & fifty cents each for settling with Elizabeth Phillips Executrix of the Estate of Ezekiel Phillips deceased which is to be paid out of said Estate by the Administrator hereof.

(p-368)   This day Thomas Howard came into Open Court and resigned his appointment of Justice of the peace for the Franklin County which resignation was received by the Court.

Ordered by the Court that Thomas Cunningham be appointed overseer of the road from George Davidson to Goshen Meeting house and that he keep the same in good repair according to law and that James Keith Esqr. give him a list of hands towork on said road.

Ordered by the Court that John Handly be appointed Overseer of the road from Major Armstrongs to Calloways pond and that he keep the same in good repair according to law to have Armstrongs and his own hands and the hands on both sides of the Stage road until he comes opposite the pond escept those on the other roads.

Ordered by the Court that Samuel Weeks be appointed Overseer to keep in repair the milk sick fence at the head of Cove Spring Creek

commonly called Buncum, and that he be overseer from Mr. Weeks plantation meandering the mountain as marked by the commissioners to the Cove
Branch & that he keep up said fence & keep the same in good repair according to law and that he have the same hands that worked under the former
Overseer.

A deed of Conveyance from Benjamin Hollingsworth & Allexander E.
Patton to Thomas King for forty acres of land lying in Franklin County
was duly proven in Open Court by the oath of Barnaby Burrow one of the
subscribing witnesses thereto to be the act and deed of the said
Benjamin Hollingsworth & Alexander E. Patton and it was also proven by
him that John Norman was a subscribing witness thereto and that he now
lives out of this state whereupon it is ordered by the Court to be
certified for registration. Let it be registered.

A deed of conveyance from Silas Tucker to Thomas King for forty
acres of land lying in Franklin County was duly proven in Open Court
by the oath of Barnaby Burrow one of the subscribing witnesses thereto
to be the act and deed of the said Silas Tucker and it was also proven
by him that Martin Connebson was a subscribing witness thereto and that
he now lives out of the State; Whereupon it is ordered by the Court
to be certified for registration. Let it be registered.

This day the amount of sales of the estate of James Philips
deceased was returned into Court which was received by the Court and
ordered to be made a part of the record.

This day the Commissioners of the school tract of land was returned
intp Court on Rock Creek which was received and ordered to be recorded.

(p-369)   A deed of conveyance from James Nelson to Samuel Davis for
one hundred and fifty acres of land lying in Franklin County was duly
proven in Open Court by the oaths of Henry Hunt & Thomas Wright subscribing witnesses thereto to be the act and deed of the said James Nelson.
Whereupon it is ordered by the Court to be certified for registration.
Let it be registered.

Ordered by the Court that John W. Jones be appointed Overseer of
the road from William Sharps to Daniel Normans and that he keep the same
in good repair according to law and that Marshall W. Howell Esqr. divide
the hands between him & James Slater.

This day the settlement made with Elizabeth Philips Esecutrix of
the Estate of Ezekiel Philips deceased was returned into Open Court was
received by the Court and ordered to be made a part of the record.

Ordered by the Court that Samuel Bradshaw & John Jones Esqrs. be
appointed to divide the hands amongst the several roads, towit, the road
from Caldwell, Bridge to Be. Nevills & from Centerville to Widow Burrows
at the head of Elk river together with the Hollingsworth & Goodman road
& the road from R. Coldwells to John Jone's and give to the several
overseers of said roads a list of hands.

This day an additional Inventory of the Estate of Ezekial Philips deceased was returned in Open Court was received by the Court and ordered to be made a part of the record.

This day Dudley Johnson Guardian for E. C. George Made his return into open Court and was qualified thereto which was ordered to be recorded.

This day the Commissioners of the George Town tract of School land made their return which was received by the Court and ordered to be recorded.

On petition of John Russell for license to keep an ordinary at his house in Franklin County. It is therefore ordered by the Court that he have license accordingly for the term of one year. who entered into bond with William H. Gillaspie & James Gillaspie his securities according to law and was qualified accordingly.

A deed of conveyance from Samuel Davis to Joseph Hickerson was for one hundred and fifty acres of land lying in Franklin County was duly acknowledged in Open Court by the said Samuel Davis to be his act and deed. Whereupon it is ordered by the Court to be certified for registration. Let it be registered.

(p-370) A bill of sale from Robert S. Sharp to Jesse Runnels for one negro girl named Drucilla was duly proven in open Court by the oaths of William Estill and John Goodwin subscribing witness thereto to be the act and deed of the said Robert S. Sharp whereupon it is ordered by the Court to be certified for registration. Let it be registered.

An inventory of the Estate of Thomas Williams deceased was this day returned into Court was received by the Court and ordered to be recorded.

This day the commissioners heretofore appointed to settle with the County Trustee for Franklin County made their report to Court together with the vouchers exhibited to them by the County Trustee which report was received by the Court and ordered to be recorded. It is also ordered by the Court that the vouchers accompanying said report be carefully preserved by the clerk of this Court.

Court adjourned until tomorrow morning nine o'clock.
James Robinson
M. W. Howell
John Dougherty

Tuesday June the third one thousand eight hundred and thirty-four Court met according to adjournment.
Present. James Robinson   )
          Marshall W. Howell &   )   Esquires
          John Dougherty   )   Justices of the peace for
Franklin County.

JOHN W & ARTHUR L. CAMPBELL   )   Debt
    Against   )
ELIJAH D. ROBBINS   )   This day came the defendant into open

Court ~~~~~ ~~~~~ in his proper person and saith he cannot gainsay the plain
say the plaintiffs action against him and confesses Judgment for four h
hundred and fourteen dollars and 44 cents the debt in the declaration
mentioned together with the further sum of two dollars & seven cents
interest thereon at the rate of six per cent per annum. It is therefore
considered by the Court that the plaintiff recover against the Defendant
their debt and interest confessed as aforesaid and also their costs by
them about their suit in this behalf expended and the said Defendant
in Mercy & C and the plaintiffs agree to stay the Execution until the
first of November next.

ROBERT S SHARP assee & c   )   Debt.
   Against   )
JOHN W. CAMDEN & Ruthy Whitney) This day came the plaintiff by his
attorney and having filed his Declaration and the defendants being Solemnly
called (p-371)   failed to appear and defend this suit but made default
and on motion of the plaintiff by his attorney it is considered by the
Court that the plaintiff recover against the defendants one hundred and
fifty dollars the debt in the Declaration mentioned together with the
further sum of three dollars & seventy five cents interest thereon at the
rate of six per cent per annum and also his costs by him about said suit
in this behalf expended and the said defendants in Mercy &.

ROBERT H. OLIVER assignee & C)   Debt
   Against   )
JOHN MCGOWAN   ) This day came the defendant plaintiff
by his attorney and having filed his Declaration and the defendant being
Solemnly called to appear and defend this suit came not but made default
And on motion of the plaintiff by his attorney. It is considered by the
Court that the plaintiff recover against the defendant fifty dollars
the debt in the Declaration mentioned together with the further sum of
sixteen dollars and fifty cents Interest thereon at the rate of six
per cent per annum and also his costs by him about his suit in this
behalf expended and the said defendant in Mercy &.

DENNIS B. MUSE   )   ~~Debt~~
   Against   )
PORTLAND J. CURLE   )   This day came the defendant & prayed an
appeal from the Judgment of the Court of Pleas and Quarter Sessions
heretofore at this Term rendered against him to the next Circuit Court
to be held for Franklin County bond & security given and the appeal
granted.

        Ordered by the Court that Thomas Finch be appointed collector
of the State, County additional & poor tax for the year 1834 who entered
into bond with James Campbell & John Goodwin his securities according to
law in the sum of five thousand dollars.

HENDRY M. RUTLEDGE   )   Debt
   Against   )
HAYDEN ARNOLD   )   This day came the plaintiff by his attorney
and having filed his declaration and the defendant being solemnly called
to appear and defend this suit came not but made default and on motion
of the plaintiff by his attorney. —It is considered by the Court that the

plaintiff recover against the Defendant two hundred and twenty-one dollars & sixty-two cents the debt in the Declaration mentioned together with the further sum of fourteen dollars and forty cents interest thereon at the rate of six per cent per annum and also his costs by him about his suit in this behalf expended and the said defendant in Mercy &.

(p-372)   HENRY M. RUTLEDGE   )   Debt
              Against   )
          HAYDEN ARNOLD   )   This day came the plaintiffs by their attorney and having filed their Declaration and the defendant being solemnly called to appear and defend this suit, came not but made default and on motion of the Plaintiffs by their attorney, It is considered by the Court that the plaintiffs recover against the defendant ninety-eight dollars & twenty four cents the debt in the declaration mentioned together with the further sum of four dollars interest thereon at the rate of six per cent per annum and also their costs by them about said suit in this behalf expended and the said defendant in Mercy &.

CROCKETT & PARK   )   Debt
    Against   )
HAYDEN ARNOLD   )   This day came the plaintiffs by their attorney and having filed their Declaration and the defendant being solemnly called to appear and defend this suit came not but made default and on motion of the Plaintiff by their attorney it is considered by the Court that the plaintiff recover against the defendant one hundred & twenty seven dollars & fourteen cents the debt in the declaration mentioned together with the further sum of five dollars and fifty cents interest thereon at the rate of six per cent per annum and also their costs by them about said suit in this behalf expended and the said defendant in Mercy &.

WAGGONERS EXECUTORS   )
    Against   )
LUNSFORD L. MATHEWS   ) This day came the plaintiffs by their attorney and on his motion a comission is awarded him to take the depositions of Jacob E. Waggoner, Riley Waggoner, & James Grant of Lincoln County Tennessee before any one Justice of the peace for said County to be read in evidence on b half of the plaintiffs on the trial of the above cause by their giving the defendant then days notice of the time and place of taking said deposition.

        Court adjourned until Court in Course
                                James Robinson
                                M.W. Howell
                                John Dougherty

(p-373)   August Term 1834

At a Court of Pleas and Quarter Sessions begun & held for Franklin
County at the Court house in the Town of Winchester on the fourth Monday
of August in the year of our Lord one thousand eight hundred and thirty
four it being the 25th of said month and of the Independance of the
United States the 59th.
Present a legal number of the Acting Justices of the peace for Franklin
County.

A deed of conveyance from Epps Tucker to Billy Pyland for three
hundred acres of land lying in Franklin County was duly proven in Open
Court by the oaths of Willis Burt and William Pyland Subscribing witness
thereto to be the act and deed of the said Epps Tucker on the day that
it bears date whereupon it is ordered by the Court to be certified for
registration. Let it be registered. Void

A deed of conveyance from Andrew Campbell to Hezekiah Faris for
forty acres of land lying in Franklin County was duly acknowledged in
open Court by the said Andrew Campbell to be his act and deed. Whereupon it is ordered by the Court that to be certified for registration.
Let it be registered.

A deed of conveyance from George W. Thompson to John Farrar for
Seventy acres of land lying in Franklin County was duly acknowledged in
Open Court by the said George W. Thompson to be his act and deed.
Whereupon it is ordered by the Court to be certified for registration
Let it be registered.

A deed of conveyance from Gabriel Tucker to Josiah Jones for one
hundred and fifty five acres of land lying in Franklin County was duly
proven in Open Court by the oaths of John Pyland & Robert Smith subscribing witnesses thereto to be the act and deed of the said Gabriel Tucker
on the day it bears date. Whereupon it is ordered by the Court to be
certified for registration. Let it be registered.

A deed of conveyance from Joel Mathews to Gabriel Tucker for one
hundred and fifty-five acres of land lying in Franklin County was duly
proven in Open Court by the oaths of Britton P. Smith and John (p-374)
Pyland Subscribing witnesses thereto to be the act and deed of the said
Joel Mathews on the day it bears date. Whereupon it is ordered by the
Court to be certified for registration. Let it be registered.

A deed of conveyance from Joseph Smith to Thomas Byron for isxty
one acres of land lying in Franklin County was duly acknowledged in
Open Court by the said Joseph Smith to be his act and deed. Whereupon
it is ordered by the Court to be certified for registration. Let it
be registered.

A deed of conveyance from George Box to Thomas Harrison for one
hundred and thirteen acres of land lying in Franklin County was duly
proven in Open Court by the oaths of John Jones & Charles McDaniel
subscribing witnesses thereto to be the act and deed of the said George
Box on the day it bears date. Whereupon it is ordered by the Court
to be certified for registration. Let it be registered.

A deed of conveyance from William Cook to David Prater for two hundred and twenty acres of land lying in Franklin County was duly proven in Open Court by the oaths of Stephen Adams one of the subscribing witnesses thereto to be the act and deed of the said William Cook on the day it bears date and it was also proven by him that he saw John S. Estill sign the same as a witness and that he now lives out of this State. Whereupon it is ordered by the Court to be certified for registration. Let it be registered.

A deed of conveyance from Irvin Baker and Sabana Baker his wife to John R. Patrick & Co. for sixty five acres of land in Franklin County was duly proven in Open Court by the oaths of George Hudspeth & John W. Smith to be the act and deed of the said Irvin Baker on the day it bears date. Whereupon it is ordered by the Court to be certified. Void

A power of attorney from Nancy Crockett to J. H. Roberts was duly proven in Open Court by the oath of Thomas J. Sartain one of Subscribing witnesses thereto to be the act and deed of the said Nancy Crocket. Whereupon it is ordered to be certified.

(p-375)   Ordered by the Court that John F. Graham be appointed constable in & for the County of Franklin in the bounds of Captain Grahams Company for the next ensuing two years who entered into bond with David Muchleroy & John Goodwin his securities according to law and was qualified accordingly.

Ordered by the Court that Andrew C. Wood be appointed constable in & for the County of Franklin in the bounds of Captain. Dennis Muse Company for the next ensuing two years who entered into bond with William N. Taylor and Richmond P. Harris his securities according to law and was qualified accordingly.

This day came on an election for the purpose of electing a constable in & for the County of Franklin in the bounds of Capt. Browns Company and on counting out the votes it was found that Albert G. Black was duly and constitutionally elected constable in the bounds of said Company who entered into bond with Andrew Mann, Jacob Awalt, Asa D. Oakley & Andrew H. McCollum his securities according to law and was qualified accordingly.

This day the Commissioners appointed to lay off to the Widow Vanzant one years support out of the Estate of Jacob Vanzant deceased this day made their report which was received by the Court.

This day the inventory of the Estate of Jacob Vansant deceased was returned into Open Court was received by the Court and ordered to be made a part of the record.

Ordered by the Court that Wm. C. Handly, Thomas D. White & William Litle be appointed commissioners to settle with Robert Taylor administrator of the Estate of Joshua Hickman Decd. and make report to the next term of this Court.

Ordered by the Court that Zachariah H. Murrell be appointed Guardian over the persons & property of Thomas T. Ezekiel H. James L.

and Sally Emeline Philips minor orphans of James Philips decd who entered into bond with Mark Hutchins & William N. Taylor his securities in the sum of two thousand dollars according to law and was qualified accordingly.

(p-376)   This day Wm. H. Murry one of the Executors named in the last will and testament of Ann Williamson deceased came into Open Court and was qualified as Executor of said will who entered into bond with Thomas Finch his security in the sum of two thousand dollars according to law.

It appearing to the satisfaction of the Court that John Conwill late of this County died Intestate and Joshua Franklin applied for letters of administration on the Estate of the said decd. It is therefore ordered by the Court that he have letters accordingly who entered into bond with Benjamin Franklin and Jacob Awalt his securitiees in the sum of one thousand dollars according to law and was qualified accordingly.

Ordered by the Court that Stewart Cowan, John M. Morrow, James Wilkinson, Council B. Ingram, Wm. B. Wilson, William W. Corn & Jas. B. Stovall or any five of them be appointed a Jury of view to view and mark a road leading from the Mohergs ford road near John Pattons to view and mark a road leading from the Mohergs ford road near John Pattons to intersect the Lusks Gap road near the Pleasant Plaines & that they view and mark the same of the most convenience of Travelers and as little as may be to the prejudice of Individuals and make report to the next term of this Court.

This day the Jury of view appointed at the last term of this Court to view a road from the mans ford road to the Fayetteville road running by Jesse Waggoner's & Jacob Waggoners Mill & to intersect the Fayetteville road at Jonothan Hortons Shop, this day made their report which was received by the Court.

This day the Jury of view appointed at the last term of this Court to the view and turn the road on the land of John Holder made their report which was received by the Court.

Ordered by the Court that Gabriel Jones, Josiah Berry, Henry Powers Jas. Hogan William Bicknel & Abram Kuykindall or any five of them be appointed a Jury of view to view and mark a road from where a road leaves the Nashville road near to W. H. Fosters to the Franklin County line near the gum swamp and that they view and mark the same with due regard to the convenience of Travelers and as little as may be to the prejudice of individuals and make report to the next Term of this court.

(p-377)   Ordered by the Court that Thomas Finch, James Sharp and Benjamin Decherd be appointed Commissioners to settle with Thomas Embry and William Duncan Executors of the last will and testament of Boley Embry deceased and that they make report either to this or to the next term of this Court.

Ordered by the Court that Isaac Henry be appointed Overseer of the road of the 1st class from the County line to the North end of Ephriam Cates lane in room and stead of John Winton and that he keep the same in in good repair according to law and that he have the same hands that worked under said Winton.

Present Samuel Norwood, Asa D. Oakley, William Crownover, Meredith Kitchins, Robinson Nevill, Elias Oldham, James B. Stovall, James Keith Jeremiah Balckard, Marshall W. Howell, Littleton G. Simpson, Andrew Mann, Andrew Campbell, William Lasiter, Wallace Estill, Zachariah H. Murrell, George W. Thompson, Jesse Jenkins, John Sanders.

Ordered by the Court that Thomas Finch be allowed the sum of forty dollars and twenty five cents for repairing the railing around the Court house and that the clerk issue a certificate to the County Trustee to pay him the same, which allowance was unanimously made by said Justices . Isd.

Present Samuel Norwood, Asa D. Oakley, William Crownover, Meredith Kitchins, Roberson Nevill, Elias Oldham, James Keith, Jeremiah Blackard Marshall W. Howell, Littleton G. Simpson, Andrew Mann, Andrew Campbell, Wallace Estill, Zachariah H. Murrill, George W. Thompson, Jesse Jenkins John Sanders and John Oliver. Ordered by the Court that Mrs. McKnight be allowed the sum of forty dollars for her support one year to be appropriated by David Goodman quarterly and that the clerk issue certificate for the same to the County Trustee for payment. Isd for 1 quarter.

Present Samuel Norwood Asa D. Oakley

William Crownover, Meredith Kitchins, Elias Oldham, Roberson Nevill, James Keith, Jeremiah Blackard, Marshall W. Howell, Littleton G. Simpson, Andrew Mann, Andrew Campbell, William Lasiter, Wallace Estill, Zachariah H. Murrell, Richmond P. Harris, Geo. W. Thompson, John Sanders, George Hudspeth and John Oliver, Ordered by the Court that Henry J. Jordan be allowed the sum of twenty dollars for keeping Henry call a child twelve months and that the clerk issue a certificate to the County Trustee to pay the same, the (p-378)   ayes & noes being taken were as follows- Ayes - William Crownover, Meredith Kitchins, Robertson Nevill, Elias Oldham, James Keith, Marshall W. Howell, Littleton G. Simpson, Andrew Campbell, William Lasiter, Wallace Estill, Zachariah H. Murrell, Richmond P. Harris, George W. Thompson, John Sanders, George Hudspeth and John Oliver. 16. Noes - Samuel Norwood, Asa D. Oakley & Jeremiah Blackard -3.

Ordered by the Court that John R. Patrick, Benjamin Decherd, & Marshall W. Howell be appointed Commissioners to settle with Peter Simmons administrator of the estate of Alexander Simmons deceased and that they make report to the present term of this Court.

Present William Crownover, Meredith Kitchins, Roberson Nevill, Elias Oldham, James Keith Jeremiah Blackard, Marshall W. Howell, Littleton G. Simpson, Andrew Mann, Andrew Campbell, Wallace Estill, Zachariah H. Murrell, Richmond P. Harris, George W. Thompson, Jesse Jenkins, John Sanders Geo. Hudspeth. John Oliver, Samuel Bradshaw, John R. Patrick, and John W. Campbell Ordered by the Court that Thomas Finch Sheriff of Franklin County purchase 12 chairs for the use of the Juries of said County and that he be allowed six dollars for the same and that the clerk issue a certificate to the County trustee to pay the same - which chairs are to be taken care of by Col. Ralph Crabb - the ayes and noes being taken were as follows. Ayes - William Crownover, Meredith Kitchins, James Keith Jeremiah Blackard, Andrew Mann. Richmond P. Harris, George W. Thompson, Jesse Jenkins, John Sanders, John Oliver, Samuel Bradshaw, John R. Patrick and John W. Campden. 13. Noes Roberson Nevill, Elias Oldham, Marshall W. Howell, Littleton G. Simpson Andrew Campbell, Wallace Estill, Zachariah H. Murrell and George Hudspeth - 8.

Ordered by the Court that Secil Bobo, Andrew Oliver, and Daniel McClain be appointed commissioners to settle with the Executors of Joel Taylor deceased and that they make report to the next term of this Court.

Present James Howard William Crownover, Meredith Kitchens, Robertson Nevill, Elias Oldham, James Keith, Jeremiah Blackard, Marshall W. Howell, Andrew Mann, Andrew Campbell, William Lasater, Wallace Estill, Zachariah H. Murrell, Richmond P. Harris George W. (p-379) Thompson, Jesse Jenkins, John Sanders, George Hudspeth John Oliver, Samuel Bradshaw and John R. Patrick,

Ordered by the Court that William B. York and John Brummit be allowed the sum of five dollars each for attending on an boarding David Meeks and that the Clerk issue certificate to the County Trustee to pay the same. Isd to York.

Ordered by the Court that Joseph Hickerson be allowed the sum of four for two wolf scalps under six months old and that the treasurer of Middle Tennessee pay him the same out of any money in the Treasury not otherwise appropriated.

Ordered by the Court that Paris A. Low be allowed the sum of three dollars for one wolf scalp over six months old and that the Treasurer of Middle Tennessee pay him the same out of any money in the Treasury not otherwise appropriated.

Ordered by the Court that James Keith be allowed the sum of four dollars for two wolf scalps under six months old and that the Treasurer of Middle Tennessee pay him the same out of any money in the Treasury not otherwise appropriated.

Ordered by the Court that the order of Court made at the last term of this Court allowing Jane Woodard fifty dollars for her support one year be allowed so that she have it a certificate quarterly for one fourth of said sum.

Ordered by the Court that Sidney Porter be appointed overseer of the road of the second class from the three mile post to the boiling fork and that he keep the same in good repair according to law and that Wallis Estill Esqr. give him a list of hands to work on said road.

Ordered by the Court that John Holder be appointed Overseer of the road of the third Class from Adam S. Capertons Mill to intersect the main road that runs through the sinking cove and that be keep the same in good

repair according to law and that James Keely and Adam S. Caperton Esqrs.
give him a list of hands to work on said road.
(p-380)

Present James Howard, Asa D. Oakley, Wm. Crownover, Meredith
Kitchings, Robertson Neville, Elias Oldham, James Keith, Marshall W.
Howell, Andrew Mann, Andrew Campbell, William Lasater, Wallis Estill,
Zachariah H. Murrell, Richmond P. Harris, Geo. W. Thompson, Jesse Jenkins
John Sanders, John Oliver, Samuel Bradshaw & John R. Patrick, Esqrs.
Ordered by the Court that William Mayhall and James Walker be allowed
the sum of one dollar & fifty cents each for their attendance as witness
in behalf of the State in the case of the state against Benjamin Allen
the Ayes & Noes being taken were unanimous in favor of the allowance.
Isd. to Mayhall.

Ordered by the Court that John W. Holder James Robinson and
Marshall W. Howell be appointed Commissioners to settle with William B.
Harris Administrator of the Estate of Thomas T. Harris decd. and that
they make report to the next Term of this Court.

Ordered by the Court that James Be. Stovall, John Oliver &
James Howard be appointed commissioners to settle with William G. Guinn
administrator of the Estate of Nathaniel Wilder dece and that they make
report to the next Term of this Court.

Ordered by the Court that Samuel Holland overseer of the road work
from the mountain to the top of the hill opposite the corner of David
Decherds fence this side the boiling fork at Horton mill and that he keep
the same in good repair according to law and that Wallis Estill Esqr.
divide the hands between him & Peter S. Decherd in proportion to their
respective roads.

Ordered by the Court that Peter S. Decherd Overseer of the road
work from where Samuel Holland Stops to Wallis Estill Esqr. house and
that he keep the same in good repair according to law and that Wallis E
Estill Esqr. divide the hands between him and Samuel Holland in proportion
to their respective roads.

Ordered by the Court that John G. Bostick Samuel Bradshaw and
Barnaby Burrow be appointed commissioners to settle with Elijah Allen
Executor of the last will and testament of James Sartain decd. and that
they make report to the present Term of this Court.

(p-381)   Ordered by the Court that William H. Taylor be appointed Overseer
of the road from the State line to where said road crosses Crosses Creek
and that he keep the same in good repair according to law and that William
Crownover Esqr. give him a list of hands to work on said road.

Ordered by the Court that John Buckner be appointed Overseer of the
road from Liberty Meeting house to Vernors in room of Joseph Bibb decd
and that he keep the same in good repair according to law and that he
have the same hands that worked under said Bibb.

This day David Muchroy came into Open Court and resigned his
appointment of constable in the bounds of Captain Grahams Company which

was received by the Court.

Ordered by the Court that the order of Court heretofore made for the support of Tabby Moore be so altered as that the money shall be drawn by Alexr. E. Patton and handed over to the wife of John G. Bostick & take her receipt for the same and that she make the appropriation.

JOHN KEY TO the use of PETERS S DECHERD)   Covenant
     against)
WILLIAM B. HARRIS)   This day came the defendant into open Court in his proper person and saith he cannot gainsay the plaintiffs action against him and confesses Judgment for eighty five dollars & fifty cents debt and also the further sum of eight dollars and forty cents interest thereon at the rate of six percent peranum. It is therefore considered by the Court that the plaintiff recover against the defendant his debt and interest confessed as aforesaid and also his costs by him about said suit in this behalf expended and the said defendant in Mercy &. and the plaintiff agrees to stay the Execution until February Term 1834 of the County Court.

A deed of conveyance from Irvin Baker & Sabina his wife to John R. Patrick & Co. for sixty-five acres of land lying in Franklin County was duly proven in Open Court by the oaths of George Hudspeth & Jno. W. Smith subscribing witnesses thereto to be the act and deed of the said Irvin Baker on the day it bears date and as to him ordered to be registered and it being represented to the Court that the said Sabina cannot attend Court to have (p-382) her privy examination taken whereupon it is ordered by the Court that a commission issue to George Hudspeth and David Bell Esqrs to take the privy examination of the said Sabina and her acknowledgement of said deed as required by law and make report to the present or to the next Term of this Court.

The last will and testament of Michael Bowlin deceased was this day produced in Open Court and the Execution thereof was duly proven by the oaths of John A. Rutherford, Richard Charles & C. B. Sawyer subscribing witnesses thereto as prescribed by law. Whereupon it is ordered by the Court that the same be recorded.

On peition of David Goodman and it appearing to the Court therefrom that the said David Goodman has erected a grist Mill on his land on Upper Beans Creek in Franklin County which is now in operation. Whereupon it is ordered by the Court that said Mill be established and that it be henceforth be considered a public mill of said County.

THOMAS CRUTCHER Assur&Co) Debt
  Against)
WALLIS WILSON)   This day came the defendant into Open Court in his proper person and saith he cannot gainsay the plaintiffs action against him and confesses Judgment for one hundred and fifty three dollars and forty six cents the balance of the debt in the declaration mentioned and also the further sum of one dollar and fifty three cents interest thereon at the rate of six per cent per annum. It is therefore considered by the Court that the plaintiff recover against the defendant his debt and interest confessed as aforesaid and also his costs by him about said

suit in this behalf expended and the said defendant in Mercy &.
Execution stayed three months.

It appearing to the satisfaction of the Court that Nancy Sanders
wife of Suddy Sanders had at one birth on the fourth day of July 1834
three children which are now alive towit George Washington, Delila &
Telitha. Whereupon it is ordered by the Court that the said Suddy Sanders
the father of said Children receive a certificate thereof.

(p-383)   Ordered by the Court that Daniel Roddy be appointed overseer
of the road from the head of Sandy branch to thefar end of Ephraim Cates
lane in room and stead of John A Rutherford and that he keep the same in
good repair according to law and that he have the same hands that worked
under said Rutherford.

Ordered by the Court that Isaac Patton be appointed overseer of
the road from the gum branch to Dabbs on Mohergs ford on Elk River in
room and stead of Daniel Finch and that he keep the same in good repair
according to law and that he have the same hands that worked under
the former overseer.

Ordered by the Court that Monday next be set apart to do County
business.   Court adjourned untill tomorrow morning ten o'clock.
                                        James Robinson
                                        Geo. W. Thompson
                                        James Keith

Tuesday August the twenty sixth one thousand eight hundred and
thirty four. Court Met according to adjournment.
Present.   James Robinson   )   Esqrs.
           George W. Thompson   )   Justice of the peace for
           James Keith   )   Franklin County.
          Proclamation being made the Sheriff made return of the State writ
of Ueniri Facias to this Court that he had summoned the following persons
being all good and lawful men of said County of Franklin and being
citizens of the County of Franklin to attend and serve as Jurors at the
present term of this Court which persons so summoned and returned as
aforesaid had been nominated for that purpose by the Justices of this
said Court of Pleas and Quarter Sessions of said County of Franklin at
its last session a list of whom was delivered to the said Sheriff of
Franklin County by the clerk of this said Court, towit, Thomas Cunningham
Edom Holder, John W. Holder, Charles Duncan, John Handly, John Russell,
Chapman McDaniel, James Morris, Thomas Williamson, James Robinson Senr.
William Darwin, Milton McQueen (p-384)   James P. Keith, Green Brazelton,
Barnaby Burrow, Archebald Hatchett, Amos Horton, George Box, William Corn
William Gibson, Thomas S. Logan, John S. Martin, John Anderson, Meredith
Catchings, Thomas Howard & Jess Reynolds, And of whom the following this
day attended, towit, Thomas Cunningham, Edom Holden, John W. Holden,
Charles Duncan, John Handly, John Russy, Chapman McDaniel, Thomas Williamson
James Robinson Senr. William Darwin, Milton McQueen James P. Keith,
Green Brazelton, Archibald Hatchett, George Box, William Corn, William
Gibson, Thomas S. Logan, John S. Martin, John Anderson, Meredith Catchings
and of whom the following persons-being all good and lawful men of said

County of Franklin were elected empanneled and sworn a grand Jury of Inquest for the body of the County of Franklin, towit, John W. Holder who was appointed foreman. Thomas Williamson, Thomas Cunningham, William Corn, Thomas S. Logan, James P. Keith, Charles Duncan, William Darwin, Archibald Hatchett, John Hadly, Meredeth Catchings, John S. Martin & Green Brazelton Who after receiving their charge retired to consult of their presentments who afterwards came into Open Court and returned a bill of indictment against Bryant B. Thompson, William B. Thompson and Richard F. McDuff for a Riot and assault & Battery a true Bill.

This day came on an election for the purpose of electing a County Trustee in & for the County of Franklin and on counting out the votes it was found that Benjamin Decherd was duly and constitutionally elected County Trustee in and for said County for the next ensuing two years.

THE STATE OF TENNESSEE) Indict for an Affray
 Against)
JOHN ANDERSON)

This day came the attorney General who prosecutes for the State on this behalf as well as the defendant in his proper person and the said defendant having heard said indictment read says he is thereof guilty and puts himself upon the grace and mercy of the Court. It is therefore considered by the Court that the defendant for such his offence be fined one cent and pay the costs of this prosecution & in Mercy &.

(p-385) JAMES CAMDEN) On affidavit of the defendant
  Against)
  BENJAMIN F. JENKINS) It is ordered by the Court the Plaintiff be ruled to give other good and sufficient securty for the prosecution of this suit in room of James Camden by the time this suit is called for trial.

HENRY C. GARNER & wife)
 Against)
MARY WILLIAM & Others) On motion of the parties by ther attornies this cause is continued untill the next term of this Court by their consent.

THE STATE OFTENNESSEE)
 Against)
BRYANT B. THOMPSON)
WM. B. THOMPSON &)
RICHARD F. MCDUFF) Thomas W. Swift acknowledges himself to owe and stand justly indebted to the State of Tennessee in the sum of one hundred and twenty five dollars to be levied of his respective goods and chattels lands and tenements to the use of said State but to be void on condition that he make his personal appearance before the Justices of our next Court of Pleas and Quarter Sessions on Thursday after the 4th Monday in November next then and there to testify and give evidence in behalf of the State on a bill of Indictment found against Bryant B. Thompson Wm. B. Thompson & Richard F. Mc uff for a riot and assault & Battery and not depart the same without leave first had and obtained.

ROBERT GIBSON _____)
  Against _____)
THOMPSON & MOORE ___)   On motion of the defendants by their
attorney this cause is continued until the next Term of this Court as on
their affidavit.

JOHN B. PATRICK & CO.)   Debt
  Against _____)
JAMES ARMSTRONG ____)
CHARLES J. GILLASPIE &)
JOHATHAN SPYKER ____)   This day came the parties by their attornies
and thereupon came a Jury, towit, Chapman McDaniel, John Anderson, Milton
McQueen, William Gibson, Edom Holder, James Robinson, John Russell,
Adam Oehmig, James Russy, Alexander Eanes, Britton Jones and George
Hockersmith who being elected trid and sworn the truth to speak upon the
issure joined upon their oaths do say they find the issue in favor
(p-386)   of the plaintiffs and assess their damages to twelve dollars
and seventeen cents besides costs. It is therefore considered by the
Court that the Plaintiffs recover against the Defendants sixty six
dollars and thirty nine the debt in the declaration mentioned together
with their damages aforesaid in form aforesaid assessed and also their
costs by them about their suit in this behalf expended and the said
dependants in Mercy &.

SAMUEL HOPPER Assu & C.)   Debt.
  Against _____)
DAVID C. HUTCHISON &)
WILLIAM H. MURRY ___)   This day came the parties by their attornies
and thereupon came a Jury, towit, Chapman McDaniel, John Anderson
Milton McQueen, William Gibson Edom Holder, James Robinson, John Russell
Adam Oehmig, James Russy, Alexander Eanes, Britton Jones & George
Hockersmith, who being elected tried and sworn the truth to speak upon
the issue joined upon their oaths do say they find the issue in favor of
the plaintiff and assess his damage to six dollars & fifty nine cents
besides costs. It is therefore considered by the Court that the plaintiff
recover against the defendants one hundred and nine dollars & sixty nine
cents the balance of the debt in the delaration mentioned together with
his damages aforesaid in form aforesaid assessed and also his costs by
them about his suit in this behalf expended and the said defendants in
Mercy &.

THE STATE OF TENNESSEE)   Indict for an affray
  Against _____)
JOHN W. CARPENTER __)   This day came the attorney General who pros-
secutes for the State on this behalf as well as the defendant in his
proper person and the said defendant having heard said indictment read
says he is therof quilty and puts himself upon the grave and Mercy of
the Court. It is therefore considered by the Court that the defendant
for such his offence be fined one cent and pay the costs of this
prosecution and that he be in custody of the Sheriff till paid or
security given for the same Whereupon Robert H. Oliver came into Court
and acknowledged himself security for the above find and costs and that
an execution issue against him for the same.

(p-387) THOMAS M. PRYOR & CO) Case
     Against)
WILLIAM P. CAMPBELL &)
GEORGE W. RICHARDSON) This day came the parties by their
attornies and thereupon came a Jury towit Thomas Williamson, Thomas
Cunningham 2, William Corn, 3, Thomas S. Logan 4, James P. Keith 5,
John W. Holder 6, John Handly 7, Charles Duncan 8, William Darwin 9,
Archibald Hatchett 10, Meredith Catchings 11 & John S. Martin 12,
Who being elected tried and sworn the truth to speack upon the issue
joined upon their oaths do say they find the issue in favor of the plaintiffs and assess them damages to nine hundred and thirty dollars beside
costs it is therefore considered by the Court that the plaintiffs recover
against the Defendants their damages aforesaid in favor aforesaid assessed
and also their costs by them about said suit in this behalf expended and
the said defendants in Mercy &.

HUDSON ALLEN)
  Vs)
JAMES RUSSY) On motion of the defendant this cause is continued
untill the next Term of this Court for want of counsel by the defendants
paying the costs.

MOSES RUNNELS) Debt
  Against)
RUTHY WHITNEY))
HAYDEN ARNOLD &)
GEORGE W RICHARDSON) This day came the plaintiff by his attorney
and having filed his Declaration and the defendants being solemnly called
to appear and defend this suit came not but made default. It is therefore
considered by the Court that the Plaintiff recover against the defendants
two hundred dollars the debt in the Declaration mentioned together with
the further sum of nine dollars & sixty six cents interest thereon at the
rate of six percent per anum also his costs by them about his suit in this
behalf expended and the said Defendants in Mercy &.

JOSEPH HINKLE)
  Against)
KINDRED H. MUSE) On motion of the defendant by his attorney this
cause is continued until the next term of this Court as on his affidavit
by his paying the costs of the Term and on his motion a commission is
awarded him to take the Depositions of John C. Beasly & John Conley before
any one Justice of the peace of Madison County Alabama by his giving the
plaintiff ten days notice of the time and place of taking said depositioned.

(p-388) JOSEPH HINKLE)
    Against)
    KINDRED H. MUSE) On motion of the plaintiff by his
attorney a commission is awarded him to take this deposition of William
M. Inge before any one Justice of the peace for Franklin County Tennessee
to be read in evidence on the trial of the above cause in favor of the
plaintiff by his giving the defendant ten days notice of the time and place
of taking said deposition.

LEWIS HARRIS   )
  Against   )
HAYDEN ARNOLD   )   On motion of the plaintiff by his attorney and it
appearing to the satisfaction of the Court that the said Lewis Harris
has paid as the security of the said Hayden Arnold the sum of one hundred
and fifty two dollars and forty three cents. Whereupon it is considered
by the Court that the said plaintiff recover against the said Defendant
the said sum of one hundred and fifty two dollars and forty three cents
and also two dollars and twenty eight cents interest thereon from the
31st day of May 1834 and also his costs by him about this motion in
this behalf expended and the said defendant in Mercy &.

        Ordered by the Court that Barnaby Burrow, Amos Horton & ~~Thomas
Howard~~ be find the sum of two dollars and fifty cents each for not
attending as Jurors who had been summoned on the orginal pannel to
attend at the present Term of the Court and that they show cause at the
next term of this Court why this judgment should not be made absolute
upon notice hereof.

JAMES SHARP Admr. of the estate of)
D.R. SLATER decd.   )
   Against   )
JOHN DRISKILL   )   This day came the plaintiff by
his attorney and dismissed his suit and not further prosecuting. It is
ordered that this suit be dismissed. It is therefore considered by the
Court that the Defendant recover against the plaintiff his costs about
his defence in this behalf expended and the said plaintiff in Mercy &.

JAMES SHARP Admin of the Estate)
of D.R. SLATER DECD   )
   Against   )
John Driskill   )   This day came the plaintiff by his
attorney and dismisses his suit and not further prosecuting it is ordered
that this suit be dismissed. It is therefore considered by the Court
that the Defendant go hence without day (p-389)   and recover against
the plaintiff his costs about his defence in this behalf expended and the
said plaintiff in Mercy &.

JAMES SHARP Admin of the   )
Estate of D. R. SLATTER DECD   )
   Against   )
JOHN DRISKILL   )   This day came the plaintiff by his
attorney and dismisses his suit and not further prosecuting it is ordered
that this suit be dismissed. It is therefore considered by the Court that
the defendant go hence without day and recover against the plaintiff his
costs by him about his defence in this behalf expended and the said plaintiff
in Mercy &.

        Court adjourned untill tomorrow morning 9 o'clock
                                James Robinson
                                James Kieth
                                M. W. Howell.

Wednesday August the twenty seventh one thousand eight hundred and thirty four. Court met according to adjournment

Present. James Robinson)
        James Keith &) Esqr.
        Marshall W. Howell) Justices of the peace for Franklin County.

THOMAS M. PRYOR & CO)   Debt
  Against)
JAMES L. BRYANT &)
JOSEPH DUNKIN) This day came the parties by their attornies and thereupon came a Jury, towit, John W. Holden, Thomas Cunningham William Corn, Thomas S. Logan, James P. Keith, William Darwin, Archibald Hatchett, John Handly, Meredith Catchings, John S. Martin Green Grazelton & Charles Duncan who being elected tried and sworn the truth to speak upon the issue joined upon their oaths do say they find the issue in favor of the Plaintiff and assess their damages to twenty seven dollars and twenty cents besides costs. It is therefore considered by the Court that the Plaintiffs recover against the Defendants eight hundred dollars the debt in the Declaration mentioned together with their damages aforesaid in form aforesaid assessed and also their costs by them about their suit in this behalf expended and the said Defendant in Mercy &.

(p-390)   HENRY M. RUTLEDGE)   Debt
        Against)
       JOHN G BOSTICK) This day came the parties by their attornies and thereupon came a Jury, to wit, John W. Halden, Thomas Cunningham, William Corn, Thomas S. Logan, James P. Keith William Darwin, Archibald Hatchett, John Handly, Charles Duncan, Meredith Catchings, John S. Martin & Green Brazelton, who being elected tried and sworn the truth to speak upon the issue joined upon their oaths do say they find the issue in favor of the plaintiff and assess his damages to nineteen dollars and seventy five cents besides costs. It is therefore considered by the Court that the Plaintiff recover against the Defendant. one hundred and ninety six dollars and eighty seven & one half cents the debt in the Declaration mentioned together with his damages aforesaid in form aforesaid assessed and also his costs by him about said suit in this behalf expended and the said Defendant in Mercy &.

HENRY M. RUTLEDGE assu & c)   Debt
  Against)
JAMES WILKINSON)
ISAAC WILKINSON) This day came the parties by their attornies and thereupon came a Jury, towit, John W. Holder, Thomas S. Logan James P. Keith, William Darwin, Archibald Hatchett, John Handly, Charles Duncan, Meredith Catchings, John S. Martin & Green Brazelton who being elected tried and sworn the truth to speak upon the issue do say they find the issue in favor of the plaintiff and assess his damages to twelve dollars and fifty cents besides costs. It is therefore considered by the Court that the Plaintiff recover against the defendants five hundred and three dollars and eighty seven cents the balance of the debt in the Declaration mentioned together with his damages aforesaid in form aforesaid assessed and also his costs by him about said suit in this behalf

expended and the said defendants in Mercy &. —

DANIEL WAGGONERS EXNS.   )
   Vs.   )
LUNSFORD MATHEWS   )   On motion of the Plaintiffs by their attorney
a commission is awarded them to take the depositions of Jacob E. Waggoner,
Riley Waggoner & James Grant before any one Justice of the peace of Lincoln
County Tennessee to be read as evidence on the trial of the above case on
behalf of the Plffs. by their giving the defendant thendays notice of the
time and place of taking said deposition.

(p-391)   JAMES A. SNOWDEN   )   Case
        Against   )
      MICAJAH L. GILLASPIE   )   This came the parties by their attorneys
and thereupon came a Jury, towit, John W. Holder, Thomas Cunningham,
William Corn, Thomas Williamson, Charles Duncan Thomas S. Logan, James P
Keith William Darwin, Archibald Hatchett, John Handly, Meredith Catchings
John S. Martin & Green Brazelton, who being elected tried and sworn the t
truth to speak upon the issue joined who after returning to consult of their
verdict afterward returned into open Court and declared they could not
agree and by the consent of the parties and with the assent of the Court
John Handly one of the Jurors aforesaid is withdrawn and the rest of the
Jury from rendering their verdict are discharged and the cause continued
for a new trial to be had thereon at the next Term of this Court.

     Ordered by the Court that the fine entered against Amos Horton on
yesterday for his non attendance as a Juror be remitted.

JOHN COTTON   )
 Against   )
JOHN NABORS &   )
MARTHA NABORS   )   Whereas on the second day of August 1834 there
was issued by John Jones Esqr an Execution in favor of the plaintiff
against the defendants for the sum of thirty five dollars and thirty
seven & one half cents debt and one dollar costs which execution was
returned to the present Term of this Court with the following levy thereon
endorsed, towit, no personal property found I have levied this alias Fi Fa
on one tract or parcel of land as the property of John Nabors and his wife
Martha Noabors or one what interest they have in and to ninety acres of
land more or less formerly belonging to Nathan Camp deceased and bounded
as follows on the north by Elk River and on the South West by Cold James
Lewis' thousand acre survey August 4th 1834.
               R.H. Oliver Deputy Sheriff
and on motion of the Plaintiff by his attorney. It is ordered by the
Court that said tract of land be condemed to satisfy said execution and
that the costs about this order of sale expended and that an order of sale
issued to the Sheriff of Franklin County to seel the same according to law.

(p-392)   CAMPBELL & HATFIELD   )
        Against   )
      RICHARD HANEY   )   Whereas on the 10th day of July 1834
there was issued by Jess Jenkins an acting Justice of the peace in and for
the County of Franklin an Execution in favor of the plaintiff against the

defendant for the sum of eight dollars and sixty six cents debt and one dollar and fifty cents costs which execution was returned to the present term of this Court with the following levy thereon endorsed, towit, no personal property found in my County whereon to levy this execution levied on a tract of land the property of the defendant situated in said County said to contain fifty acres lying on the West fork of Duck River and bounded as follows beginning at a large poplar lettered S D standing on the South side of the boiling Spring branch of the barron fork of Duck River & runs North across said branch at 2 poles in all 89½ poles to a white oak & Chestnut thence West crossing the road leading from the Stone part to Lumleys stand at 45 poles in all 89½ poles to a post oak & Black oak thence South 89½ poles to two hickorys and black oak thence east 89½ poles to the beginning being the tract of land granted to Samuel Davis No of grant 1034 on the 9th day of Feb. 1835.

B. F. Jenkins ,Const.

And on motion of the Plaintiff by his attorney it is ordered by the Court that said tract of land be condemed to satisfy said execution and the cost about this order of Sale expended. And that an Order of Sale issue to the Sheriff of Franklin County to seel the same according to law.

CAMPBELL & HATFIELD)
  Against)
FRANCIS HANEY) Whereas on the 10th day of July 1834 there was issued by Jess Jenkins an acting Justice of the peace for Franklin County an Execution in favor of the plaintiff against the defendant for the sum of nine dollars & forty cents debt and one dollar and fifty cents costs which Execution was returned to the present Term of this Court with the following Levy thereon endorsed, towit, no personal property found in my County whereon to levy this execution levied on a tract of land of the property of the said defendant situate in said County said to contain fifty acres lying on the West fork of Duck River and bounded as follows beginning at a large poplar lettered S D standing on the South side of the boiling spring branch of the Barron fork of Duck River and runs north across said branch (p-393) at 2 poles in all 89½ poles to a white oak and chestnut thence west crossing the road leading from the Stone Fort to Lumleys stand at 45 poles in all 89½ poles to a post oak and black oak thence East 89½ poles to the beginning being the tract of land granted to Samuel Davis no. of grant 1034 on the 9th day of Feb. 1835.

B. F. Jenkins Ct.

And on motion of the plaintiff by his attorney it is ordered by the Court that said tract of land be condemed to satisfy said Execution and the costs about this order of sale expended and that an order of sale issue to the Sheriff of Franklin County to sale the same according to law.

EDWIN EANES)
  Against)
KINDRED H. MUSE) On motion of the Plaintiff by his attorney and it appearing to the satisfaction of the Court that the said Edwin Eanes has paid as the security of the said Kindred Muse the sum of one hundred and twenty three dollars and forty one cents. Whereupon it is considered by the Court that the said Plaintiff recover against the said Defendant the said sum of one hundred and twenty three dollars & forty one cents and also his costs by him about this motion in this behalf expended and the said defendant in Mercy &.

THOMAS HURST) Debt
 Against)
ZACHARIAH H. MURRELL admin of the)
Estate of James Philips deceased &)
WILSON HUDSON) This day came the parties by
their attornies and thereupon came a Jury, towit, John W. Holder Thomas
Williamson, Thomas Cunningham, Wm. Corn, Thomas S. Logan, James P. Keith
William Darwin, Archibald Hatchett John Handly, Meredith Catchings
John S. Martin & Green Brazelton, who being elected tried and sworn the
truth to speak upon the issue Joined upon their oaths do say they find the
issue in favor of the Plaintiff and assess his damages to sixteen dollars
& fifty cents beside costs it is therefore considered by the Court that
the plaintiff recover against the Defendant four hundred and fifteen dollars
the balance of the debt in the Declaration mentioned together with his
damages aforesaid in form aforesaid assessed and also his costs by him
about said suit in this behalf expended and the said defendants in Mercy &
to be levied of the proper goods and chattels rights and (p-394) credits
of James Philips deceased in the hands of said administrator to be
administered.

JEREMIAH SMITH) Motion
 Against)
JAMES BOX) This day came the defendant by his attorney and
moved the Court for a rule to compel the Plaintiff to give good and
sufficient security for the prosecution of this suit which is granted.
Whereupon it is ordered by the Court that the said Plaintiff give said
security by the next Term of this Court.

JOSEPH B. HERNDON)
 Against)
BARNETT FORSYTH) This day came the defendant by his attorney and
moved the Court to Continue this cause until the next Term of this Court
and from the reasons set forth in his statement which is received as an
affidavit. It is ordered by the Court this cause be continued untill the
Next Term of this Court.

    Court adjourned untill t-morrow nine o0clock

                   James Robinson
                   M. W. Howell
                   James Keith

    Thursday August the twenty eight one thousand eight hundred and
thirty four, Court met according to adjournment.
Present. James Robinson)
       James Keith &) Esquires
       Marshall W. Howell) Justice of the peace for Franklin County

THE STATE OF TENNESSEE) Indict for an Affray
 Against)
JORDON MORRIS) This day came the attorney General who
prosecutes for the State in this behalf as well as the defendant in his
proper person and the said defendant having heard said Indictment read says

he is thereof guilty and put himself upon the grave and mercy of the Court. It is therefore considered by the Court that the defendant for such his offence be fined one cent and pay the costs of the prosecution and to remain in custody of the Sheriff till paid or security given for the same. Whereupon Minyard Gilliam came into Court & acknowledged himself securty for the fine and costs in the above case and that a Fi Fa issue against him for the same.

(p-395) THE STATE OF TENNESSEE   )   Indictment for an Affray
              Against   )
         WILSON MORRIS   )

This day came the Attorney General who prosecutes for the State in this behalf as well as the defendant in his proper person and the said defendant having heard said Indictment read says he is thereof guilty and puts himself upon the grave and mercy of the Court. It is therefore considered by the Court that the Defendant for such his offence be find one cent and pay the costs of the prosecution and that he remain in custody of the Sheriff till paid or security given for the same. Whereupon Jordon Morris came into Court and acknowledged himself security for the above fine and costs and that an execution issue against him for the same.

THE STATE OF TENNESSEE   )   Indictment for an Affray
    Against   )
THOMAS BURROWS   )   This day came the Attorney General who prosecutes for the State in this behalf as well as the defendant in his proper person and the said defendant having heard said Indictment read says he is thereof not guilty and puts himself upon the Country and the Attorney General doth the like and thereupon came a Jury, towit, John W. Holder 1, Thomas Williamson 2, Thomas Cunningham 3, William Darwin 6, William Corn 4 Thomas S. Logan 5, Archibald Hatchett 7, John Handly 8, Meredith Catchings 9 Edom Holder 10, James Robinson Senr. 11 & Chapman McDaniel 12. Who being elected tried and sworn the truth of and upon the premises to speak upon their oaths do say they find the defendant guilty in manner & form as charged in the Bill of Indictment. It is therefore considered by the Court that the Defendant for such his offence be fined one cent and pay the costs of this prosecution, and that he remain in custody of the Sheriff till paid or security given for the same Whereupon William B. Willis came into Court and acknowledged costs in the above case and that an Execution issue against him for the same.

THE STATE OF TENNESSEE   )   Indictment for an Affray
    Against   )
MADISON GOODMAN   )   This day came the Attorney General who prosecutes for the State in this behalf, as well as the defendant in his proper person and the said Defendant having heard said Indictment read says he is therof not guilty and puts (p-396) himself upon the Country and the attorney General doth the like an thereupon came a Jury, towit, Milton McQueen 1, James P. Keith 2, William Hendly 3, William Lyons 4, Andrew McCollum 5, Charles Woods 6, John D. Fennell 7, Henry Runnels 8, Elijah Hammons 9, James Walker 10, Alexander Eanes 11, and Richard P. Holder 12, Who being elected tried and sworn the truth of and upon the premises to speak who after retiring to consult of their verdict afterwards returned into Open Court and declared they could not agree and by the consent of

the parties and with the assent of the Court Milton McQueen one of the
Jurors aforesaid is with drawn and the rest of the Jury from rendering
their verdict are discharged and the cause continued for a new trial to
be had thereon at the next Term of this Court.

THE STATE OF TENNESSEE)   Indictment for an Affray
   Against)
BENJAMIN MORRIS)   This day came the Attorney General who prosecutes
for the State in this behalf as well as the defendant in his proper person
and the said Defendant having heard said Indictment read says he is thereof
not guilty and puts himself upon the Country and the Attorney General doth
the like and thereupon came a Jury, to wit, John W. Holder 1, Thomas
Williamson 2, Thomas Cunningham 3, William Corn 4, William Darwin 5,
Archibald Hatchett 6, John Handly 7, Meredith Catchings 8, Edom Holder 9,
James Robinson Senr 10, Chapman McDaniel 11 & Hugh Richardson 12, who
being elected tried and sworn the truth of and upon the premises to speak
upon their oaths do say they find the defendant guilty in manner and form
as charged in the bill of Indictment. It is therefore considered by the
Court that the defendant for such his offence be fined one cent and pay
the costs of this prosecution and that he remain in custody of the Sheriff
till paid or security given for the same. Whereupon William McClelen
came into Court and acknowledged himself security for the fine and costs
in the above case and that an Execution issue against him for the same.

THE STATE OF TENNESSEE)
   Against)
MADISON GOODMAN)   This day Madison Goodman, Council B. Goodman
& James Sarton came into Open Court and acknowledged themselves to owe
and stand justly indebted to the State of Tennessee in the following
sums towit the said Madison Goodman in the sum of two hundred and fifty
(p-397) dollars and the said Council B. Goodman & James Sartan in the sum
of one hundred and twenty five dollars each to be levied off their respective goods and chattels lands and tenements to the use of said State but
to be void on condition that Madison Goodman make his personal appearance
before the Justice of our next Court of pleas and quarter sessions to be
held for the County of Franklin on Thursday after the Fourth Monday in
November next then and there to answer the State on a bill of Indictment
found against him for an affray and not depart the same without leave
first had and obtained.

THE STATE OF TENNESSEE)
   Against)
CHARLES WOODS)   This day Charles Woods and Thomas Finch came
into Open Court and acknowledged themselves to owe and stand justly indebted to the State of Tennessee in the following sums, towit, Charles Woods
the defendant in the sum of two hundred and fifty dollars & Thomas Finch
his security in the sum of one hundred and twenty five dollars to be levied
of their respective goods and chattles lands and tenements to the use of
said State but to be void on condition that the said Charles Woods make
his personal appear ance before the Justice of our next Court of pleas
Quarter Sessions to be held for the County of Franklin at the Court house
in the Town of Winchester on Thursday after the fourth Monday in November
next then and there to answer the State on a Presentment found against
him for gaming and not depart the same without leave first had and obtained.

This day Benjamin Decherd who was heretofore on Tuesday elected County Trustee came into Court and entered into bond with Mark Hutchins his Security in the sum of six thousand dollars according to law.

The deef of conveyance from Strother Key to John Winn Key for his interest in the Estate of Walter Key deceased was duly acknowledged in Open Court by the said Strother to be his act and deed. Whereupon it is ordered by the Court to be so certified.

(p-398)   THE STATE OF TENNESSEE)   Indictment for an Affray
         Against   )
        MADISON GOODMAN   )
        WILLIAM B. WILLIS   )
        BENJAMIN J. JACAWAY   )
        JAMES SARTAIN   )   This day came the Attorney General

who prosecutes for the State in this behalf, as well as the defendants in their proper person and the said Defendants having heard said Indictment read say they are thereof not guilty and put themselves upon the Country and the Attorney General doth the like and thereupon came a Jury, towit, Thomas Williamson 1, Thomas Cunningham 2, William Corn 3, Thomas S. Logan 4, William Darwin 5, Archibald Hathcett 6, John W. Holder 7, John Hendley 8, Meredith Catchings 9, Edom Holder 10, James Robinson 11 & Chapman McDaniel 12, Who being elected, tried and sworn the truth of and upon the premises to speak upon their oaths do say they find the Defendants guilty in manner and form as charged in the Bill of Indictment. It is therefore considered ty the Court that Madison Goodman, Wm. B. Willis & Benjamin J. Jacaway for such their offence be fined two dollars & fifty cents each, and pay the costs of this prosecution and that James Sartain for such his offence be fined one cent and pay the costs of this prosection and that they remain in custody of the Sheriff till paid or security given for the same. Whereupon Robert H. Oliver came into Court & acknowledged himself Security for the fine & costs against Madison Goodman & Wm. B. Willis & Whereupon Madison Goodman came into Court and acknowledge himself security for the fine and cost against James Sartain and that an Execution issue against them for the same.

THE STATE OF TENNESSEE   )
  Against   )
MADISON GOODMAN   )   This day came the attorney General who
prosecutes for the State in this behalf and James Dean having been Summoned as a witness to give evidence in behalf of the State against Madison Goodman on a bill of Indictment found against him for an affray to appear at this Term who having been solemnly called failed to appear according to the tenor and effect of his said subpoena and on motin of the attorney General it is considered by the Court that he forfiet the sum of one hundred and twenty five dollars. And that a Scieri Facias issue against him returnaable to the Next Term of this Court to show cause if any he can why said Judgment should not be made absolute.

(p-399)   STATE OF TENNESSEE   )
         Against   )
        CHARLES WOODS   )   This day came the attorney General
who prosecutes for the State in this behalf and William B. Thompson having been summoned as a witness to give evidence in behalf of the State

against Charles Woods on a Presentment found against him for Gaming to appear at this Term who having been solemnly called failed to appear according to the tenor and effect of his said subpoena and on motion of the attorney General It is considered by the Court that he forfeit the sum of one hundred and twenty five dollars. And that a Seieri Facias issue against him returnable to the next Term of this Court to show cause if any he can why said Judgment should not be made absolute.

THE STATE OF TENNESSEE   )
   Against   )
JOHN HUGHS   )   This day came the attorney General who prosecutes for the State in this behalf as well as the defendant and William B. Thompson having been summoned as a Witness to give evidence in behalf of the State against the said John Hughs on a presentment found against him for Gaming to appear at this Term who having been solemnly called failed to appear according to the tenor and effect of his said subpoena And on motion of the Attorney General. It is considered by the Court that he forfeit the sum of one hundred and twenty five dollars and that a Sciere Facias issue against him returnable to the next Term of this Court to show cause if any he can why said Judgment should not be made absolute.

THE STATE OF TENNESSEE   )
  Against   )
CHARLES WOODS   )   This day came the attorney General who prosecutes for the State in this behalf and William B. Thompson having been summoned as a witness to give evidence in behalf of the State against the said Charles Woods on a Presentment found agiast him for gaming to appear at this Term who having been solemnly called failed to appear according to the tenor and effect of his said subpoena. And on motion of the attorney General, it is ordered by the Court that an attachment Nici issue against him returnable to the next Term of this Court.

(p-400)   THE STATE OF TENNESSEE   )
           Against   )
           JOHN HUGHS   )   This day came the attorney General who prosecutes for the State in this behalf and William B. Thompson having been summoned as a witness to give evidence in behalf of the State against the said John Hughs on a Presentment found against him for gaming to appear at the Term who having been solemnly called failed to appear according to the tenor and effect of his said Subpoena. And on motion of the attorney General it is ordered by the Court that an Attachment Nici issue against him returnable to the Next Term of this Court.

          Court adjourned untill tomorrow morning nine o'clock.
                                        James Robinson
                                        James Keith
                                        M.W. Howell.

          Friday August the twenty ninth one thousand eight hundred and thirty four Court met according to adjournment.

Present James Robinson   )   Esquires
      James Keith &   )
      Marshall W. Howell   )   Justices of the peace for Franklin County

THE STATE OF TENNESSEE   )   On motion
   Against   )
CHARLES WOODS   )   It is ordered by the Court that the forfeiture
taken against Wm. B. Thompson on yesterday be set aside and that the order
directing an attachment to issue be recinded & made void.

THE STATE OF TENNESSEE   )   On motion
   Against   )
JOHN HUGHS   )   It is ordered by the Court that the forfeiture
taken against Wm. B. Thompson as a witness in this case on yesterday be
set aside & that the order directing an attachment to issue be recinded
& made void.

THE STATE OF TENNESSEE   )
   Against   )
CHARLES WOODS   )   This day William B. Thompson & Henry Runnels
came into Open Court and acknowledged themselves to owe and stand justly
indebted to the State of Tennessee in the following sums, towit, the said
William B. Thompson in the sum of two hundred and fifty dollars & Henry
Runnels in the sum of one hundred and twenty five dollars to be levied of
their respective goods and chattels lands and tenements to the use of said
State, but to be void on condition that William B. (p-401 Thompson make
his personal appearance before the Justices of our next Court of pleas and
quarter sessions to be held for the County of Franklin at the Court house
in the Town of Winchester on Thursday after the fourth Monday in November
Next then and there to prosecute and give evidence in behalf of the State
on a Presentment found against Charles Woods for Gaming and not depart
the same without leave first had and obtained.

THE STATE OF TENNESSEE   )
   Against   )
JOHN HUGHS   )   This day Wm. B. Thompson, Henry Runnels
came into open Court and acknowledged themselves to owe and stand justly
indebted to the State of Tennessee in the following sums, towit,
Wm. B. Thompson in the sum of two hundred and fifty dollars and Henry
Runnels in the sum of one hundred and twenty five dollars to be levied
of their respective goods and chattels lands and tenements to the use of
said State but to be void on condition that the said Wm. B. Thompson make
his personal appearance before the Justices of our next Court of Pleas and
Quarter Sessions to be holden pon the county of Franklin at the Court house
in the town of Winchester on Thursday after the fourth Monday in November
next then and their to prosecute and give evidence in behalf of the state
on a Presentment found against John Hughs and not depart the same without
leave first had and obtained.

JOHN J. LASATER   )   Appeal Debt
   Against   )
ERVIN ADAMS   )   This day came the parties by their attornies and
thereupon came a Jury, towit, Thomas Williamson 1, Thomas Cunningham 2,
James P. Keith 3, William Darwin 4, John Hendly 5, Meredith Catchings 6.

Edom Holder 7, James Robinson Senr. 8, Chapman McDaniel 9, Milton McQueen
10, James S. Cowling 11, & William M. Finch 12, Who being elected tried
and sworn the truth to speak upon the matter of controversy joined upon
their oaths do say they find for the Defendant, it is therefore considered
by the Court that the Defendant go hence without pay and recover against
the plaintiff and Laban Jones security for the appeal his costs by him
about his defence in this behalf expended and the said Plaintiff in Mercy
&. from which Judgment the plaintiff prayed an appeal to the next curcuit
Court to be held for Franklin County which is granted by this giving bond
& security according to law.

(p-402)   HENRY M. RUTLEDGE Assu & C)
                Against   )
           JAMES WILKINSON &   )
           ISAAC WILKINSON   )   This day came the Defendant by
his attorney and prayed an appeal from the Judgment heretofore at this
Term rendered against him to the next Curcuit Court to be held for this
County, bond & security given and the appeal granted.

THOMAS HURST   )
 Against   )
ZACHARIAH H. MURRELL   )
Admin of the Estate of   )
JAMES PHILIPS decd &   )
WILSON HUDSON   )   This day came the defendants by their
attorney and prayed an appeal from the Judgment of the Court of Pleas and
Quarter Sessions heretofore at this Term rendered against them to the
next Curcuit Court to be held for this County, bond and security given
and the appeal granted. A. Bill of Sale from Joseph Cowling to Benjamin
Powell for four negro boys named Jerry, Ned, Samuel & Lewis was duly
acknowledged in Open Court by the said Joseph Cowling Whereupon it is
ordered by the Court to be certified for registration. Let it be registered.

JAMES H. ESTILL Assee & C)   Ca. Sa.
   Against   )
THOMAS P. WHITNEY   )   This day came the plaintiff by his
attorney and it appearing to the satisfaction of the Court that there was
issued by James Robinson an acting Justice of the peace for Franklin County
an Execution of Capias Ad Satisfaciendum on the 9th day of June 1834 and
directed to any lawful officer of said County commanding him to take the
body of Thomas P. Whitney if to be found in his county and him safely
keep until he should pay James H. Estill assee & C. ninety one dollars
& eighty one & one fourth cents debt and fifty cents costs of suit to
satisfy a Judgment lately obtained against him by said James H. Estill
assee & c. before said James Robinson which Ca.Sa. came into the hands of
Robert S. Sharp a constable of said County on the same day issued and
was by him executed on the body of the said defendant on the 10th day
of June 1834 to satisfy said Ca. Sa. and the said Thomas P. Whitney
then and there executed and tendered his bond to the said Robert S. Sharp
constable as aforesaid with Anderson F. Willis, Joseph R. Drake &
Elisha Anderson his securities for his personal appearance before the
Justices of our Court of pleas and quarter sessions of Franklin County
at the August Sessions therof 1834 according to an act of assembly (p-403)

in such cases made and provided and it appearing to the Court that the
defendant failed to make his appearance agreeable to the tenor and effect
of his said bond so entered into as aforesaid and as he was by law bound
to do. It is therefore considered by the Court that the Plaintiff recover
against the said Defendant and Anderson F. Willis, Joseph R. Drake &
Elisha Anderson his securities as aforesaid the aforesaid sum of ninety
one dollars & eighty one & one fourth cents and also the further sum of
seven dollars interest thereon at the rate of six per cent per anum and
all lawful costs and also his costs about said motion in this behalf
expended and the said defendants in Mercy &.

   Court adjourned untill tomorrow morning 9 o'clock.
            James Robinson
            James Keith
            M. W. Howell.

   Saturday August the thirteeth one thousand eight hundred and thirty
four. Court met according to adjournment.
Present - James Robinson   ) Esquires
   James Keith &   )
   Marshall W.Howell   ) Justices of the peace for Franklin County

JAMES H. ESTILL & C   )   Debt
 Against   )
JOHN LEFEVER &   )
HAYDEN ARNOLD   ) This day came the defendants into Open Court
in their proper persons and saith they cannot gainsay the Plaintiffs
action against them and confess Judgment for one hundred and fifty
dollars debt and two dollars and fifteen cents interest thereon at the
rate of six per cent per anum. It is therefore considered by the
Court that the Plaintiff recover against the defendants his debt and
interest confessed as aforesaid and also his costs by them about said
suit in this behalf expended and the said defendant in Mercy &. and the
Plaintiff agrees to Stay the Execution untill the first of Nov. next.

   A power of attorney from Robert B. Duncan, Edy Duncan & Lucy Duncan
to William Duncan and Jess Oldham was duly acknowledged in Open Court by
the said Robert, Edy & Lucy Duncan to be their act and deed. Whereupon
it is ordered to be certified.

(p-404) THOMAS CRUTCHER assee & c)   Debt
    Against   )
   EDMOND RUSSELL &   )
   NATHAN GREEN   ) This day came the Plaintiff by
his attorney and having filed his declaration and the Defendants being
solemnly called to appear and defend this suit came not but made default
it is therefore considered by the Court that the plaintiff recover against
the defendant one hundred and forty five dollars the debt in the Declaration
mentioned together with the futher sum of one dollar & ninety three
damages which he hath sustained by occasion of the detention of his debt
and also his costs by them about said suit in this behalf expended and
the said Defendant in Mercy &.

BENJAMIN & PETER S DECHERD)   Case
   Against   )
THOMAS J. KENNERLY   )   This day came the plaintiffs by their attorney having filed their Declaration and the Defendant being solmnly called to appear and defend this suit came not but made default. And on motion of the plaintiffs by their attorney. It is considered by the Court that the plaintiffs recover against the defendant such damages as they may have sustained by reason of the non performance of the assumption in the Declaration mentioned which damages are to be enquired of by a Jury at the next Term of this Court.

BENJAMIN DECHERD   )   Case
, Against   )
THOMAS J. KENNERLY   )   This day came the Plaintiff by his attorney and having filed his Declaration and the defendant being solemnly called to appear and defend this suit came not but made default and on motion of the plaintiff by his attorney it is considered by the Court that the plaintiff recover against the defendant such damages as he may have sustained by reason of the non performance of the assumptions in the Declaration mentioned which damages are to be enquired of by a Jury at the next Term of this Court.

JOHN W. & ARTHUR L. CAMPBELL)   Debt
   Against   )
JOHN D. STOVALL   ) This day came the Plaintiffs by their attorney and having filed their Declaration and the Defendant being solemnly called to appear and defend this suit came not but made (p-405) default and on motion of the plaintiffs by their attorney. It is considered by the Court that the plaintiffs recover against the Defendant two hundred and seventy five dollars the debt in the Declaration mentioned together with the further sum of eleven dollars interest thereon at the rate of six per cent per anum and also their costs by them about said suit in this behalf expended and the said defendant in mercy &.

GEORGE KEESSED   )   Debt
Against   )
THOMAS GAITHER   ) This day came the Plaintiff by his attorney and having filed his Declaration and the Defendant being solemnly called failed to appear and defend this suit but made default. And on motion of the Plaintiff by his attorney it is considered by the Court that the plaintiff recover against the Defendant three hundred dollars the debt in the Declaration mentioned together with the futher sum of twelve dollars interest at the rate of six per cent per anum and also his costs by him about said suit in this behalf expended and the said Defendant in Mercy &.

(p-405)   Court adjourned untill Monday morning ten o'clock.
                                 James Robinson
                                 James Keith
                                 M. W. Howell

     Monday September the first, one thousand eight hundred and thirty four. Present eleven of the acting Justices of the peace for Franklin County.

JOHN J. LASATER)
   Against)
ERVIN ADAMS) This day came the Plaintiff and entered into
bond and security for the appeal heretofore prayed at this Term which is
granted.

This day Elijah D. Robbins who was heretofore at the last Term of this
Court elected coroner for Franklin County came into Open Court and entered
into bond with John Handly and Dudley Johnson his Securties in the sum
of two thousand five hundred dollars according to law.

(p-406) Ordered by the Court that the fine heretofore at this Term
entered against Barnaby Burrow for his non attendance as a Juror summoned
to attend at this Term be remitted.

Ordered by the Court that William Hendley be allowed eight dollars
for four wolf scalps under four months old out of any money in the
Treasury of Middle Tennessee not otherwise approprated.

Ordered by the Court that Barister Partain be appointed overseer
of the road of the second class from Thomas Knights to Elk River in room
and stead of Joel Chitwood and that he keep the same in good repair
according to law and that he have the same hands that worked under said
Chitwood.

Ordered by the Court that John W. D. Stamper be appointed overseer
of the road of the first class from Elk river to where Wilkinsons mill
road corsses the same to Coldwells Bridge and that he keep the same in
good repair according to law and that Samuel Corn Esqr. give him a list
of hand to work on said road.

Ordered by the Court that Anderson F. Willis an overseer of the
road have the following hands to wit, Jess Jenkins, Wm. & Benjamin F.
Jenkins, James Lindley, Mason Flour & Sons, Granville Hogan, James
Sanders, Robertson Nevill & Wm. Harp.

Ordered by the Court that the following persons be Jurors to the
next Curquit Court to wit, David Decherd, Wiley J. Hines, Ryon Caperton
Abram Shook, Joseph Francis, Daniel Martin Senr. John Lee, William
Larkin, George Simmons, Richard C. Holder, John Staples, Jacob Awalt,
Daniel Weaver, William Buchanan, James Sharp Senr. Thomas Howard, James
Stamps, Benjamin Hasty, William Crownover, James Kelly, Peter S. Decherd,
William Henley Wiley Cunningham, John Lefever, James P. Keith, and David
Muckleroy, and that the Sheriff summon them to attend the same and make
due return to the same and that James Oliver & James H. Estill constables
be appointed to attend on said Court and that the Sheriff summon them
to attend the same and make due return to the same.

(p-407) Ordered by the Court that the following persons be appointed
Jurors to attend at the next Term of this Court towit, John Larkin 1,
William Simmons Junr. 2, Peter Simmons 3, Samuel A. Harris 4, Peter
Huston 5, David Robinson 6, James Campbell 7, Alexander Donoldson Senr. 8
William L. Sargeant 9, Thomas Muse 10, Madison Porter 11, Charles
Crisman 12, William M. Finch 13, Thomas Duncan 14, Bird Francis 15,

Samuel Miller, 16, Robert Cowan 17, Squire B. Hawkins 18, William Hendon 19, Nelson Carter 20, James S. Cowling 21, Saul Camp 22, John Morris Jur. 23, Edward Morris 24, James Russy 25, John Francis 26, and that Benjamin Franklin & James Campbell constables be appointed to attend on said Court and that the Sheriff summon them to attend the same and make due return to the same.

This day the amount of Sales of the Estate of Martin Adams deceased was returned into open Court was received by the Court and ordered to be made a part of the record.

This day the amount of Sales of the Sales of the Estate of Thomas Williams deceased was returned into Open Court was received by the Court was received by the Court and ordered to be made a part of the record.

This day the commissioners appointed to settle with Joseph Smith Guardian for James Brazier & Lucinda Brazier made their report which was received by the Court and ordered to be made apart of the record.

The commissioners appointed to settle with Elijah Allen administrator of the Estate of James Sartain deceased their day made their report which was received by the Court and it is ordered by the Court that said administrator be allowed a further credit of four dollars & 32½ cents amt. paid John Jones and also one dollar & Seventy five cents amt. paid on account of the widows one year support.

This day the amount of Sales of the Estate of Alexander S. Acklin deceased was returned into open Court was received by the Court and ordered to be made part of the record.

A Bill of sale from John W. Jones to Benjamin Powell for one negro girl named Mary was duly acknowledged in Open Court by the said John W. Jones to be his act and deed and ordered to be registered. Let it be registered.

(p-408)   It appearing to the satisfaction of the Court that Henry Burrow late of this County died intestate and Priscilla Burrow and Barnaby Burrow applied for letters of administration on the Estate of the said deceased It is therefore ordered by the Court that they have letters accordingly who entered into bond with Jethor Goodman their security in the sum of twelve hundred dollars according to law and was qualified accordingly.

Ordered by the Court that David O. Anderson, George Hudspeth, John Stavall, Hezekiah Faris, William Simmons, Thomas J. Hall and Isaac Vanzant or any five of them be appointed a Jury of view to view and change the road from Salem to the mouth of Beans Creek to turn off at the upper corner of Aaron McClures field and intersect the road at Beans Creek and that they view and turn the same with due regard to the convenience of travalers and as little as may be to the prejudice of individuals and that they make report of their proceedings to the next Term of this Court.

Ordered by the Court that John Sylor, William Lucus, William West, Robert Thompson, James Young Holloway Power and Benjamin Lucus or any five of them be appointed a Jury of view to view and mark a road from Fares mill on Beans Creek up said creek to William Simmons and that they view and mark the same with due regard to the convenience of travalers and as little as may be to the prejudice of individuals and that they make report of their proceedings to the next Term of this Court.

Ordered by the Court that Jackson Kenedy of the age of fifteen years be bound to Richmond P. Harris untill he arrives to the age of twenty-one years. Whereupon the said Richmond P. Harris entered into Indentures with the Chairman of Franklin County Court to learn him the said apprentice the art and ministery of the cotton spinning business and to learn him to read, write, and cipher through the rule of three and to give him at the end of his time one horse worth seventy five dollars & saddle and bridle and one new suit of clothes.

(p-409)   It appearing to the Court from the Inquesition of the Jury returned by the Sheriff to the present Term of the Court taken in pursuance of the order made at the last Term of this Court in relation to the insanity or lunacy of Edmond Russell a citizen of this County and the summons and proceedings had thereon: that the said Edmond Russell is insane and of unsound mind, and incapble of making contracts or managing his own affairs, and it also appearing that the said Edmond Russell owns and possesses three and about a half town lots adjoining each other in Winchester on which is the brick house where he now lives of the value of $4000, a tract of land of about 100 acres on dry creek value at $500, two hundred acres of one cent land valued at $25, a negro woman Peggy value at $400, a negro boy at $200, a negro child at $100 household and kitchen furniture including library $700, water cart and gray horse $30, stock of Cattle & hogs $35, gig and harness under execution $200 but which has been since taken and sold, all which will more fully appear by said inquest and return of the Sheriff of record in this Court. Whereupon it is ordered by the Court that Nathan Green James Taylor and Benjamin Decherd, be appointed guardain of the said Edmond Russell on their entering into bond in the penalty of twelve thousand dollars condition as the law direct.

THOMAS CRUTCHEN Assee & c   )
  Against   )
EDMOND RUSSELL &   )
NATHAN GREEN   )   On motion of the defendants by their
attorney it is ordered by the Court that the Judgment taken by default in this case be set aside and that the defendant be permitted to plead and that the same shall stand for trial at the next Term of this Court.

Court adjourned untill tomorrow morning ten o'clock.
                                        James Robinson
                                        M. W. Howell
                                        James Keith

(p-410)
      Tuesday September the seond one thousand eight hundred and thirty four Court met according to adjournment
Present - James Robinson   )   Esquires
          Marshall W. Howell   )
          James Keith   ) Justices of the peace for Franklin
                                            County

BENJAMIN DECHERD   )
  Against   )
THOMAS J. KENNERLY   )   This day came the Defendant by his attorney
and moved the Court to set aside the Judgment by default heretofore at
this Term rendered against him. Whereupon it is ordered by the Court
that said Judgment be set aside and that the defendant be permitted to
plead and that the same shall stand for trial at the next Term of this
Court.

BENJ. & P. S DECHERD   )
  Against   )
THOMAS J. KENNERLY   )   This day came the defendant by his attorney
and moved the Court to set aside the Judgment by default heretofore at
this Term rendered against him. Whereupon it is ordered by the Court
that said Judgment be set aside and that the Defendant be permitted to
plead and that the same shall stand for trial at the next term of this
Court.

GEORGE KESSED   )
  Against   )
THOMAS GAITHER   )   This day came the defendant by his attorney and
moved the court to set aside the Judgment by default heretofore at this
Term rendered against him Whereupon it is ordered by the Court that said
Judgment be set aside and that the Defendant be permitted to plead and
that the same shall stand for trial at the next Term of this Court.

THE STATE OF TENNESSEE   )
  Against   )
JOHN HUGHS   )   This day Edwin Eanes came into Open Court
and acknowledged himself to owe and stand justly indebted to the State
of Tennessee in the sum of two hundred and fifty dollars to be livied
of his respective goods and chattels lands and tenements to the use of
Said State but to be void on condition that John Hughs make his personal
appearance before the Justices of our next Court of pleas and quarter
sessions to be held for the County of Franklin at the Court house in
Winchester on Thursday after the fourth Monday in November next then
and there to answer the State on a Presentment found against him for
gaming and not depart the same without leave first had and obtained.

(p-411)   JAMES GILLASPIE   )   Debt
          Against   )
        KINDRED H MUSE   )
        WM. B. THOMPSON   )
        HARMAN LOKEY &   )
        JOPKIN L. TURNEY   )   This day came the plaintiff by his
attorney and having filed his Declaration and the Defendants being solemnly
called to appear and defend this suit came not but made default. Whereupon
it is considered by the Court that the plaintiff recover against the
Defendant one hundred and fifty dollars the debt in the Declaration
mentioned together with the further sum of six dollars interest thereon
at the rate of six per cent per anum and also his costs by them about
said suit in this behalf expended and the said defendants in mercy &.

Court adjourned untill Court in course.

                  James Robinson
                  M. W. Howell
                  James Keith

November Term 1834   State of Tennessee

At a Court of Pleas and Quarter Session began and held for
Franklin County on the fourth Monday of November in the year of our
Lord one thousand eight hundred and thirty four it being the 24th day
of said month and of the Independance of the United States the 59th.

Present thirteen of the acting Justices of the peace from
Franklin County.

A deed of conveyance from James Woods Trustee to James Matlook
for one hundred and eighteen and one third acres of land lying in
Franklin County was duly acknowledged in Open Court by the said James
Woods Trustee & C to be his act and deed whereupon it is ordered by the
Court to be certified for Registration. Let it be registered.

A deed of conveyance from John Faulkenberry to Spencer Rogers
for twenty acres of land lying in Franklin County was duly proven in
Open Court by the oaths of Thomas B. Simpson & Robert Stone subscribing
witnesses thereto to be the act and deed of the same John Faulkenberry
on the day that it bears date. Whereupon it is ordered by the Court
to be certified for registration. Let it be registered.

(p-412)   A deed of conveyance from John Brincy to James Henry for
seventy acres of land lying in Franklin was duly acknowledged in Open
Court by the said John Brincy to be his act and deed whereupon it is
ordered by the Court to be certified for registration. Let it be
registered.

A deed of conveyance from William Faris to William McKelvy for
fifty acres of land lying in Franklin County was duly acknowledged in
Open Court by the said William Faris to be his act and deed. Whereupon
it is ordered by the Court to be certified for registration. Let it be
registered.

A deed of conveyance from Thomas Rich & Catharine his wife to
Joseph Noe for thirteen acres of land lying in Franklin County was duly
proven in Open Court by the oaths of Connebus Homan & Wm. C. Handly
Subscribing witnesses thereto to be the act and deed of the said
Thomas Rich & Catharine his wife on the day that it bears date whereupon
it is ordered by the Court to be certified for registration. Let it
be registered.

A deed of conveyance from Jess Oldham to China Whalen for twenty
five acres of land lying in Franklin County was duly proven in Open
Court by the oaths of Elias Oldham Sr. and Elias Oldham Jr. Subscribing
witnesses thereto to be the act and deed of the said Jess Oldham on
the day that it bears date. Whereupon it is ordered by the Court to
be certified for registration. Let it be registered.

A deed of conveyance from Henry M. Rutledge to Jess Reynolds for
three hundred and twenty eight acres and one hundred & fifty four poles
of land lying in Franklin County was duly proven in Open Court by the

oaths of Hayden Arnold & Peter Willis Subscribing witnesses thereto to be the act and deed of the said Henry M. Rutledge on the day it bears date. Whereupon it is ordered by the Court to be certified for registration. Let it be registered.

A deed of conveyance from William C. Lipscomb to John R. Patrick for eighty acres of land lying in Franklin County was duly acknowledged in Open Court by the said Wm. C. Lipscomb to be his act and deed. Whereupon it is ordered by the Court to be certified for registration. Let it be registered.

(p-413) A deed of Trust from Robert Malone to John Goodwin for the personal property therein named for the benefit of Benjamin & Peter L. Dechered was duly acknowledged in Open Court by the said Robert Malone & John Goodwin to be their act and deed on the day it bears date. Whereupon it is ordered by the Court to be certified for registration. Let it be registered.

Ordered by the Court that Wallis Wilson be appointed overseer of the Court that Wallis Wilson be appointed overseer of the road of the third class from Salem to Buncomb in room and stead of George Foster and that he keep the same in good repair according to law and that he have the same hands that worked under said Foster.

Ordered by the Court that Dyer Moore be appointed overseer of the road of the third class from William Sharps to Daniel Normans in room and stead of John W. Jones and that he keep the same in good repair according to law, and that he have the same hands that worked under said Jones.

Ordered by the Court the Josiah Benny be appointed overseer of the road of the second class from the Stone fort to Bennys branch in room and stead of Reuben Cardin and that he keep the same in good repair according to law, and that he have the same hands that worked under the former overseer.

Ordered by the Court that Richard P. Holden be appointed overseer of the road of the second class from a hickory tree above Buckners to Rowland Lanes in room & stead of John L. Bowen and that he keep the same in good repair according to law and that he have the same hands that worked under the former overseer.

Ordered by the Court that Willis Burt be appointed overseer of the road of the second class from the Williford Place to Shasteens Old Place in room and Stead of Robert Smith and that he keep the same in good repair according to law and that he have the same hands that worked under the former overseer.

Ordered by the Court that William Arnold be appointed overseer of the road of the second class from the old county line of Franklin to the Bedford County line in room and stead of Benjamin Hasty and that he keep the same in good repair according to law & that Wm. Lasater Esqr. give a list of hands to work on said road.

(p-414)   Ordered by the Court that Joseph Newman be appointed overseer of the road of the first class from the boiling fork of Elk river to Thomas Knights and that he keep the same in good repair according to law, and that Marshall W. Howell Esq. give him a list of hands to work on said road.

Ordered by the Court that Thomas Cunningham Overseer of the road be authorized to buy a sledge hammer for the use of said road and that he bring in his bill at the next term of this Court.

Ordered by the Court that David Weaver be appointed overseer of the road of the second class from Mannsford to Wm. F. Longs Tanyard and that he keep the same in good repair according to law. And that Andrew Mann Esq. give him a list of hands to work on said road.

Ordered by the Court that Edward Swann be appointed overseer of the road from Pattons lane to Elk river and that he keep the same in good repair according to law and that James B. Stovall Esq. give him a list of hands to work on said road.

Ordered by the Court that Boyed Wilson be appointed Overseer of the road from Elk river to the Pleasant Plains and that he keep the same in good repair according to law. And that James B. Stovall Esq. give him a list of hands to work on said road.

Ordered by the Court that Hezekiah Faris be appointed overseer of the road of the third class from Lucus field to the mouth of Beans creek in room & stead of James Hobbs and that he keep the same in good repair according to law and that he have the same hands and that he that worked under said Hobbs.

Ordered by the Court that James B. Stovall, John Oliver & James Howard be appointed commissioners to settle with the administration of the Estate of Mathe Wilder deceased and make report to this on the next Term of this Court.

This day Samuel Handly came into Open Court and resigned his commission as a Justice of the peace for Franklin County which resignation was received by the Court.

This day Robinson Nevils came into Open Court and resigned his commission as a Justice of the peace for Franklin County which resignation was received by the Court.

(p-415)   Ordered by the Court that Soloman Banks, John McCrary, Thomas Embrey, Thomas Howard, Murry Embrey, Elias Oldham & Thomas Knight or any five of them be appointed a Jury of view to view and make a road from Maj. Sharps Mill crossing the mill pond so as to intersect the present road opposite Christopher Achlins and that they view & make the same with most convenience of travalers and as little asmay be to the prejudice of individuals and that they make return to this or the next Term of this Court.

This day Joseph Hickerson brought into Open Court four wolf scalps over four months old, and the Court being satisfied from his statement upon oath. It is ordered by the said Court to be allowed the sum of twelve dollars therefor out of any money in the Treasury of Middle Tennessee not otherwise appropriated.

Ordered by the Court that Benjamin Nevils be released from four dollars and fifty cents the tax on one Stud horse overcharged on the tax list for the year 1833 and that the collector have acredit for the same on his accounts. Isd.

Ordered by the Court that the allowance heretofore made to Tabby Moore be stoped.

Ordered by the Court that Andrew Byers & Laban Jones be appointed commissioners of the poor house to act with Wm. Lasater and said Andrew Byens was qualified according to law.

Ordered by the Court that John R. Patrick, Richard C. Holder & George Simmons be appointed commission to Settle with John S. Martin Guardain for Diannah Martin orphan of John Martin dead and that they make their report to this on the next Term of this Court.

Ordered by the Court that Peter Simmons, David O. Anderson and John Staples be appointed commissioners to settle with Susan Trigg Administratrix of the Estate of James L. McWharten dead and that they make their report to this on the next Term of this Court.

Ordered by the Court that Monday next be set apart to do County business.

On motion it is ordered by the Court that Olly Haws be appointed Guardian over the person & property of Amanda Terresa, & Thomas Jefferson Haws orphans of Harrison Haws dead who entered into bond with Andrew Woods her security in the sum of Sixty dollars according to law.

(p-416) It appearing to the Satisfaction of the Court that Francis A. Moore late of this county departed this life intestate since the last Term of this Court and on motion of Elias Moore brother of said Decedent who made oath and gave bond with John G. Bostick, Barnaba Burrows, David Bunniss, Jethro Goodman, Littlebenny Bostick, Anderson S. Goodman & Benjamin F. Moore his security in the penalty of five thousand dollars condtioned as the law directs letters of administration and therefore granted to the said Elias Moore.

It appearing to the satisfaction of the Court that Catharine Shropshire departed this life intestate. And on motion of Joseph R. Shropshire son of said Decedent for letters of administration on the Estate of said deceased. It is therefore ordered by the Court that he have letters accordingly who entered into bond with Henry Runnels and William R. Gillaspie his securities in the sum of four hundred dollars according to law and was qualified accordingly.

On motion it is ordered by the Court that John H. Martin be

appointed Guardian over the person and property of Diannah Martin minor orphan of John Martin deceased who entered into bond with John Staples and Aaron Thompson his Securities in the sum of twelve hundred dollars according to law.

On motion it is ordered by the Court that Martha Garner be appointed Guardian over the person and property of Susan Jane, Celia Ann, George Franklin, William Wallace & Diannah Harrison Garner minor orphans of Jrons Garner deceased who entered into bond with James Woods and John H. Martin her Securities in the sum of four thousand dollars according to law.

On motion it is ordered by the Court that Mary Vanzant be appointed Guardain over persons and property of Maria Louisa, Francis Adaline, Mary Anna & William Thomas Vanzant minor orphans of Jacob Vanzant deceased who entered into bond with James Robinson & Benjamin F. Wofford her Securities in the sum of twenty thousand dollars according to law.

Ordered by the Court that William M. Cowan be appointed constable in & for the County of Franklin in the bounds of Captain Hines Company for the next ensuing two years who entered into bond with John B. Hawkins & Squire B. Hawkins his securities according to law and was qualified accordingly.

(p-417) Ordered by the Court that James M. Jones be appointed constable in & for the county of Franklin in the bounds of Captain Stephens Company for the next ensuing two years who entered into bond with Josiah Benny & Thomas Wright his securities according to law and was qualified accordingly.

Ordered by the Court that Benjamin Orear be appointed constable in & for the county of Franklin in the bounds of Captian Knights company for the next ensuing two years.

Ordered by the Court the James Oliver be appointed constable in & for the County of Franklin in the bounds of Captain Naoots Company for the next ensuing two years.

This day came on an election for the purpose of electing a constable in & for the County of Franklin in the bounds of Captain Sartain's Company and on counting out the votes it was found that Littlebenny Bostich was duly and constitutionally elected constable in the bounds of said company for the next ensuing two years.

This day Barnaby Bunrow Guardian for the heirs of John Grahan dead made his return for the year 1833 which was received by the Court and ordered to be made a part of the record also a return for the year 1834 which was also received and ordered to be made part of the record.

This day the amount of Sales of the Estate of Henry Bunrow deceased was returned into Open Court was received by the Court & ordered to be made part of the record.

This day the settlement made with Robert Taylor administrator of the estate of Joshua Hickman deceased was returned into Open Court was received by the Court and ordered to be made a part of the record.

This day the amount of Sales of the Estate of John Conwell deceased was returned into Open Court was received by the Court and ordered to be made a part of the record.

(p-418)   Present Zachariah H. Murrell, Marshall W. Howell, John R. Patrick, Asa D. Oakley, Samuel Bradshaw, James Robinson, James Keith, Jess Jenkins, David Bell, George Hudspeth, William Lasater Richmond P. Harris & Elias Oldham Esqrs.

Ordered by the Court that Polly Ryal be allowed the sum of forty five dollars for her Support one year to be appropriated by Zachariah H. Murrill quarterly and that the Clerk issue certificates quarterly to the county Trustee to pay the same which allowance was unanimously made by said Justices.

Present ~~Zachariah H. Murrill~~, Marshall W. Howell, John R. Patrick Asa D. Oakley, Samuel Bradshaw, James Robinson, James Keith, Jess Jenkins, David Bell, George Hudspeth, William Lasaten, Richmond P. Harris & Elias Oldham Esqrs.

Ordered by the Court that John Handly & Benjamin Powell be allowed the following sums, to wit, John Handly seventeen dollars and fifty cents for seven days attendance & Benjamin Powell twelve dollars & fifty cents for five days attendance as commissioners of the public revenue for Franklin County and that the Clerk issue certificate to the same. Which allowance was unanimously made by said Justices.

(p-419)   Present Marshall W. Howell, John R. Patrick, Asa D. Oakley, Samuel Bradshaw, James Robinerson, James Keith, Jess Jenkins, David Bell, George Hudspeth, William Lasaten, Richmond P. Harris, George Thompson & Elias Oldham Esqrs.

Ordered by the Court that Ervin J. Frierson attorney General be allowed the sum of fifty dollars for his Exificio Services for the year 1833 and that the Clerk issure a cirtificate to the County Trustee to pay him the same which allowance was unanimously made by said Justices.

Ordered by the Court that Robert W. Thompson, John Silor, James H. Young, Isaac Silor, Wm. West, Hezekiah Faris, Wm. Simmons, or any fine of them be appointed a Jury of view to view and turn the road that leads from Salem to the mouth of Beanes Creek to turn off at the ford of the creek opposite Faris Mill and that they view and turn the same to the most convenience of Travalers and as little as may be to the prejudice of Individuals and that they make report to the next term of this Court.

This day the Jury of view appointed at the last Term of this Court to view and mark a road from the Mohergs ford road near John Pattons to intersect the Lusk gap road near the Pleasant Plains made their report which was received by the Court.

Present Zachariah H. Murrell, Marshall W. Howell, John R. Patrick Asa D. Oakley, Samuel Bradshaw James Robinson, James Keith, Jess Jenkins, David Bell, George Hudspeth, William Lasaten, Richard P. Harris & Elias Oldham Esqrs.

Ordered by the Court that James Byron be allowed one dollar & fifty cents for one day services as commissioner of the poor house and that William Lasaten Treasurer of said poor house pay him the same. Which allowance was unanimously made by said Justices. Isd to Powel.

Present /////////// /. /////// Marshall W. Howell, John R. Patrick, Asa D. Oakley, Samuel Bradshaw, James Robinson, James Keith, Jess Jenkins, David Bell, George Hulspeth, William Lasaten, Richmond P. Harris, George W. Thompson & Elias Oldham Esqrs.

Ordered by the Court that John Handly & Benjamin Powell be allowed the following sums, to wit, John Handly seventeen dollars and fifty cents for seven days attendance & Benjamin Powell twelve dollars & fifty cents for five days attendance as commissioners of the public revenue for Franklin County and that the clerk issure centificate to the County Trustee to pay them the same, which allowance was unanimously made by said Justices.

This day the last will and testament of Wm. B. Harris dead was produced in Court by the Executors therein named and thereupon came J James Flagg and George Simpson Subscribing witnesses thereto and being first duly sworn deposed and say that the said deceased William B. Harris declared and published this as his last will and testament and at the time of signing the same he the said William B. Harris was of sound and disposing mind and memory, and that he signed the same in their presence and they as witnesses thereto signed the same in his presence and at his request whereupon it is ordered by the Court that the same be recorded.

This day the resignation of Bryant B. Thompson as guardian of two of the minor heirs of Nathaniel Wilder deceased was this day produced in Open Court and duly proven by the oaths of Wm. B. Thompson & Wm. Farris subscribing witnesses thereto to be the act and deed of the said Bryant B. Thompson & ordered to be certified.

(p-420)   This day the Jury of view appointed at the last Term of this Court to view and make a road from Farris Mill on Beans Creek up said creek to Wm. Simmons made their report in the following words, towit, in pursuance of an order of the Court of Pleas & Quarter Sessions for Franklin County to us directed to view a road from Faris Mill on Beans Creek to Wm. Simmons up sd. Creek report that after having been duly qualified we have viewed said road and that we think the present road from the mouth of Beans Creek to Salem as far as Joshua Gore's field and from thence across through the upper corner of said field to the ford leading to Wm. Simmons lane the same way the old road formerly run is the best & most convenient way Oct. 7th 1834

John Siler
Holloway Power
James H. Young
Robert W. Thompson
William West
Benjamin Lucus
Wm. H. Lucus

To which Joshua Gore one of the persons whose land said road runs through objects and says he will be injured thereby and prays a Jury to assess damages. It is therefore ordered by the Court that a writ issure to the Sheriff of Franklin County commdanding him to summon a Jury of twelve for holders to go upon the land of the said Joshua Gore and ascertain what damages he has sustained by reason of said road passing through his land and that they make report his land and that they make report to the next Term of this Court.

Court adjourned until tomorrow morning 10 o'clock.
James Robinson
Geo. W. Thompson
James Keith

Tuesday November the twenty fifth one thousand eight hundred and thirty four Court met according to adjournment.

Present -   James Robinson   )   Esquires
              George W. Thompson   )
              James Keith   )   Justices of the peace for
Franklin County.

State of Tennessee

Proclamation being made the Sheriff of Franklin County made return of the State writ of Venirefacia to this Court that he had summoned the following persons (p-421) being all good and lawful men of said County of Franklin and being citizens of said County of Franklin to attend ahd serve a Jurors at the present Term of this Court which persons so summoned and returned as aforesaid had been nominated for that purpose by the Justices of this said Court of Pleas and Quarter Sessions of said County of Franklin at its last Session a list of whom was delivered to the said Sheriff of Franklin by the Clerk of this said Court, to wit, John Larkins, Wm. Simmons Junr, Peter Simmons, Samuel A. Harris, Peter Heistan, David Robinson, Joseph Campbell, Alexander Donaldson Senr. Wm. S. Sargeant, Thomas Mused, Madison Porter Charles Crisman, Wm. M. Finch, Thomas Duncan, Bird Francis, Samuel Miller, Robert Cowan Squire B. Hawkens, William Hendon, Nelson Carter, James S. Cowling, Saul Camp John Morris Junr. Edward Morris, James Russy & John Francis and of whom the following this day attended, to wit, Wm. Simmons Junr. Peter Simmons, Samuel A. Harris, David Robinson, Joseph Campbell, Alexander Donaldson Senr. Wm. S. Sargeant, Thomas Musd. Madison Porter Charles Crisman, Wm. M. Finch, Thomas Duncan, Bird Francis, Samuel Miller Squire B. Hawkins, William Henden, Nelson Carter, Jas. S. Cowling, John Morris Junr. Edward Morris, James Russy & John Francis and of whom the following persons being all good and lawful men of said County of Franklin were elected empanneled and sworn a grand Jury of Inquest for the body of the County of Franklin, to wit, William M. Finch who was appointed foreman, William S. Sargeant, Nelson Carter, James Russy, John Morris Jr. Alexander Donaldson Senr. Edward Morris, Joseph Campbell Thomas Duncan, Charles Cristman, James S. Cowling, Bird Francis & Samuel Miller who after receiving their charge retired to consult of their presentments.

Ordered by the Court that Saul Camp, Samuel A. Harris John Larkins, Peter Simmons & Wm. Simmosn be released from serving as Jurors during the present Term of this Court.

Ordered by the Court that Peter Heistan and Robert Cowan Jurors summond to attend at the present Term of this Court be fined the sum of two dollars and fifty cents each for their non attendance and that a Sci fa issure against them returnable to the next Court.

(p-422)   HENRY S. CAMDEN   )
               Vs   )
           BENJAMIN F. JENKINS   )   On motion of the defendant by his
attorney and upon his statement which is taken as an affidavit. It is ordered that this cause be continued untill the next Term of this Court.

JAMES B. STOVALL   )   Case
    Against   )
JOHN D. STOVALL   )   This day came the parties by their attornies and

thereupon came a Jury, to wit, Thomas Muse 1, Squire B. Hawkins 2, John Francis 3, William Henden 4, David Robinson 5, John M. Bennett 6, Baraham Shook 7, Barnett Forsyth 8, William Greenlee 9, Thomas L. Duncan 10, James Camden 11 & Joseph Miller who being elected tried and sworn the truth to speak upon the issure. Joined upon their oaths do say they find the issure in favor of the plaintiff and assoess his damages to three hundred and sixteen dollars & twenty cents besides costs. It is therefore considered by the Court that the plaintiff recover against the defendant his damages aforesaid in form of one said assocessed and also his costs by him about said Suit in this behalf expended and the said defendant in mercy &.

A deed of Trust from James H. Badget to John a McNiel for the personal property therein named was duly acknowledged in Open Court by the said James H. Badget and John McNeil to be their act and deed. Whereupon it is ordered by the Court to be certified for registration. Let it be registered.

The day Benjamin Orear who was on yesterday appointed constable in the bounds of Captain Knights Company came into Court and entered into bond with George McCrutchion and William McClelen his Securities according to law and was qualified accordingly.

This day Littleberry Bostich who was on yesterday elected constable in the bounds of Captain Sartains Company came into Open Court and entered into bond with James Oliver and John Goodwin his securities according to law and was qualified accordingly.

An additional list of Sales of the Estate of Joseph Blake decd. was this day returned into Open Court was received by the Court and ordered to be made a part of the record.

(p-423)   This day Elias Oldham came into Open Court and resigned his commission a Justice of the peace for Franklin County which was received by the Court.

JOSEPH HINKLE   )
  Against   )
KINDRED H. MUSE   ) On motion of the defendant by his attorney this cause is continued untill the next Term of this Court on his affidavit by his paying the costs of the Term, and on his motion a commission is awarded him to take the deposition of John C. Beasley & John Conly before any one Justice of the peace for Madison County Alabama to be read as evidence on the trial of the above cause on behalf of the defendant by his giving the plaintiff ten days notice of the time and place of taking said deposition.

JOHN J. HAYTER assee & C.   )   Debt
  Against   )
THOMAS P. WHITNEY   )
LEVI C. ROBERTS   )
HAYDEN ARNOLD &   )
PORTLAND J. CURLE   ) This day came the plaintiff as well as

Thomas P. Whitney & Levi C. Roberts by their attornies and there upon
came a Jury towit, William L. Sargeant 1, Nelson Carter 2, John Morris 5
Wm. M. Finch 6, Joseph Campbell 7, Thomas Duncan 8, Charles Crisman 9,
James S. Cowling 10, Bird Francis 11, & Samuel Miller 12, Who being
elected tried and sworn the truth to speak upon the issure joined between
the said Plaintiff & Thomas P. Whitney & Levi C. Roberts two of the
defendants the other two defendants not having pleaded to this action
upon their oaths do say they find the issure in favor of the said Thomas
P. Whitney & Levi C. Roberts Wherefore it is considered by the Court
that the said Thomas P. Whitney & Levi C. Roberts go hence without day
and recover against the plaintiff their costs about said suit in this
behalf expended and the said depot in mercy &. Whereupon the said
Hayden Arnold & Portland J. Curle the other defendants in this suit and
who have not pleased to this action a aforesaid being solemly called to
appear and defend this suit came not but made default, wherefore on
motion of the plaintiff by his attorney it is considered by the Court
that the plaintiff recover against the said Hayden Arnold and Portland
Js Curle the sum of one hundred dollars the debt in the Declaration
mentioned together with the further sum of forty dollars & eighty three
cents damages being the interest thereon at the rate of six percent peranum and also his costs by them about said suit in this behalf expended
and the said Hayden Arnold & Portland J. Curle im.

(p-424)   This day James Oliver who was on yesterday elected constable
came into Court and entered into bond with John Oliver & Littleberry
Bostick his securities according to law. Court adjourned untill tomorrow
morning 10 o'clock.

                                            James Robinson
                                            James Keith
                                            Geo. W. Thompson

        Wednesday, November the twenty sixth, one thousand eight hundred
and thirty four Court met according to adjournment.
Present - James Robinson   )   Esquires Justices of
          James Keith &   )   peace for Franklin County.
          George W. Thompson   )

EPHRAIM H. FOSTER assee & C   )
  Assigned   )
  Against   )
WILLIAM JACKSON &   )
JOHN B. WILKERSON   )   This day came the Plaintiff by his
attorney and dismisses his suit and not further prosecuting it is ordered
that this suit be dismissed and the defendant assumes the costs. It is
therefore considered by the Court that the plaintiff recover against
the defendant his costs by about said suit in this behalf expended and
the said defendant in mercy &.

BENJAMIN DECHERD   )
  Against   )
THOMAS J. KENNERLY   )   This day came the plaintiff by his attorney
and dismisses his suit and not furthers prosecuting it is ordered that
this suit be dismissed and the Defendant assumes the costs. It is therefore considered by the Court that the Plaintiff recover against the

Defendant his costs by him about said suit in this behalf expended and the said Defendant in Mercy &.

BENJAMIN & PERER S. DECHERED)
  Against   )
THOMAS J. KENNERLY   ) This day came the plaintiffs by
their attorney and dismiss their suit and not further prosecuting. It is ordered that this suit be dismissed, and the Defendant assume the costs. It is therefore considered by the Court that the plaintiffs recover against the Defendant their costs by them about said suit in this behalf expended and the said defendant in Mercy &.

(p-425)   JOSEPH B. HERNDON)
          Against   )
          BARNETT FORSYTH   ) On motion of the parties by their attornies this cause is transfered to the next Court to be held for this county Court by their consent.

HUDSON ALLEN   )   Case
  Against   )
JAMES RUSSY   ) This day came the parties by their attornies and thereupon came a Jury, to wit, Madison Porter 1, Thomas Muse 2, Squire B. Hawkins 3, John Francis 4, William Henden 5, David Robinson 6 William Lee 7, Elijah D. Hammons 8, William Greenlee 9, Barnett Forsyth 10 Joseph Duncan 11, & Richard B. Moore 12, who being elected tried and sworn the truth to speak upon the issure joined upon their oaths do say they find the issure in favor of the plaintiff and asscess his damages to sixty one dollars & forty four cents besides costs. It is therefore considered by the Court that the Plaintiff recover against the Defendant his damages aforesaid in from aforesaid asscessed and also his costs by him about said suit in this behalf expended and the said defendant in Mercy &.

JOHN W. PEARSON   )
  Against   )
CORNELUS HOMAN   ) On motion of the parties by their attornies the cause is transfered to the next Circuit Court to be held for this Country by their consent.

JAMES A. SMOWDEN   )
  Against   )
JOHN WINFORD   ) On motion of the parties by their attornies this cause is continued untill the next Term of this Court by their consent.

JAMES MCDANIEL   )   Debt
  Against   )
BENJAMIN J. JACAWAY) This day came the parties by their attornies and thereupon came a Jury to wit William M. Finch 1, William S. Sargeant 2, Nelson Carter 3, John Morris Junr. 4, Alexander Donaldson Senr. 5 Edward Morris 6, Joseph Campbell 7, Thomas Duncan 8, Charles Christmas 9, James S. Cowling 10, Bird Francis 11 & Samuel Miller 12, Who being elected tried and sworn the truth to speak upon the issure joined upon their oaths do say they find the issure in favor of the plaintiff and asscess

his damages to thirty one dollars & Seventy five cents besides costs.
It is therefore considered by the Court that the Plaintiff recover
against the Defendant two hundred and fifty dollars the balance of the
debt in the Declaration mentioned together with his damages aforesaid
in form aforesaid his costs about said suit expended & the said debt
in mercy &.

(p-426)   THOMAS CRUTCHER Assee & C.)   Debt
              Against   )
           EDMOND RUSSELL &   )
           NATHAN GREEN   ) This day came the plaintiff by
his attorney and having filed his Declaration and the Defendants being
solemnly called to appear and defend this suit come not but made default
It is therefore considered by the Court that the plaintiff recover against
the defendants one hundred and forty five dollars the debt in the
Declaration mentioned together with the further sum of four dollars
Interest thereon at the rate of six percent peranum and also his costs
by him about said suit in this behalf expended and the said Defendants
in mercy &.

EPHRAIN H. FOSTER   )   Debt
  Against   )
BARNABY BUNROW   ) This day came the parties by their attornies
and thereupon came a Jury to wit William M. Finch 1, William S. Sargeant 2,
Nelson Carter 3, John Morris Junr. 4, Alexander Donaldson Senr. 5,
Edward Morris 6, Joseph Campbell 7, Thomas Duncan 8, Charles Crisman 9,
James S. Cowling 10, Bird Francis 11, & Samuel Miller 12, Who being
elected tried and sworn the truth to speak upon the issure joined upon
their oaths do say they find the issure in favor of the plaintiff and
assoess his damages to ~~ninety four dollars and fifty six cents the debt~~
~~in the~~ one dollar & eighty seven and one half cents besides costs. It
is therefore considered by the Court that the Plaintiff recover against
the Defendant ninety four dollars & fifty six cents the debt in the
Declaration mentioned together with his damages aforesaid in form
aforesaid assessed and also his costs by him about said suit in this
behalf expended and the said defendant in Mercy &.

WILLIAM KNOX Assignee & C)   Debt
  Against   )
HENRY HENREFORD   ) This day came the parties by their
attornies and thereupon came a Jury to wit, Wm. M. Finch 1, William S.
Sargeant 2, Nelson Carter 3, John Morris Junr. 4, Alexander Donaldson
Senr. 5, Edward Morris 6, Joseph Campbell 7, Thomas Duncan 8, Charles
Crisman 9, James S. Cowling 10, Bird Francis 11, & Samuel Miller 12,
Who being elected tried and sworn the truth to speak upon the issure
joined upon their oaths do say they find the issure in favor of the
plaintiff and assess his damages to six dollars & five cents besides
costs. It is therefore considered by the Court that the plaintiff recover
against the Defendant one hundred and twenty six dollars and sixty six
cents the balance (p-427) of the Debt in the Declaration mentioned
together with his damages aforesaid in form aforesaid assecessed and
also his costs by him about said suit in this behalf expended and the
said Defendant in mercy & C.

ROBERT WEAKLY) Debt
  Against)
NANCY SIMPSON) This day came the parties by their attornies
and thereupon came a Jury to wit, William M. Finch 1, William S. Sargeant
2, Nelson Carter 3, John Morris Junr 4, Alexander Donaldson Senr. 5,
Edward Morris 6, Joseph Campbell 7, Thomas Duncan 8, Charles Crisman 9,
James S. Cowling 10, Bird Francis 11, & Samuel Miller 12, Who being
elected tried and sworn the truth to speak upon the issure joined upon
their oaths do say they find the issure in favor of the plaintiff and
assess his damages to thirty two dollars and thirty five cents besides
besides costs. It is therefore considered by the Court that the plaintiff recover against the Defendant one hundred dollars the debt in the
Declaration mentioned together with his damages aforesaid in form
aforesaid assessed and also his costs by him about said suit in this
behalf expended and the said Defendant in mercy &.

THOMAS S. LOGAN Assignee &) Debt
  Against)
JAMES GILLASPIE &)
MICAJAH L. GILLASPIE) This day came the parties by their
attornies and thereupon came a Jury to wit, William M. Finch 1,
William S. Sargeant 2, Nelson Carter 3, John Morris Junr 4, Alexander
Donaldson Senr. 5, Edward Morris 6, Joseph Campbell 7, Thomas Duncan 8,
Charles Crisman 9, James S. Cowling 10, Bird Francis 11, Samuel Miller 12
Who being elected tried and sworn the truth to speak upon the issure
joined upon their oaths do say they find the issure in favor of the
plaintiff and assess his damages to seven dollars and eighty seven
cents besides costs. It is therefore considered by the Court that the
Plaintiff recover against the defendants two hundred and twenty five
dollars and twenty five cents the balance of the debt in the declaration
mentioned together with his damages aforesaid in form aforesaid assessed
and also his costs by him about said suit in this behalf expended and
the said Defendant in mercy &.

GEORGE KEESSEE) Debt.
  Against)
THOMAS GAITHER) This day came the parties by their attornies and
thereupon came a Jury (p-428) to wit, William M. Finch 1,
William S. Sargeant 2, Nelson Carter, 3, John Morris Junr. 4, Alexander
Donaldson Senr. 5, Edward Morris 6, Joseph Campbell 7, Thomas Duncan 8,
Charles Crisman 9, James S. Cowling 10, Bird Francis 11, & Samuel
Miller 12, Who being elected tried and sworn the truth to speak upon
the issure joined upon their oaths do say they find the issure in favor
of the plaintiff and assess his damages to sixteen dollars and fifty
cents besides costs. It is therefore considered by the Court that the
Plaintiff recover against the Defendant three hundred dollars the debt
in the Declaration mentioned together with his damages aforesaid in
form aforesaid assessed and also his costs by him about said suit in
this behalf expended and the said Defendant in mercy &.

EPHRAIM HL FOSTER) Debt
  Asignee &)
ROBERT TURNER) This day came the parties by their attornies and
thereupon came a Jury to wit, William M. Finch 1, William S. Sargeant 2,
Nelson Carter 3, John Morris Junr. 4, Alexander Donaldson Senr. 5

Edward Morris 6, Joseph Campbell 7, Thomas Duncan 8, Charles Crisman 9
James S. Cowling 10, Bird Francis 11 & Samuel Miller 12, Who being elected
tried and sworn the truth to speak upon the issure joined upon their
oaths do say they find the issure in favor of the Plaintiff and assess
his damages to four dollars and twenty five cents besides cost. It is
therefore considered by the Court that the plaintiff recover against
the Defendant eighty two dollars the debt in the Declaration mentioned
together with his damages aforesaid in form aforesaid assessed and also
his costs by him about said suit in this behalf expended and the said
Defendant in mercy &.

THOMAS S. LOGAN Asignee & C)   Debt
   Against   )
RICHARD B. MOORE   )   This day came the parties by their
attornies and thereupon came a Jury, towit, William M. Finch 1,
William S. Sargeant 2, Nelson Carter 3, John Morris Junr 4, Alexander
Donaldson Senr. 5, Edward Morris 6, Joseph Campbell 7, Thomas Duncan 8,
Charles Crisman 9, James S. Cowling 10, Bird Francis 11, & Samuel Miller 12,
Who being elected tried and sworn the truth to speak upon the issure
in favor of the plaintiff and assess his damage to seven dollars and
fifteen cents besides costs. It is (p-429)   therefore considered by
the Court that the plaintiff recover against the Defendant one hundred
and ten dollars the debt in the Declaration mentioned together with
his damages aforesaid in form aforesaid assessed and also his costs by
him about said suit in this behalf expended and the said Defendant in
mercy &.

ANDERSON W. REED   )   Debt
   Against   )
BENJAMIN J. JACAWAY   )   This day came the parties by their attornies
and thereupon came a Jury to wit, William M. Finch 1, William S. Sargeant
2, Nelson Carter 3, John Morris Junr 4, Alexander Donaldson Senr. 5
Edward Morris 6, Joseph Campbell 7, Thomas Duncan 8, Charles Crisman 9
James S. Cowling 10, Bird Francis 11, & Samuel Miller 12, Who being
elected tried and sworn the truth to speak upon the issure Joined upon
their oaths do say they find the issure in favor of the plaintiff and
the issure in favor of the plaintiff and assess his damages to fifteen
dollars besides costs. It is therefore considered by the Court that
the plaintiff recover against the defendant five hundred dollars the
balance of the debt in the Declaration mentioned together with his
damages aforesaid in form aforesaid assessed and also his costs by him
about said suit in this behalf expended and the said defendant in mercy &.

JAMES ARMSTRONG   )   Debt
   Against   )
MICAJAH L. GILLASPIE   )   This day came the parties by their attornies
and thereupon came a Jury, to wit, William M. Finch 1, William L.
Sargeant 2, Nelson Carter 3, John Morris Junr. 4, Alexander Donaldson
Senr. 5, Edward Morris 6, Joseph Campbell 7, Thomas Duncan 8, Charles
Crisman 9, James S. Cowling 10, Bird Francis 11, & Samuel Miller 12,
Who being elected tried and sworn the truth to speak upon the issure
joined upon their oaths do say they find the issure in favor of the
plaintiff and assess his damages to eighty dollars & sixteen cents
the balance of the debt in the Declaration mentioned together with

with his damages aforesaid in form aforesaid assessed and also his costs
by him about said suit in this behalf expended and the said defendant
in mercy &.

This day James Oliver who was heretofore on Monday last elected
Constable in the bounds of Captain Nancis Company came into Court and
was qualified according to law.

(p430)　JOHN J. HAYTER Asee & C　)　On motion of Livi C. Roberts by
　　　　Against　　　　　　　　　)　　his attorney.
　　　　THOMAS P. WHITNEY　　　　)
　　　　LEVI C. ROBERTS　　　　　)
　　　　HAYDEN ARNOLD &　　　　　)
　　　　PORTLAND I. CURLE　　　　)　It is ordered by the Court that he
have privelege to withdraw the note from the files in this case and it
is also ordered that the Clerk of this Court retain a copy of said note
and the endorsements thereon.

DANIEL WAGGONER &　　　　　　　)　　　　Case
DAVID WAGGONER　　　　　　　　)
Executors of DANIEL　　　　　)
WAGGONER SEnr. Decd.　　　　　)
　Against　　　　　　　　　　　　)
LUNSFORD S. MATHEWS　　　　　　)　　This day came the parties by
their attornies and thereupon came a Jury, to wit, William M. Finch 1,
William S. Sargeant 2, Nelson Carter 3, John Morris Junr 4,
Alexander Donaldson Senr. 5, Edward Morris 6, Joseph Campbell 7,
Thomas Duncan 8, Charles Crisman 9, James S. Cowling 10, Bird Francis 11,
& Samuel Miller 12, Who being elected tried and sworn the truth to
speak upon this issure joined upon their oaths do say they find the
issure in favor of the Defendant. It is therefore considered by the
Court that the defendant go hence without day and recover against the
plaintiffs his costs by him about his defence in this behalf expended
and the said plaintiffs in mercy &. to be levied of the proper goods
and chattels rights and credits of Daniel Waggener Senr. Decd. in
the hands of said Executors to be administered, from which judgment the
plaintiffs prayed an appeal to the next Curcuit Court to be held for this
County which is granted.

This day Samuel Corn came into Open Court and resigned his commission
of the Justice of the peace for Franklin County which was received by
the Court.

This day the Grand Jury came into Open Court and returned a Bill
of Indictment against Enoch Hardcastle for an assult & Battery. A True
Bill.

A Bill of Sale from Barnett Forsyth to James Forsyth for his
interest in four negroes was duly acknowledge in Open Court by the
said Barnett Forsyth to be his act and deed, Whereupon it is ordered
by the Court to be certified for registration. Let it be registered.

Ordered by the Court that Joseph R. Shropshire befined the sum
of two dollars and fifty cents for his non attendance as a Petit Juror

when summoned by the sheriff. ~~and that a few to leave out all the return~~
~~are to the next term of the~~

(p-431)   JOSEPH DUNCAN   )   Motion
              Against   )
           JAMES S. BRYANT &   )
           HAYDEN ARNOLD   ) On motion of the said plaintiff by his
attorney and it appearing to the satisfaction of the Court that on the
27th day of August 1834 that Thomas M. Pryor & Co. Recovered against
James S. Bryant and Joseph Duncan in an action of debt by them prossecuted
in the Court a Judgment for eight hundred and twenty seven dollars and
twenty cents debt and damages and also seven dollars twenty seven & one
half cents costs of suit as will more fully appear by the record of said
formen suit which judgment is founded upon the following note to wit,
$800 on or before the 1st day of February next we promise to pay Thomas
M. Pryor & Co. or order eight hundred dollars which may be discharged
in merchantable bailed cotton delivered in Winchester this 4th day of
February 1833 which if paid in cotton is at the cash price.

                                        Hayden Arnold (Seal)
H. Arnold   James S. Bryant (Seal)
                                        Jos. Duncan (Seal)

Whereupon came a Jury of good & lawful men, to wit, Madison Porter 1,
Thomas Muse 2, Squire B. Hawkins 3, John Francis 4, William Hendon 5,
David Robinson 6, Wm. Lee 7, Huston Allen 8, Solomon Hogue 9, Elijah
D. Hammons 10, Wm. Greenlee 11, & Barnett Forsyth 12, Who being elected
tried and sworn well and truely to try & find whether said Joseph Duncan
excuted said note as the Security only of the said James S. Bryant and
Hayden Arnold, upon their oaths do say that the said Duncan did excute
the said note as the Security only of the said James S. Bryant & Hayden
Arnold. It further appeared to the Court that said Judgment and costs
have been satisfied by the said Joseph Duncan Whereupon it is considered
by the Court that the plaintiff recover against the Defendants eight
hundred and sixty six dollars & forty two cents that being the amount
of the judgment & costs aforesaid and interest on the same from the 7th
day of November 1834 up to this time, and also the costs of this motion
in this behalf expended and the said defendants in mercy &.

ROBERT GIBISON   )
  Against   )
GEORGE W. THOMPSON &   )
FRANCIS A. MOORE   ) This day came the plaintiff by attorney and
suggisted to the Court here that since the last Term of this Court
Francis A. Moore one of the Defts. in this suit have departed the life
intostate and the other defendant agrees that this suit may be prosecuted
against him without making the representive of more a party thereto.
(p-432)   Court adjourned until tomorrow morning 10 o'clock
                                        Geo. W. Thompson
                                        James Robinson
                                        James Keith

      Thursday November the 27th one thousand eight hundred and thirty
four Court met according to adjournment.

Present - James Robinson) Esquires
        James Keith &)
        Marshall W. Howell) Justices of the peace for Franklin
                           County

THE STATE OF TENNESSEE) Indict for an Affray
  Against)
WILLIAM P. CRAIGG) This day came the attorney General who
prosecutes for the State in this be half and with the assent of the Court
enters a noteprosegue in this case.

THE SATE OF TENNESSEE) Present for Gaming
  Against)
JOHN HUGHS) This day came the attorney General who
prosecutes for the State in this behalf as well as the defendant in his
proper person and the said Defendant having heard the said Indictment
read says he is thereof not guilty and puts himself upon the Country
and the attorney General doth the like and thereupon came a Jury, to wit,
Madison Porter, 1, Thomas Muse 2, Squire B. Hawkins 3, John Francis 4,
William Hendon 5, David Robinson 6, William Darwin 7, Madison Goodman 8
Hayden Arnold 9, Andrew G. Mitchell 10, Lunsford Mathew 11, & Richard
B. Moore 12, Who being elected tried and sworn the truth ~~to speak upon~~
~~this issure upload upon their oaths do say they find it~~ of and upon the
promises to speak upon their oaths do say they find the defendant guilty
in manner and form as charged in the Bill of Indictment. It is therefore
considered by the Court that the Defendant for such his offence be fined
five dollars and pay the costs of this prosecution.

THE STATE OF TENNESSEE) Present of Gaming
  Against)
CHARLES WOODS) This day came the attorney General who
prosecutes for the State in this behalf as well as the defendant in his
proper person and the said Defendant having heard said Indictment read
says he is thereof guilty and puts himself upon the grave and mercy of
the Court. It is therefore considered by the Court that the Defendant
for such his offence be finded five dollars & pay the costs of this
prosecution and in mercy &.

(p-433) THE STATE OF TENNESSEE) Indict for an affray
        Against)
        WILLIAM B. THOMPSON) This day came the attorney General
who prosecutes for the state on his behalf expended as well as the defendant in his property person and the said defendant having heard said
Indictment read says he is thereof guilty and puts himself upon the grave
and mercy of the Court. It is therefore considered by the Court that the
defendant for such his offince be fined one cent and pay the costs of this
prosecution and that he remain in custody of the Sheriff till paid or
security given for the same whereupon William Faris came into Court and
acknowledged himself security for the above fine and costs and that a
fi fa issure against him for the same.

THE STATE OF TENNESSEE) On motion of the parties by their attornies
  Against)
MADISON GOODMAN)

this cause is continued untill the next Term of this Court by their Consent.

THE STATE OF TENNESSEE)
  Against)
MADISON GOODMAN)   This day Madison Goodman & Robert H. Oliver came into Open Court an acknowledged themselves to owe and stand justly indebted to the State of Tennessee in the following sums to wit, Madison Goodman in the sum of two hundred & fifty dollars & Robert H. Oliver his security in the sum of one hundred and twenty five dollars to be levied of their respective goods & Chattels lands and tenements to the use of said State but to be void on condition that Madison Goodman make his personal appearance before the Justices of our next Court of please and quarter sessions to be held for the County of Franklin at the Court house in Winchester on Thursday after the fourth Monday in February next then and there to answer the State on a bill of Indictment found against him for an Affray and not depart the same without leave first had and obtained.

This day the grand Jury came into Open Court and returned a Bill of Indictment against William Kirkandal for an assault & Battery not a true Bill also a Bill of Indictment against Andrew H. McCollum for malicious mischief a true Bill.

(p-434)   A deed of conveyance from Benjamin Franklin to Micajah L. Gillaspie for Sixity three acres of land lying in Franklin County was duly acknowledged in Open Court by the Said Benjamin Franklin to be his act and deed. Whereupon it is ordered by the Court to be certified for registration. Let it be registered.

Whereas at the may term 1834 of this Court it was made satisfactorly appear to said Court that Edmond Russell of said County is insane. Whereupon the Court ordered that a writ of Inquisition should issue directed to the Sheriff of Franklin County to commanding him to summon twelve face holders to ascertain the alledged Lunacy that in pursuance thereof the Clerk of this Court issured said writ which was placed in the hands of said Sheriff who in obedience thereto summoned twelve face holders, being good and lawful men of said County who being sworn well and truly to enquire and ascertain whether the said Edmond Russell is a lunatic or Insane and also to ascetain the value of the Estate of the said Edmond Russell upon their oaths do say that they said Edmond Russell is insane and of unsound mind and is incapable of making contracts or managing his own affairs and that he possesses real and personal property to the value of six thousand one hundred and ninety dollars as specified and ascertained in their return which writ and inquisition was returned to the August Term of the Court and thereupon said Court appointed Benjamin Decherd, Nathan Green & James Taylor were appointed Guardians over the person and property of the said Edmond Russell and who were required by said Court to enter into bond and security in the penalty of twelve thousand dollars who failed to entere into bond as required by the order of the Court, and now at this day Benjamin Decherd be appointed guardian over the person and property of the said Edmond Russell who thereupon came into open Court and applied to be appointed guardian as aforesaid whereupon in pursuance of the proceedings aforesaid it is ordered by the Court

that the said Benjaman Decherd entered into bond with John Goodwin &
Mark Hutchins his securities in the sum of five thousand dollars according to law.

       Court adjourned untill tomorrow morning 10 o'clock.
                                      M. W. Howell
                                    James Keith
                                    James Robinson

       Friday Nov. 28th 1834 Court met according to adjournment.   Present-
Jas. Robinson Jas. Keith & M. W. Howell, Esqrs. Justices of the peace
for Franklin County.

(p-435)   JAMES A. SNOWDEN   )   Case
             Against   )
          MICAJAH L. GILLASPIE   ) This day came the parties by their
attornies and thereupon came a Jury, to wit, William M. Finch, 1
William S. Sargeant 2, Nelson Carter 3, John Morris Junr. 4,
Alexander Donaldson Senr. 5, Edward Morris 6, Joseph Campbell 7,
Thomas Duncan 8, Charles Crisman 9, James S. Cowling 10, Bird Francis 11
& Samuel Miller 12, Who being elected tried and sworn the truth to speak
upon the issure Joined upon their oaths do say they find the issure in
favor of the plaintiff, and assess his damages to seventy nine dollars
& forty five cents besides costs. It is therefore considered by the Court
that the plaintiff recover against the defendant his damages aforesaid
in form aforesaid assessed and also his costs by him about said suit in
this behalf expended and the said defendant in mercy &. from which
judgment the Defendant prayed an appeal to the Next Curcuit Court to be
held for this County which is granted by his giving bond & Security to
the Clerk within a week from the rise of the Court.

JAMES ARMSTRONG   )
  Against   )
MICAJAH L. GILLASPIE   )   This day came the defendant by his attorney
and payed an appeal from the Judgment of the Court heretofore at this
Term rendered against him to the next Curcuit Court to be held for
this County which is granted him by his entering into bond & Security
to the Clerk within a week from the rise of this Court.

THOMAS S. LOGAN Assee & C.)
  Against   )
JAMES GILLASPIE &   )
MICAJAH L. GILLASPIE   )   This day came the defendants by their
attorney and prayed an appeal from the Judgment of the Court heretofore
at this Term rendered against them to the next Curcuit Court to be held
for this County which is granted them by this entering into bond
& Security to the Clerk within a wekk from the rise of this Court.

       Court Adjourned untill tomorrow morning 10 o'clock.
                                    James Robinson
                                    M. W. Howell
                                 - James Keith

(p-436)   Saturday November the twenty ninth one thousand eight hundred
and thirty four Court met according to adjournment.
Present - James Robinson   )   Esquires Justices
            James Keith &   )   of the peace for Franklin County
            Marshall W. Howell   )

A deed of conveyance from Thomas Williamson to David Robinson for
one hundred eighty two & one half acres of land lying in Franklin County
was duly acknowledged in Open Court by the said Thomas Williamson to be
his act and deed. Whereupon it is ordered by the Court to be certified
for registration. Let it be registered.

JAMES CAMPBELL &   )   Motion
JOHN GOODWIN   )
 Against   )
EDMOND RUSSELL   )   This day came the plaintiff by their attorney
and moved the Court for Judgment against the defendant, and it appearing
to the satisfaction of the Court that the defendant Edmond Russell the
former Clerk of this Court has collected five hundred and fifty one dollars
& twenty five cents in tax fees belonging to the plaintiffs which he has
failed to pay over or account for to the said plintiffs. Wherefore
it is considered by the Court that the plaintiff recover against the
defendant said sum of five hundred and fifty one dollars and twenty five
cents and also their costs by them about this motion in this behalf
expended and the said Defendant in mercy &.

Court adjourned untill Monday morning 10 o'clock.
                                        James Robinson
                                        M. W. Howell
                                        James Keith

Monday December the first one thousand eight hundred and thirty
four. Court met according to adjournment. Present a legal number of
acting justices for Franklin County a Deed of conveyance from Henry M.
Rutledge to Robert Lackey Junr. for one hundred and ten acres of land
lying in Franklin County was duly acknowledged in Open Court by the said
Henry M. Rutledge to be his act and deced. Whereupon it is ordered by the
Court to be certified for registration. Let it be registered.

(p-437)   A deed of conveyance from John R. & Thomas H. Patrick to
George Noe. for Sixity five acres of land lying in Franklin County was
duly proven in Open Court by the oaths of Petr. Simmons & Joshua Gore
subscribing Witnesses thereto to be the act and deed of the said
John R. & Thomas H. Patrick on this day. Whereupon it is ordered by the
Court to be certified for registration. Let it be registered.

A bill of Sale from James Street & Rhody Street his wife to
Benjamin Wileman for one negro woman named Milly was duly proven in
Open Court by the oaths of Peter Burrows & Manaley Wileman subscribing
witnesses thereto to be the act and deed of the said Isaac & Rhody Street
on the day that is bears date. Whereupon it is ordered by the Court to
be certified for registration. Let it be registered.

A Bill of Sale from Rhoda Street to Benjamin Wileman for one negro girl named Claresy was duly proven in Open Court by the oaths of Peter Burrows & Manaley Wileman Subscribing witnesses thereto to be the act and deed of the said Rhoda Street on this day that it bears date whereupon it is ordered by the Court to be certified for registration. Let it be registered.

Ordered by the Court that the following persons be appointed Jurers to the next County Court, to wit, Thomas Garner 1, Charles B. Faris 2, Willis Holden 3, Abraham Shook 4, Wm. Brazelton 5, Robert Cowan 6, James P. Keith 7, John P. Davidson 8, Samuel Hollin Junr. 9, Wiley Denson 10, Benjamin Porter 11, Sidney Porter 12, James Morris 13, Joseph M. Bickley 14, Nicholas W. Mathews 15, Lunsford L. Mathews 16, Lewis Robbins 17, Miles Francis 18 , Sims Kelly 19, Robert C. Coldwell 20, David McGowan 21, Henry Herriford 22, James Bledsoe 23, Wm. Buchanan 24, Portland J. Curle 25, & Thomas Sanders Senr. 26, and that James Campbell & Benjamin Franklin constables be appointed to attend on said Court and that the Sheriff summon them to attend the same and make due return to the next Term of this Court.

Ordered by the Court that the following persons be appointed Inspectors & Clerks to held and election on the first Thursday & Friday in March next for the satification on rejection of the new or amended constitution of the State of Tennessee to wit, at the Precinct at Coldwells (p-43) Bridge: James B. Stovall, William Gibson & Sims Kelly Inspectors. Edward Long, Franklin Moore, & Joseph Floyd Clerks at the Precinct at Cunninghams, Jess Gotchen, John W. Camden & Jess Jenkins Inspectons, George W. Richardson, William Jenkins & James Shead Junr. Clearks, at the Precinct at the Stone Fort, John Hickerson, William H. Murry & Gabriel Jones Inspectors, Mriah Sherrill, Wklliam Hickerson & Thomas Wright Clerks at the Precinct at Winfords, William Orear, Jeremiah Blackard & Samuel Corn inspectors. John D. Stovall Edward Harris & Reuben Darnaby Clerks. At the Precinct at Crow Creek Wm. Crownover, Daniel Riggle & Amos Richardson Senr. Inspectors Moses Taylor, William Jackson Junr. & Reuben Richardson Clerks, at the Precinct in the Sinoking Cove, James Kelly, Randolph Champion & Peter Sells Inspectors, Adam S. Caperton, Anthony Stewart & John West Clerks. At the Precintet in Winchester John Turner, Wm. Street Senr. & William Buchanan Inspectors, Edwin Eanes Jess Sharp & John D. Germell Clerks at the Precinct at Salem. John Staples, Isaac Vanzant Senr. & John S. Martin Inspectors. Andrew W. Caperton. John R. Patrick & William C. Handly, Clerks. At the precintot on lost creek Spencer Robers, Rice Simpson & Reuben Strambler Inspectors, William N. Taylor, John O. Young & Littleton G. Simpson Clerks. At the Precinct on rook Creek, Soloman Holden. Abner Lasater & William Lasater Inspectors. Augustus Donnell, Thomas Gaither & Dennis B. Muse Clerks and that the Sheriff Summon them to attend the same.

Ordered by the Court that John G. Brazelton be appointed overseer of the road of the second class from Winchester to William Streets' Gin and that he keep the same in good repair and the he have Mrs. Ewings hands according to law John S. Sutphen, Benjamin Powells, James Taylor's William Streets and one half Wm. Brazelton's hands.

Ordered by the Court the William M. Finch be appointed overseer of the road of the second class from Winchester to Elk River and that he have the same hands that worked under the former overseer.

Ordered by the Court that James Robinson, Mark Hutchins & John Goodwin be appointed commissions to settle with James Sharp administrator of the Estate of David R. Slatter Decd. & that they make report to the next Term of this Court.

(p-439)   Ordered by the Court that Richard H. McLaughlin of the age of sixteen years the first day of October last be bound to Joseph Bradford untill he arives to the age of twenty one years who entered into Indentures with the Chairman of Franklin County to learn him the said apprentice the art and mistery of Saddle making and to give him 10 months Schooling and fifty dollars in cahs & one good suit of Clothes at the end of his time.

Ordered by the Court that William McLaughlin of the age of ten years the 7th day of June last be bound to Thomas S. Logan untill he arrive to the age of twenty one years. Who entered into Indentures with the Chairman of Franklin County Court to learn him the said apprentice the art and mistery of carriage making to learn him to read, write, & cipher as for as the rule of three and to give him a good suit of Clothes and a horse, saddle and bridle worth seventy five dollars at the end of his apprenticeship.

Ordered by the Court that John B. Hawkins & Lewis Perkins commissions of the school tract of land in Talleys cove retain sixty dollars of the school fund in their hands for their trouble in attending to and prosecuting a suit for part of said School tract against John Bowens & others.

Ordered by the Court that Town lots be taxed according to the plan of the Town of Winchester.

Ordered by the Court that John Goodwin and John Handley be appointed commissions to settle with George Gray & James Robinson Executors of the last will and testament of John Mathews decd. and that they make report to the next Term of this Court.

Ordered by the Court the hereafter the two first days of each Term of this Court be set apart to do County business to wit Monday & Tuesday

This day Elias Moore administration of the Estate of Francis A. Moore deceased came into Open Court and resigned his appointment of Administrator of said decedent. Whereupon Thomas Willson a credition of said decedent made application for letters of administrator on Estate of said decedent. It is therefore ordered by the Court that he have letters accordingly who entered into bond with Hopkins L. Turney & John Goodwin his Securities (p-440) in the sum of ten thousand dollars according to law and was qualified accordingly.

This day a Suplemental inventory of the Estate of Jacob Vansant deceased was returned in Open Court was received by the Court was and ordered to be made a part of the record.

This day two lists of Sales of the Estate of Jacob Vanzant deceased was returned in open Court was received by the Court and ordered to be made a part of the record.

Ordered by the Court that Reuben Webb be appointed Overseer of the road from Elk River to Shasteens road from Elk River to Shasteens Old place in room of Elijah Philips that he keep the same in good repair according to law and that he have the same hands that worked under the foreman Overseer.

An assignment of a plat & certificate of Survey from Britton Jones to Richard Sharp for his interest in fifty acres of land lying in Franklin County was duly acknowledged in open Court by the said Britton Jones to be his act and deed whereupon it is ordered by the Court to be certified.

This day a Suplemental inventory of the estate of John Mathews deceased was returned into open Court was received by the Court and ordered to be made a part of the record.

This day the commissioners appointed to settle with Peter Simmons administrator of the Estate of Alexander Simmons deceased made their report to Court which was received by the Court and ordered to be made a part of the record.

This day the resignation of James Howard as a Justice of the peace for Franklin County was produced in open Court and received by the Court.

This day the commisioners appointed to settle with Thomas Embrey & William Duncan executors of the last will and testament of Boley Embrey deceased made their report which was received by the Court and ordered to be made a part of the record.

An assignment of a plat & certificate of Survey from John T. Carter by his attorney in fact George W. Carter to William Buchanan for two hundred acres of land lying in Franklin County, (p-441) was duly acknowledge in open Court by the said George W. Carter attorney in fact as aforesaid to be his act and deed. Whereupon it is ordered by the Court to be certified.

A Suplemental inventory of the Estate of Henry Burrow deceased was this day returned into open Court was received by the Court and ordered to be made a part of the record.

Ordered by the Court that the following receipt be recorded to wit Recd. of Barnaby Burrow Guard. two hundred and eighty five dollars sixty three cents in full of a legacy due me from the Estate of John Graham deceased I say recd. by me October 22nd 1834.

                              Archibald Graham

It appearing to the satisfaction of the Court that John Upton late of this county died interstate and Mark Hutchins made application for letters of Administration on the Estate of said deceased. Whereupon it is ordered by the Court that he have letters accordingly who entered into bond with Benjamin Decherd & John Goodwin his secuities in the sum of five thousand dollars according to law and was qualified accordingly.

Ordered by the Court that William Rials, Coonrod Hice, John Roleman, Cicero Johnston & William Chastian be appointed a Jury of view to view and mark a road starting out from the Winchester road at Johnston's and Francis line & running so as to intersect a new road at the County line and that they view and mark the same with due regard to the convenience of Travalers and as little as may be to the prejudice of Individuals and make report to the next Term of this Court.

This day the Jury of view appointed at the last Term of this Court to mark a road from where a road leaves the Nashville road near to W. H. Foster to the Franklin County line this day made their report which was received by the Court.

(p-442)   Ordered by the Court that Abraham Shook, James Keith, Wallace Estell M.D. James Taylor, Benjamin Dechered, Porter Keith & Daniel Keith be appointed a Jury of view to view and mark a road leading from Winchester past James Taylors Geo. Davidsons & on to the top of the mountain up the Keiths trace untill it intersects with the road leading from Dr. Rows trace on to Billfort and that they view and mark the same with due regard to the convenience of Travalers and as little as may be to the prejudice of individuals and that they make report immediately. Whereupon they made their report which was received by the Court and the road established.

Ordered by the Court that John P. Davidson be appointed Overseer of the road of the second Class from Winchester to Esqr. Keiths Barn and that he keep the same in good repair according to law and that he have Capt. Davidsons hands Wm. Taylor Wm. Streets hands. Ben Powells hands. B. Dechers hands. John Goodwins hands, Ben Porters, Thomas Logans hands, Wm. Brazelton & Sons.

Ordered by the Court that Abraham Shook be appointed Overseer of the road of the second class from Squire Keiths barn to top of the mountain and that he keep the same in good repair according to law, and that he have John L. Keith & Hands, Thomas Stone, Daniel W. Keith Ben Wears, hands, James Keith Benjamin Green, Thos. N. Holt, John Mason Jas. P. Keith, Daniel Keiths A. Shooks hands Joseph Francis & Sons Joseph Holden & Sons, Dempsy Holden & Sons. Wm. Anderson, Morgan Corn Oliver Corn, John Francis, Linn Berryhill, Sampson Thompson, Bird Francis, Miles Frances, Wm. T. Francis, Wm. Lee. Edom Holder, George Young, John Row, James Bledsoe, Theodore L. Jackson, Zachariah Wortham & Madison Porter.

JOSEPH A. ALDRICH   )
  Against   )
JOSEPH S. MEDCALF   )   Whereas there was issured by the Clerk of Franklin County Court an Execution in favor of the plaintiff against the defendant on the 10th day of October 1834 and sixty two & one half cents costs of suit which Execution was returned to the present Term of this Court with the following levy thereon endorsed to wit, there being no personal property found in my County upon which (p-443)   to levy this

Fi Fa therefore levied on a house and lot in the Town of Salem in said
County the same that sd Metcalf purchased from J. H. Kilpatrick and upon
which John McClure now resides Nov. 12th 1834.

Conrs. Homan D.S.

And on motion of the plaintiff it is ordered by the Court that said tract
of land be condemed to satisfy said execution and the costs about this
motion expended and that an order of sale issure to the Sheriff of
Franklin County to sell the same according to law.

This day the Jury of view appointed at the present Term of this
Court to view and mark a road from Major Sharps Mill crossing the mill
pond so as to intersect the present road apposite Christopher Acklin's
made their report and to the confirmation of whichChristopher Acklin
whose land said road runs through objects and prays the Court for a writ
of Ad Qud. Damnum to issure to the Sheriff of Franklin County to summon
a Jury of twelve free holders to turn the road or assess the damages he
has sustained by reason of said road and make report to the Next Term of
this Court.

This day the Jury Summond by the Sheriff to assess the damages that
Joshua Gore has sustained by reason of a road marked and laid out from
Faris Mill on Benas Creek to Wm. Simmon's report that said Gore has
sustained damage to the amount of ten dollars and the money not being
paid down in Court the Court refused to confirm said road.

Ordered by the Court that Ezekiel E. Thacken be appointed Overseer
of the road from the Franklin County line to the top of the ridge to
where Daniel Harpoles part of the road intersects said road and that
he keep the same in good repair according to law and that Thomas Wright
Esqr. give him a list of hands to work on said road.

Ordered by the Court James M. James be appointed overseer of the
road from where Ezekiel E. Thacken stops to the Nashville road and that
he keep the same in good repair according to law and that Thomas Wright
Esqr. give him a list of hands to work on said road.

(p-444)   Court adjourned untill tomorrow morning 10 o'clock.

M.W. Howell
James Keith
Meredith Catching.

Tuesday December the second one thousand eight hundred and thirty
four. Court met according to adjournment.
Present - Mashall W. Howell   ) Esquires
         James Keith &   ) Justices of the peace Franklin
         Meredith Catchings   ) County

On the petition of Marshall W. Howell one of the executors of
William Trigg deceased praying the sale of certain salves in said
petition mentioned to wit Esther and her four children Margaret, Betsy,
Emily, & Amelia, and it appearing to the satisfaction of the Court
that said slaves could not be divided among the legatees in said will
without a sale thereof. Whereupon the Court doth order adjudge and

direct that said Executor sell said slaves at the Court door in the
town of Winchester after giving ten days notice of the time and place of
sale by written advertisements to the highest bidder on a twelve months
credit taking bond and approved security from the purchaser on purchasers.

ISAAC B. GORE) Covenant
  Against)
RUTHY WHITNEY &)
ANDERSON F. WILLIS) This day come the plaintiff by his attorney
and having filed his declaration and the defendants being solemnly called
to appear and defend this suit came not but made default. and on motion
of the plaintiff by his attorney. It is considered by the Court that
the plaintiff recover against the defendants such damages as he has sustained by reason of the non performance of the covenant in the Declaration
mentioned which damages are to be enquired of by a Jury at the next Term
of this Court.

EPHRAIM H. FOSTER Asses & C) Debt
  Against)
JOHN WEST) This day came the plaintiff by his
attorney and having filed his declaration and the defendant being solemnly
called to appear and defend this suit came not but made default. And on
motion of the plaintiff by his attorney it is considered by the Court that
the plaintiff recover against the defendant one hundred and thirty eight
dollars and ninety one cents the debt in Declaration mentioned together
with the further sum of twenty seven dollars & seventy seven cents damages
(p-445) he has sustained by reason of the detention of his debt and also
his costs by him about said suit in this behalf expended and the said
defendant in Mercy & Execution Stayed untill next Court.

JAMES WOODS & CO) Case
  Against)
WILLIAM CENTER) This day came the plaintiff by their attorney
and having filed their Declaration and the Defendant being solemnly called
to appear and defend the suit came not but made default and on motion
of the plaintiff by their attorney it is considered by the Court that
the plaintiff recover against the defendant such damage as they have
sustained by reason of the non performance of the assumptions in the
Declaration mentioned which damages are to be enquired of by a Jury at
the next Term of this Court.

ISAAC VANZANT SURVING Partner) Attachment
  of ISAAC VANZANT & CO.)
  Against)
E. P. BACON) In this case time is given until the
next Term of this Court for the Garnished to answer.

VANZANT HARRIS & CO.) Attachment
  Against)
E. P. BACON) In this case time is given untill the next
term of this Court for the Garnished to answer.

A power of attorney from Mark Malone to Robert Malone was duly
acknowledged in Open Court by the said Mark Malone to be his act and deed.

Whereßpon it is ordered by the Court to be certified.

Court adjourned untill Court in course.

James Keith
Andrew Campbell
Meredith Catching

(p-446)   February Term 1835

State of Tennessee

At a Court of pleas and quarter sessions begun & held for Franklin County on the fourth Monday of February in the year of our Lord one thousand eight hundred and thirty five it being the twenty third day of February and of the Independance of the United States of 59th. Present a legal number of acting Justices of the peace in & for said County.

A Bill of Sale from Moses Morris to Rowlin Morris for one negre girl named Chaney was duly acknowledged in Open Court by the said Moses Morris to be his act and deed. Whereupon it is ordered by the Court to be certified for registration. Let it be registered.

A deed of conveyance from Edmond Dickey to Peter Simmons for acres of land lying in Franklin County was duly proven in Open Court by the oaths of John R. Patrick & George Hudspeth subscribing witnesses thereto to be the act and deed of the said Edmond Dickey on the day that it bears date. Whereupon it is ordered by the Court to be certified for registration. Let it be registered.

A Bill of Sale from William M. Raines to Samuel Miller for one negro boy named Bob was duly proven in Open Court by the oaths of Joseph Miller & William Laster Subscribing witnesses thereto to be the act and deed of the said William M. Raines on the day that it bears date. Whereupon it is ordered by the Court to be certified for registration. Let it be registered.

A deed of conveyance from Barbee Collins to Jephtha V. Horton for one hundred & twenty acres of land lying in Franklin County was duly proven in Open Court by the oaths of Amos Horton and Andrew Woods to be the Act and deed of the said Barbee Collins on the day that it bears date. Whereupon it is ordered by the Court to be certified for registration. Let it be registered.

(p-447)   A deed of conveyance from Peter R. Booker to Benjamin Wilson for fifty acres of land lying in Franklin County was produced in Open Court and appearing to have been duly acknowledged and certified in the County of Murry & State of Tennessee. It is therefore ordered by this Court that the same be certified for registration. Let it be registered.

A deed of conveyance from Mitchell K. Jackson to George Young for twenty acres of land lying in Franklin County was duly acknowledged in Open Court by the said Mitchell K. Jackson to be his act and deed Whereupon it is ordered by the Court to be certified for registration. Let it be registered.

A deed of conveyance from William Larkin to Ancil Stovall for one hundred and ten acres of land lying in Franklin County was duly acknowledged in Open Court by the said William Larkin to be his act and deed. Whereupon it is ordered by the Court to be certified for registration. Let it be registered.

A deed of conveyance from Granville Lipscomb to William Simmons

for two hundred and forty eight acres and 140 poles of land lying in
Franklin County was duly proven in Open Court by the oaths of Hastings
M. Sargeant & Chapman McDaniel subscribing Witnesses thereto to be the
act and deed of the said Granville Lipscomb on the day it bears date.
Whereupon it is ordered by the Court to be certified for registration.
Let it be registered.

A deed of conveyance from Reuben Simmons to Susan Trigg for one
hundred and seventy five acres of land lying in Franklin County was
duly acknowledge in Open Court by the said Reuben Simmons to be his act
and deed. Whereupon it is ordered by the Court to be certified for
registration. Let it be registered.

Ordered by the Court that John Lyons be appointed overseer of the
road of the second class from the Widow Kettons on the Moherds road to
the Gum Swamp branch in room of William Cowling and that he keep the
same in good repair according to law and that he have the same hands
that worked under the former overseer.

(p-448)   Ordered by the Court that Thomas Muse Senr. be appointed
overseer of the road of the second class from Sharps Mill to Holders
in room and stead of Ransom Rice and that he keep to same in good repair
according to law and that he have the same hands that worked under the
former overseer.

Ordered by the Court that Samuel Austell be appointed overseer of
the road from his own house to where it intersects the Stage road leading
to Hillsboro and that he keep the same in good repair according to law
And that he have the same hands that worked under the former Overseer.

Ordered by the Court that Henry Robertson be appointed Overseer
of the Road from the pond Springs to the five mile post in Room of Loranzo
D. Philips and that keep the same in good repair ac ording to law. & that
he have the same hands that worked under the former Overseer.

Ordered by the Court that Thomas Branch be appointed Overseer of
the road of the second class from Joseph Millers to Bradley's Creek in
room of Samuel Austin and that he keep the same in good repair according
to law and that he have the same hands that worked under the former overseer.

Ordered by the Court that Benjamin Dechered be appointed overseer
of the road of the first Class from Major Armstrongs to James W. Estills'
in room of James England and that he keep the same in good repair
according to law & that he have the same hands that worked under the former
overseer.

Ordered by the Court that the order of Court made at the last term
of this Court appointing Joseph Numan Overseer of the road from the
boiling fork to Thomas Knights be recinded and made void & that all that
past of said road from the Boiling fork to the end of Dardis lane be
attacked to John D. Finnels part of the road (Bridge road) and that said
Finnels keep the same in good repair according to law & that he have
James Dardis's hands in addition to the hands he now has.

(p-449)
Ordered by the Court that Edward Morris be appointed overseer of the road of the second class from Doctor Beckleys to John Francis in the room of Hastings M. Sargeant & that he keep the same in good repair according to law & that he have the same hands that worked under the former overseer.

Ordered by the Court that David Hunt be appointed overseer of the road ~~of the first class~~, from Cox's on the stage road to William Woods & that he keep the same in good repair according to law & that John R. Patrick, David Bell George Hudspath and William Larkin Esqr. give him a list of hands to work on said road.

Ordered by the Court that John Haws be appointed overseer of the road from Wm. Woods to the stage road near Esqr. Staples and that he keep the same in good repair according to law and that John R. Patrick, David Bell, George Hudspeth & Wm. Larkin Esqrs. give him a list of hands to work on said road.

Ordered by the Court that John R. Patrick David Bell, George Hudspeth & Wm. Larkins Esqrs. make a real lotment of hands to work on all the roads below Salem and that they furnish each overseer with a list accordingly.

Ordered by the Court that John Berger be appointed overseer of the road of the third class from the forks of the road at Shattens old place to where it crosses the cane hollow and that he keep the same in good repair according to law and that he have the same hands that worked under the former overseer.

Ordered by the Court that Thomas Harris be appointed overseer of the same part of the road that George Box was formerly overseer of in room of said Box and that he keep the same in good repair according to law. And that he have the same hands that worked under the former overseer.

Ordered by the Court the William S. Mooney be appointed overseer of the same part of the road that Elijah Muckleroy was formerly overseer of in room of said Muckleroy and that he keep the same in good repair according to law. And that he have the same hands that worked under the former overseer.

Ordered by the Court that John Goodwin, Willie B. Wagner & William N. Taylor be appointed commissioners to settle with the administrators of James Philips deceased and that they make report to the next Term of this Court.

(p-450) Ordered by the Court that Reuben Strambler be appointed a commissioners of the tract of School land on coffers Creek in room of Joseph Hilton removed and that he be permitted to come in at any time during this Court and enter into bond & give security.

Ordered by the Court that James Woods, John Handley & Dudley Johnson be appointed commissioners to settle with the executors of William Arnett deceased and that they make report either to this or the next term of this Court.

Ordered by the Court that John Goodwin, Mark Hutchins & James
Robinson be appointed commissioners to sittle with James Sharp Guardian
for John T. Slatter a minor orphan of David R. Slatter deceased, and
that they make their report to the present term of this Court.

Ordered by the Court the James Sharp, Thomas Finch & Benjamin
Decherd be appointed commissioners to settle with Thomas Embrey & William
Duncan executors of the last will and testament of Boby Embry deceased
and that they make their report to the next Term of this Court.

Ordered by the Court that John Goodwin, Jess T. Wallace & Cabb H.
Jones be appointed commissioners to settle with the admin of Elijah Runnels
deceased. And that they maked report to the present term of This Court.

Ordered by the Court that Sims Kelly, William S. Mooney & John G.
Bostick be appointed commissioners to settle with Barnaby Bunrow
former guardian of Juliann Graham minor orphan of John Graham deceased
and make report to this on the next term of this Court.

Ordered by the Court that John Frame, Benjamin Franklin & James
Morris be appointed commissioners to settle with Joseph Franklin administrator of the Estate of Elizabeth Franklin deceased, and that they make
report to this on the next term of this Court.

Ordered by the Court that Elizabeth Muckleroy be privileged to
turn the road leading from Centerville to Pelham from the corner of
Thomas King's field untill it comes opposite to her house & then with
her apple orchard fence and to intersect the old road at the corner of
her fence.

(p-451)   Ordered by the Court that Thomas Lusk be allowed the sum of
three dollars for one old wolf sheep out of any money in the treasury
in Middle Tennessee not otherwise appropriated.

Ordered by the Court that William Sartin have a credit of four
dollars and fifty cents for money paid out by him as treasury of the
Poor House.

Ordered by the Court Mary Elizabeth Baxter be carried by
Elizabeth Phillips to Richmond P. Harris's and that he take her to the
Poor House.

This day came on an Election for the purpose of electing a constable
in the bounds of Captain Millers Company & on counting out the votes it
was found that James Sargeantwas duly and constitutionally elected
constable in the bounds of said company for the next ensuing two years.

Ordered by the Court that William H. Handley be appointed constable
in and for the County of Franklin in the bounds of Captain McClands
Company for the next ensuing two years who entered into bond with
John Handley and John R. Patrick his securities according to law and
was qualified accordingly.

Ordered by the Court that Alexander Donaldson be appointed constable in and for the County of Franklin in the bounds of Captain Woods old Company, now Gillaspie, for the next ensuing two years who entered into bond with John Armstronge and Dudley Johnson his surities according to law as was qualified accordingly.

Ordered by the Court that tomorrow be set apart to do Country business.

This day came on an election for the purpose electing a quorum t0 hold the Court of pleas and quarter sessions for Franklin County for the next twelve months. And on Counting out the votes it was found that James Robinson, James Keith Marshall M. Howell, Esqrs. were duly and constitutionally elected a quorum to hold said Court.

Ordered by the Court that John F. Graham be appointed guardain over the person and property of Julia Ann Graham a minor orphan of John Graham decd. Who entered into bond with John Goodwin his security in the sum of five hundred dollars according to law.

Ordered by the Court that Minnifred Phillips be appointed guardian over the person and property of Nancy Manervey and Martha Elizabeth Philips * decd. Who entered into bond with William McElroy her security in the sum of two thousand dollars according to law.

(p-452)   It appearing to the satisfaction of the Court that Wiatt Ballard lat of this county died intestate and John Ballard applied for letters of administration on the Estate of said deceased. It is therefore ordered by the Court that he have letters accordingly who entered into bond with Robert Lackey Jr. & Thomas C. Yeates his securities in the sum of six hundred dollars according to law and was qualified accordingly.

Ordered by the Court that George W. Richardson, John W. Camden, Jess Jenkins, William Anderson, Barnett Forsyth & Benjamin T. Hollins or any five of them be appointed a Jury of view to view and turn the stage road leading through the lands of Daniel Roddy & William Kenedy and that they view and turn the same with a due regard to the conveyance of Travalers and as little as may be to the prejudice of individuals, and that they make report of their proceedings to the next term of this Court.

On the petition of Mitchell K. Jackson it is ordered by the Court that he have the liberty to change the road according to the prayer of said petition on his own lands running as it now does from Davidsons to Gashen untill it comes to the West side of his plantation thence South about 20 or 25 poles so as to round on the South side of said Plantation and to come into the old road on the East side of the planation.

Ordered by the Court that Samuel A. Harris, Legrand King, Henry Larkins, David Hunt, Wm. Lipscomb, Evertt Horton & Jephtha Horton or any five of them be appointed a Jury of view to view and turn the road leading from Salem to Paint Rock on the land of William Woods, and that they view and turn the same having due regard to the convenience of Travalers and as little as may be to the prejudice of individuals and

* minor orphans of James Philips

that they make report of their proceedings either to this or the
next term of this Court.

This day the return of Jas. Wilkinson Isaac Wilkinson &
Isaac Miller Guardians of the minor heirs of John Wilkinson decd.
was returned into Open Court was received by the Court & ordered to
be made a part of the record.

This day the Jury of view appointed at the last term of this
Court to view and mark a road starting out from the Winchester road
at Johnsons & Frames Line & running so as to intersect a new road
at the county Line this day made their report which was confirmed by
the Court.

(p-453)   This day the Jury of view appointed at the last Term of
this Court to view and turn the road that leads from Salem to the
mouth of Beans Creek to turn off at the ford of the creek appoint
Faris's Mill this day made their report which was confirmed by the
Court.

Present William Crownover, Wm. Lasater, Meredith Catchings,
Geo. W. Thompson Marshall W. Howell, James Keith, Andrew Campbell,
Zachariah H. Murrel, Blackard David Bell, Littleton G. Simpson ,
John R. Patrick, John Oliver, Samuel Bradshaw, Jeremiah & Richmond
P. Harris Esquires.

Ordered by the Court that Ralph Grable be allowed the sum of
twenty two dollars for sweeping the Courthouse six Courts and that
the Clerk issure a certificate to the County Trustee to pay him the
sum the ayes & noes being taken were unanious in favor of the
allowance. Isd.

Present William Crownover, Wm. Laster, Meredith Catchings
George W. Thompson, Marshall W. Howell/ James Keith, Andrew Campbell
Zachariah H. Murrell David Bell, John Oliver, Saml. Bradshaw,
Jeremiah Blackard, John R. Patrick & Richmond P. Harris Esquires.

Ordered by the Court that George Gillaspie be allowed the sum
of twenty dollars for clothing, boarding, and schooling 4 orphan
children of Thomas McLaughlin $3\frac{1}{2}$ months and that the Clerk issure a
certificate to the County Trustee to pay him the same, The ayes &
noes being taken were unanimous in favor of the allowance.

Present William Crownover, Wm. Lasater, Meredith Catchings,
George W. Thompson, Marshall W. Howell, James Keith, Andrew Campbell
Zachariah Nl Murrell, John Oliver, Samuel Bradshaw, Jeremiah Blackard
John R. Patrick, Richmond P. Harris & William Simmons Esqrs.

Ordered by the Court the Gideon N. Pully be allowed the sum
of twenty five dollars for keeping a infant by the ane of Perkins
fifteen months and that the Clerk issure a certifiedtto the County
Trustee to pay him the same the ayes & noes being taken those who
voted in the affirmative are Wm. Lasater, George W. Thompson,

Marshal W. Howell, James Keith, Andrew Campbell, Zacharah H. Murrell John R. Patrick & Richmond P. Harris, and those who voted in the negative are William Crownover Meredith Catchings, John Oliver, Samuel Bradsahw & Jeremiah Blackard.

Present the above named Justices. Ordered by the Court that Moorning Miller be allowed the sum of one dollar & fifty cents the tax on three negroes overcharged on the tax list for the year (pg454)   1834 and that the Clerk issure a certificate to the county Trustee to pay him the same. The ayes & noes being taken were unanimous in favor of the allowance.

Present the above named Justices. Ordered by the Court that Samuel Rosborough be allowed the sum forty dollars the amount assessed by the Jury as the avlue of two acres of his land for a boat yard and that the clerk issure a certificate to the County Trustee to pay him the same which was unanimously made by said Justices.

HELLSMAN KING   )
 Against   )
William Williams   ) Whereas on the twenty third day of February 1835 there was issured by William Corwnover an acting Justice of the peace in & for the County of Franklin an Execution in favor of the Plaintiff against the Defendant for the sum of twenty two dollars & fifty cents debt and one dolar cost which Execution was returbed to the present Term of the Court with the following levy thereon endorsed, to wit, no personal property found to make the within Execution and leved on one tract of land and near to M. Kitchens Esqr. on 23rd February 1835.
                                        Wm. Wilkinson
And on motion of the plaintiff by his attorney. It is ordered by the Court that said tract of land be condemed to satisfy said Execution and the costs about this order of sale expended and that an order of sale issure to the sheriff of Franklin County to snel the same according to law.

JOHN CAIN   )
 Against   )
PHILIP TAYLOR   ) Whereas on the 9th day of January 1835 there was issured by John W. Camden an acting Justice of the peace in and for the county of Franklin an Execution in favor of the plaintiff against the defendant for the sum of eighty dollars and ninety cents debt and one dollar cost which Execution was returned to the Present Term of this Court with the following levy thereon endorsed to wit, No personal property found in my county whereon to levy this Fi Fa levied on a lot of land of the said defendant setuated near Hillsboro in said County adjoining a lot of land belonging to John W. Camden stage road running through the said Town of Hillsboro southerly by the land of Jess Jenkins and Westerly by the lands of John W. Camden, it being the place where the said Taylor now lives and by estimation containing about three acres. January 9th 1835 B. F. Jenkins Const. for Franklin County. And on motion of the Plaintiff by his attorney. It is ordered by the Court that said lot of land be condemed to satisfy said Execution and the costs about this order of sale expended & that an order of issure to the sheriff of Franklin County to sell the same according to law.

(p-455)   JAMES H. ARNOLD   )
              Against   )
           JOHN FORSYTH   )   Whereas on the 20th day of February 1835
there was issue by Jess Jenkins an acting Justice of the peace in and
for the County of Franklin an Execution in favor of the Plaintiff against
the Defendant for the sum of six dollars debt and one dollar costs. Which
Execution was returned to the present Term of this Court with the following levy thereon endorsed, to wit, no personal property found in my
county, Whereon to levy this Fi Fa levied on a tract of land the property
of the defendant situate and lying on upper Beans Creek in Franklin County
bound on the west by John Deen on the South by James Cunningham on the
east by Raghly Cunningham & William Stphenson & on the north by Thos.
P. Stphenson supposed to contain one hundred & twenty acres this 20th day
of Feby. 1835.

                              B. F. Jenkins Cst.
And on motion of the plaintiff by his attorney. It is ordered by the
Court that said tract of land be condemed to Satisfy said Execution and
the costs about this order of sale expended and that an order of sale
issure to the Sheriff of Franklin County to sell the same according to
law.

        Ordered by the Court that Richmond P. Harris be appointed treasurer
& Willis Burt & Laban Jones be appointed commissioners of the poor house
for Franklin County and/that/they/appoint/a/Treasurer/for/said/poor/house
and that they be empowered to settle with the former commissioners of
said poor house and take to proceeds into their own hands.

        This day the last will and testament & the three codicils thereto
of Wallis Estill Senr. deceased was produced in Open Court by the executors therein named whereupon came Nathan Green, Madison Porter, &
Jonathan Decherd three of the subscribing witnesses thereto who being
duly sworn depose and say that the said Wallace Estill Senr. deceased
declared & published this as his last will & testament and at the time
of acknowledgeing the same he the said Wallace Estill Senr. was of sound
and desposing mind and memory and that he acknowledged the same in their
presence and they as witnesses thereto signed the same in his presence
and at his request, Whereupon came Nathan Green, Peter S. Decherd,
Jonathan Decherd & Benjamin Decherd Subscribing witnesses to the first
codicil who being first duly sworn deposed and say that the said Wallace
Estill Senr. deceased declared and published this as his first codicil
to his last will and testament and at the time of acknowledgeing the same
he the said Wallace Estell Senr was of Sound and disposing mind & memory
and that he acknowledged the same in their presence, and they as witnesses
thereto signed the (p-456) same in his presence and at his request.
Whereupon came Jonathan, Decherd, Peter S. Decherd & Benjamin Decherd
subscribing witnesses to the second codicil to said will who being first
duly sworn depose and say that the said Wallace Estill Senr. declared
and published this as the second codicil to his last will and testament
and at the time of acknowledging the same he the said Wallace Estill
Senr. was of sound and disposing mind & memory and that he acknowledged
the same in their presence and they as witnesses thereto signed the
same in his presence and at his request. Whereupon came Nathan Green
& Wallace Estill subscribing witnesses to the third codicil to said
will who being first duly sworn depose and say that the said Wallace

Estill Senr. declared and published this as the third codicil to his last will and testament and at the time of acknowledging the same he the said Wallace Estill Senr. was of sound and disposing mind and memory and that he acknowledged the same in their presence and they as witnesses thereto signed the same at his request. Whereupon it is ordered by the Court that said last will and Testament and the three codicils thereto be recorded.

On the petition of Sundry citizens of this County praying for the erection of a Bridge across the boiling fork of Elk River at or near where the stage road crosses the same & it appearing to the Court that the sum of about four hundred dollars has been raised by subscription for the purpose aforesaid to be paid into the hands of James Robinson James Sharp and Joseph Klepper commissioners selected by the subscribers to said Bridge, and it appearing to the Court that the erection of a good bridge at the place aforesaid would be of great publick utility & convenience. It is therefore resolved by the Court the following Justices, to wit, Meredith Catchings, George W. Thompson, Marshall W. Howell, James Keith Andrew Campbell, Zachariah H. Murrell, David Bell, John Oliver Samuel Bradshaw, Jeremiah Blachard, John R. Patrick, James B. Stovall James Keely & Richmond P. Harris being present & unanimously concurring therein that a sum not exceeding two hundred and fifty dollars to be paid out of the county revenue to be laid and collected the present year be and the same is hereby appropriated to aid in the erection of said Bridge provided that it shall be the duty of said commissioners shall be the duty of said commissioners forthwith to proceed in the erection of the same upon such plan as they may agree upon & after agreeing upon the plan they shall let the building of said bridge to the lowest bidder taking bond with good security for the faithfull preformance of the work and Whatever sum the building of said (p-457)   Bridge may cost over the above said sum of $400 and not exceeding said sum of $250 to be paid as aforesaid by the county Trustee out of the county Revenue to be collected for the present year to said commissioners upon their reporting to the Court that said Bridge has been erected according to contract.

The commissioners appointed at the last Term of this Court to Settle with James Sharp administrator of the Estate of David R. Statten decd this day made their report in open Court whereupon it is ordered by the Court that the same in all things be affirmed, and that the same be recorded.

This day the Jury summoned by the sheriff to go upon the land of Christopher Acklin and turn the road or assess the damages said Acklin has sustained in consequence of said road passing consequence of said road passing through his land this day made their report which is in all things confirmed by the Court whereupon Richard Sharp paid down in Court here five dollars being the amount of damages assessed by the Jury aforesaid.

Court adjourned untill tomorrow morning 11 o'clock.
                              Andrew Campbell
                              James Keith
                              John W. Camden

Tuesday February the 24th one thousand eight hundred and thirty five Court met according to adjournment. Present a legal number of acting Justices of the peace in and for said County.

A deed of Trust from Hugh Richard son to Robert H. Oliver for the personal property therein named for the benefit of Henry M. Ruttedge was duly acknowledge in open Court by the said Richardson & Oliver to be their act and deed whereupon it is ordered by the Court to be certified for registration. Let it be recorded.

A deed of conveyance from Jonathan Martin to Richard Varnell for fifty acres of land lying in Franklin County was duly acknowledge in Open Court by the said Jonathan Martin to be his act and deed, whereupon it is ordered by the Court to be certified for registration.

Ordered by the Court that William A. Francis be appointed Overseer of the same part of the milk Sick fence (p-458) that William Thurman was formerly overseer of and that he keep the same in good repair according to law and that he have his own hands Michael Williams, Absalom Williams Peter Williams and the Widow Williams hands, John Francis, Linsfield Berryhill, Sampson Thompson, Bird Frances, Wm. Thurman & his hands Oliver Corn, Edom Holder, Wm. Lee, George Young & William Anderson.

Ordered by the Court that Willis Holder be appointed overseer of the same part of the milk sick fence that Joseph Francis was formerly overseer of and that he keep the same in good repair according to law and his hands are Joseph Francis Senr. Joseph Francis Jr. Wm. R. Francis Mitchell Holder, James P. Keith, John Mason, James Keith Esq. hands Benjamine Wear hands, A. Shook & hahds Daniel Keith, Morgan Corn & Dempsy Holder.

Ordered by the Court that the following persons be Jurors to the next Circuit Court to whit, Adam Oehmig, John Hanley, Mark Hutchins Benjamin Powell, John Turner Dudly Johnson, John Farris William Brazelton Andrew Campbell, James Kieth, William Street, John W. Holder, Thomas Green David Decherd, Joseph Miller, James Sharp, William Orear, Herndore Green Jess Oldham, Wm. Ducan, George Roland, Benjamin Wear, Richmond P. Harris, Sims Kelley, George Mosely & John Stovall, Salem and that James Oliver and John G. Brazelton be appointed constables to attend on said Court and that the Sheriff summons them to attend the same and make dure returns of the same.

Ordered by the Court that the following persons be appointed Jurors to attend at the next county Court to witt, Soloman Wagner, Nelson Carter, Hezekiah Farris, John Emberson, William Darwin, John D. Ferrel, John Armstrong, Wm. Therman, Christopher Acklin, George Davidson, James Taylor Maddison Porter, James Logan, John Frame, Joseph Franklin, Daniel Keith, Julius C. Sims, James Woods, James Estill, Peter Simmons, Henry Fancy, James Knight, Clement Arledge, Joab Short, Peter Sells & Michael Williams and that Alexander Donaldson & Wm. M. Cowan be appointed constables to attend on said Court and that the Sheriff summons them to attend the same and make due return to the next term of this Court.

(p-459)   Ordered by the Court that the following Justices of the peace

be appointed to take in a list of taxable property in and for the county
of Franklin in the different companies for the year 1835 to wit, John
Dougherty in Capt. Winfords Company, James Keith in Capt. Shooks Company,
James F. Green in Capt Faris company William Simmins in Capt. Gillaspies
Company John R. Patrick in Capt. Kavanaugh Company George Hudspeth in
the Salem Company William Larkin in Capt. McCluds Company Zackerish H.
Murrel in Capt. Tips Company Andrew Mann in Capt. Browns Company,
Richmond P. Harris in Capt. Muse Company, Wm. Lasater in Capt. Gathers
old Company James Robinson in Capt. Hines Company M. W. Howell in Capt.
Martins Company Asa D. Oakley in Capt. Brooks Company, John Sanders in
Capt. Sartins Company, John W. Comden in Capt. Deans Company Jess Jenkins
in Capt. Burris Company Thomas Wright in Capt. Childres Old Company
James Kelley in Capt. Childs Company Meredith Catchings in Capt. Govers
Company George W. Thompson in Capt. Wm. B. G. Muses Old Company James B.
Stoval in Capt. Stamps Company John Oliver in Capt. Millers Company
Jeremiah Blacherd in Capt. Knights Company & Samuel Bradshaw in
Capt. Gillams Old Company and that they make due return to the next term
of this Court.

Ordered by the Court that James Dean be appointed overseer of the
road of the second class from his fathers house to the Blue Spring
on the Georgia road in room of Christopher Sanders and that he keep the
same in good repair according to law and that he the same hands that
worked under the former overseer.

Ordered by the Court that Henry Herriford, Robert C. Colwell
and Samuel Holland be released from attending on the Jury during the
present Term of this Court.

Ordered by the Court that James Roberds be appointed overseer of
the same part of the road that George Box was formerly overseer of and
that he keep the same in good repair according to law and that he have
the same hands that worked under the former overseer.

Ordered by the Court that John Russell be appointed overseer of
the road of the first class from John Armstrongs to Callaways Pond in
the room of John Hanley and that he keep the same in good repair
according to law and that (p-460) he have the same hands that worked
under the former overseer.

Ordered by the Court that the order appointing commissioners to
settle with the administrator of Elijah Runnels be extended so that said
Commissioners may make their Report to the next Term of this Court.

This day came on an Election for the purpose of Electing a
constable in and for the County of Franklin in the Bounds of Capt. Brooks
Company and on counting out the votes it was found that James Morris was
duly and Constitutionally elected constable in the bounds of said
Company for the next ensuing two years who entered into Bond with
Alexander Donaldson and Benjamine Franklin his securities according to
law and was qualified accordingly.

This day James Sargent Who was elected constable on yesterday
came into Open Court and entered into bond with James Oliver & John Oliver

his securities according to law and was qualified accordingly.

Ordered by the Court that the following receipts be Recorded to wit Nashville Inn 8th of December 1834 received of W. B. Wagner Clerk of Franklin County Court three hundred and sixty one dollars ninety eight cents being the amount of State Tax by him collected from the 27th day of May 1834 to the 1st day of October ensuing agreably to his return this day ordered for said times.
$361.98   Tho Crutcher Treasurer.

Recd Winchester 22nd December 1834 of Willie B. Wagner Clerk of the County Court of Franklin County Seventeen dollars and fifty cents the amount of fines collected by him due to said County since the 27th day of May to the 1st of December 1834 as per Commissioners Report to me Benjmin Decherd.

County Trustee

The Report of the commissioners appointed at the present term of this Court to settle with James Sharp former Guardian of John T. Slatter orphan of David R. Slatter Decd was this day returned into Open Court was received by the Court and ordered to be recorded.

(p-461)   HOLLIS & WALLAS   )
           Against   )
           JOHN FORSYTH   ) Whereas there was issued by John W. Camden an acting Justice of the peace in & for said County on the 28th day of January 1835 an Execution in favor of the plaintiff against the defendant for the sum of twenty three dollars twenty five & one fourth cents debt and one dollar cost. Which execution was returned to the present term of this Court with the following levy thereon endorsed to wit, no personal property found in my county whereon to levy this Fi Fa. levied on a tract of land of the said deft lying on the waters of upper Beans Creek in said County bounded on the West by John Dean's on the South by James Cunningham's on the East by Raleigh Cunningham's & Wm. Stephenson, on the north by Thos. P. Stephenson supposed to be 120 acres.
                                    James M. Shead, Const.
And on motion of the plaintiff by his attorney. It is ordered by the Court that said tract of land be condemed to satisfy said Execution & what an order of sale issue to the Sheriff of Franklin County to sell the same according to law.

PRICE & CAIN   )
  Against   )
JOHN FORSYTH   ) Whereas there was issued on the 29th day of January 1835 by John W. Camden an acting Justice of the peace in & for the County of Franklin and Execution in favor of the plaintiff against the defendant for the sum of twelve dollars and ninety eight and three fourth cents debt and one dollar cost which execution was returned to the presents Term of this Court with the following levy thereon Endorsed, to wit, no personal property found in my county whereon to levy this Fi Fa levied on a tract of land of the said defendant lying on the waters of upper Beans Creek in said County bounded on the West, by John Dean on the South by James Cunningham on the East by Raleigh Cunningham & Williams Stephenson on the North by Thos. P. Stphenson suppose to contain 120 acres

29th January 1835.

B. F. Jenkins Cst.

And on motion of the plaintiff by his attorney it is ordered by the Court that said tract of land be condemed to satisfy said execution and that an order of Sale issue to the Sheriff of Franklin County to sell the same according to law.

This day the ~~list of the~~ Settlement made with the executors of the last will and testament of John Mathews deceased was returned into Open Court was received by the Court and was ordered to be recorded.

(p-462)   This day Wallace Estill Jr. one of the Executors appointed by the last will and testament of Wallace Estill Senior Deceased came into Open Court and entered into bond with Isaac K. Vanzant Senior, Mark Hutchins, Maddison Porter and Benjamine Powell his securities in the sum of twenty thousand dollars according to law and was qualified accordingly.

This day Matilda Lucy and Thomas Jefferson Embrey being of the age of fourteen years came in open Court and chose Thomas Embrey their Guardian and it is ordered by the Court that he be appointed Guardian over the persons and property of Winney Betsey and Isabilla Embrey Minor orphans of Boley Embrey Decd who entered into bond with Thomas Finch & Thomas Howard his securities in the sum of fifteen hundred dollars according to law.

Ordered by the Court that Thomas Finch have a credit for forty one dollars six & $\frac{1}{2}$ cents on a settlement of his a accounts with the County Trustee for delinquents and twice listed property on ~~over charges~~ the tax list for year 1834.

Ordered by the Court that Thomas Finch Sheriff of Franklin County and collector of Publick taxes be charged with one hundred and eighty eight dollars that being the amount of taxes collect by him on property not listed for the year 1834.

Ordered by the Court that the following tax be laid to pay Jurors for the year 1835 to wit, on white polls $12\frac{1}{2}$ cents on black polls 25 cents on land $12\frac{1}{2}$ cents & on town lots 25 cents.

Ordered by the Court that the following tax be laid to pay Jurors for the year 1835 to wit, on white polls $12\frac{1}{2}$ cents on black polls 25 cents on land $12\frac{1}{2}$ cents & on town lots 25 cents.

Ordered by the Court that the following tax be laid for County purposes for the year 1835, to wit, white polls $6\frac{1}{4}$ cents. Black polls 18-3/4 cents land $12\frac{1}{2}$ cents & town lots 25 cents.

Ordered by the Court that the following tax be laid to pay the poor for the year 1835 to wit, on white polls $6\frac{1}{4}$ cents Black polls $6\frac{1}{4}$ cents. Land $6\frac{1}{4}$ cents and on Town lots $12\frac{1}{2}$ cents.

WINGATE & GASKILL)
  Against)
GEORGE W. THOMPSON) This day came the plaintiff by their attorney
and dismissed their suit and not further prosecuting it is orderdd that
this suit be dismissed and the defendant assumes the cost it is therefore
considered by the Court that the plantiffs recover against the defendant
their cost by them about said suit in this behalf expended and the said
defendant in Mercy &.

(p-463) Present Marshal W. Howell, James Keith, George Gray,
James F. Green, Asa D. Oakley, Andrew Campbell, George W. Thompson,
Samuel Norwood, Andrew Mann, Richmond P. Harris, John Oliver, Zachariah
H. Murrell & John W. Camden Esqr.

Ordered by the Court that Willie B. Wagner Clerk of Franklin County
Court be allowed the sum of two dollars & fifty cents for furnishing the
treasurer a list of the amount of tax for the year 1834 and also one
dollar for rendering to the County Trustee an account of the fines
forfeitures and amercements due and payable to the use of the County and
that the County Trustee pay him the same which allowance was unanimously
made by said Trustee.

Ordered by the Court that Geter Lynch of the age of sixteen years
next April be bound to Hudson Allen & Portland J. Curle untill he arrives
to the age of twenty one years who entered into Indentures with the
Chairman of Franklin County Court to learn him the said apprentice the
art and mistery of making harness & triming, to learn him to read & write
& to cipher through the rule of three and to give him thirty dollars
in money at the end of his time.

HENRY L. CAMDEN)
  Against)
BENJAMIN F. JENKINS) This day came the parties into Open Court and
mutually agree that all matters in dispute between them in this suit be
refered to the final determination of Stewart Cowan & John G. Gostick
and such other persons as they may choose whose award thereupon shall be
made the final judgment of the Court returnable to the Next Term of this
Court.

Ordered by the Court that Wm. Emmerson be permitted to turn the
road from the Lowry road commencing on the North South line between Daniel
Martin & John Emmerson running about two hundred yards and then running
on John Emmerson's land by where his Son Wm. Emmerson lives and into the
Lowry road this side of John Emmersons.

On petition of Mary Vanzant widow and relict of Jacob Vanzant
deceased for Dower & of Benjamin F. Wafford & Emily his wife & Isaac
Vanzant two of the heirs of said Decedent for partition of the real
estate. This day came the parties aforesaid in their proper persons
and presented here into Court their petitions aforesaid, and it appearing
to the satisfaction of the Court that the said Mary is the administrator
of said decedents estate and Guardian to Maria Louisa, Francis, Adaline
Polly Ann (p-464) and William Thomas the minor children of said Decedent
and the said Isaac Vanzant & Benjamin F. Wafford & wife being here present

in Court in their proper persons and consenting to the assignment of
dower as played for by said petitioner it is decreed & ordered by the
Court that the Sheriff of this County Summon a Jury of five Good &
lawful men to met on the premises in said petition described who being
first duly sworn according to law shall proceed to allot and set off
to said Petitioner one third part of the several tracts of land and Town
lot in said petition mentioned & described either in one entere tract,
or parcels as they in their Judgment may think right. And the said
Mary for herself & as Guargian of her minor children aforesaid being
now here present in Court in her proper person & Consenting to the prayer
of said Isaac Vanzant and Benjamin F. Wafford & wife for Petition of said
real estate it is further ordered and decreed by the Court that the same
commissioners appointed to allot the dower to the widow do at the same
time make partition of said real estate amongst the heirs according to
law assigning to each his or her partion in severalty and that they return
a fair plat & report of their proceedings to the next term of this Court.

On petition of Jesse T. Wallace for a license to keep an ordinary
at his house in Franklin County. It is thereupon ordered by the Court
that he have license accordingly for the Term of one year from the date
hereof who entered into Bond with George Gray his Security according to
law and was qualified accordingly.

On petition of Henry Runnels for a license to keep an ordinary
at his house in Franklin County it is therefore ordered by the Court the
that they have license accordingly for the term of one year.

On petition of Shipp and Ragsdale for a license to keep an
Ordinary at their house in Franklin County. It is thereupon ordered by
the Court that they have license accordingly for the Term of one year.

Court adjourned until tomorrow morning nine o'clock.
James Keith
M. W. Howell
Andrew Campbell

(p-465)   Wednesday February the twenty fifth one thousand eight hundred
and thirty five. Court met according to adjournment.
Present - James Keith   ) Esquires Justice of
         Marshall W. Howell &) the peace for Franklin Cty
         Andrew Campbell   )

State of Tennesse
Proclamation being made the Sheriff of Franklin County made return
of the States writ of Veniree facias to this court that he had summond
the following persons being all good and lawful men of said County of
Franklin and being citizens of said County of Franklin to attend and
serve as Jurors at the present term of this Court which persons so
summoned and returned as aforesaid had been nominated for that purpose
by the Justices of this said Court of pleas and quarter sessions of
Franklin County at its last Session a list of whom was delivered to the
Sheriff of Franklin County by the Clerk of this said Court, to wit,

Thomas Garner, Charles B. Faris, Willis Holder, Abraham Shook,
Wm. Brazelton, Robert Cowan, James P. Keith, John P. Davidson, Samuel
Holland Jr. Wiley Denson, Benjamin Porter, Sidney Porter, James Morris,
Joseph M. Bickley, Nicholas W. Mathews, Lunsford L. Mathews, Lewis Robbins
Miles Francis, Sims Kelly, Robert C. Coldwell, David McGowan, Henry Herford,
James Bledsoe, Wm. Buchanan, Portland J. Curel & Thomas Sanders, and of
whom the following this day attended, to wit, Thomas Garner, Charles B
Faris, Willis Holder, Abraham Shook, William Brazelton, Robert Cowan
James P. Keith, John P. Davidson, Wiley Denson, Benjamin Porter,
Joseph M. Beckley, Nicholas W. Mathews, Lunsford L. Mathews,
Lewis Robbins, Miles Francis, Sims Kelly James Bledsoe, Wm. Buchanan,
Portland J. Curel & Thomas Sanders and of whom the following persons
being all good & lawful men of said County of Franklin were elcted
empanneled and sworn a grand Jury Jury of Inquestto inquire for the
body of the County of Franklin to wit Abraham Shook who was appointed
foreman, Thomas Garner, Willis Holder, Wm. Brazelton, James P. Keith
Wily Denson, Benjamin Porter, Joseph M. Bickley, Nicholas W. Mathews,
Lunsford L. Mathews, James Bledsoe, Wm. Buchanan & Thomas Sanders who
after receiving their charge retired to consult of their presentments.

(p-466)   A deed of conveyance from Alexander Young to Thomas Hopkins
for two lots in the Town of Winchester was duly acknowledged in open
Court by the said Alexnader Young to be his act and deed whereupon it
is ordered by the Court to be certified for Registration. Let it be
registered.

        A Bill of Sale from Peter Willis to James Howard for one negro
girl named Phebe was duly acknowledged in open Court by the said Peter
Willis to be his act and deed whereupon it is ordered by the Court to
be certified for registration. Let it be registered.

ROBERT S. SHARP   )
 Against   )
JAMES D. LUCAS &   )
HAYDEN ARNOLD   )   Where as on the 27th day of January 1835 there
was issued by James Robinson an acting Justice of the peace in & for
the County of Franklin and execution in favor of the plaintiff against
the defendents for the sum of sixty dollars & twelve & one half cents
debt and one dollar cost, which execution was returned to the present
Term of this Court with the following levy thereon endorsed, to wit,
Feb. the 4th 1835 executed by levying on one town lot in Hillsboro and
two dwelling houses on the same adjoining the land of John & James Camden
to wit, beginning on a stake in the stage road at the corner of James
Camdens stable running north with said road 12½ poles thence west thence
south thence east so as to include one acre levied on as the real estate
of Jas. D. Lucas J. G. Brazelton Cst. and on motion of the Plaintiff by
his attorney. It is ordered by the Court that said tract of land be
condemed to satisfy said execution and that an order of sale issue to
the sheriff of Franklin County to seel the same according to law.

LETTY WHITE   )
 Against   )
ZACHARAH H. MURRELL ADM.   )
& WENNY PHILIPS ADMRX   )
OF JAS. PHILIPS DECD.   )This day came the defendant by their attorney

and on their motion this cause is continued until the next Term of this Court as on their affidavit.

WALKERS ADMRS)
Vs)
ROBINSON & DARDIS) On motion of the parties by their attornies this cause is continued untill the next term of this Court by their consent.

Ordered by the Court that David M. McGowan who was summoned to attend as a Juror at this Court be fined the sum of two dollars & fifty cents for his non attendance as such & that a Scire Facias against him returnable to the next term of this Court to show cause why said Judgment should not be made absolute.

(p-467) JOSEPH HINKLE) Covenant
Against)
KINDRED H. MUSE) This day came the parties by their attorney and thereupon came a Jury to wit, Miles Francis, Robert Cowan Charles B. Farris, John P. Davidson, Edward Berk, Andrew H. McCollum, William M. Finch, George Tucker, Pleasant Hill, Benjamin Sherwood, John Turner and Benjamin Powell who being elected tryed and sworn the truth to speak upon the issue joined upon their oaths do say they find the issue in favor of the plantiff and assess his damages to four hundred and eighty dollars and twenty four cents besides cost it is therefore considered by the Court that the plantiff recover against the defendant his damages aforesaid in form assessed and also his cost by him about said suit in this behalf expended and the said defendant in mercy &.

JOHN F. GRAHAM ASSIGNEE & C) Debt
Against)
BARNABY BURROW)This day came the parties by their attorney and thereupon came a Jury to wit, Miles Francis, Robert Cowan, Charles B. Farris, John P. Davidson, Edward Berk Andrew H. McCollum, William M. Finch George B. Tucker, Pleasant Hill, Benjamin Sherwood, John Turner, and Benjamin Powell who being elected tryed and sworn the truth to spak upon the issue joined upon their oaths do say they find the issue in favor of the plantiff and assess his damages to three dollars & thirty eight cents besides the cost. It is therefore considered by the Court that the plantiff recover against the defendant one hundred and sixty nine dollars the debt in the declaration mentioned together with his damages aforesaid in form assessed and also his cost by him about said suit in this behalf expended and the said defendant in mercy &.

JAMES WOODS & CO)
Against)
WILLIAM CARTER) This day came the plantiff by their attorney and dismissed their suit and not further it prosecuting it is ordered by the Court that this suit be dismissed.

BENJAMIN DECHERED)
Against)
EDWARD RUSSELL) On motions of their attorney this cause is continued until the next Term of this Court by their consent.

HENRY M. RUTLEGE)
 Against)
EDWARD RUSSELL) On motion of the parties by their attorney this
cause is continued untill the next term of this court by their consent.

(p-468)   WM. M. & MATT FINCH)
           Executors of the last will)
           and testament of EDWARD FINCH)
           deceased Against)
           MECAJAH L. GILLASPIE) This day came the plaintiff
by this attorney and dismiss their suit and not further prosecuting.
It is ordered that this suit be dismissed and each party assumes one
half of the costs. It is therefore considered by the Court that the
plaintiff recover against the defendant his part of the costs by said
suit in this behalf expended and the said deft in mercy &. and it is
also considered by the Court that the Defendant recover against the
plaintiff their part of the costs about said suit in this behalf expended
and the said plaintiffs in mercy & to be levied of the goods and chattels
of Edward Finch decd. in the hands of said Executors to be administered.

JOHN TARWATER)
 Admin of LEWIS TARWATER DECD.)
 Against)
WILLIAM GREENLEE) On motion of the defendant by his
attorney. This cause is continued untill the next term of this Court
as on his affidavit, and on motion of the parties by their attornies a
general order is granted them to take depositions to be read as evidence
on the trial of the above cause by the adverse party giving the other
ten days notice if in this state and thirty days if out of State of the
time and place of taking said depositions.

ISAAC B. GORE) Covenant
 Against)
RUTHY WHITNEY &)
ANDERSON F WILLIS) This day came the parties by their attornies
and thereupon came a Jury, to wit, Miles Francis, Robert Cowan,
Charles B. Faris, John P. Davidson, Edward Burk Andrew H. McCullum,
Wm. M. Finch, George B. Tucker, Pleasant Hill, Benjamin Sherwood,
John Turner & Benjamin Powel who being elected tried and sworn ~~the truth~~
~~to speak uppothe issues joined upon their~~ will and truly to enquire of
damages in this case, upon their oaths do say the plaintiff hath sustained damages by reason of the non performance of the covenant in the
declaration mentioned to the amount of five hundred and eighty five
dollars & twenty nine cents besides costs, it is therefore considered
by the Court that the plaintiff recover against the defendants his
damages aforesaid in form aforesaid assessed and also his costs by
him about said suit in this behalf expended and the said defendant in
Mercy &.

WM. D. MARHUM)
 Against)
JOHN NUGENT) On motion of the plantiff by his attorney to dismiss
the appeal in this case because there was not grant or prayer for an appeal

in this cause and being argued and by the Court fully understood. It
is therefore ordered by the Court that said appeal be dismissed and
that a procedento be awardedto the Justice who rendered the Judgment.
And it is further considered by the Court that the Plaintiff recover
against the defendant his costs about said appeal in this behalf expended
and the said defendant in mercy &.

ROBERT GIBSON   )
 Against   )
GEORGE W. THOMPSON   ) This day came the plaintiff by his attorney
& the said deft and mutually agree all matters in dispute between them
in this suit be refered to the Arbitrament and award of Benjamin Decherd
Mark Hutchins & Thomas Wilson whose award thereupon shall be made the
Judgment of the Court, which is by the Court ordered accordingly made
returnable to the next Term of this Court provided that Crokett & Park
who are entitled to the beneficial interest of this suit consent to this
reference before the Arbitrators act thereupon.

JOHN TURNER ASSEE & C   )
 Against   )
WILLIAM A COLDWELL   )
GEORGE B. TUCKER &   )
MADISON PORTER   ) This day come William A. Coldwell, George B.
Tucker and say that they cannot gainsay the plaintiffs action against
them and confess judgment for the sum of one hundred thirty dollars and
twenty two cents and thereupon Madison Porter came into Open Court and
waves the necessity of an origional writ and confesses judgment jointly
with the other defendants for said sum it is therefore considered by
the Court that the plaintiff against the defendant said sum of one hundred
thrity dollars & twenty two cents confessed as a foresaid and also his
cost by him about said suit in this behalf expended and the said defendants
in Mercy & Execution stayed until next term of this Court.

On the petition of Marshall W. Howdard the acting executor of the
last will and testment of William Trigg deceased praying to alter &
change the order and judgement of the Court made at the last Term of
This Court directing certain negroes to be sold and it appearing to
the satisfaction of the Court that the negro girl margaret ought not.
(p-480) to be sold she being the property of the widow during her life
or widowhood and it further appeared to the Court that said negor woman
Esther has an infant child the six and name of which is unknown, whereupon
the Court doth order adjudge and direct that so much of the former order
of this Court as directs said negro Margaret to be sold be and the same
is hereby recinded annulled and made void, and it is further ordered that
said infant child slave be sold with the other negroes mentioned in the
former order of this Court agreeable to the Terms of said former order.

         Court adjourned until tomorrow morning 10 oclock
                              James Keith
                              Andrew Campbell
                              Sam Norwood

         Thursday February the 26th one thousand eight hundred and thirty

five Court met according to adjournment.
Present - James Keith   )   Esquires Justices of
       Andrew Campbell   )   peace for Franklin County
       Marshall W. Howell)

THE STATE OF TENNESSEE   )
  Against   )
MADISON GOODMAN   ) This day came the attorney General who
prosecutes for the State in this behalf and with the consent of the
Court enters a noteprosigue in this case.

THE STATE OF TENNESSEE   )
  Against   )
ANDREW H MCCULLUM   ) This day Andrew H. McCullum & James Morris
came into Open Court and acknowledged themselves to owe and stand justly
indebted to the State of Tennessee in the following sums to wit, the
said Andrew H. McCullum in the sum of two hundred and fifty dollars and
James Morris his security in the sum of one hundred and twenty five dollars
to be levied of their respective goods and chattels lands and tenaments
to the use of said State but to be void on condition that the said
Andrew H. McCullum make his personal appearance before the Justices of
our next Court of please and quarter sessions to be held for the County
of Franklin on Thursday after the fourth Monday in May next then and
there to abide by and perform the judgment of said Court and not depart
the same without leave first had and obtained.

(p-471)   THE STATE TENNESSEE   ) Present for an Affray
           Against   )
           MICAH TAUL   ) This day came the attorney general
who prosecutes for the State in this behalf as well as the said defendant
in his proper person and the said defendant having heard said presement
read says he is thereof guilty and puts himself upon the grace and mercy
of the Court. It is therefore considered by the Court that the defendant
for such his offence be fined one cent and pay the costs of this prosecution and the said defendant in mercy &.

This day the grand Jury came into Open Court and returned a
Presentment against Micah Taul & Joseph R. Shropshire for an affray a
true Bill. Also a Presentment against Jesse Ferrel & Elias Oldham Jr.
for an affray a true Bill.

A deed of Mortgage from Elias Smith to John Sanders for the
personal property therein named was duly acknowledged in Open Court by
the said Elias Smith to be his act and deed whereupon it is ordered by
the Court to be certified for registration. Let it be registered.

The return of Marshall W. Howell Guardian of the minor heirs of
Wm. Trigg decd this day made his return to Court for the years 1834 &
1835 which was received by the Court and ordered to be recorded.

This day Colewell P. Shipp and Moses C. Ragsdale who obtained
a license on Tensday last to keep an Ordinary at their house came into
Open Court and entered into Bond with Thomas Finch, James Morris and
Nicholas W. Mathews his securities according to law and was qualified
accordingly.

This day Henry Runnels who obtained a license on Tuesday last to keep an Ordinary at his house came into Open Court and entered into bond with Micajah L. Gillaspie his security according to law and was qualified accordingly.

Court adjourned untill tomorrow morning 9 oclock.

M. W. Howell,
James Keith
Andrew Campbell

(p-472)   Friday February the 27th one thousand eight hundred and thirty five Court met according to adjournment.
Present - James Keith   )   Esquires Justices
         Andrew Campbell   )   of the peace for Franklin
         Marshall W. Howell   )   County.

JOSEPH HINKLE   )
 Against   )
KINDRED H. MUSE   )   This day came the defendant into Open Court and moved the Court to grant him an appeal to the next Circuit Court to be held for Franklin County upon the following affidavit to wit.

HINKLE   )
 Vs   )
MUSE   )   In this case the defendant makes oath that owing to his poverty he is not able to give security or bear the expences of this law suit in conveying it up to the Circuit Court, and that he is justly intitled to be releived against a greater part of the judgment rendered agt. him in this case at the present Term of this Court Sworn to in Open Court this 27th Feb. 1835   K. H. Muse
W.B. Wagner Clerk,
Which is granted by the Court without his giving security.

ROBERT L. SHARP ASSIGNEE & C)   Debt
 Againsts   )
HAYDON ARNOLD   )
JAS H. ARNOLD &   )
JAS. R. DRAKE   )   This day came the plaintiff by his attorney and having filed his declaration and the defendants being solemnly called to appear and defend this suit came not but made default. It is therefore considered by the Court that the plaintiff recover against the defendant one hundred dollars the debt in the declaration mentioned together with the further sum one dollar interest thereon at the rate of six per cent per annum and also his cost by him about said suit in this behalf expended and the said defendant in Mercy &.

ROBERT H. OLIVER   )   Debt
 Against   )
JOHN D. STOVALL &   )
CATHARINE DRAKE   )   This day came the plaintiff by his attorney and having filed his declaration and the defendants being solemnly called to appear and defend this suit came not but made default. It is therefore considered by the Court that the plaintiff recover against the defendants

ninty dollars and seventy two cents the debt in the declaration mentioned together with the further sum of ninety cents interest thereon at the rate of six per cent per annum and also his cost by him about said suit in this behalf expended and the said defendants in mercy &.

(p-473)   BAZABEL PRAYTON to the use)   Debt
       of CLAIBORN STINNETT   )
            Against   )
        SAMUEL SWANN   ) This day came the plaintiff by his attorney and having filed his Declaration and the defendant being solemnly called to appear and defend this suit. Came not but made default It is therefore considered by the Court that the plaintiff recover against the defendant one hundred dollars the debt in the Declaration mentioned together with the further sum of one dollar Interest thereon at the rate of six percent peranum also his costs by him about said suit in this behalf expended and the said Defendant in mercy &.

EATON A WOOD Who sues to   )   Debt
the use of R. P. HARRIS   )
    Against   )
POLLARD RHODES &   )
ISHAM HARRIS   ) This day came the plaintiff by his attorney and having filed his Declaration and the Defendant being solemnly called to appeare and defend this suit, came not but made default It is therefore considered by the Court that the plaintiff recover against the defendant one hundred & seventy two dollars & twenty five cents the balance of the debt in the Declaration mentioned, together with the further sum of one dollar and seventy seven cents. Interest thereon at the reate of six percent peranum and also his costs by him about said suit in this behalf expended and said defendants in mercy &.

JOHN W. & A. S. CAMPBELL   )   Debt
 Against   )
ISAAC LOLLAR   ) This day came the plaintiff by their attorney and having filed their declaration and the defendants being solemnly called to appear and defend this suit came not but made default It is therefore considered by the Court that the plaintiffs recover against the defendant one hundred dollars the debt in the Decoration mentioned together with the further sum of five dollars & fifty cents interest thereon at the rate of six percent peranum and also their cost by them about said suit in this behalf expended and the said defendant in Mercy &.

      The return of Osborn D. Henndon Guardian for the minor heirs of Pomgret Henndon Decd was this day produced in open Court was received by the Court and ordered to be recorded.

(p-474)   ROBERT L. SHARP ASSEE & C)
        Against   )   Debt
        WILLIAM BICHNILL &   )
        HAYDON ARNOLD   )
) This day came the plaintiff by his attorney and having filed his declaration and the defendants being solemnly called to appear and defend this suit came not but made default

It is therefore considered by the Court that the plaintiff recover against the defendants one hundred dollars the debt in the declaration mentioned together with the further sum of one dollar interest at the rate of six per cent per annum and also his cost by him about said suit in his cost by him about said suit in his behalf expended and the said defendants in mercy &.

This day James H. Estill came into Open Court and resigned his appointment of constable for Franklin County which was received by the Court.

Court adjourned untill Court in Course

M. W. Howell
James Keith
Andrew Campbell

May Term 1835

State of Tennessee

At a Court of pleas and quarter sessions begun & held for Franklin County on the 4th Monday of May in the year of our Lord one thousand eight and thirty five it being the twenty fifth day of said month and the 59th year of the Independance of the United States.

Present thirteen of the acting Justices of the peace for Franklin County

A deed of conveyance from William Larkins to Elijah N. Stovall for one hundred and sixty acres of land lying in Franklin County was duly acknowledged in Open Court by the said William Larken to be his act and deed. Whereupon it is ordered by the Court to be certified for registration Let it be registered.

By the oaths of Robert Dougan & Preston Hatchett subscribing witnesses thereto to be the act and deed of the said James Dougan on this day t̶h̶a̶t̶/̶i̶t̶/̶b̶e̶a̶r̶s̶/̶d̶a̶t̶e̶/̶w̶h̶e̶r̶e̶u̶p̶o̶n̶ It is ordered by the Court to be certified for registration. Let it be registered.

A Bill of Sale from George W. Thompson to Benjamin O. Nevill for one Negro boy named Randol was duly acknowledged in Open Court by the said George W. Thompson to be his act and deed. Whereupon it is ordered by the Court to be certified for registration. Let it be registrated.

Ordered by the Court that Henry Peacock be appointed overseer of the road from the Baptist meeting house to the foot of the mountain in room of Afry Bass and that he keep the same in good repair according to law and that he have the same hands that worked under the former overseer.

A deed of conveyance from Andrew Oliver to John Hickerson for two hundred acres of land lying in Franklin County was duly acknowledged in Open Court by the said Andrew Oliver to be his act and deed, Whereupon it is ordered by the Court to be certified for registration. Let it be registered.

(p-475) A deed of conveyance from Mary Noe to David Arnett for thirty acres of land lying in Franklin County was duly proven in Open Court by the oaths of Preston Hatchett & Robert Dougan subscribing Witnesses thereto to be the act and deed of the said Mary Noe on this day Whereupon it is ordered by the Court to be certified for registration. Let it be registered.

A deed of conveyance from James Dougan to David Arnett for forty acers of land lying in Fra klin County was duly proven in Open Court.

Ordered by the Court that Holloway Power be appointed Overseer of the road from the county line to John Silons lane in room of Henry Benny and that he keep the same in good repair according to law and that he have the same hands that worked under the former overseer.

Ordered by the Court that Samuel Taylor be appointed overseer of the road of the first class from John Armstrongs to Calloways Pond in room of John Russell and that he keep the same in good repair according to law and that he have the same hands that worked under the former overseer.

(p-476)   Ordered by the Court that Sarah Taylor be appointed overseer
of the road of the third class from the State line to John Larkins in
room of Elisha Stovall and that he keep the same in good repair according
to law and that he have the same hands that worked under the former overseer.

Ordered by the Court that Philip Roberts be appointed overseer of
the road from John Burrows to Benjamin Burrow's old place in room of
John Burrows and that he keep the same in good repair according to law
and that he have the same hands that worked under the former overseer.

Ordered by the Court that Ninrod Sandridge be appointed overseer
of the road, of the second class from Timms Ford to Limebaugh's in room
of Col. Stramler and that he keep the same in good repair according to
law and that he have the same hands that worked under the former overseer.

Ordered by the Court that Alexander E. Patton be appointed overseer
of the same part of the road which William S. Mooney was formerly overseer
and that he keep the same in good repair according to law and that he
have the same hands that worked under the former overseer.

Ordered by the Court that Richard H. Limmins be appointed overseer
of the road of the second Class from Lee's ford and Elk River to the
Williford Old place in the room of Andrew C. Wood and that he keep the
same in good repair according to law and that he have the same hands that
worked under the former overseer.

Ordered by the Court that Jacob Killian be appointed overseer of
the road of the ~~second class~~ first Class from Benjamin Nevills to Dry
Creek in room of James Wilkinson and that he keep the same in good repair
according to law and that he have the same hands that worked under the
former overseer.

(p-477)   Ordered by the Court that John Dewitt be appointed overseer
of the road of the second class from the road leading from Manns ford
to Lynchburg to intersect the Fayetteville road near Brandons' and that
he keep the same in good repair according to law and then Lemuel Brandon
and David Prater allot the hands to work on said road.

Ordered by the Court that Asa D. Oakley Esqs. be appointed to
allot and divide the hands to work under Edward Morris Overseer of the
Fayetteville road an the overseer of the Boat landing road and the
overseers of the road leading by Popler Grove.

Ordered by the Court that James Patty foreman an overseer of a
road in this county deliver up to David Mackleroy overseer of another
road one sledge hammer and crow bar in his possession.

Ordered by the Court that George Hudspeth David Bell and William
Larkin be appointed to allot and divide the hands between all the overseers
below Salem in Franklin County.

Ordered by the Court that Council B. Ingram be appointed overseer of the road of the first class from Bradlys Creek to John Lefebr's in room of Anderson F. Willis and that he keep the same in good repair according to law & that he have the same hands that worked under the former Overseer.

Ordered by the Court that Joshua Turner be appointed overseer of the road of the second class from Stone Fort to the Big Prairy (p-478) and that he keep the same in good repair according to law and that Thomas Wright give a list of hands to work on said road.

Ordered by the Court that William M. Finch be appointed overseer of the was of the second class from the end of Hayters lane to Lees ford in the room of Matt Finch and that he keep the same in good repair according to law and that he have the same hands that worked under the former overseer.

Ordered by the Court that James B. Stovall, John Oliver, John G. Bostick be appointed commissioners to settle with William G. Givins administrator of the estate of Nathaniel W. Wilder deceased and that they make report to this or the next term of this Court.

Ordered by the Court that John Handly Benjamin Powell be appointed commissioners to settle with the County offercers for the year 1835.

Ordered by the Court the Richard C. Holder, John Staples G. John L. Martin be appointed commissioners to settle with the executor of the estate of John Feamster deceased and that they make their report to this or the next term of this Court.

Ordered by the Court that the Indenture binding Westly Gutry to Richard B. Moore be rescinded and made void and that said Moore be released from said Indenture all of which was by consent of the parties.

This day John Burrows produced in Open Court one old Wolf scalp and from his statements upon oath the Court being satisfied thereupon ordered that he have a certificate to the Treasurer of Middle Tennessee for $3.00 out of any money in the Treasury not otherwise appropriated.

(p-479)   Ordered by the Court that Richmond P. Harris, Willis Burt & James Byrom be appointed commissioners of the poor house who were qualified according to law. It is also ordered that Richmond P. Harris be appointed Treasurer of said board of commissioners who entered into bond with Thomas Finch his securety in the sum of one thousand dollars according to law.

Ordered by the Court that Coldwell P. Shipp be appointed constable in & for the County of Franklin in the bounds of the Town Company for the next ensuing two years who entered into bond with Portand J. Curle, Nicholas W. Mathews & James Lewis his securities according to law and was qualified accordingly.

Ordered by the Court that John F. Anderson be appointed constable in & for the County of Franklin in the bounds of Captain Gofers Company for the next ensuing two years who entered into bond with Armon Gipson

& Fredench F. Hendricks his securities according to law and was qualified accordingly.

Ordered by the Court that James Campbell be appointed constable in & for the County of Franklin in the bounds of Captain Faris Company for the next ensuing two years who entered into bond with Andrew Campbell & Alexander Donaldson his securities according to law and was qualified accordingly.

This day the settlement made with Secil Bobo administrator of the estate of Hardin Taylor decd was produced in Open Court was received by the Court and ordered to be recorded.

This day the settlement made with Alexander E. Patton former administrator of the estate of Alexander Floyd deceased was produced in Open Court was received by the Court and ordered to be recorded.

This day the return of Joseph Gentry Guardian of Jane and Nancy Roach minor heirs of John Roach deceased was produced in open was received by the Court and ordered to be recorded.

(p-480)   This day the inventory and amount of sales of the estate of Wyatt Ballard deceased was produced in Open Court was received by the Court and ordered to be recorded.

This day the settlement made with the administrators of the estate of Elijah Runnels decd was produced in OpenCourt was received by the Court and ordered to be recorded.

This day the amount of sales of the estate of James Surrat deceased was produced in Open Court was received by the Court and ordered to be recorded.

This day the settlement made with Barnaby Barrow former guardian of Juliann Graham Minor orphan of John Graham deceased was produced in Open Court was received by the Court and ordered to be recorded.

Ordered by the Court that the following recpt be recorded, to wit, received of Barnaby Barrow former guardian of Juliann Graham in full assets in his hands as per settlement by commissioners report $244.12
This 26 March 1835
John F. Graham
Late Guardian

This day the settlement made with the Executors of Boley Embry deceased was produced in Open Court was received by the Court and ordered to be recorded.

This day Wiley J. Hines guardian of James C. Neaves orphan of James Neaves deceased made his return on oath which was rec. by the Court and ordered to be recorded.

This day the settlement made with the administrator of the estate of Joel Taylor dece. was produced in Open Court was received by the Court and ordered to be registered recorded.

(p-481)   On the petition of Joseph Bratton to turn the turnpike road commencing where it leanes the Moherds ford road to the road that leads from Coldwell's bridge to Winchester, It is therefore ordered by the Court that said petition be granted and that said road be established according to the prayer of said petition.

On petition of John Anderson to turn the road leading down crow creek on his own land, and it appearing to the Court that he has Opened a new road and on better ground. It is therefore ordered by the Court that said new way be established according to the prayer of the petition.

Present George Hudspeth, Meredith Catchings, Richmond P. Harris, Wm. Crownover, James Keith, George W. Thompson, James Byron David Bell, Wm. Laster, Littleton G. Simpson, Andrew Mann, Samuel Bradshaw & Marshall W. Howell Esquires.

Ordered by the Court that Thomas Finch be allowed the sum of seven dollars for wood and candles furnished for the county of Franklin for the use of the Court, which was unanimously allowed by said Justices.

Ordered by the Court that the County Trustee refund to Thomas Finch collector of the taxes one dollar & eighty cents the tax on 266 acres of land & 2 black poles twice listed on the tax lists for the year 1834. Isd

Present George Hudspeth, Meredith Catchings, Richmond P. Harris, Wm. Crownover, James Keith, George W. Thompson, James Byron, David Bell Wm. Laster, Littleton G. Simpson, Andrew Mann, Samuel Bradshaw & Marshall W. Howell Esqrs. Ordered by the Court that Willie B. Wagner Clerk of the County Court of Franklin County be allowed the sum of seven dollars for a record book furnished for the clerks office of said County which allowance was unanimously made by said Justices. Isd.

Present, Meredith Catchings, Richmond P. Harris, Wm. Crownover, James Keith George W. Thompson, James Byron David Bell, Wm. Laster, Little-ton G. Simpson, Andrew Mann, Samuel Bradshaw, Marshall W.   (p-482) Howell, Andrew Campbell & John Oliver, Esquires. Ordered by the Court that Willie B. Wagner pø/ḱ/l̸l̸øẃéd̸ Clerk of Franklin County Court be allowed the sum of twenty dollars for making out and delivering to the sheriff a complete list of the polls & taxable property for which each person is liable and for recording the same for 1834 which allowance was unanimously made by said Justices except James Keith who voted in the negative.

Present, George Hudspeth, Meredith Catchings, Richmond P. Harris, Wm. Crownover, James Keith, George W. Thompson James Byron, David Bell, Wm. Lasater Littleton G. Simpson, Andrew Mann Samuel Bradshaw, Marshal W. Howell Andrew Campbell, John Oliver & Wm. Simmons Esqrs.

Ordered by the Court that Willie B. Wagner Clerk of Franklin County Court be allowed the sum of fifty dollars for his Exeficio services for the year ending at this term of the Court which allowance was unanimously made by said Justices except George W. Thompson who voted in the Negative. Isd.

Present - George Hudspeth, Meredith Catchings, Richmond P. Harris
Wm. Crownover, James Keith, George W. Thompson, James Byron David Bell,
Wm. Lasiter, Littleton G. Simpson Andrew Mann, Samuel Bradshaw, Marshall
W. Howell, Andrew Campbell ~~John Daugherty James Kelly~~ Esqrs Ordered by
the Court that Thomas Finch sheriff of Franklin County be allowed the sum
of fifty Dollars for his exofficio services for the year ending at this
Term of the Court which allowance was unanimously made by said Justices.

Present George Hudspeth, Meradithe Catchings, Richmond P. Harris
Wm. Crownover, James Keith, George W. Thompson, James Byram, David Bell
Wm. Lasiter, Littleton G. Simpson, Andrew Mann, Samuel Bradshaw,
Marshall W. Howell, Andrew Campbell, John Daugherty and James Kelly
Esquire Ordered by the Court that Madison Porter be allowed the sum of
eight dollars for one sledge and croe bar for the use of the public road
which allowance was unanimously made by said justices.

(p-483)   It appearing to the satisfaction of the Court that the following
named children of Thomas Finch have a legacy coming to them in the State
of Missouri. It is therefore ordered by the Court that Thomas Finch be
appointed Guardian over the persons and property of following named
children to wit, Mary E. Matt L., Rebecca C., Sarah E., Thomas H., &
Susan L. Finch who entered into bond with John Goodwin & Richmond P.
Harris his securities in the sum of one thousand dollars according to law.

Ordered by the Court that William G. Guinn be appointed guardian
over the persons and property of Daniel Modely who entered into bond
with William Greenlee and Frederick F. Hendrick his securities in the
sum of one thousand dollars according to law.

Court adjourned untill tomorrow morning ten o'clock.
                                        John Daughtery
                                        M. W. Howell
                                        James Byrom

Tuesday May the twenty sixth one thousand eight hundred and thirty
five. Court met according to adjournment.
Present - seven of the acting Justices of the peace for Franklin County

A deed of conveyance from Ambrose James to Absalom Faris Senr. for
one hundred and forty five acres of land lying in Franklin County was
duly proven in Open Court by the oaths of Edwin Eanes and John Handley
subscribing Witnesses thereto to be the act and deed of the said Ambrose
James on the day that it bears date. Whereupon it is ordered by the Court
to be certified for registration. Let it be registered.

This day Cornelias Homan came into Court and resigns his appointment
of Deputy Sheriff of Franklin County which was received by the Court.

This day David O. Anderson came into open Court and took the
necessary oaths of qualification as deputy sheriff of Franklin County.

(p-484)   This day Williamson S. Oldham came into Open Court and took
the necessary oaths of qualification as deputy Clerk of Franklin County.

(p-484)   This day Williamson S. Oldham came into Open Court and took the necessary oaths of qualification as Deputy Clerk of Franklin County Court.

Ordered by the Court that James Wilkinson be appointed overseer of this road from Benjamin Nevills to Coldwell's Bridge and that John Oliver & Samuel Bradshaw Esqrs. allot the hands to work said road.

Ordered by the Court that James Robinson John Goodwin & Willie B. Wagner be appointed commissioners to settle with John Frame administrator with the Will annexed of the estate of Ezekiel Phillips decd and that they make their report to the next term of this Court.

Ordereed by the Court that Daniel O. Anderson, John Staples & Peter Simmons be appointed commissioners to settle with Susan Trigg Adminstratrix of the Estate of James L. McWhorten decd and that they make report to the next term of this Court.

Ordered by the Court that Joseph Klipper, Wm. Reeves & John Goodwin be appointed commissioners to settle Hance McWhorten administrator of the Estate of James Patton decd and that they make report to the next term of this Court.

Ordered by the Court, that James B. Stovall, John Oliver & John G. Bostick be appointed commissioners to settle with Wm. G. Guinn administrator of the estate of Nathaniel Wilden decd and also to make partition and division among the heirs of said estate and that they make their report to the next term of this Court.

Ordered by the Court that Mark Hutchins William Estill, Benjamin Decherd, John P. Gandy, Thomas L. Logan, Madison Porter & Wm. T. Wills be appointed a Jury of view to mark and lay off a road from the public square to the grave yard near Winchester and that the view and mark the same and make report to the next Term of this Court rescinded & make void.

(p-485)   Ordered by the Court that the following persons be appointed judges and Clerks to hold the election on the first Thursday in August 1835 for Governor mmebers to congress and members to the general assembly to wit,   Winchester Precinct Judges Thomas Howard, Solomon Wagner & Capt. James Taylor, Judges Jesse Sharp, John Daugherty and John D. Fennnell At the precinct at Winford's Edmond P. Lee, Milton McQueen and William Orear Judges J. W. D. Stamper Benjamin B. Knight and William J. Grills Clerk, at Rock Creek Precinct, Benj. Majors Willis Burt & James Byram Judges, A. W. Majors, Augustus Dorrill & Milus M. Hall Clerks, At Big Crow Creek Precinct, George Garner, David Lynch and William Crownover Judges, Moses Taylor Reuben Richard & Andrew Kincaid. At Wagners Precinct Rice Simpson, Dan'l Weaver and L. G. Simpson, Judges, William N. Taylor David Prater and John O. Young Clerks. At the Precinct at Salem, John Staples, David Hurt and Isaac Vanzant, Judges, Andrew Woods C. Homan and George Staples, Clerks, At the Precinct at Coldwell Bridge Sam'l Bradshaw William G. Gunn and John Oliver Judges, William S. Mooney, Thompson Evans and A. E. Patton, Clerk at the precinct at Cunningham's James Howard, John O. Johnson and Stewart Cowan Judges, Jesse Reynolds, R. N. Wallis Robert Lackey Jr. Clerks. At the Precinct at the Stone Fort John Lowry

J. Jones and Thos. Right Judges, William P. Hickerson, Wm. Hickerson and
Willis Hickerson Clerks. At the Precinct at Adam G. Capertons. P. Sells
Sr. Randolph Champion & Stewart Judges James Kelly, George West and
Bledsoe Stewart, Clerks, and that the Sheriff summon them to attend.

Ordered by the Court that the following persons be appointed Jurors
for the next term of this Court, to wit, Joseph Klipper, Benjamin Decherd
Paschal Green Thomas Cunningham, Julius C. Simmons, Edmund P. Lee,
J. W. D. Stamper, John Lee (pay the warrent) Wm. L. Hannah, Joseph
Francis Sr. Bird Francis, Joseph Sewell, John K. Burton, Joseph Huddleston
Thomas Wilson, William A. Coldwell, William Hendon, John I. Hayter,
John Mason, Asakel Aldrich, Frances Turner, Thomas N. Holt, George
McCutcheon, William Champion, John L. Bowers and Milton McQuin, and that
Caldwell (p-486) P. Shipp and James Campbell be appointed constable to
attend an said Court and that the Sheriff summon them to attend and make
due returns to the Next Term of this Court.

This day the report of the commissioners of the school tract near
Rowlands was produced in Open Court was received by the Court and ordered
to be recorded.

This day the settlement with the executors of the estate of Wm.
Arnett deceased, was produced in Open Court was received and ordered to
be recorded.

This day the return of Dudley Johnson guardian of Etherbert C.
George was produced in Open Court was received by the Court and ordered
to be recorded.

This day an additional Inventory of the estate of Ezekiel Phillips
deceased was produced in Open Court was received by the Court and ordered
to be recorded.

This day an additional list of sales of the estate of James Phillips
deseased was produced in Open Court was received by the Court and ordered
to be recorded.

This day the settlement made with Zacharia H. Murrell one of the
administrators of the estate of James Phillips deceased was produced in
Open Court was received by the Court and ordered to be recorded.

The commissoners appointed at the last term of this Court to
make petition of the real estate and slaves of Jacob Vanzant deceased
between the heirs of said decendent and to allot and assign to the widow
her dower in said lands and her share in said slaves, made the followhing
report which was received by the Court and no objections being made thereto
is ordered to be affirmed and recorded to wit, In obedience to an order
of the February sessions of 1835 of our County Court appointing the
undersigned commissioners to lay off and assign to Mary Vanzant widow
and relich of the late Jacob Vanzant dedeased her dower in the real estate
of her deceased husband and also to divide the balance (p-487) of his
real estate between the rest of his heirs Present this Court the following. Report of their proceedings we went upon the premises of the said
deceased about the 9th of March following and gave them that full exami-

nation that the nature of the case required and ascertained by an accurate
survey the tracts of land the said Jacob ~~Vanzant~~ died seized or in
possession of to contain seven hundred and ten acres. We then assigned
the widow her dower or one third part beginning at a stake & Hickory
pointers standing in the section line where the Paint)Rock Road by the
way of woods, Meeting house, crosses the Buncomb Road south of the mouth
Vanzants lane and runs north two hundred and sixteen poles to a stake
standing ten poles north sixty degrees east of the head of the Rattlesnake or big Spring thence east one hundred and fifty eight poles to a
hickory stump in the west boundary of John W. Holders land & South with
the same passing his South West corner, in all one hundred and thirty
one poles to a stake in a filed thence east forty two poles to a hickory
in a lane thence south eighty five poles to a stake & pointers in the
section line and with the same and the Buncomb Road west two hundred
poles to the beginning including the mansion house where the deceased
lived and all the out houses appertaining thereto containing Two hundred
and thirty six acres and a sufficient quantity of timber cleared land &
which is truly represented by the black dated lines in the plat, We then
proceeded to divide among or between the legates as follows having one
region to water timber and quality of soil &. Lot No. 2 fell to Adeline
67½ acres beginning at the North East corner of the two hundred and
thirty six acres Dower tract and runs north with Holders line, fifty Seven
and one third poles stake and pointers the noe west one hundred eighty
seven poles to a stake in Mrs. Triggs line & with the same south in all
fifty seven and one third poles to a stake in the water below the spring
in the North boundary of No. 5 thence East to and with the North boundary
of the two hundred and thirty six acres in all one hundred & eighty seven
poles to the beginning containing sixty seven and one third acres.
(p-488)   Lot no. 3 fell to Isaac beginning at the north east corner of
No. 2 in holders line & runes north with the same fifty seven and one
third poles to a stake and pointed thence west one hundred and eighty
seven poles to a stake in Mrs. Triggs line & with the same South fifty
seven and one third poles to the northwest corner of lot No. 2 and with
the north boundary of the same east one hundred and eighty seven poles
to the beginning containing sixty seven and one third acres. Lot no. 4
fell to Wofford 67½ acres bebinning at a hickory in John W. Holders
west boundary the same bing north east corner to the old tract as occupant
claim & runs west to and with John Haws south boundary in all one hundred
and eighty seven poles to a stake in Mrs. Griggs east boundary south with
the same fifty seven & one third poles to the North west corner of lot No. 3
Isaac's tract and with the north boundary of the same east one hundred
and eighty seven poles to his north east corner in Holders line & with
the same north fifty seven and one third poles to the beginning containing sixty seven and one third acres. Lot No. 5 to Williams Thomas 111
acres beginning at the stake & hickory pointers in the section line south
of the mouth of Vanzants Lane. The same being the Beginning corner to
the 236 acre dower tract & runs north with the west boundary of the same
two hundred and sixteen poles to the north west corner a stake standing
ten poles north sixty degrees east of the head of the Rattlesnake Spring
thence west to the southwest corner of No. 2. In the water below the
spring and down the spring branch with Mrs. Griggs line south sixty degrees
west when reduced to a straight line in all forty two poles to the north
east corner of lot No. 7 mill tract south with the east boundary of the
same one hundred and forty four poles to a stake standing north eastward

of Knykendalls old house thence west with the south boundary of the
mill track passing the south west corner in all one hundred and seventy
one poles to a stake & pointer thence south seventy two poles to a
stake and two post oaks on the Buncomb Road in the section line & with
the same East One hundred and sixty three poles to the beginning including the Knykendal Old Houses & one hundred and Eleven acres of land and
the spring. Lot No. 6 feel to Polly Ann beginning at the South west
corner of the section the tract lises in and runs (p-489)   north with
the Range line crossing the Rattlesnake spring branch 174 poles in all
one hundred and ninty four poles to a stump north west corner of the
Patton Tract of land thence east one hundred and fourteen poles to the
north east corner on Mrs. Triggs line thence south, crossing said branch
below the mill at 13 poles in all one hundred and eighteen poles to a
post oak south west corner to the mill tract in Pattons Old line thence
west with the line of No 5 sixty one poles to a stake & pointers thence
south seventy two poles to a stake and two post oaks on the Buncomb Road
in the section line & with the same west fifty seven poles to the beginning including Pattons Old House and one hundred and eleven acres of
land. No. 7 mill tract fell to mariah 50 acres beginning at the north
east corner of the Patton tract on Mrs. Triggs line & runs South with
the East boundary of lot No. 6 crossing the said branch below the mill
in all one hundred and eighteen poles to a post oak in Pattons Old line
thence east sixty two poles to the stake corner Northeast of Knykendalls
Old house thence north with another line of lot No. 5 William Thomas
tract in all one hundred and forty four poles to the north west corner
in the mill pond and down the same south sixty degrees west including
the mill gin press, distillery & fifty acres of land to the beginning.
It was the desire of the commissioners to have laid off each lot as every
lot of equal value but finding that impossible or hard to do in order,
therefore to make each lot as near as they could of equal value they
have laid on or traced Lot No. 5 William Thomas Knykendalls place $23
and lot No. 6 Polly Ann's Patton place $57 forty dollars to be paid over
to Lot No. 2 Adalines and $20 to be paid over to No. 3 and four each Isaac
and Woofords lots. The above lots or tracts of land is truly represented
in the annexed plats or correction as marked and numbered &. The commissioners is advised of no other tracts of land that belongs to the deceased
except a small lot in the Town of Winchester being part of Lot No in
the plan of said Town and too small to Divide. (p-490)   and recomend
it to be sold and the proceeds divided among the heirs &. All which is
respectfully submitted

We were four days engaged   George Gray
in laying off the dower   Geo. Hudspeth
and dividing the land & 7   J. Handly
tracts or lots   John S. Martin

        State of Tennessee
        The undersigned having been appointed by the County Court of
Franklin County at the Feby Term 1835 Commissioners to divide the negro
property belonging to the Estate of Jacob Vanzant deceased among his
legal representatives beg leave to report that they have discharged the
duty assigned them, and have alloteed to Mary Vanzant the Widow of said
Jacob the following named negroes at the following prices to wit,

```
Peter A man at          ------------------------------------------- $ 700.00
Henery a man at         ------------------- ------------------------   425.00
Winny, a woman at       -------------------------------------------    250.00
Gusta a man at          -------------------------------------------    650.00
Betsy a girl at         -------------------------------------------    250.00
Cyntha a girl at        -------------------------------------------    175.00
Amounting in all to the sum                                        $2425.00
```

To Isaac Vanzant son of said Jacob the following named negroes at the
following named prices, to wit,

```
Andrew, a boy at        -------------------------------------------  $ 550.00
Ben    a boy at         -------------------------------------------    562.00
Hamilton, a man at------------------------------------------------     625.00
Amounting to thesums of                                            $1737.00
```

To B. F. Wosford and Emily his wife the daughter of said Jacob the
following negroes to the following prices to wit

```
Lew a man at            ------------------------------------------- $700.00
James a man at          -------------------------------------------   650.00
Step a man at           -------------------------------------------   450.00
Amounting in value of the sum of                                  $1800.00
```

To Maria Louisa Vanzant daughter of the said Jacob the following
negroes at the following prices, to wit,

```
Susan & child           -------------------------------------------$350.00
Jack a boy at           ------------------------------------------- 300.00
Nancy a girl at         ------------------------------------------- 200.00
Milly a girl at         ------------------------------------------- 325.00
Sam a man at            ------------------------------------------- 750.00
Amounting in value to the sum of                                  $1925.00
```

(p-491)   To Frances Adaline Vanzant a daughter of the said Jacob the
following negroes at the following prices, to wit,

```
Lucy & child            ------------------------------------------- $ 525.00
Napoleon a boy at ------------------------------------------------    250.00
Herculse a boy at ------------------------------------------------    200.00
Lewis a boy at          -------------------------------------------   150.00
Anne a girl at          -------------------------------------------   300.00
Bob a man at            -------------------------------------------   675.00
Amounting in value to the sum of                                  $2100.00
```

To Polly Anne Vanzant daughter of the said Jacob the following negroes
at the following prices, to wit,

```
Eliza & child           ------------------------------------------- $600.00
Roena a woman at        -------------------------------------------   500.00
Arthur a man at         -------------------------------------------   650.00
John a boy              -------------------------------------------   500.00
Amounting in value to the sum of                                  $2250.00
```

To Wm. Thomas Vanzant son of the said Jacob the following negroes
at the following prices, to wit,

```
Moses a man at          -------------------------------------------$725.00
Abraham a boy at        ------------------------------------------- 275.00
George a boy at         ------------------------------------------- 300.00
Alfred a boy at         ------------------------------------------- 275.00
Abram a boy at          ------------------------------------------- 225.00
Anderson a boy at ------------------------------------------------- 125.00
Amounting in value to the sum of                                  $1925.00
```

In dividing the negroes aforesaid they were in the first place valued at
the above prices the heirs then drew by turns the negroes above alloted
to them, the widow as the guardian of the four minors drawing for them
which is respectfully submitted, 5th May 1835.

George Hudspeth
John Staples
John L. Martin
J. Handley

Whereupon it is ordered by the Court that the administratrix of said estate pay to the commissioners George Gray, George Hudspeth, John Staples, John L. Martin & John Handly seven dollars & fifty cents each for their services in making pertition of said estate.

Ordered by the Court that the following receipts be recorded, to wit, Nashville Inn, 15th of May 1835. Received of Thomas Linch Seriff of Franklin County Nine hundred and sixty one dollars eighty one cents being the amount of state tax in said county for the year 1834 which by law he is bound to account for agreeably to the (p-492)   Clerk return for said year 1834.
$961.81   Thos. Crutcher Treasurer.

Received of Thomas Finch Sheriff and collector of the public taxes in and for the County of Franklin and State of Tennessee for the year 1834 the sum of one hundred and seventy seven dollars and ninety eight cents being the full amount of money by him collected on School lands for said year of 1834 after deducting his commission on the same
                              Feb. 27th 1835
                    Hugh Frances Treasurer & Clerk
                    For the board of common school commissioners
                    for Franklin County.

Rec'd Winchester 22nd May 1835 of Thomas Finch Sheriff & Collector of the County tax for Franklin County for the year 1834 nine hundred thirty seven dollars 30½ cents after deducting his commissons being the amt of County & Jurors tax and tax collected on property not listed.
                    Benjamin Decherd
                              County Trustee.

On petition of Nimrod Sandridge for permission to keep a public ferry at Tims Ford on Elk river on the road leading from Winchester to Fayetteville. It is ordered by the Court that said petition be granted and that he have permission to keep a public ferry at said ford. Who entered into bond with Elijah D. Robbins & Nathan Sandrige his security in the sum of two thousand dollars according to law.

Ordered by the Court Richard Parish of the age of twelve years be bound to David Paris untill he arrives to twenty one years of age who entered into indentures with the chairman of Franklin County Court to educate the Richard Parish to read, write and cypher as far as the Rule of three in Pike's Arithmetic and on his arriving at lawful age to give him a good suit of Broadcloth cloths, one horse worth seventy dollars and a good sadle & bridle.

On petition of John Russell for leave to keep an ordinary at his house in Franklin County, It is ordered that he have license accordingly for the Term of one year who entered into bond with Thomas Finch, Hopkins L. Turney his securities according to law and was qualified accordingly.

(p-493)   This day the last will and testament of Adam Gross Decd was produced in Open Court by the executors therein named Whereupon came James Robinson, Joseph Kleppen & Michael Custer, Subscribing witnesses thereto who being first duly sworn depose and say that the said Adam Gross declared and published this as his last will and testament and at the same time of signing the same he the said Adam Gross was of sound and disposing mind and memory and that he signed the same in their presence and they as witnesses thereto signed the same in his presence and at his request whereupon it is ordered by the Court to be recorded Whereupon came James Robinson & Joseph Kleppen the executors therein named and entered into bond with James Sharp their security in the sum of five thousand dollars according to law and were qualified accordiggly

Whereas at a former Term of this Court John Jones was appointed guardian of Elizabeth Robbins of said County an old lady who was incapable of managing her own affairs and it appearing to the Court that said guardian has failed to make his returns as required by law, Whereupon on motion it is ordered by the Court that John Jones, Guardian as aforesaid be removed from his appointment as such that he be released from all responsibility as such from this time forth. And on motion it is ordered by the Court that David Mackleroy be appointed Guardian of said Elizabeth Robbins who entered into bond with Isaac H. Roberts & John Goodwin his securities in the sum of two thousand dollars according to law.

Ordered by the Court that George W. Thompson, Wm. L. Mooney & Barnaby Bursow be appointed commissioners to settle with John Jones farmer Guardian of Elizabeth Robbins and that they make their report to the next Term of this Court.

Court adjourned until tomorrow morning 10 o'clock.
                                        John Dougherty
                                        M. W. Howell
                                        James Keith

(p-494)   Wednesday May the twenty seventh one thousand eight hundred and thirty five Court met according to law Adjournment.
Present - John Dougherty   )   Esquires
         Marshall W. Howell   )
         James Keith   )   Justices of the peace for Franklin
                                     County

    State of Tennessee
    Proclamation being made the Sheriff of Franklin County made return of the States writ of Veniris facises to this Court that he had summoned the following persons being all good and lawful men of said county of Franklin and being citizens of said County to attend and serve as Jurors at the present term of this Court which persons so summoned and returned as aforesaid had been nominated for the purpose by the Justices of this said Court of pleas and Quarter sessions of said County of Franklin at the last session a list of whom wasddlivered to the sheriff of this said county by the Clerk of this said Court, to wit, Solomon Wagner, Nelson Carter, Hezekiah Faris, John Emmerson, William Darwin, John D. Fennell, John Armstrong, William Thurman, Christopher Acklin, George

Davidson, James Taylor, Madison Poter, James Logan, John Frances,
Joseph Franklin, Daniel Keith, James Woods, James Estill, Peter Simmons
Henry Fancy, James Knight, Clement Arledge, Joab Short, Peter Sells and
Michael Williams and of whom the following persons being good and lawful
men of said county of Franklin were elected, empanneled, sworn and
charged as a grand Jury of Inquest for the body of the County aforesaid
to wit, James Taylor who was appointed foreman, James Estill, John Emmerson
Michael Williams, Clement Arledge, William Darwin, (p-495) John Francis
George Davidson, William Thurman, Peter Sells, Christopher Acklin,
Henry Fancy and Soloman Wagner who having received their charge retired
to consult of their presentment. Ordered by the Court that the following persons be released from serving as Jurors during the present Term
of this Court, to wit, Hezekiah Fariss, Daniel Keith, Julius C. Sims
James Woods, Peter Simmons and Joab Short.

JAMES STANLEY) Debt
Against)
BENJAMIN J. JACAWAY)
JAMES WILKERSON &)
ISAAC WILKERSON) This day came the parties by their attorney
and thereupon came a Jury to wit, John D. Fennell 1, John Armstrong 2,
Madison Porter 3, Joseph Franklin 4, Nelson Carter 5, James Knight 6
James Logan 7, Daniel Roddy 8, James Akin 9, Daniel Roddy 8 James Akin 9
Joseph R. Shropshire 10, Thomas Green 11 & Wiley J. Hines 12 who being
elected, tried and sworn the truth to speak upon the issue joined upon
their oath do say they find the issue in favor of the plaintiff and assess
his damages to twenty eight dollars and forty two cents besides cost.
It is therefore considered by the Court that the plaintiff recover against
the defendant four hundred and six dollars the debt in the Declaration
mentioned together with the damages aforesaid in form aforesaid assessed
and also his costs by him about said suit in this behalf expended and
the said defendants in mercy &.

THOMAS M. PRYOR & CO.) Case
Against)
JOHN BLACK &)
LUSK COLVELL) This day came the parties by their attornies
and thereupon came a Jury, to wit, John D. Fennell 1, John Armstrong 2
Madison Porter 3, Joseph Franklin 4, Nelson Carter 5, James Knight 6
James Logan 7, Daniel Roddy 8, James Akin 9, Joseph R. Shropshire 10,
Thomas Green 11 & Wiley J. Hines 12, who being elected tried and sworn
the truth to speak upon the issue joined upon their oaths do say they
find the issue in favor of the plaintiff and assess their damages to
two hundred and seven dollars (p-496) besides costs. It is therefore
considered by the Court that the plaintiffs recover against the defendants
their damages aforesaid in form aforesaid assess and also their costs by
them about said suit in this behalf expended and the said defendants in
Mercy &.

HENRY BRAZELTON) Debt
Against)
ARTHUR K. LOLLAR)
& ISAAC LOLLAR) This day came the parties by their attornies
and thereupon came a Jury to wit, Andrew McGowan 1, Basil E. Lucus 2,

Samuel Stephen 3, Wm. Faris 4, William Greenlo 5, Joel Chitwood 6, George Custer 7, Martin Gross 8, Edmond Dyer 9, James Gillaspie 10, Solomon Hogh 11, John Turner 12 who being elected, tried and sworn the truth to speak upon the issue joined upon their oaths do say they find the issue in favor of the plaintiff and assess his damage to ten dollars and sixty two cents besides costs. It is therefore considered by the Court that the plaintiff recover aga'nst the defendants one hundred and twenty five dollars the debt in the Declaration mentioned together with his damages aforesaid in form aforesaid assessed and also his costs by him about said suit in this behalf expended and the said defendants in mercy &.

WILLIAM KNOX ASSUE & C   )   Debt
 Against   )
ORREN EMBREY &   )
JOSEPH CAMBELL   ) This day came the parties by their attornies
and thereupon came a Jury, to wit, Andrew MdGowan 1, Basil E. Lucus 2, Samuel Stephens 3, William Faris 4, William Greenlu 5, Joel Chitwood 6 George Custer 7, Martin Gross 8, Edmond Dyer 9, James Gillaspie 10, Solomon Hogh 11 & John Turner 12 who being elected, tried and sworn the truth to speak upon the issue joined upon their oaths do say they find the issue in favor of the plaintiff and assess his damages to ten dollars and twenty cents besides costs. It is therefore considered by the Court that the plaintiff recover against the defendant one hundred and twenty dollars the debt in the Declaration mentioned together with his damages aforesaid in form aforesaid assessed and also his costs by him about said defendant in mercy &. from which judgment the defendant prayed an appeal to the next Circuit Court to be held for this County.

[p-497)   JAMES M. CRAWLEY)   Debt
    Against   )
    ISAAC VANZANT   ) This day came the parties by their attornies
and thereupon came a Jury to wit, Andrew McGowan 1, Basil E. Lucus 2, Samuel Stephens 3, William Faris 4, William Greenlu 5, Joel Chitwood 6 George Custer 7, Martin Gross 8, Edmond Dyer 9, James Gillaspie 10, Solomon Hogh 11, & John Turner 12 who being elected tried and sworn the truth to speak upon the issue joined upon their oaths do say they find the issue in favor of the plaintiff and assess his damages to four dollars & thirty seven cents besides costs. It is thereupon considered by the Court that the plaintiff recover aga'nst the defendant one hundred and seventy five dollars the debt in the Declaration mentioned together with his damages aforesaid in form aforesaid assessed and also his costs by him about said suit in this behalf expended and the said defendant in Mercy &. from which judgment the defendant prayed an appeal to the next circuit Court to be held for said County.

JAMES WOODS   )   Debt
 Against   )
JOSEPH CAMPBELL   )
JAMES CAMPBELL &   )
JOHN HANDLY   ) This day came the parties by their attornies
and thereupon came a Jury, to wit, Andrew McGowan 1, Basil E. Lucus 2, Samuel Stephens 3, William Faris 4, William Greenlu 5, Joel Chitwood 6, George Custer 7, Martin Gross 8, Edmond Dyer 9, James Gillaspie 10.

Solomon Hogh 11, & John Turner 12, who being elected, tried and sworn
the truth to speak upon the issue joined upon their oaths do say they
find the issue in favor of the plaintiff and assess his damage to eight
dollars & seventy one cents besides costs. It is therefore considered
by the Court that the plaintiff recover against the defendants one
hundred and two dollars and fifty cents the debt in the Declaration
mentioned together with the damages aforesaid in form aforesaid assessed
and also his cost by him about said suit in this behalf expended and the
said Defendant in Mercy &.

JOSEPH MILLER ASSU & C   )   Debt
 Against   )
DAVID WARREN   )
THOMAS S. LOGAN &   )
JAMES LOGAN   )   This day came the parties by thier
attornies and thereupon came a Jury, to wit, Andrew McGowan 1, Basil
E. Lucus 2, Samuel Stephens 3, William Faris 4, William Greenlu 5,
Joel Chitwoods 6, (p-498) George Custer 7, Martin Gross 8, Edmond
Dyer 9, James Gillaspie 10, Solomon Hogh 11, & John Turner 12 , who
being elected tried and sworn the truth to speak upon the issue joined
upon their oaths do say they find the issue in favor of the plaintiff
and issue his damages to three dollars and sixty two cents besides costs.
It is therefore considered by the Court that the plaintiff recover against
the defendants one hundred and forty five dollars the debt in the
Declaration mentioned together with his damages aforesaid in form aforesaid assessed and also his cost by him about said suit in this behalf
expended and the said defendants in Mercy & from which judgment the
defendants prayed an appeal to the next Circuit Court to be held for
this County.

RICHARD C. ARNETT ASSU & C)   Debt
 Against   )
HELBARD PETTY   )   This day came the parties by thereupon
came a Jury, to wit, Andrew McGowan 1, Basil E. Lucus 2, Samuel Stephens 3,
William Faris 4, William Greenlu 5, Joel Chitwood 6, George Custer 7,
Martin Gross 8, Edmond Dyer 9, James Gillaspie 10, Solomon Hogh 11
& John Turner 12 who being elected tried and sworn the truth to speak
upon the issue joined upon their oaths do say they find the issue
in favor of the plaintiff and assess his damages to four dollars & forty
one cents besides costs. It is therefore considered by the Court that
the plaintiff recover against the defendant one hundred and seventy six
dollars and fifty cents the debt in the Declaration mentioned together
with his damage aforesaid in form foresaid assessed and also his costs
by him about said suit in this behalf expended and the said defendant
in Mercy &. from which judgment the defendant prayed an appeal to the
next circuit Court to be held for this County bond & security given and
the appeal granted.

NATHAN GILLISPIE to the   )   Debt
use of A. L. CAMPBELL   )
 Against   )
MICAJAH L. GILLASPIE   ) This day came the parties by their
attornies and there upon came a Jury to wit, Andrew McGowan 1, Basil E.
Lucus 2, Samuel Stephens 3, William Faris 4, William Greenlu 5,

Joel Chitwood 6, George Custer 7, Martin Gross 8, Edmond Dyer 9
James Gillaspie 10, Soloman Hogh 11 & John Turner 12 who being elected
tried and sworn the truth to speak upon the issue joined upon their oaths
do say they find the issue in favor of the plaintiff and assess his
damages to five dollars & six cents besides costs, (p-499)   It is
therefore considered by the Court that the plaintiff recover against the
defendant two hundred dollars the debt in the Declaration mentioned
together with his damages aforesaid in form aforesaid assessed and also
his costs by him about said suit in this behalf expended and the said
defendant in mercy & from which Judgment the defendant prayed and
appeal to the next circuit Court to be held for said County, Bond & Security given and the appeal granted.

HENRY T. WIGGIN   )   Debt
  Against   )
JOSEPH COWLING   )
WM. K. COWLING   )
JAMES S. COWLING &   )
WILEY J. HINES   )   This day came the parties by their attornies
and thereupon came a Jury, to wit, Andrew McGowan 1, Basil E. Lucus 2,
Samuel Stphens 3, William Faris 4, William Greenlu 5, Joel Chitwood 6,
George Custer 7, Martin Gross 8, Edmond Dyer 9, James Gillaspie 10,
Solomon Hogh 11 & John Turner 12 who being elected tried and sworn the
truth to speak upon the issue joined upon their oaths do say they find
the issue in favor of the plaintiff and assess his damages to forty dollars
and twelve cents besides costs. It is therefore considered by the Court
that the plaintiff recover against the defendant four hundred and seventy
two dollars and twelve cents the debt in the Declaration mentioned together
with his damages aforesaid in form aforesaid assessed and also his cost
by him about said suit in this behalf expended and the said defendant in
mercy &.

DRAKE F. RANDOLPH   )   Debt
  Against   )
ABIRAM SHORES   )   This day came the parties by their attornies
and thereupon came a Jury, to wit, Andrew McGowan 1, Basil E. Lucus 2,
Samuel Stephens 3, William Faris 4, William Greenlu 5, Joel Chitwood 6,
George Custer 7, Martin Gross 8, Edmond Dyer 9, James Gillaspie 10,
Solomon Hogh 11 & John Turner 12, who being elected, tried and sworn
the truth to speak upon the issue joined upon their oaths do say they
find the issue in favor of the plaintiff and assess his damages to ten
dollars & fifty cents besides costs. It is therefore considered by the
Court that the plaintiff recover against the defendant one hundred and
thirty one dollars & seventy five cents together with his damages
aforesaid in form aforesaid assessed and also his costs by him about
said suit in this behalf expened and the said Defendant in mercy &.

(p-500)   ALEXANDER C. MCEWIN ASSIGNEE & C   )   Debt
       Against   )
       BENJAMIN H. GREEN   )   This day came the plaintiff
by his attorney and the defendant in his proper person and thereupon came
a Jury to wit, Andrew McGowan 1, Basil E. Lucus 2, Samuel Stephens 3
William Faris 4, William Greenlu 5, Joel Chitwood 6, George Custer 7
Martin Gross 8, Edmond Dyer 9, James Gillaspie 10, Solomon Hogh 11 &

John Turner 12 who being elected, tried and sworn the truth to speak upon the issue joined upon their oaths do say they find the issue in favor of the plaintiff and assess his damages to three dollars and seventy nine cents besides costs. It is thereupon considered by the Court that the plaintiff recover against the defendant one hundred and five dollars the debt in the declaration mentioned together with his damages aforesaid in form aforesaid assessed and also his costs by him about said suit in this behalf expended and the said Defendant in mercy &.

JOSEPH H. BRADFORD) Debt
  Against)
MARY VANZANT ADMINISTRIX)
of the Estate of JACOB VANZANT DECD) This day came the parties by their attornies and thereupon came a Jury, to wit, Andrew McGowan 1, Basil E. Lucus 2, Samuel Stephens 3, William Faris 4, William Greenlu 5 Joel Chitwood 6, George Custer 7, Martin Gross 8, Edmond Dyer 9 James Gillaspie 10, Solomon Hogh 11 & John Turner 12 who being elected tried and sworn the truth to speak upon the issue joined upon their oaths do say they find the issue in favor of the plaintiff and assess his damage to eight dollars & eighty eight cents besides costs. It is therefore considered by the Court that the plaintiff recover against the plaintiff recover against the defendant seventy four dollars and sixty two cents the balance of the debt in the Declaration mentioned together with his damages aforesaid in form aforesaid assessed and also his costs by him about said suit in this behalf expended and the said defendant in Mercy & to be levied of the proper goods & chattels rights and credits of Jacob Vanzant deceased in the hands of said administratrix to be administered.

DANIEL RODDY)
  Vs)
SAML CAMP) This day came the defendant by his attorney and upon his affidavit this cause is continued until the next term of this Court.

LETTY WHITE)
  Vs)
Z. H. MURRELL ADMIN &)
WINNY PHILIPS ADMINX) This day came the plaintiff by her attorney and upon the affidavit of John Wisemon this cause is continued untill the next term of this Court.

(p-501) THE STATE OF TENNESSEE)
    VS)
    JOSEPH R. SHROPSHIRE) This day Joseph R. Shropshire and Hopkins L. Turney came into Court and acknowledge themselves to owe and stand Justly indebted to the State of Tennessee in the following sums, to wit, the Said Joseph R. Shropshire in the sum of two hundred and fifty dollars and Hopkins L. Turney this security in the sum of of one hundred and twenty five dollars to be levied of their respective goods and chattels lands and tenements to the use of said State but to be void on condition that Joseph R. Shropshire make his personal appearance before the Justices of our next Court of pleas and quarter sessions to be held for the Court of Franklin at the Court house in

in Winchester on Thursday after the fourth Monday of August next then
and there to answer the state of Tennessee on a bill of Indictment
found against him for an affray and not depart the same without leave
first had and obtained.

JOHN TARWATER ADMINISTRATOR   )   Debt
of the Estate of LEWIS TARWATER DECD)
 Against   ))
WILLIAM GREENLEE   )   This day came the parties by
their attornies and thereupon came a Jury, to wit, Johnd B. Fennell 1,
John Armstrong 2, Madison Poter 3, Joseph Franklin 4, Nelson Carter 5
James Knight 6, James Logan 7, Daniel Roddy 8, James Akin 9, Joseph
R. Shropshire 10, Thomas Green 11 & Wiley J. Hines 12 who being elected
tried and sworn the truth to speak upon the issues joined upon their
oaths do say they find ~~the issue in form of the plaintiffs~~ that the said
Defendant hath not well and truly paid the debt in the Declaration
mentioned and upon their oath aforesaid do say that they further find
that the said defendant is entitled to an soffset of one hundred and
eighteen dollars and assess the plaintiffs damage to the sum of forty
three dollars & sixty two & one half cents ~~and cost cost~~ Whereupon it is
considered by the Court that the plaintiff recover against the said
defendant the sum of two hundred dollars together with the further sum
of forty three dollars & sixty two and one half cents the damage assessed
by the Jury aforesaid and also his costs by him about said suit in this
behalf expended and the said defendant in mercy &.

JOHN W. & A. L. CAMPBELL   )   Debt
 Against   )
GEORGE BARBER &   )
CHARLES FARIS   )   This day came the parties of by their
attornies and thereupon came a Jury, to wit, James Estill 1, (p-502)
John Emerson 2, Michael Williams 3, Clement Arledge 4, William Darwin 5
John Frame 6, William Thurman 7, James Taylor 8, Peter Sells 9,
Christophen Acklin 10, Henry Fancy 11, & Solomon Wagner 12, who being
elected, tried and sworn the truth to speak upon the issue joined
between the said Plaintiffs and the said defendant George Barber and
by the consent of the parties and with the assent of the Court the Jury
is permitted to disperse untill to morrow morning 10 o'clock.

CAIN & PRICE   )   Debt
 Against   )
PETER WILLIS &   )
ANDERSON F. WILLIS   )   This day came the defendant Peter Willis into
open Court in his proper person and south he cannot gainsay the plaintiff
action against him and confesses Judgment for one hundred and eighty nine
dollars & fifty cents together with the further sum of five dollars &
fifty six cents interest thereon at the rate of six percent perannum,
Whereupon William Greenlu came into Open Court and confesses Judgment
jointly with the said Peter Willis for said sum of one hundred and eighty
nine dollars & fifty cents and also the said sum of fifty six cents
interest thereon at the rate of six percent perannum confessed as aforesaid
and also their costs by them about said suit in this behalf expended and
the said defendants in mercy &. and the plaintiffs agree to stay the
execution for debt untill Christmas next.

An assignment of a plat and certificate of survey from Elijah Mason to Daniel McElhea for fifty acres of land lying in Franklin County was only proven in Open Court by the oath of Isaac McElyea one of the subscribing witnesses thereto.

JAMES A. SNOWDEN & C)
  Against)
JOHN WINFORD SR.) This day came plaintiffs by their attorney and dismissed their suit and not further prosecuting it is ordered that this suit be dismissed whereupon it is considered by the Court that the defendant recover against the plaintiffs his costs by him about his defence in this behalf expended and the said plaintiffs in mercy &.
  (p-503)

WALLIS ESTILL)
  Vs)
RICHARD C. HOLDER) This day came the plaintiff by his attorney and dismisses his suit and not further prosecuting it is ordered that this suit be dismissed and the defendant assumes the costs whereupon it is considered by the Court that the plaintiff recover against the defendant his costs by him about said suit in this behalf expended and the said defendant in mercy &.

WALLIS ESTILL JR)
  Vs)
JAMES M. CRAWLY) This day came the plaintiff by his attorney and dismisses his suit and not further prosecuting it is ordered that this suit be dismissed and the defendant assumes the cost. Whereupon it is considered by the Court that the plaintiff recover against the defendant his costs by him about said suit in this behalf expended and the said defendant in Mercy &.

JAMES MOORE to the use)
of HENRY A RAINES)
  Vs)
HENRY RUNNELS) This day came the defendant into open Court and saith he cannot gainsay the plaintiffs action against him and confesses judgement for one hundred dollars the debt in the declaration mentioned together with the further sums of four dollars and seventy cents Interest thereon at the rate of six percent peranum whereupon it is considered by the Court that the plaintiff recover against the defendant his debt and interest confessed as aforesaid and also his costs by him about said suit in this behalf expended and the said defendant in mercy & and the plaintiff agrees to stay the execution untill next November Court.

WILLIAM JACKSON)
  Against)
JOHN COOK) Whereas on the 29th day of September 1834 there was issued by Richmond P. Harris an acting Justice of the peace in and for the County of Franklin an execution in favor of the plaintiff against the defendant for $30 debt and 50 cents costs of suit which execution was returned to the present term of this Court with the following (p-504) levy thereon endorsed, to wit, executed by levy on 20 acres of deeded land including the place where John Cook Jr. now resides and 35 acres

where Henry Cook Sr. formerly lived adjoining the lands of John Atkins,
William Laseter Henry Cook and others and on head of Rock Creek as there
could not be any personal property found to levy this fi fa on therefore I
levy on the said land returnable at May Court 1835 this the 24th February 1835.
J.Byram C.F.C.
And on motion of the plaintiff by his attorney it is considered by the Court
that said tracts of land be condemned to satisfy said execution and that an
order of sale issue to the sheriff of Franklin County to sell same according
to law.

NANCY PRICE)
 Against   ) On motion of the defendant by his attorney this
JOSEPH R. SHROPSHIRE) cause is continued until the next term of this
Court on his affidavit and on his motion a commission is awarded him to
take the depositions of Robert T. Mitchell & Mary W. Mitchell before anyone
justice of the peace in the State of Alabama the County in which they reside
being unknown to be read in evidence on the trial of the above cause on
behalf of the Defendant by his giving the plaintiff then days notice of the
time and place of said depositions Court adjourned until tomorrow morning
10 o'clock.   John Daughtery M. W. Howell James Keith

   Thursday May the twenty eight one thousand eight hundred and thirty
five Court met according to adjournment. Present John Dougherty, M.W.Howell
James Keith Esquires Justices of the peace, Franklin County.

THE STATE OF TENNESSEE) Indict for an Affray
 Against   )
ALBERT G. BLACK   ) This day came the Attorney General who presents for
the State in this behalf as well as the defendant in his proper person and
the said defendant having heard said Indictment read says he is therefore
guilty, (p-505) and puts himself upon the grace and mercy of the Court.
It is therefore consd. by the Court that the defendant for such his offence
be fined one dollar and pay the costs of this prosecution. Whereupon John
Rulemon came into Court and acknowledged himself security for the fine and
costs in this case and that a fi fa issue against him for the same.

THE STATE OF TENNESSEE) Presentment for gaming
 Vs.   )
WILLIAM MCCOY   ) This day came the Attorney General who prosecutes
for the State in this behalf as well as the defendant in his proper person
and the said defendant having heard said Presentment read says he is there
of guilty and puts himself upon the grace and mercy of the Court. Whereupon
it is considered by the Court that the defendant for such his offence be
fined Ten Dollars and pay the cost of this prosecution Whereupon Portland
J. Curle came into Court and acknowledged himself security for the fine and
cost in this case and that a fe fa issue against him for the same.

THE STATE OF TENNESSEE) Indictment for malicious mischief
 VS   )
ANDREW H. MCCOLLUM) This day came the attorney General who prosecutes
for the State in this behalf as well as the defendant in his rpoper person
and the said defendant having heard said indictment read says he is there of
not guilty and puts himself upon the Country and the attorney General doth
the like and thereupon came a Jury, to wit. John D. Fonnell, John Armstrogg
Nelson Carter, James Logan Madison Porter, George W. McCaully, William Faris
Joel Chitwood.

William Center, Charles Woods, James P. Aikin and Samuel Brannon, Who being elected tried and sworn the truth of and upon the premises to speak who after retiring to consult of their verdict afterwards returned into Court and declared they could not agree and by the consent of the parties and with the assent of the Court John D. Fennell one of the Jurors is withdrawn and the rest of the Jury from rendering of their verdict are discharged and the cause continued for a new trial to be had thereon at the next Term of this Court.

(p-506)   THE STATE OF TENNESSEE   )
                Vs   )
           JESSE FERRAL   ) Presentment for an affray this day came the Attorney General who prosecutes for the State in this behalf as well as the defendant in his proper person and the said defendant having heard said presentment read says he is thereof not guilty and puts himself upon the Country and the attorney General doth the like and thereupon came a Jury, to wit, James Estill, John Emmerson, Michael Williams, Clement Arledge, William Darwin, John Frame, William Darwin John Frame, William Thurman, James Taylor, Peter Sells, Christopher Acklin, Henry Fancy and Solomon Wagner, who bein g elected tried and sworn the truth of and upon the premises to speak upon their oaths do say they find the defendant not guilty in manner and form as charged in the presentment. It is therefore consider ed by the Court that the defendant go hence with out day.

        This day John Rolemon came into Court and acknowledged himself to owe and stand justly indebted to the State of Tennessee in the sum of one hundred and twenty five dollars to be levied of his proper goods and chattles, lands & tenements to the use of said State but to be void on condition that he make his personal appearance before the justices of our next Court of pleas and quarter sessions to be held for the County of Franklin at the Court house in Winchester on Thursday after the fourth Monday in August next then and there to prosecute and give evidence in behalf of the State on a Bill of Indictment found against Reason Ishams for an Affray and not depart the same without leave first had and obtained.

NANCY PRICE   )   Case
Against   )
DAVID C. LEWIS   )   This day came the parties by their attornies and thereupon came a Jury, to wit, John D. Fennell 1, John Armstrong 2, Joseph Franklin 3, Nelson Carter 4, James Knight 5, James Logan 6, James P. Akin 7, Joseph C. January 8, Robert Poe 9, Edward Morris 10 Andrew H. McCollum 11 & David Harris 12 who being elected tried and sworn the truth to speak upon the issure Joined upon their oaths do say they find the issure in favor of the plaintiff and assess her damages to thirty dollars. It is therefore considered by the Court that the plaintiff recover against the defendant her damages a foresd. in form aforesaid assessed and also her costs by her about said suit in this behalf expended and the said defendant in mercy &.

(p-507)   THE STATE OF TENNESSEE)
              Against   )
           ANDREW H. MCCOLLUM   ) This day A. H. McCollum & James Morris came into Open Court and acknowledged themselves to owe and

stand justly indebted to the State of Tennessee in the following sums to
wit Andrew H. McCollum in the sum of $250 and James Morris his security
in the sum of $125 to be levied of their respective goods and chattels
lands and tenements to the use of said State but to be void on condition
that Andrew H. McCollum make his personal appearance before the Justices
of our next Court of pleas and quarter sessions to be held for the county
of Franklin at the Court house in Winchester on Thursday after the fourth
Monday in August next then and there to answer the State on a bill of
Indictment found against him for malicious mischief and not depart the
same without leave first had and obtained.

This day the inventory of the Estate of Francis A. Moore decd.
was produced in Open Court was received by the Court and ordered to be
recorded.

This day the Jury of view appointed at the last Term of this Court
to view and turn the road leading from Salem to Paint Rook ~~road~~ was
received by the Court.

This day the Grand Jury came into Open Court and returned a Bill
of indictment against Albert G. Black & Reason Ishams for an Affray a
true Bill also a Bill of Indictment against William McCoy and David
Foster for an Affray a true Bill.

JOSEPH MILLER ASSIGNEE & CO)
 Vs)
David Warren)
THOMAS LOGAN &)
JAMES LOGAN) This day David Warren one of the defendant
came into Court and prayed an appeal from the judgment of the Court
heretofore at this term rendered against him to the next circuit Court
to be held for this County bound and security given and the appeal granted.

PRICE & CAIN)
 Vs)
E. E. THACKER) Whereas on the 20th day of March 1835 there was
issued by Jesse Jenkins an acting Justice of the peace in and for the
County of Franklin and execution against the defendant in favor of the
plaintiff for the sum of thirty dollars debt an 50 cents costs of suit
which execution was returned to the present term of this Court with the
(p-508) following levy thereon endorsed, to wit, came to hand the same
day issued and no personal property found levied on a tract of land
containing 195 acres be the same more or less lying on the bark camp fork
of Duck River bounded on the North by the lands of Joel Taylor on the
East by William Bradshaw on the South by John Raley on the West by Vacant
land as the property of E. E. Thacker 23rd May 1835.   B.F. Jenkins. C.S .T
and on motion of the plaintiff by their attorney it is considered by the
Court that said tract of land be condemned to satisfy said execution and
that an order of sale issue to the Sheriff of Franklin County to sell
the same according to law.

ESCUE & BRITTON)
 Vs.)
JAMES KELLEY &)
JOEL KELLEY SENR.) Whereas on the 22nd day of January 1835 there

was issued by the olerk of Franklin County Court on execution in favor
of the plaintiff against the defendant for the sum of $43.87½ debt and
one dollar 12½ cents costs of suit upon a judgement rendered by George
Gl Black who was then an acting Justice of the peace in and for said
County but has since resigned which execution was returned to the present
term of this Court with the following levy thereon endorsed to wit,
executed by levy on 28 acres of deeded land and 231 acres of school
land as the property of Joel Kelley at the Inst. of the plaintiffs being
the same tract of land where C. C. Gerant now lives on the waters of Rock
Creek as there could not be no personal property found to levy this Fi Fa
on therefore I leyy on the said land returnable at the May Court 1835 24 of
February 1835   J. Byyom   C. F. C.
and on motion of the plaintiffs by their attorney it is considered by the
Court that said tracts of land be condemned to satisfy said execution
and that an order of sale issue to Sheriff of Franklin County to sell
the same according to law.

ROBT. GIBSON   )
  Against   )
GEORGE W. THOMPSON   )   This day came the parties by their attornies
and agree that the order of reference made by the last term of this Court
in this case be reviewed and that said reference have until the next Term
of this Court to make their award.

(p-509)   J. W. & A. S. CAMPBELL)   Debt
          Against   )
          GEORGE BARBER &   )
          CHARLES FARIS   )   This day came the parties by their
attornies and thereupon came the same Jury who were on yesterday elected
tried and sworn the truth to speak upon the issue joined between the said
plaintiffs and the said defendant Barber upon their oaths do say that they
find the writing obligatory declared on to be the act & deed of the said
Barber and assess their damages by reason of the detention of their debt
to twenty two dollars and ninty eight cents whereupon it is considered
by the Court that the plaintiffs recover against the defendant Barker
Seven hundred & sixty six dollars & twenty four cents the balance of
twenty four cents the balance of the debt in the declaration mentioned
together with their damages aforesaid in form afrcesaid assessed and
also their costs by them about said suit in this behalf expended and the
said defendant Barber in mercy & from which judgment the said defendant
prayed and appeal to the next circuit Court to be held for Franklin County
bond and security given and the appeal granted.

HENRY S. CAMDEN   )
Against   )
BENJAMIN F. JENKINS   )   This day the referees to whom was refered
all matters in dispute between the parties in this suit made the following
award, to wit:
HENRY S. CAMDEN   )   Trover
Against   )
BENJAMIN F. JENKINS &   )
JAMES H. HESTILL   )   We Stewart Cowan & John G. Bostick abritrators
in the above case appointed by the Court of pleas and quarters sessions
of the County of Franklin to settle said case do award that the plaintiff

Henry S. Camden recover of James H. Estill the sum of fourteen dollars
eighty & forith cents and that each of the parties pay one half of the
Court costs and that each party pay their own witnesses given under
our hands this 7th day of March 1835.   John G. Bostick
                                               Stewart Cowan
We agree to stand to and abide by above award this 7th day of March 1835
                                         J. H. Estill (Seal)
                                         H. S. Camden (Seal)
Recd. five dollars in part of the within on above award 7th March 1835
                                         H. S. Camden
Whereupon it is considered by the Court that said award be made the final
determination of the Court (p-510) and that the plaintiff recover against
James H. Estill his part of the Court costs and his own witnesses. And
that James H. Estill recover against the plaintiff his part of the Court
costs and his own witnesses and they said parties in mercy &.

EATON A. WOOD to the use   )
of RICHM P. HARRIS   )
 Against   )
POLLARD RHODES &   )
ISHAM HARRIS   )   Cecil Bobo having been summoned as a
garnishee in this case makes oaths that he entered into a written contract
with said Rhodes to work for him as a tanner for the term of four years
that said Rhodes failed to comply with his contract that he owe him a note
of 140 dollars and an acct. of $99.89 cents that said Rhodes refused to
come to a settlement with him and affiant believes that upon a fair
settlement of their accounts he does not owe said Rhodes one cent but
that Rhodes is indebted to him thereupon it is considered by the Court
that said Cecil Bobo be discharged from said garnishee.

WILLIAM FARIS   )   Case
 Against   )
GEORGE BARBER &   )
CHARLES FARIS   )   This day came the parties by their attornies
and thereupon came a Jury, to wit, James Estill 1, John Emerson 2,
Michael Williams 3, Clement Arledge 4, Wm. Darwin 5, John Frame 6,
Wm. Thurman 7, James Taylor 8, Peter Sells 9, Christopher Acklin 10,
Henry Fancy 11 & Solomon Wagner 12 who being elected tried and sworn
the truth to speak upon the issue joined upon their oaths do say they
find the issue in favor of the defendants. It is therefore considered
by the Court that the Defendant go hence without pay and recover against
the plaintiff their costs by them about their defence in this behalf
expended and the said plaintiff in mercy &.

THE STATE OF TENNESSEE   )   Sce Fa
 Against   )
JAMES DEAN   )   This day came the defendant by his attorney
and moved the Court for to set aside the forfeiture in this case and upon
arugment thereupon had it is considered by the Court that the forfeiture
by set aside by the defendant paying the costs of this suit & in mercy &.

(p-511)   Court adjourned until tomorrow morning 10 o'clock
                              John Dougherty
                              M. H. Howell
                              James Keith

Friday May the twenty ninth one thousand eight hundred and thirty five Court met according to adjournment.

Present - John Dougherty) Esqrs Justices of
        Marshall W. Howell) peace for Franklin County.
        James Keith)

RICHARD HL WALLACE) Debt
  Against)
HAYDEN ARNOLD &)
JAMES CAMDEN) This day came the plaintiff by his attorney
and having filed his Declaration and the defendant being solemnly called
to appear and defend this suit came not but made default, Whereupon it
is considered by the Court that the Plaintiff recover against the
defendant one hundred dollars and fifty dollars the debt in the
Declaration mentioned together with the further sum of three dollars
and Seventy five cents Interest thereon at the rate of six percent
peranum and also his costs by him about said suit in this behalf expended
and the said defenandt in mercy &.

PRESTLEY E. GEORGE to the use) Debt
of J. W. & A. L. CAMPBELL)
  Against)
THOMAS FINCH) This day came the defendant into
Open Court and waves the necessity of an original Writ and confesses
Judgment for one hundred dollars debt and four dollars and fifty cents
Interest thereon at the rate of six percent peranum, Whereupon it is
considered by the Court that the plaintiffs recover against the defendant
their debt and interest confessed as aforesaid and also their costs by
them about said suit in this behalf expended and the said defendant in
Mercy and the plaintiffs agree to stay the execution untill next Court

PETER S. DECHERD) Debt
  Against)
JOHN JONES) This day came the defendant by his attorney
in fact and waives the necessity of an original writ and confesses
Judgment for two hundred and twelve dollars and sixty five cents debt
and thirty dollars and eighty two cents interest thereon (p-512) at the
rate of six per cent per anum whereupon it is considered by the Court
that the plaintiff recover against the defendant his debt and interest
comfessed as aforesaid and also his costs by him about said suit in
this behalf expended and the said defendant in mercy &.

J. W. & A. L. CAMPBELL) Debt.
  Against)
C. B. H. AKE) This day came the plaintiffs by their
attorney and having filed their declaration and the defendant being
solemnly called to appear and defend this suit came not but made
default, whereupon it is considered by the Court that the plaintiffs
recover against the defendant ninety three dollars & eighty seven cents
the debt in the Declaration mentioned together with the further sum of
one dollar and sixty two cents Interest thereon at the rate of six per
cent per anum and also their costs by them about said suit in this behalf
expended and the said defendant in mercy &.

THOMAS M. PRYON & CO.   )   Debt
  Against   )
  C. B. H. AKE   )   This day came the plaintiffs by their
attorney and having filed their Declaration and the defendant being solemnly
called to appear and defend this suit came not but made default. Whereupon
it is considered by the Court that the plaintiffs recover against the
defendant sixty four dollars and ninety three cents the debt in the
Declaration mentioned together with the further sum of one dollar and
fifty cents interest thereon at therrate of six per cent per anum and
also their costs by them about said suit in this behalf expended and the
said Defendant in mercy &.

LITTY WHITE   )
 Against   )
Z. H. MURREL ADMIN &   )
 JAMES PHILIPS DECD   ) On motion of the plaintiff by her attorney
this cause is continued untill the next term of this Court on the affidavit
of John Wiseman by the plaintiff paying the cost of this term. Whereupon
it is considered by the Court that the Defendants recover against the
plaintiff their costs about their defence at this term expended and the
said plaintiff in mercy &.

(p-518)   MADISON PORTER   )   Debt
          Against   )
          C. B. H. AKE   )   This day came the plaintiff by his attorney
and having filed his Declaration and the defendant being solemny called
to appear and defend this suit came not but made default. Whereupon
it is considered by the Court that the plaintiff recover against the
defendant twenty six dollars and thirty three cents the balance of the
debt in the Declaration mentioned together with the further sum of sixty
five cents interest thereon at the rate of six per cent per anum and also
his cost by him about said suit in this behalf expended and the said
defendant in mercy &.

     A Power of Attorney from Frances Rawlins to Joel Mason was duly
acknowledged in Open Court by the said Francis Rowlins to be her act and
deed whereupon it is ordered by the Court to be certified.

ROBERT S. SHARP   )   Ca Sa
  Against   )
JOHN D. STOVALL   ) Whereas Robert S. Sharp recovered a Judgment against
John D. Stovall before James Robinson Esqr. on the 10th day of May 1834
for the sum of ninety nine dollars and afterwards on the 28th day of
February 1835 the said Plaintiff obtained from James Robinson Esqr. a
Capias Ad Staisfaciendum founded upon said judgment directed to any lawful
Officer to execute and return which came into the hands of Thomas Finch
Sheriff of Franklin County on the same day issued who thereupon executed
the same by arresting the body of the said John D. Stovall who thereupon
entered into bond with Portland J. Curle his security conditioned to
make his personal appearance at the next Court of pleas and quarter
sessions to be held for Franklin County at the Court house in the Town
of Winchester on the fourth Monday in May the Next ensuing then and there
to make payment of the debt and cost called for in said Execution or to
take the oath of Insolvency or to make a surrender of his property as

prescribed by the laws of this State all which the said John D. Stovall
failed to do as the condition of said bond required. Whereupon the said
Robert S. Sharp by his attorney moved the Court for Judgment against the
said John D. Stovall and the said Portland J. Curle his security as aforesaid (p-514)   for the amount of the Judgement mentioned in said, Ca Sa
and bond aforesaid, together with the interest thereon and the costs before
the Justice, Wherefore it is considered by the Court that the said Robert
S. Sharp recover against the said John D. Stovall and the said Portland
J. Curle the sum of ninetvy nine dollars together with the sum of six
dollars and nineteen cents interest thereon at the rate of six per cent
per annum from the rendition of said Judgment by said Justic up to the
present time together with the sum of one dollar cost before the Justic
and also his cost about this motion in this expended and the said defendant
in mercy &.

THOMAS FINCH   )   Motion
 Against   )
WILLIAM WINFORD   ) This day came the plaintiff by his attorney
and moved the Court for Judgment against the said defendant and it appear-
ing to the Court that the said Plaintiff upon this day confessed a
Judgment in favor of Prestly E. George who sues to the use of John W. &
A. L. Campbell for the sum of one hundred dollars debt & four dollars
and fifty cents interest as the security of the said William Winford.
Whereupon it is considered by the Court that the said Plaintiff recover
against the said defendant said sum of one hundred and four dollars &
fifty cents also the costs of the suit of Presly E. George against said
Finch and the costs of this motion in this behalf expended for all of
which execution may issue.

JAMES WOODS   )
 Against   )
JOSEPH CAMPBEIL &   )
JOHN HANDLEY   ) This day came the defendant by their attorney
and prayed an appeal from the Judgment of the Court heretofore at this
term rendered against them to the next Circuit Court to be held for
Franklin County which is granted by their entering in to bond and Security
to the Clerk in one week from this time.

WILLIAM KNOW ASSEE & C   )
 Against   )
ORREN EMBREY &   )
JOSEPH CAMPBELL   ) This day came the defendant by their
attorney and prayed an appeal from the Judgment heretofore at this term
rendered of the Court against them to the next Circuit Court to be held
for Franklin County which is granted them by their entering into bond
and security to the Clerk within one week from this time.

(p-515)   JAMES M. CRAWLEY   )
          Against   )
          ISAAC VANZANT   ) This day came the defendant by his attorney
and prayed appeal from the judgment of the Court heretofore at this Term
rendered against him to the next Circuit Court to be held for Franklin
County which is granted him by his entering into bond & Security to the
Clerk within one week from this time.

JOHN OLIVER)   Case
Against)
C. B. H. AKE) This day came the plaintiff by his attorney and having
filed his Declaration and the defendant being solemnly called to appear
and defend this suit came not but made default this suit came not but
made default and on motion of the Plaintiff by his attorney. It isconsidered
by the Court that the Plaintiff recover against the defendant such damages
as he may have sustained by reason of the now performance of the assumpsions
in the Declaration mentioned which damages are to be enguired of by a Jury
at the next Term of this Court.

JOSEPH KLIPPER)   Case
Against)
C. B. AKE) This day came the plaintiff by his attorney and
having filed his Declaration and the defendant being solemnly called to
appear and defend this suit came not but made default and on motion of the
Plaintiff by his attorney..It is considered by the Court that the plaintiff
recover against the Defendant such damages as he may have sustained by
reason of the non performance of the assumptions in the Declaration
mentioned which damages are to be enguired of by a Jury at the next Term
of this Court.

    This day Benjamin Decherd County Trustee made his return upon oath
of the monies received and paid but by him far the 1834 which was received
by the Court and ordered to be recorded.

    Ordered by the Court that Thomas Finch Sheriff of Franklin County
be appointed to collect the State County Jurors and poor tax for the year
1835 for said County who entered into bond with John Goodwin & Solomon
Wagner his securities in the sum of five thousand dollars according to
law and was qualified accordingly.

(p-516)   Court adjourned untill Court in Course.

                           John Daugherty
                           James Keith
                           M. W. Howell

August Term 1835

State of Tennessee
At a Court of pleas and quarter sessions begun & held for Franklin County on the fourth Monday in August in the year of our Lord one thousand eight hundred and thirty five it being the twenty fourth day of said month and the Sixtieth year of the Independence of the United States. Present thirteen of the acting justices of the peace for Franklin County.

A deed of conveyance from Sanford W. Young to Connor Bean for 50 acres of land lying in Franklin County was duly proven in Open Court was duly proven in Open Court by the oaths of John Weaver and William Bean subscribing witnesses thereto to be the act and deed of the said Sanford W. Young on the day that it bears date whereupon it is ordered by the Court to be certified for registration. Let it be registered.

A deed of conveyance from Joseph H. Bradford to Jonathan Syker for his undivided mouty in 1000 acres of land lying in Tipton County and State of Tennessee was duly proven in Open Court by the oaths of Edwin Street and William Street subscribing witnesses there to to be the act and deed of the said Joseph H. Bradford on the day that it bears date. Whereupon it is ordered by the Court to be certified for registration in Tipton County. Let it be registered.

A deed of conveyance from Joseph McVay to Wiley B. McCorner for 20 acres of land lying in Franklin County was duly acknowledged in Open Court by the said Joseph McVay to be his act and deed whereupon it is ordered by the Court to be certified for registration. Let it be registered.

A deed of conveyance from Barnes Clark to Conner Bean for 25 acres lying in Franklin County was duly proven in Open Court by the oaths of Wm. Bean and John Weaver subscribing witnesses thereto to be the act and deed of the said Barns Clark on the day that it bears date thereupon it is (p-517) ordered by the Court to be certified for registration. Let it be registered.

An assignment of a plat and certificate of a survey from Elijah Mason to Daniel McElyea for 50 acres of land lying in Franklin County was duly proven in Open Court by his oath of Wm. Larkins a subscribing witness thereto to be act and deed of the said Elijah Mason on the day that it bears date whereupon it is ordered by the Court to be certified.

A deed of conveyance from James Cardin to Lewis Carden for 70 acres of land lying in Franklin County was duly proven in Open Court by the oaths of Henry Powers and John Brown subscribing witnesses thereto to be the act and deed of the said James Cardin on the day that it bears date whereupon it is ordered by the Court to be certified for registration. Let it be registered.

A deed of conveyance from John Driskill to Aaron Thompson for 200 acres of land lying in Franklin County was duly proven in Open Court by the oaths of William C. Handley and Edmund Dyar subscribing witnesses thereto to be the act and deed of the said John Driskill on the day that it bears date whereupon it is ordered by the Court to be certified for registration. Let it be registred.

A deed of conveyance from James Lockhart to Henry Powers for 10 acres of land lying in Franklin County was duly proven in Open Court by the oaths of of Joseph Hickerson and John Hickerson subscribing witnesses thereto to be the act and deed of the said James Lockhart on the day that it bears date whereupon it is ordered by the Court to be certified for registration. Let it be registered.

A deed of conveyance from James Cardin to Lewis Cardin for 125 acres of land lying in Franklin County was duly proven in Open Court by the oaths of Henry Powers and John Brown to be the act and deed of the said James Cardin on the day that it bears date whereupon it is ordered by the Court to be certified for registration. Let it be registered.

A deed of conveyance from James Cardin to Lewis Cardin for 125 ac res of land lying in Franklin County was duly proven in Open Court by the oaths of Henry Powers and John Brown to be the act and deed of the said James Cardin on the day that it bears date whereupon it is ordered by the Court to be certified for registration. Let it be registered.

(p-518) A deed of relinquishment from William C. Lipscomb to John Driskill was duly acknowledged in Open Court by the said William C. Lipscomb to his act and deed whereupon it is ordered by the Court to be certified for registration. Let it be registered.

Ordered by the Court that Newton Majors be appointed overseer of the road of the second class from Bobo's to Benjamin Majors in the room of Joab, Short and that he keep the same in good repair according to law, and that he have the same hands that worked under the former overseer.

Ordered by the Court that Miles Hatchcock be appointed over seer of the raod in room of Alexander Grant and that ht keep the same in goo d repair according to law and that he have the same hands that worked under the former overseer.

Ordered by the Court that George West be appointed overseer of the road of the second class from the State line of Alabama to the foot of the mountain in the room of Jeremiah Matthews and that he keep the same in good repair according to law and that he have the same hands that worked under the former overseer.

Ordered by the Court that Wm. Holloday be appointed overseer of the Huntsville road from Beans Creek to where the Fayetteville road turns out in the room of David O. Anderson and that he keep the same in good repair according to law and that he have the same hands that worked under the former overseer.

Ordered by the that John W. Camden and Jesse Jenkins Esqrs. be appointed to allot hands to concil B. Ingram overseer of the road.

(p-519) Ordered by the Court that Ervin Adams be appointed overseer of the road of the second class from the widow Caldwell's to the Hill on the East side of Big Hurricane Creek in the room of Robert Atkins and that he keep the same in good repair according to law and that Jas. Byram and Littleton G. Simpson Esqrs. give him a list of hands to work on said road

Ordered by the Court that Wm. Woods Jr. be appointed overseer of the road from W. Woods to cross in the room of Hunt and that he keep the same in good repair according to law and that he have the same hands that worked under the former overseer.

Ordered by the Court that John C. Dickey be appointed overseer of the road of the first class from the 8 mile post to Beans Creek in the room of Jas. M. Crawley and that he keep the same in good repair according to law and that he have the same hands that worked under the former overseer.

Ordered by the Court that John W. Camden Esqrs. allot hands to Samuel Austill overseer of the road.

Ordered by the Court that Robertson Nevile be appointed overseer of the road from Wilman's to Samuel Austells and that he keep the same in good repair according to law and that he have the same hands that worked under the former overseer.

Ordered by the Court that Coonrod Hise purchase a crow bar and sledge hammer for the use of said road and that be bring in his account at the next Term of this Court for allowance.

Ordered by the Court that Walter Swan be appointed overseer of the road from the bridge on the Maherds Ford Road for three miles on said road and that he keep the same in good repair according to law and that Jas. B. Stovall allot hands to work on the same.

(p-520)   Ordered by the Court that Jas. S. Cowling be appointed overseer of the road from the Rocky point on the Maherds ford road to the road leading to Caldwells Bridge and that he keep the same in good repair according to law and that he have the same hands that worked under the former overseer.

Ordered by the Court that Allen Young be appointed overseer of the road of the second Class from Sqr. Francis to Mansford in the room of Andrew Mann and that he keep the same in good repair according to law and that he have the same hands that worked under the former overseer.

Ordered by the Court that Harmon Lokey be appointed overseer of the road of the second class from Soloman Holders to the Cross road leading from William Lasater's to William Gibson and that he keep the same in good repair according to law and that he have the same hands that worked under the former overseer.

Ordered by the Court that John Doughterty & James Robinson Esqrs. be appointed to allot hands to the overseer of the road of the third class which leads by Soloman Wagners.

This day Marshall W. Howell came into Open Court and resigned his commission of Justice of the peace of Franklin County Which resignation was received by the Court.

Ordered by the Court that Caldwell P. Shipp be released from serving as constable during the present term of this Court and that John G. Brazelton be appointed in his place during this term.

This day the settlement made with Wm. G. Gwinn administrator of the estate of Nathaniel Wilder deceased was produced in Open Court was received by the Court and ordered to be recorded and it is also ordered by the Court that the allowance of (p-521) $125.00 made to said administrator by the commissioners by confirmed.

This day Daniel Martin Sr. brought into Open Court four wolf scalps, to wit, one old one and three young ones and the Court being satisfied from the statements of John S. Martin upon oath order that said Daniel Martin Sr. have a certificate to the treasurer of Middle Tennessee for Nine dollars for the same. Isd.

Ordered by the Court that Benjamin F. Jenkins be appointed constable in and for the County of Franklin in the bounds of Captain Dean's company for the next ensueing two years who entered into bond with Jesse Jenkins & Thomas Finch his securities according to law & was qualified accordingly.

Ordered by the Court that Jesse Reynolds, James B. Stovall & Samuel Bradshaw Esqrs. be appointed to examine the Bridge built a cross Elk River at Maherds ford and that they make report to the Next Term of this Court.

Ordered by the Court that Benjamin Decherd, James Robinson & James Sharp be appointed commissioners to settle with the Executors of the last Will and testament of William Knight deceased, and that they make their report to the next term of this Court.

Ordered by the Court that the commissioners of the school tract of land at the Pond Springs be allowed the sum of five dollars peranum each for their services as commissioners.

It appearing to the satisfaction of the Court that Thomas Hoockersmith late of this County died intestate and George Hookersmith Sr. applied for letters of administration on the estate of said deceased It is therefore ordered by the Court that he have letters accordingly who entered into bond with John M. Kavanaugh his security in the sum of one hundred dollars according to law and was qualified accordingly.

(p-522) It appearing to the satisfaction of the Court that Alexander Floyd late of this county died intestate and George M. Thompson applied for letters of administration on the estate of said deceased it is therefore ordered by the Court that he have letters accordingly who entered into bond with John M. Morrow, Stewart Cowen and Joseph Floyd his securities in the sum of five thousands dollars according to law and was qualified accordingly.

It appearing to the satisfaction of the Court that William Littlepage late of this county died intestate and Daniel M. Roddy and Joseph Duncan applied for letters of administration on the estate of sadd deceased. It is therefore ordered by the Court that they have letters accordingly who entered into bond with George M. Thompson and Barnet Forsyth their securities in the sum of twelve hundred dollars according to law and were qualified according to law and were qualified accordingly.

Ordered by the Court that George Hudspeth be appointed guardian over the person and property of Carter Hudspeth a lunatic of Franklin County. Who entered into bond with George M. Foster hissecurity in the sum of six hundred dollars according to law.

Ordered by the Court that Rowland Lane Joseph Coker, Jacob Sanders, William K. Cowling and Richard P. Holder be appointed a Jury of view to review the road leading through the land of James Greenlee also on the North side of the river through the land of John J. Hayter to the Bridge across the river and that they view the same having due regard to the convenience of Travellars and as little as may be to the prejudice of individuals and that they make their report to the next term of this Court.

A Bill of sale from Joseph Cowling to William Orear for a negro woman named Sue was duly acknowledged in Open Court by the said Joseph Cowling to be his act and deed Whereupon it is ordered by the Court to be certified for registration. Let it be registered.

(p-523) This day the last Will and Testament of William M. Rains deceased was produced in Open Court whereupon came Benjamin Decherd and Zacharih Wortham the subscribing witnesses thereto who being first duly swörh depose and say that the said William M. Rains signed the same in their presence and that he the said William M. Rains at the time of signing the same was of sound and disposing mind and memory and that they signed the same as witnesses in his presence and at his request whereupon it is ordered by the Court to be recorded.

This day the last Will and Testament of William Hedger deceased was produced in Open Court whereupon came John M. Morrow and Stewart Cowen the subscribing witnesses thereto who being first duly sworn depose and say that the said William Hedger Signed the same in their presence and that he the said William Hedger at the time of signing the same was of sound and disposing mind and memory and that they signed the same as witnesses thereto in his presence and at his request Whereupon it is ordered by the Court to be recorded Whereupon James Howard and William W. Harris the Executors therein named came into Open Court and were qualified as Executors of said last Will and testament who entered into bond with George W. Thompson their security in the sum of One thousand dollars according to law.

This day an additional sale of the Estate of Jacob Vanzant deceased was returned in to Open Court was received by the Court and ordered to be recorded.

Present Andrew Mann, Richmond P. Harris, James Kelley, John Daugherty, James Robinson, James Byrom, Jesse Jenkins, William Lasater, Zachariah H. Murrell, James Keith, Samuel Bradshaw and George W. Thompson Esqrs.

Ordered by the Court that John Handly one of the County commissions be allowed the sum of two dollars and fifty cents for one days services settleing with County Clerk (Page 524) the fines and forfectures for the year 1834 and also the forther sum of two dollars and fifty cents for one days services in settling with the County Trustee for the year 1835 and that the Clerk issure a certificate to the County Trustee to pay the sums which allowance was unanimously made by said Justices.

Present Andrew Mann Richmond P. Harris, James Kelley, John Daughterly, James Robinson, James Byram, Jesse Jinkins, William Laster, Zachariah H. Murrell, James Keith, Samuel Bradshaw & George W. Thompson, Ordered by the Court that Erwin J. Frierson Attorney General be allowed the sum of fifty dollars for his exofficio services for the year ending at the present Term of this Court and that the Clerk issure a certificate to the County Trustee to pay the same. Which allowance was unanimously made by the said Justices.

Present Andrew Mann, Richmond P. Harris, James Kelley, John Daughterty James Robinson James Byrom, Jesse Jinkins William Lasater Zachariah H. Murrell James Keith Samuel Bradshaw and George W. Thompson Esqrs. Ordered by the Court that the following persons be allowed the the following sums, in the following cases to wit, in the case of the State of Tennessee against Richard Malone Clerk of the Circuit Court $5.12½. Attorney General Frierson $2.50 Sheriff Finch $3.00. In the case of the State of Tennessee against John Simmons and Peter Simmons Clerk of the Circuit Court $8.06. Attorney General Frierson $2.50 Sheriff Hudspeth $2.25 Sheriff Homan $2.87½ Wallis Wilson a witness for the State 4 days $2.00 Johns S. Martin do 4 days $2.00 George Hudspeoth do 4 days $2.00 James Britton do 4 days $2.00 in the case of the State of Tennessee against Portland J. Curle & Claiborn Herbert. The Clerk of the Circuit Court $1.75 Attorney General Frierson $2.50. In the case of the State of Tennessee againgt Francis Gidion Clerk of the Circuit Court $5.25 Atty General Frierson $2.50 Sheriff Finch $1.50. In the case of the State of Tennessee against David Austin (p-525) The Clerk of the Circuit Court $5.00 Atty. General Frierson $2.50 Sheriff Finch one dollar Sheriff Jones Fifty cents Sheriff Homan $.50 cts. and that the clerk issure separate certificates for each of them to the county Trustee to pay the same. Which allowance was unanimously made by said Justices. Isd to Frierson to Finch Isd to Homan Isd to Hudspeth.

Present Andrew Mann, Richmond P. Harris, James Kelley, John Daughterty James Robinson, James Byron, Jesse Jenkins, Wm. Lasater, Zachariah H. Murrell, James Keith, Samuel Bradshaw & George W. Thompson Esqr. Ordered by the Court John Goodwin Clerk of the Circuit Court for Franklin County be allowed the sum of one dollar & fifty cents for a record book furnished for said office and that the clerk issure a certificate to the County Trustee to pay him the same which allowance was unanimously made by said Justices. Isd.

This day Jesse Jenkins, Jesse Reynolds & Hosea Stamps three of the commissions of the School tract of land at the Pond Springs made their return to Court of the proceeds of said tract of land and was qualified thereto which returnwas received by the Court & ordered to be recorded.

This day the amount of Sales of the Estate of Catharine Shropshire deod. was returned into open Court, was returned into open Court, was received by the Court and ordered to be recorded.

On the Petition of George Hudspeth administrator of all and singular the goods & Chattels rights and credits of Robert Hudspeth deceased praying the sale of certain negroes in said Petition mentioned to wit, Grave & Jacob. And it appearing to the satifaction of the court the said slaves could not be divided among the legatees of said Estate, without a sale thereof, Whereupon the Court doth order adjudge and direct that said administrator sell said slaves at the Court house door in the Town of Winchester after giving ten days notice of the time and place of sale by written advertisements to the highest bidder on a twelve months credit taking bond and approved security from the purchaser or purchasers.

On the petition of Wm. Hudspeth, George Hudspeth, Seaton Hudspeth, Wm. Collins & his wife Elizabeth, George Collins & his wife Elizabeth, George Collins & his wife Polly, Green W. Caperton & his wife Anna, Sandridge Arnett & his wife Jane & Estill (p-526) Scrivner and his wife Licity & Carter Hudspeth and William Ranson & his wife Sarah & Samuel Hudspeth heirs at law of Robert Hudspeth deceased and Nancy Hudspeth widow of said decedent. And it appearing to the satisfaction of the Court that some years ago Robert Hudspeth departed this life intestate being sized and possessed of a tract of two hundred acres of land lying and being in the County of Franklin Tennessee situated on or near the head of Beans Creek adjoining the lands of George Foster, Jesse Ginn & Zachariah Brown, Wherefore said Petitioners pray the Court to appoint a Jury of five free holders to divide the land among said heirs and allot to the widow her dower agreeably to the prayer of said petition. Whereupon it is ordered by the Court that David O. Anderson Archibald Hatchett, David O. Anderson Archibald Hatchett, David Arnett John Staples & George Foster be appointed to divide the lands of said intestate among said heirs allotting to the widow her dower according to law and that they make report of their proceeding to the next term of this Court.

This day the last will and testament of Michael Awalt deceased was produced in Open Court Whereupon came William Jenkins one of the subscribing witnesses thereto who being first duly sworn deposith and saith that Michael Awalt signed the same in his presence and that at the time of signing the same he the said Michael Awalt was of sound and disposing mind & memory and that he signed the same as a witness thereto in his presence and at his request and he also says the Robert Frost was a subscribing witness, thereto and that he saw him sign his name as a witness thereto & that he now lives beyond the limits of the State. Whereupon it is ordered by the Court to be recorded, Whereupon Michael Awalt the Executor named in said will came into Court and was qualified as Executor of said will who entered into bond with Zachariah H. Murrell & Peter Limbough his securities in the sum of three hundred dollars according to law.

Ordered by the Court that Thomas Wilson Mark Hutchins, Marshall W. Howell, Thomas L. Logan, Madison Porter, William H. Street and Henry Bunnels be appointed commissions to ascertain the value and comdemn a sufficient quantity of ground for the purpose of erecting the ground for the purpose of erecting the abutment of the Brdige on the North side of the Boiling Fork of Elk River Winchester and to turn the road so as to correspond therewith and that they make their report to (p-527) the present term of this court.

This day a Paper writing purporting to be the last will and testament of Elizabeth Bowling was produced in Open Court and offered for Probate Whereupon came Elizabeth Gilliland and objects to the probate thereof Whereupon it is ordered by the Court that an issure be made up to try whether said paper writing is the last will and Testament of said Elizabeth Bowlin deod.

This day came Aaron Goin a free man of yellow complexion about twenty two or three years of age and Nancy Goin his sister a free woman of yellow complesion about twenty six years of age and adduced prof of their freedom and the Court being satisfied from said prof that they are the offspring of Aaron & Nancy Goin who are free people of color doth order that the above facts be recorded and that they have a certificate here of this day the last Will and Testament of Mary Wilson deo'd was produced in Open Court whereupon came Barnett Forsyth one of the subscribing witnesses thereto who being first duly sworn deposeth and saith that the said Mary Wilson signed the same in his presence and that at the time of signing the same she the said Mary Wilson was of sound and desposing mind and memory and that he signed the same as a Witness thereto in her presence and at her request and it is ordered by the Court that a Subscribing Witness thereto to appear at the Next Term of this Court.

This day the last Will and testament of Hannah Woods dec'd was presented in open Court for Probate, and it appearing to the Court that Richard C. Arnett and Abigail Gibbon the subscribing witnesses to said Will are unable to attend the Court for the purpose of proving the same and that the said Richard C. Arnett is an inhabitant of the State of Mississippi and that the said Abigail Gibbons is expected to remove beyond the Jurisdiction of this Court before the next Term thereof - Whereupon it is ordered by the Court that a commission issue to any justice of the peace for the County of Fayette to take the deposition of the said Richard C. Arnett and also that a commission issue to take the deposition of the said Abigail Gibbon for the purpose of proving the execution of said Will (p-528)   Satisfactory evidence was adduced in Open Court to prove that Winny Warner since intermarried with Mansfield Thompson was the wife of the late Thomas Warren a Soldier in Capt. Selden's company of the Rifle regiment who died in the service, it is said about 16th of Jan. 1816 and at the time of his death he had the four following children to wit, Hannah Warren who has since intermarried with Sidina Shiply of County Illinois, William Warren a citizen of Warren County Tenn. Anna Warren and Elizabeth Warren heirs at law in fee to the said Thomas Warren deceased of Capt. Seldens Company the rifle regiment who died as aforesaid.

Court adjourned untill tomorrow morning 11 o'clock
                              James Robinson
                              John Daugherty
                              James Keith

Tuesday August the twenty fifth one thousand eight hundred and thirty five. Court met according to adjournment.
Present - Five of the acting Justices of the peace for Franklin County.

Ordered by the Court that Francis Turner be released from serving on the Jury during the present Term of this Court.

Ordered by the Court that Richmond P. Harris Esqrs be appointed one of the Quorum Court to hold the Courts of Pleas and Quarter Sessions of Franklin County untill February Term 1836 of said Court in room of Marshall W. Howell resigned.

Ordered by the Court that John G. Bostick be appointed overseer of the same part of the road that David Willis was formerly Overseer of and that he keep the same in good repair according to law and that he have the same hands that worked under the former Overseer.

Ordered by the Court that John G. Bostick, William S. Mooney & Barnaby Burrow be appointed Commissioners to settle with David Muckleroy who was appointed by the circuit Court of Franklin County to take care of the property belonging to the Estate of Alexander Floyd, Dec'd during the pendancy of a suit in relation to his Will and that they make their report to the next Term of this Court. (p-529)

Ordered by the Court that Thomas Finch be appointed to make a contract with some person to convey a Pauper from Samuel Harris to the poor house of Franklin County and that he report the expences to the next term of this Court.

Ordered by the Court that James Robinson, John Goodwin & Willie B. Wagner be appointed commissioners to settle with John Frame Administrator with the will annexed of the Estate of Ezikiel Philips deceased and that they make their report to the next Term of this Court.

Ordered by the Court that Frances Turner be appointed Overseer of the Lowery road from Capt. Davidsons to where it intersects the stage road and that he keep the same in good repair according to law and the James F. Green Esqr. allot hands to work on said road.

Ordered by the Court that Wm. H. Byrom be appointed Overseer of the road from Esquire Majors to the Widow Caldwells in room of John Adkins and that he keep the same on good repair according to law and that he have the same hands that worked under the former Overseer.

This day Thomas Finch Sheriff of Franklin County produced in open Court the following receipts, to wit, Received August the 8th 1835 of Thomas Finch Sheriff of Franklin County a certificate of the number of votes poled for Governor in the County of Franklin on Thursday the 6th day of August 1835 directed to the speaker of the Senate of the State Legislature of the Senate of the State Legislature of Tennesse and dated the 8th day of August 1835 which will be sent on by the first mail.   W. Estill, P. M.

Received of Thomas Finch Sheriff of Franklin County his return of the number of votes polled in Franklin County for Governor at the General

Election held in said Counth on the 1st Thursday of August 1835 ,
8th August 1835.   Hopkins L. Turner.

This day an inventory of the Estate of Adam Gross dec'd was
returned into Open Court was received by the Court and ordered to be
recorded. (p-530)

This day the amount of sales of the Estate of Adam Gross dec'd was
returned into Open Court was received by the Court and ordered to be
recorded.

This day the settlement made with the Executor of John Feamster
dec'd was produced in Open Court was received by the Court and ordered
to be recorded.

Ordered by the Court that the following Persons be Jurors to the
next circuit Court, to wit, Stewart Cowan, James Howard John Burrows,
Thomas Burrows, Barnaby Burrow, Jesse Gotcher Harris Gilliam, James Bill
Larson Rowe, George S. Miller, Thomas Wright, John Hickerson, Lewis
Davidson, Laban Jones James Cowan, Wiley J. Hines, Green Brazelton,
Abram Shook, Benjamin Elbott, Anthory Stewart, John S. Martin, John
Staples, Thomas Garner, Wallis Estill Jr. James Woods, James Sharp, Senr.
and that James Oliver & Wm. M. Cowan be appointed constables to attend
on said Court & that the Sheriff summon them to attend the same and make
due return to the same.

Ordered by the Court that the following persons be appointed Jurors
to the next County Court, to wit,- Edwin M. Tatum, James Taylor, James P
Keith, John K. Burton, William Frances, Miles Francis, John D. Ferrell,
Willis Holden, Solmon Holden, Joab Short, Wiley Denson, David Robinson
Littleton Faris, Edward M. Wade, Absolom Faris Senr. Joseph Bradford,
John P. Davidson, John B. Wilkinson, John Howard, William Taylor,
John Frame, James V. Acklin, Admond R. Lee, Joseph Acklin, Hamilton
Stewart, Bdedsoe Stewart and that James N. Chiles & John G. Brazelton be
appointed constable to attend on said Court and that the Sheriff summons
them to attend the same and make due returns to the next term of this Court

On motion of John Goodwin Esquire and it appearing to the satisfaction of the Court, that Williamson S. Oldham, is a man of Honesty
probity and good demeanor, and that he is twenty one years of age, and
that he has been a resident citizen of Franklin County for the last
twelve months. It is therefore ordered by the Court that the said
Williamson S. Oldham receive a certificate hereof from the Clerk of this
Court.

(p-531)   This day the Commissioners appointed at present Term of this
Court to ascertain the value and condem a sufficient quantity of ground
for the purpose of erecting the abutment of the bridge on the North side
of the boiling fork of Elk river at Winchester and to turn the road to
correspond therewith made their report which was received by the Court
and ordered to be confirmed. Wherefore it is ordered by the Court that
James Dardis upon whose land said abutment is to erected be allowed
the sum of twenty four dollars the damages assessed by the commissioners

aforesaid.

It appearing to the satisfaction of the Court that John Saxton late of this County died intestate and Edwin Eanes applied for letters of administration on the Estate of said Decd Whereupon it is ordered by the Court that be have letters accordingly Who entered into bond with James Oliver his security in the sum of Four hundred dollars according to law and was qualified accordingly.

This day Henry A. Raines one of the Executors named in the last will and testament of Wm. M. Raines decd. came into open Court and was qualified as executor of said Will Who entered into bond with John Goodwin & Benjamin Dechered his securities in the sum of Five thousand dollars according to law and Edwin M. Tatum the other Executor named in said Will refused to Qualify.

Court adjourned untill tomorrow morning nine o'clock
James Keith
John Doughterty
R. P. Harris

Wednesday August the 26th 1835 Court met according to adjournment Present - Jas Keith, John Doughterty & R. P. Harris Esqrs.

The State of Tennessee
Proclamation being made the Sheriff of Franklin County made return of the States writ of Venire Facias to this Court that he had summoned the following persons being all good and lawful men of said County of Franklin and being citizens of said County of Franklin to attend and serve as Jurors at the present term of this Court which persons so summoned and returned as aforesaid had been nominated for that purpose by the Justices of this said Court of pleas and quarter sessions of said County of Franklin at its last session a list of whom was delivered to the Sheriff of this said County (p-532)   by the Clerk of this said Court, towit, Joseph Klipper Benjamin Dechered, Paschal Green, Thomas Cunningham, Julius C. Sims, Edmond P. Lee, J. W. D. Stamper, John Lee, Wm. L. Hannah, Joseph Francis senr. Bird Francis, Joseph Sewell, John K. Burton, Joseph Huddleston Jr. Thomas Wilson, Wm. A. Caldwell, Wm. Hendon, John J. Hayter, John Mason, Asahel Aldrich Francis Turner, Thomas N. Holt, George McCutcheon, Wm. Champion, John S. Bower & Milton McQueen, and of whom the following this day attended, to wit, Joseph Klipper, Paschal Green, Thomas Cunning-ham, John Lee, Wm. L. Hannah, Joseph Francis Sr. Bird Francis, Huddleston Jr. Joseph Wewell John K. Burton, Thomas Wilson, Wm. A. Caldwell, Wm. Hendon John Mason, Asahel Aldrich, Thomas N. Holt, George McCutcheon, Wm. Champ-ion & Milton McQueen, and of whom the following persons being good and lawful men of said County of Franklin were elected empanneld Sworn and charged to enquire for the body of the County aforesaid, to wit, George McCutheon who was appointed foreman, Paschal Green, Thomas Cunningham John Lee, Joseph Francis Senr. Bird Francis Joseph Sewell, John K. Burton Joseph Huddleston Jr. Wm. A. Caldwell, Asahel Aldrich, Thomas N. Holt & Wm. Champion who after receiving their charge returned to consult of their charge returned to consult of their presentments who afterwards came int o open Court and returned a bill of Indictment against Charles Gurrant for Malicious Mischief a true Bill.

Ordered by the Court that James P. Keith & Abraham Shook be appointed Jurors in room of John Mason & Milton McQueen and that Joseph Klipper, Thomas Wilson & Wm. Henden be released from serving as Jurors &c during the present term of this Court.

WM. FARIS)
  Against)
FARLAIGH B. WADE) This day came the plaintiff by his attorney and dismissed his suit and not further prosecuting. It is ordered the this suit be dismissed. Wherefore it is considered by the Court that the defendant go hence with out day and recover against the Plaintiff his costs by him about his defence in this behalf expended and the said Plaintiff in Mercy &.

ROBERT S. SHARP ASSEE & C) Debt
  Against)
JAMES CAMDEN &)
HAYDEN ARNOLD) This day came the parties by their attorneys and thereupon came a Jury, to wit, Wm. L. Hannahl, James P. Keith 2, Abraham Shook 3, Edward Garrett 4, John Haws 5, Farley B. Wade 6, Joseph Campbell 7, Wm. Thurman 8, James Estill 9, Benjamin Franklin 10, Daniel M. Roddy 11, & Alexander (p-533) Winford 12, Who being elected tried and sworn the truth to speak upon the issure joined upon their oaths do say they find the issure in favor of the Plaintiff and assess his damages to six dollars. It is therefore considered by the Court that the Plaintiff recover against the Defendant one hundred and fifty dollars the debt in the Declaration mentioned together with his damages aforesaid assessed by the Jury aforesaid and also his costs by him about said suit in this behalf expended for all of which execution may issue &.

RICHARD HL WALLACE) Debt
  Against)
GEORGE W. RICHARDSON &)
JAMES RICHARDSON) This day came the parties by their attorneys and thereupon came a Jury, towit, Wm. L. Hannah 1, James P. Keith 2, Abraham Shook 3, Edward Garrett 4, John Haws 5, Farlaigh B. Wade 6, Joseph Campbell 7, Wm. Thurman 8, James Estill 9, Benjamin Franklin 10, Daniel M. Roddy 11 & Alexander Winford 12 who being elected tried and sworn the truth to speak upon the issure joined upon their oaths do say they find the issure in favor of the Plaintiff and assess his damages to three dollars & twenty four cents. It is therefore considered by the Court that the Plaintiff recover against the defendant sixty six dollars & forty cents the balance of the debt in the Declaration mentioned together with his damages aforesaid assessed by the Jury aforesaid and also his costs by him about said suit in this behalf expended for all of which execution may issue &.

HAYDEN ARNCLD to the) Debt
use of H. M. RUTLEDGE)
  Against)
BERRY KING)
) This day came the parties by their attorneys and thereupon came a Jury to wit, Wm. L. Hannah 1, James P. Keith 2, Abraham Shook 3, Edward Garrett 4, John Haws 5, Farlaigh B. Wade 6, Joseph Campbell 7, Wm. Thurman 8, James Estill 9, Benjamin Franklin 10,

Daniel M. Roddy 11 & Alexander Winford 12 who being elected tried and
sworn the truth to speak upon the issure joined upon the issure joined
upon their oaths do say they find the issure in favor of the plaintiff
and assess his damage to four dollars & twenty cents. It is therefore
considered by the Court that the Plaintiff recover against the defendant
one hundred and forty dollars the debt in the Declaration mentioned
together with his damages aforesaid assessed by the Jury aforesaid and
also his costs by him about said suit in this behalf expended for all
of which execution may issure &.

(p-534)   ROBERT S. SHARP ASSEE & C   )   Debt
             Against   )
           HAYDEN ARNOLD, JAMES L.   )
             BRYANT, STEWART SOWAN &   )
           GEORGE W. RICHARDSON   )   This day came the parties by
their attorneys and thereupon came a Jury, to wit, Wm. L. Hannah 1,
James P. Keith 2, Abraham Shook 3, Edward Garrett 4, John Haws 5,
Farlaigh B. Wade 6, Joseph Campbell 7, Wm. Thurman 8, James Estill 9
Benjamin Franklin 10, Daniel M. Roddy 11 & Alexander Winford 12, who being
elected tried and sworn the truth to speak upon the issure joined upon
their oaths do say they find the issure in favor of the plaintiff and
assess his damages to twelve dollars. It is therefore considered by the
Court that the Plaintiff recover against the defendant three hundred
dollars the debt in the Declaration mentioned together with his damages
aforesaid assessed by the Jury aforesaid and also his costs by him about
suit in this behalf expended for all of which execution may issue &.

JOHN W. & A. L. CAMPBELL   )   Debt
  Against   )
ARCHIBALD W. NANCY   )   This day came the parties by their attornies
and thereupon came a Jury, to wit, Wm. L. Hannah 1, James P. Keith 2,
Abraham Shook 3, Edward Garrett 4, John Hows 5, Farlaigh B. Wade 6, Joseph
Campbell 7, William Thurman 8, James Estill 9, Benjamin Franklin 10,
Daniel M. Roddy 11 & Alexander Winford 12 who being elected tried and
sworn the truth to speak upon the issue joined upon their oaths do say
they find the issue in favor of the Plaintiffs and assess them damages to
four dollars and thirty one cents. It is thereupon considered by the
Court that the plaintiff recover against the defendant one hundred and
twenty nine dollars & fifty nine cents the debt in the declaration mentioned
together with their damages aforesaid assessed by the Jury aforesiad and
also their costs by them about said suit in this behalf expended for all
of which execution may issue &.

J. W. & A. L. CAMPBELL & CO.)   Covenant
  Against   )
JAMES ESTILL   )   This day came the parties by their
attornys and thereupon came a Jury, to wit, Wm. L. Hannah 1, James P.
Keith 2, Abraham Shook 3, Edward Garrett 4, John Hows 5, Farlaigh B.
Wade 6, Joseph Campbell 7, Wm. Thurman 8, Hayden Arnold 9, Benjamin Franklin
10, Daniel M. Roddy 11 & Alexander Winford 12 who being elected tried and
sworn the truth to speak upon the issue joined upon their oaths do say
they find the issue in (p-535) favor of the Plaintiffs and assess their
damages to one hundred and forty four dollars and thirty three cents. It
is therefore considered by the Court that the Plaintiffs recover against
the Defendant their damages aforesaid assessed by the Jury aforesaid and
also their costs by them about said suit in this behalf expended for all

of which Execution may issue &.

ARNOLD & BRYANT to the)   Debt
USE OF JOSEPH HICKERSON)
  Against)
STEWART COWAN)   This day came the parties by their attorneys
and thereupon came a Jury, to wit, Wm. L. Hannah 1, James P. Keith 2,
Abraham Shook 3, Edward Garrett 4, John Haws 5, Farlaigh B. Wade 6,
Joseph Campbell 7, William Thurman 8, James Estill 9, Benjamin Franklin 10
Daniel M. Roddy 11, & Alexander Winford 12 who being elected, tried and
sworn the truth to speak upon the issue joined upon their oaths do say
they find the issue in favor of the Plaintiff and assess his damages to
eleven dollars and twenty five cents. It is therefore considered by the
Court that the Plaintiff recover against the defendant three hundred
dollars the debt in the Declaration mentioned together with his damages
aforesaid assessed by the Jury aforesaid and also his costs by him about
said suit in this behalf expended for all of which execution may Issue &.

ROBERT S. SHARP)   Debt
  Against)
BARNETT FORSYTH)   This day came the parties by their attorneys and
thereupon came a Jury, to wit, Wm. L. Hannah James P/ Keith 2,
Abraham Shook 3, Edward Garrett 4, John Hows 5, Farlaigh B. Wade 6,
Joseph Campbell 7, William Thurman 8, James Estill 9, Benjamin Franklin 10
Daniel M. Roddy 11 & Alexander Winford 12 who being elected, tried and
sworn the truth to speak upon the issue joined upon their oaths do say
they find the issue in favor of the Plaintiff and assess his damages to
four dollars and ninety nine cents. It is therefore considered by the
Court that the Plaintiff recover against the defendant one hundred and
eleven dollars the debt in Declaration mentioned together with his damages
aforesaid assessed by the Jury aforesaid and also his costs by him
about said suit in this behalf expended for all of which execution May issue &.

THOMAS M. PRYOR & CO.)   Debt
  Against)
SAMUEL BRADSHAW, JOSEPH BRADSHAW)
JOHN BRADSHAW, WM. A. COLDWELL)
GEORGE B. TUCKER & WILEY J. HINES)   This day came the parties by their
attorneys and thereupon came a Jury to wit, Wm. L. Hannah 1, (P-536)
James P. Keith 2, Abraham Shook 3, Edward Garrett 4, John Hows 5,
Farlaigh B. Wade 6, Joseph Campbell 7, Wm. Thurman 8, James Estill 9,
Benjamin Franklin 10, Daniel M. Roddy 11 & Alexander Winford 12 who
being elected tried and sworn the truth to speak upon the issue joined
upon their oaths do say they find the issue in favor of the Plaintiff
and assess their damages to four dollars and eighty cents. It is therefore considered by the Court that the Plaintiffs recover aginst the
Defendants one hundred and twenty dollars the debt in the Declaration
mentioned together with their damages aforesaid assessed by the Jury
aforesaid and also their costs by them about said suit in this behalf
expended for all of which execution May issue &.

JAMES ARMSTRONG)   Debt
Against)
MICAJAH L. GILLASPIE)   This day came the parties by their attorneys and
thereupon came a Jury to wit, William L. Hannah 1, James P. Keith 2,

Abraham Shook 3, Edward Garrett 4, John Hows 5, Farlaigh B. Wade 6
Joseph Campbell 7, William Thurman 8, James Estill 9 Benjamin Franklin 10
Daniel M. Roddy 11 & Alexander Winford 12 who being elected tried and
sworn the truth to speak upon the issue joined upon their oaths do say
they find the issue in favor of the plaintiff and assess his damages
to five dollars and sixty tree cents. It is therefore considered by
the Court that the plaintiff recover against the Defendant two Hundred
and sixty six dollars and sixty six and two third cents the debt in the
Declaration mentioned together with his damages aforesaid assessed by
the Jury aforesaid and also his costs by him about said suit in this
behalf expended for all of which execution may issue &.

JONATHAN GORE   ) Case
 Against   )
EDWARD GARRETT   ) This day came the Defendant into open Court and
saith he cannot gainsay the Plaintiffs action against him and confesses
judgment for four hundred and seventy six dollars and eighty seven one
half cents. It is therefore considered by the Court that the Plaintiff
recover against the Defendant said sum of four hundred & Seventy six
dollars & 87½ cents confessed as aforesaid and also his costs by him
about said suit in this behalf expended for all of which execution may
issue &.

(p-537) JOHN THOMISSON   ) Debt
     Against   )
    HAYDEN ARNOLD &   )
    STEWART COWAN   ) This day came the parties by their
    James B. Bryant
attorney and thereupon came a Jury, to wit, Wm. L. Hannah 1, James P.
Keith 2, Abraham Shook 3, Edward Garrett 4, John Haws 5, Farlaigh B. Wade 6
Joseph Campbell 7, Wm. Thurman 8, James Estill 9, Benjamin Franklin 10
Jas. T. Russell 11, Alexander Winford 12 who being elected tried and
sworn the truth to speak upon the issure joined upon their oaths do say
they find the issure in favor of the Plaintiff and assess his damages to
five dollars and eighty two cents. It is therefore considered by the
Court that the Plaintiff recover against the Defendant one hundred and
twenty five dollars the debt in the Declaration mentioned together with
his damages aforesaid assessed by the Jury aforesaid and also his costs
by him about said suit in this behalf expended for all of which execution
may Issue &.

DANIEL M. RODDY   )
 Against   )
SAUL CAMP   ) This day came the defendant by his attorney and
moved the Court to continue this cause untill the next term of this Court
and from the reasons set forth in the affidavit of said defendant. It is
ordered by the Court that said cause be continued untill the next term
of this Court by the defendant paying the costs of this Term about said
suit expended. Wherefore it is considered by the Court that the Pliff.
recover against the deft. the costs according at this term for which
execution may issue and on motion of the said defendant a commission is
awarded him to take the deposition of Hayden Arnold Delie neesse to be
read as evidence on behalf of the defendant on the trial of the above
cause by his giving the plaintiff five days notice of the time and place
of taking the same

LITTY WHITE   )
 Against   )
Z. H. MURRELL ADMIN &)
WINNY PHILIPS ADMIN OF)
JAMES PHILIPS DECD   ) This day came the defendants by their
attorney and moved the court to continue this cause untill the next term
of this Court. It is therefore considered by the Court that the said
cause be continued untill the next term of this Court as on their affidavit
And on their motion a commission is awarded them to take the deposition
of Joseph Hilton before any one Justice of the peace for Shelby County
and State of Tennessee to be read as evidence on the trial of the above
cause inbehalf of the defendants by their giving the plaintiff thirty days
notice of the time and place of taking the same.

(p-538) ROBERT BIBSON   )
     Against   )
     GEORGE W. THOMPSON) On motion of the plaintiff by his
attorney the order of refeference in this case is continued untill the
next Term of this Court.

   Ordered by the Court that George W. Thompson be appointed to take
care of the Estate of Elizabeth Bowlin Decd. during the controversy in
relation to her last will and testament all of which was done by the
consent of the parties.

JOHN HERRIFORD)
Against   )
LEROY MAY   ) On motion of the defendant by his attorney this cause
is continued untill the next Term of this Court on his affidavit and on
his motion a commission is awarded him to take the deposition of
James Campbell before any one Justice of the peace for Davidson County
to be read as evidence on the trial of the above cause by his giving the
Plaintiff ten days notice of the time and place of taking the same. and
on his motion leave is granted him to amend the Pleadings in this cause.

NANCY PRICE   )
 Against   )
JOSEPH R. SHROPSHIRE) This day came the Plaintiff by her attorney and
moved the Court to continue this cause. And upon her statement which is
taken as an affidavit. It is ordered by the Court that this cause be
continued for trial at the next Term of this Court.

VANZANT HARRIS & CO.)
 Against   )
E. P. BACON   ) On motion of the Plaintiffs by thier attorney
it is ordered by the Court that this cause by continued for trial untill
the next Term of this Court.

ISAAC VANZANT Surviving   )
Partner of JACOB VANZANT & CO.)
 Against   )
E. P. BACON   ) On motion of the Plaintiff by his attorney
it is ordered by the Court that this cause be continued for trial at the
next Term of this Court.

JOSEPH BICKLEY ADMIN OF)
E. L. BICKLEY DECD.)
  Against)
JOHN HAWS) This day came the plaintiff by his attorney
and moved the Court to continue this cause upon the affidavit and from
the reasons set fourth is said affidavit. It is ordered by the Court that
this cause be continued for trial at the next Term of this Court.

(p-539)   Court adjourned untill tomorrow morning nine o'clock.
                                        James Keith
                                        John Dougherty
                                        R. P. Harris.

        Thursday, August the twenty seventh one thousand eight hundred
and thirty five court met according to adjournment.
Present - James Keith
          John Dougherty &   ) Esquires Justices of the peace
          Richmond P. Harris   )

THE STATE OF TENNESSEE   ) Present for Gaming
  Against)
GAIMAN SCROGGINS) This day came the attorney General who
prosecutes for the State in this behalf and with the assent of the Court
enters a noeprosequi in this case.

THE STATE OF TENNESSEE   ) Indict for a Riot & A. & B.
  Against)
BRYANT B. THOMPSON &)
RICHARD F. MCDUFF)
) This day came the attorney General who
prosecutes for the State in this behalf and with the assent of the Court
enters a noleprosequi in this case.

THE STATE OF TENNESSEE) Present for Gaming
  Against)
MERREL EMBREY) This day came the attorney General who
prosecutes for the State in this behalf and with the assent of the
Court enters a Noleprosequi in this case.

THE STATE OF TENNESSEE) Indict for an Affray
  Against)
ELIAS OLDHAM JR.) This day came the Attorney General who
prosecutes for the State in this behalf and with the assent of the Court
enteres a Noleprosequi in this case.

THE STATE OF TENNESSEE)
  Against)
ANDREW H. MCCOLLUM) This day came the Attorney General who
prosecutes for the State in this behalf and moved the Court to continue
this cause untill the next Term of this Court. It is therefore ordered
by the Court that this cause be continued untill the next term of this
Court as on the affidavit of the prosecutor.

(p-540)

THE STATE OF TENNESSEE   )
 Against   )
ANDREW H. MCCOLLUM   )   This day Andrew H. McCollum and Micajah L. Gillaspie came into Open Court and acknowledged themselves to owe and Stant Justly indebted to the State of Tennessee in the following sums to wit, Andrew H. McCollum the Defendant in the sum of two hundred & fifty dollars & Micajah L. Gillaspie his Security in the sum of $125 dollars to be levied of their respective goods & Chattels lands and tenements to the use of said State but to be void on condition that the said Andrew H. McCollum make his personal appearance before the Justices of our next Court of Pleas and Quarter Sessions to be held for the County of Franklin at the Courthouse in the Town of Winchester on Thursday after the fourth Monday in November next then and there to answer the State of Tennessee on a Bill of Indictment found against him for Malicious mischief and abide by and perform judgment of said Court and not depart the same without leave first had and obtained.

THE STATE OF TENNESSEE   ) Present for an Affray
 Against   )
JOSEPH R. SHROPSHIRE   ) This cause is continued by the consent of the parties untill the next Term of this Court.

CRUTCHER & ALLISON   )
  Against   )
LEROY S. CAMDEN   )
JAMES H. ARNOLD   )
STEWART COWAN &   )
JOHN W. CAMDEN   )   This day came the Plaintiff by their attorney and moved this Court for an order to take the disposition of Alpha Kingly before anyone Justice of the peace of Davidson County which is by the Court ordered accordingly by the Plaintiffs giving the defendants ten days notice of the time and place of taking the same.

THE STATE OF TENNESSEE   ) Indict for an Affray
 Against   )
WILLIAM MCCOY &   )
DAVID FOSTER   )   This day came the Attorney General who prosecutes for the State is this behalf as well as the said defendant in their proper persons and the said defendants having heard said Indictment read say they are thereof not guilty and put themselves upon the Country and the Attorney General doth the like and thereupon came a Jury, to wit, Thomas N. Holt Bird Francis, Joseph Sewell John K. Burton Thomas Cunningham, Joseph Francis, Paschal Green, Joseph Huddleston Jr. George McCutcheon, Wm. Champion, Asahel Aldrich & John Lee, who being elected tried and sworn the truth of and upon the promises to speak (p-541) upon their oaths do say they find the Defendants guilty in manner and form as charged in the bill of Indictment, It is therefore considered by the Court that the Defendants for such their offense be find the sum of five dollars each and pay the costs of this prosecution, Whereupon James Gillaspie came into Open Court and acknowledged himself security for the fine and costs in the above cause, for all of which execution may issure &.

THE STATE OF TENNESSEE)
  Against)
JOSEPH R. SHROPSHIRE) This day Joseph R. Shropshire & James
Gillaspie came into Open Court and acknowledged themselves to owe and
stand justly indebted to the State of Tennessee in the following sums,
to wit, Joseph R. Shropshire the defendant in the sum of $250 and
James Gillaspie his security in the sum of $125 to be levied of their
respective goods and chattels lands and tenements to the use of said
State but to be void on condition that the said Joseph R. Shropshire
make his personal appearance before the Justices of our next Court of
Pleas and Quarter Sessions to be held for the County of Franklin at the
Court house in the Town of Winchester on Thursday after the fourth
Monday in November next then and there to answer the State of Tennessee
on a Presentment found against him for an affray and abide by and
perform the Judgment of said Court and not depart the same without leave
first had and obtained.

THE STATE OF TENNESSEE)
  Against)
REASON ISOMS) This day came the attorney General who
prosecutes for the State of this behalf and with the assent of the court
enters a noleprosequi in this case.

THOMAS M. PRYON & CO.) Debt
  Against)
JAMES ESTILL) This day came the defendant in open Court in
his proper person and saith he cannot gainsay the Plaintiffs action
against him and confesses Judgment for one hundred and ten dollars and
sixteen cents the debt in the Declaration mentioned and together with
the further sum of nine dollars and thirty cents interest thereon at
the rate of six per cent per anum. Whereupon it is considered by the
Court that the Plaintiff recover against the Defendant their debt and
Interest confessed as aforesaid and also their costs by them about said
suit in this behalf expended for all of which execution may issure &.
the Plffs. agree to stay the execution untill next Cristmas.

(p-542) THOMAS M. PRYON & CO.) Debt
    Against)
    JAMES ESTILL) This day came the Plaintiff by their
attorney and the defendant in his proper person and saith he cannot gainsay the Plaintiffs action against him and confesses judgment for one
hundred and forty dollars and fifty six cents the debt in the Declaration
mentioned together with this further sum of three dollars and fifty one
cents interest thereon at the rate of six per cent per anum. It is therefore considered by the Court that the Plaintiffs recover against the
Defendant their debt and interest confessed as aforesaid and also their
costs by them about said suit in this behalf expended and the said
defendant in mercy &. and the Plaintiffs agree to stay the execution
untill next Cristmas.

HENRY M. RUTLEDGE) Debt
  Against)
EDMOND RUSSELL) This day came the parties by their attorneys
and thereupon came a Jury, to wit, Wm. L. Hannah 1. Abraham Shook 2,

James P. Keith 3, Reason Isoms 4, Micajah L. Gillaspie 5, Andrew H. McCollum 6, Benjamin Franklin 7, Joseph R. Shropshire 8, Hayden Arnold 9 John J. Hayter 10, Joseph Campbell 11 & Lewis Perkins 12 who being elected tried and sworn the truth to speak upon the issure joined upon their oaths do say they find the issure in favor of the Plaintiff and assess his damages to one hundred and twelve dollars and eighty five cents. It is therefore considered by the Court that the Plaintiff recover against the defendant three hundred and thirty one dollars and ninety four cents the balance of the debt in the Declaration mentioned together with his damages aforesaid assessed by the Jury aforesaid and also his costs by him about said suit in this behalf expended for all of which Execution may issured.

CRUTCHER & ALLISON)   Case
  Against)
HAYDEN ARNOLD &
JAMES L. BRYANT)   This day came the Plaintiff by their attorney and having filed their Declaration and the Defendants being solemnly called to appear and defend this suit came not but made default. It is therefore considered by the Court that the Plaintiff recover against the Defendants such damages as they may have sustained by reason of the non performance of the assumptions in the Declaration mentioned which damages are to be enquired of by a Jury at the next Term of this Court.

(p-543)   J. W. & A. L. CAMPBELL & CO.)
         Against)
         JAMES ESTILL)   This day came the defendant by his attorney and prayed an appeal from the judgment of the Court heretofore at this Term rendered against him to the next circuit Court to be held for this County bond & security given and the appeal granted.

This day the Grand Jury came into Open Court and returned a Bill of Indictment against Benjamin F. Jenkins for an assault & Battery a True Bill also a Presentment against Martha Taylor for retailing liquor.

SPYKER & DECHERD   )   Sci Fa
  Against)
JOSEPH R. SHROPSHIRE
  ADMINISTRATOR OF)
CATHARINE SHROPSHIRE DECD.)   This day came the Plaintiff by their attorney and moved the Court to revive the Judgment in the Scire Facias mentioned against the said defendant and it appearing to the satisfaction of the Court that the Scire Facias has been regularly served upon the defendant, who failed to show cause why said Judgment should not be revived against him Wherefore it is considered by the Court that said Judgment be revived against the said Joseph R. Shropshire administrator as aforesaid and that the said Plaintiffs recover against said defendant administrator as afore said the sum of one hundred and twenty nine dollars the amount of the Judgment in the Scire Facias mentioned, together with the further sum of thirty dollars & ninety six cents interest thereon at the rate of six per cent per anum from the rendition of said Judgment up to this time, and also the further sum twelve dollars and eighteen cents the costs about said suit expended, and also the costs about this Sci Fa in this behalf expended for all which an execution may issure &.

JAMES ARMSTRONG   )
 Against   )
MICAJAH L. GILLASPIE   )   This day came the Parties by their attorneys
and the Plaintiffs attorney moved the Court to set aside the Judgment
rendered in this cause at the present Term of this Court and it appearing
to the Court that the said plaintiff since the last term of this Court has
departed this life, Whereupon it is ordered by the Court that said
Judgment be set aside and the said plaintiff by his attorney suggests the
death of the said Plaintiff which is admitted to be true. It is therefore
ordered by the Court that this cause be continued untill the next Term
of this Court.

(p-544)   THE STATE OF TENNESSEE)
            Against   )
       WILLIAM P. STOVALL   )   This day came the attorney General
who prosecutes for the State in this behalf and James Williams who was
recognized to appear and prosecute and give evidence in behalf of the
State against the said defendant for an assault & Battery being solemnly
called failed to appear according to his said recognizance wherefore it
is considered by the Court that he forfeit his said recognizance wherefore it is considered by the Court that the State of Tennessee recover
against the said James Williams fifty dollars the penalty in said recognizance mentioned and that a Scire Facias issue aga'nst him returnable to
the next Term of this Court to Show cause if any he can why said Judgment
should not be made absolute.

THE STATE OF TENNESSEE   )
    Against   )
WM. P. STOVALL   )   This day came the Attorney General who
prosecute for the State in this behalf and moved the Court to enter a
noleprosequi in this cause wherefore it is considered by the Court that
he be permitted to enter a noleprosequi in this cause Whereupon the
Attorney General moved the Court to tax Pleasent Sutherland the prosecutor with the costs in the case for failing to appear and prosecute the
said defendant Whereupon it is considered by the Court that the States
of Tennessee recover/Pleasant Sutherland the costs about said suit expended
for which an execution may issure &.

JOSEPH KLEPPER   )   Case
 Against   )
C. B. H. AKE   ) This day came the Plaintiff by his attorney and
thereupon came a Jury, to wit, Wm. L. Hannah 1, Abraham Shook 2,
James P. Keith 3, Reason Isom 4, Michajah l. Gillaspie 5, Andrew H.
McCollum 6, Benjamin Franklin 7, Joseph R. Shropshire 8, Hayden Arnold 9
John J. Hayten 10, Joseph Campbell 1, & Lewis Perkins 12 who being
elected tried and Sworn well and truly to inquire of damages in this
cause upon their oaths do say the plaintiff hath sustained damages by
reason of the non performance of the assumptions in the Declaration
metioned to the amount of twenty eight dollars and twenty cents. It is
therefore considered by the Court that the plaintiff recover against
the defendant his damages aforesaid assessed by the Jury aforesaid and
also his costs by him about said suit in this behalf expended for all
of which execution may issure &.

(p-545)   JOSEPH HINKLE   )   Covenanat
          Against   )
          KINDRED H. MUSE   )   This day came the Plaintiff by his
attorney and having filed his Declaration and the defendant being solemnly
called to appear and defend this suit came not but made default, wherefore
it is considered by the Court that the Plaintiff recover against the
defendant three hundred and twenty three dollars the damages which he
has sustained by reason of the non performance of the covenants in the
Declaration mentioned and also his costs by him about said suit in this
behalf expended and the said defendant in mercy &.

        A additional list of Sales of the Estate of Wm. Trigg decd. was
returned into Open Court was received by the Court and ordered to be
recorded.

PORTLAND J. CURLE   )   Motion
 Against   )
JOHN D. STOVALL   )   This day came the plaintiff by his attorney
and it appearing to the satisfaction of the Court that at the last term
of this Court Robert S. Sharp obtained a Judgment against John D. Stovall
and Portland J. Curle upon a bond for the appearance of the said John D.
Stovall under the insolvent laws for the sum of one hundred and six dollars
& forty one cents debt also for the further sum of $3.59 cents cost. And
it appearing also to the satisfaction of the Court that the said Curle was
the security only of said John D. Stovall in the said bond & that he has
paid & satisfied the Judgment in full. It is therefore considered by the
Court that the said Curle recover against the said Stovall the aforesaid
sum of one hundred & six dollars & forty one cents. & also the further sum
of $3.59, being the amount paid by the said Curle as security for said
Stovall as aforesaid and also his costs by him about his motion in this
behalf expanded for all of which Execution may issure.

        Court adjourned untill Court in course.
                                    James Keith
                                    R. P. Harris
                                    John Dougherty

November Term 1835
(p-546)   State of Tennessee
At a Court of Pleas and Quarter Session begun & held for Franklin
County on the fourth Monday in November A. D. 1835 it being the twenty
third day of said month and in the sixtieth year of the Independance of
the United States of America. Present thirteen of the acting Justices of
the peace for Franklin County.

A deed of conveyance from Allen Yowell to Ezekiel E. Thacker for
one hundred and twenty five acres of land lying in Franklin County was
duly proven in Open Court by the oaths of William Bicknell & Jordon
Anderson subscribing witnesses thereto to be the act and deed of the said
Allen Yowell on the day that it bears date. Whereupon it is ordered by
the Court to be certified for registration. Let it be registered.

A deed of conveyance from Allen Yowell to Ezekeel E. Thacker for
one hundred acres of land lying in Franklin County was duly proven in
Open Court by the oath of William Bicknill and Jordon Anderson Subscribing witnesses thereto to be the act and deed of the said Allen Yowell on
the day that it bears date. Whereupon it is ordered by the Court to be
certified for registration. Let it be registered.

A deed of conveyance from Richard Charles to John Tarwater for
eighteen acres of land lying in Franklin County was duly acknowledged in
Open Court by the said Richard Charles to be his act and deed. Whereupon
it is ordered by the Court to be certified for registration. Let it be
registered.

A deed of conveyance from Richard Charles to Ephraim Cate for
twenty eight & one half acres of land lying in Franklin County was duly
acknowledged in open Court by the said Richard Charles to be his act and
deed. Whereupon it is ordered by the Court to be certified for registration
Let it be registered.

A deed of conveyance from William Jenkins to Richard Charles for one
hundred and thirty acres of land lying in Franklin County was duly proven
in open Court by the oaths of Isaac Henry & William Charles subscribing
witnesses thereto to be the act and deed of the said William Jenkins on
the day that it bears date Whereupon it is ordered by the Court to be
certified for registration. Let it be registered.

(p-547)   A deed of conveyance from Robert Puckett to Richard Charles for
one hundred acres of land lying in Franklin County was duly proven in
Open Court by the oaths of William Charles & Isaac Henry subscribing
witnesses thereto to be the act and deed of the said Robert Puckett on
the day that it bears date. Whereupon it is ordered by the Court to be
certified for registration. Let it be registered.

A deed of conveyance from William Jenkins to Richard Charles for
fifty three acres of land lying in Franklin County was duly proven in
Open Court by the oaths of William Charles & Isaac Henry subscribing
Witnesses thereto to be the act and deed of the said William Jenkins on
the day that it bears date Whereupon it is ordered by the Court to be
certified for registration. Let it be registered.

A deed of conveyance from Nicholas Lasater to Wm. H. Byron one hundred and sixty five acres of land lying in Franklin County was duly proven in Open Court by the oaths of Henry Byron & W. L. Lasater subscribing witnesses thereto to be the act and deed of the said Nicholas Lasater on the day that it bears date. Whereupon it is ordered by the Court to be certified for registration. Let it be registered.

A deed of Trust from David G. Harris to John R. Patrick for one house and lot in Salem Franklin County Tennessee was duly acknowledged in Open Court by the said David G. Harris & John R. Patrick to be their act and deed. Whereupon it is ordered by the Court to be certified for registration. Let it be registered.

A deed of conveyance from James A. Drake to John R. Patrick for two hundred two & one half acres of land lying in Franklin County was duly proven in open Court by the oaths of George Hudspeth one of the subscribing witnesses thereto to be the act and deed of the said James B. Drake on the day that it bears date. Whereupon it be certified.

A deed of conveyance from Leroy D. Bean to Robert Turner for sixty acres of land lying in Franklin County was duly acknowledged in Open Court by the said Leroy D. Bean to be his act and deed. Whereupon it is ordered by the Court to be certified for registration. Let it be registered.

(p-548)   Ordered by the Court that Daniel Finch be appointed overseer of the road from Elk River to Pattons lane in room of Edward Swan and that he keep the same in good repair according to law and that James B. Stovall Esqr. give a list of hands to work on said road.

Ordered by the Court that Wiley Purdom be appointed overseer of the road of the first class from the county line to the North End of Ephraim Cates lane in room of Isaac Henry and that he keep the same in god repair according to law and that he have the same hands that worked under the former overseer.

Ordered by the Court the Edmond Dyer be appointed overseer of the road of the second Class from Winchester to William Street's Gin in room of John G. Brazelton and that he keep the same in good repair according to law and that he have the same hands that worked under the former overseer.

Ordered by the Court that Enos England be appointed overseer of the road from Winchester to said England's own house in room of Benjamin Deckerd and that he keep the same in good repair according to law and that he have the same hands that worked under said Decherd.

Ordered by the Court that James Bledsoe be appointed overseer of the road from George Davidsons to Goshen meeting house in room of Thomas Cunningham and that he keep the same in good repair according to law and that he have to same hands that worked under the said Cunningham.

Ordered by the Court that Elias Smith be appointed overseer of the road from his mill to near where the road intersects Mrs. Goodmans in room of Franklin Payne and that he keep the same in good repair according to law and that he have the same hands that worked under the said Payne.

Ordered by the Court the William Thompson be appointed overseer of the road of the second class from Caldwell's Bridge to the foot of the mountain at James Pettys and that he keep the same in good repair according to law and that John Oliver Esqr give him a list of hands to work on said road.

Ordered by the Court that John M. Morrow be appointed overseer of the road of the second class from James Howards (p-549) to Benjamin Nevill's and that he keep the same in good repair according to law and that George W. Thompson Esqr allot hands to work on said road.

Ordered by the Court that Harvey Cowan be appointed overseer of the road from the Big Pond to David Decherd in room of Farly B. Wade and that be keep the same in good repair according to law and that he have the same hands that worked under the said Wade together with Tom Greens'.

Ordered by the Court that John B. Hawkins be appointed overseer of the road from Hugh Montgomienys to the Big Pond in room of James Montgomery and that he keep the same in good repair according to law and that he have the same hands that worked under said Montgomeny.

Ordered by the Court that Nathan Gillaspie be appointed overseer of the road of the second class from Lessford on Elk River to the Williford place in room of Richard Sims and that he keep the same in good repair according to law and that he have the same hands that worked under said Sims.

Ordered by the Court that George West Overseer of a road in the sinking cove be permitted to purchase a Sledge hamer crow bar & two matooks for the use of said road and that he present his account at the next Term of this Court for allowance.

This day David O. Anderson & George Mosely came into Court and resigned their appointment as School commissioners of the School tract of land at the mouth of Beans Creek which resignations was received by the court and the court doth order upon sufficient cause shown that John Silon the other commissioner of said tract of School land be removed and that William McElroy, Wm. H. Lucus & Hezekiah Faris be appointed commissioners of said tract of School land in room of said former commissioners

Ordered by the Court that William M. Cowan be appointed a constable to attend on this court in room of James N. Chiles who is unable to attend on account of sickness.

This day William H. Wisemen came into Open Court and took the necessary oaths of qualification as an attorney of this Court. Whereupon he is admitted as an attorney of this Court.

(p-550) Ordered by the Court that Absalom Blythe be released from paying to the collector of taxes for the year 1835 seven dollars & twenty five cents the tax on three thousand eight hundred and seventy acres of new entered land overcharged on the tax list for said year and that a certificate hereof be a good voucher for the sheriff on a settlement of his account.

Ordered by the Court that Joseph Bradford be released from all
released from all responsibility on his Indentures binding to him
William Brooks and that said Indintures be recinded & made void.

Ordered by the Court that James Robinson be appointed to purchase
a standard of weights and measures for the County of Franklin and when
said purchase is made that he bring in his account for allowance.

This day came on an election for the purpose of electing a constable
in & for the county of Franklin in the bounds of Millers company for
the next ensuing two years and on accounting out the votes it was found
that Armon Gipson was duly and constitutionally elected constable in &
for said County in the bounds of said company who entered into bond with
John Oliver, Charles Darnell & Larson Rowe his securties in the sum of
one thousand dollars according to law and was qualified accordingly.

This day came on an election for the purpose of electing a constable
in & for the County of Franklin in the bounds of Captain Muses Company and
on counting out the votes it was found that Allison Muse was duly and
consittutionally elected constable in the bounds of said company for the
next ensuing two years who entered into bond with Richmond P. Harris &
Joab Short his securities in the sum of one thousand dollars according
to law and was qualified accordingly.

Ordered by the Court that Joseph Klepper Thomas Wilson & Joseph
Bradford be appointed commissioners to lay off to Mrs. Martha Isacks one
years support out of the Estate of Jacob be Isacks decd and that they make
report to the next Term of this Court.

Ordered by the Court that William S. Mooney Thompson Ivins &
William D. Markum be appointed commissioners to settle with David
Muckleroy who was appointed to take care of the Estate of Alexander Floyd
decd. and that they make their report to the next Term of this Court.

(p-551)   Ordered by the Court that George Hudspeth Peter Simmons &
Richard C. Hodler be appointed Commissioners to settle with David G. Harris
& James B. Harris Executors of the last will and testament of James Harris
deceased and that they make their report to the next Term of this Court.

Ordered by the Court that Peter Simmons, John Staples & John S.
Martin be appointed commissioners to settle with Susan Trigg administratrix of the Estate of James S. McWhorter deceased and that they make their
report to the next term of this Court.

Ordered by the Court that Richmond P. Harris, Willis Burt &
Joseph Smith be appointed commissioners to settle with Milas M. Hall
administrator of the Estate of Abner Davidson deceased and that they make
their report to the next term of this Court.

Ordered by the Court that Zachariah Wortham be appointed overseer
of the road from Logans to the creek and that he keep the same in good
repair according to law and that he have his own hands.

Ordered by the Court that John R. Patrick, Cornelias Homan &
John Staples be appointed commissioners to value and divide the negroes

between the heirs of Thomas G. Jones deceased and that they make their report to the Next Term of this Court.

Ordered by the Court that Benjamin F. Hollins George W. Richardson & John W. Camden be appointed commissioners to settle with the administrator of the Estate of Wyatt Ballard decd and that they make their report to the next Term of this Court.

This day the amount of Sales of the Estate of John Saxton deceased was returned into open Court was received by the court and ordered to be made a part of the record.

This day the commissioners of the tract of School land at the mouth of Beans Creek made their return which was received by the Court and ordered to be made a part of the record.

This day the amount of Sales of the Estate of William Littlepage decd. was returned into Open Court was received by the Court and ordered to be made a part of the record.

(p-552) This day the commissioners of the tract of School land on rock creek made their return into Open Court which was received by the Court and ordered to be made a part of the record.

This day the commissioners appointed to settle with John Frame administrator with the Will annexed of the Estate of Ezekeel Philips deceased made their report which was received by the Court and ordered to be recorded.

Ordered by the Court that the order made at the last Term of this Court to sell the negroes belonging to the Estate of Robert Hudspeth deceased be so altered as to make it legal for said negroes to be sold on the premises where said Robert Hudspeth lived at the time of his death.

It appearing to the satisfaction of the Court that Jacob C. Isacks late of this County died intestate and Martha Isacks the Widow of said deceased & Benjamin Decherd applied for letters of administration on the estate of said decedent. Whereupon it is ordered by the Court that they have letters accordingly who entered into separate bonds to wit, Martha Isacks with Christopher Bullard her security in the sum of five thousand dollars and Benjamin Decherd with Mark Hutchins his security in the sum of five thousand dollars according to law and was qualified accordingly.

Ordered by the Court that Martha Isacks be appointed Guardian over the persons and property of Corella, Harrett Newel, Ann Pryor, Andrew Jackson & Rachel Abegail Isacks orphans of Jacob C. Isacks deceased who entered into bond with Christopher Bullard her security in the sum of ten thousand dollars according to law.

This day the Last Will & Testament of Fleet W. Neighbors deceased was produced in Open Court by the executor therein named whereupon came Peter Burroughs & Eli Silmon subscribing witnesses thereto who being first duly sworn deposed and say that the said Fleet W. Neighbors signed the same in their presence and that at the time of signing the same be the the said Fleet W. Neighbor was of Sound & disposing mind & memory and

168

that they signed the same as witnesses thereto at his request. Whereupon it is ordered by the Court to be recorded whereupon came Benson Neighbors the executors therein named and was qualified as Executor to execute said last Will & Testament who entered into bond with John M. Morrow & Saul Camp his securities in the sum of one thousand dollars according to law.

(p-553)   On petition of James Yericks to keep an ordinary at his house in Franklin County it is therefore ordered by the Court that he have license accordingly for the term of one year who entered into bond with Wm. M. Cowan & Benjamin F. Gibson be securities in the sum of five thousand dollars according to law & was qualified accordingly.

This day Anderson F. Willis came into Open Court and was qualified as executor of the last will and testament of Alexander Floyd deceased, who entered into bond with Peter Willis & Joseph Floyd his securities in the sum of eight thousand dollars according to law.

Present Zacharah H. Murrell, Andrew Mann, Andrew Campbell, John R. Patrick, James Robinson, Richmond P. Harris, Wm. Lasater Samuel Norwood John Dougherty George Gray, George Hudspeth John Oliver & James B. Stovall Esqrs.

Ordered by the Court that Thomas Finch Sheriff of Franklin County be allowed the sum of five dollars of removing Hannah Arnold, from Samuel A. Harris to the poor house on rock creek and that the County Trustee pay him the same the Ayes & Noes being taken were unanimous in favor of the allowance Isd.

Present Zacharah H. Murrell, Andrew Mann, Andrew Campbell, John R. Patrick, James Robinson, Richmond P. Harris, Wm. Lasater, Samuel Norwood, John Daugherty, George Gray, George Hudspeth, John Oliver James B. Stovall & James Kelly Esqrs.

Ordered by the Court that Mrs. Eunice Witten be allowed the sum of seventy five dollars for the support of her Self and daughter for twelve months to be approprated By William Buchanan and that the Clerk issure a certificate to the County Trustee to pay the same the ayes & noes being taken those who voted in the affirmative are Zacharah H. Murrell, Andrew Mann, Andrew Campbell, James Robinson, Samuel Norwood, John Oliver, James B. Stovall & James Kelly and those who voted in the negative are John R. Patrick, Richmond P. Harris Wm. Lasater & George Hudspeth. Isd.

Present Zacharah H. Murrell, Andrew Mann, John R. Patrick, James Robinson, Richmond P. Harris, William Lasater, Samuel Norwood, John Dougherty, George Gray, George Hudspeth, John Oliver, James B. Stovall & James Kelly Esqrs.

Ordered by the Court that Lucinda Wilson a pauper of Franklin County be allowed the sum of forty dollars for her support one year to be approprated by James B. Stovall and that the clerk issue a certificate to the County Trustee to pay the same the ayes & noes being (p-554) taken those who voted in the affirmative are Andrew Mann, James Robinson Samuel Norwood, John Dougherty, George Gray, John Oliver, James B. Stovall and James Kelly and those who voted in the negative are Zacharah H. Murrell John R. Patrick, Richmond P. Harris Wm. Lasater & George Hudspeth.

Present Zachariah H. Murrell, Andrew Mann, Andrew Campbell, James Robinson Richmond P. Harris, Wm. Lasater, Samuel Norwood, John Dougherty George Gray, George Hudspeth, John Oliver, James B. Stovall & James Kelly Esqrs. Ordered by the Court that John Byrom be allowed the sum of seventy dollars for building a cabbin at the poor house in Franklin County and that the Clerk issure a certificate to the County Trustee to pay him the same which was unanimously allowed by said Justices. Isd.

Present Zachariah H. Murrell Andrew Mann, Andrew Campbell, James Robinson Richmond P. Harris, Wm. Lasater, Samuel Norwood John Dougherty, George Gray, George Hudspeth, John Oliver, James B. Stovall & James Kelly Esqrs.

Present Zachariah H. Murrell Andrew Mann, Andrew Campbell, James Robinson Richmond P. Harris, Wm. Lasater, Samuel Norwood, John Dougherty George Gray, George Hudspeth, John Oliver, James B. Stovall & James Kelly Esqrs.

Ordered by the Court that Alexander W. Majors be allowed the sum of Sixty two dollars & fifty cents the balance for his services as keeper at the poor house for the year 1835 and that the Clerk issure a certificate to the County Trustee to pay him the same which allowance was unanimously made by the Justices.

Present Zacharah H. Murrell, Andrew Mann, Andrew Campbell, ~~John R. Patrick~~ James Robinson, Richmond P. Harris, Wm. Lasater, Samuel Norwood, John Dougherty, George Gray, George Hudspeth, John Oliver James B. Stovell & James Kelly Esqrs.

Ordered by the Court that James L. Williamson jailor of Franklin County be allowed five dollars & eighty seven & one half cents for keeping Alexander McCambridge in jail five days and for four Turn Keys and for two locks bout for the use of said jail and that the Clerk issure a certificate to the County Trustee to pay him the same which allowance was unanimously made by said Justices. Isd.

Present Zachariah H. Murrell, Andrew Mann, Andrew Campbell, John R. Patrick, James Robinson, Richmond P. Harris, Wm. Lasater, Samuel Norwood John Dougherty, George Gray, George Hudspeth, John Oliver James B. Stovall & James Kelly Esqrs.

Ordered by the Court that Willie B. Wagner clerk of Franklin County Court be allowed the sum of twenty dollars for making out & delivering to the Sheriff a complete list of polls & taxable property for the year 1835 & recording the same and that the county Trustee pay the same which allowance was unanimously made by said Justices.

(p-555) Present Zachariah H. Murrell, Andrew Mann, Andrew Campbell John R. Patrick, James Robinson, Richmond P. Harris, Wm. Lasater, Samuel Norwood, John Dougherty George Gray, George Hudspeth, John Oliver James B. Stovall & James Kelly Esqrs.

Ordered by the Court that Coonrod Hice be allowed the sum of eight dollars for purchasing one sledge hammer and crow bar for the use of the public road and that the County Trustee pay him the same which allowance was unanimously made by said justices. Isd.

(p-556)   We the Surveyor & commissioners by an ordered by the County Court after being duly sworn did divide the lands of Robert Hudspeth deceased agreeable to said orders between the widow & said heirs to the best of our knowledge taken three days to do the same. Given under our hands this 19th Nov. 1835.

                         D. O. Anderson Suvr.
                         David Arnett
                         Arod. Hatchett
                         George Foster
                         John Staples
Whereupon the Court doth order that D. O. Anderson the Surveyor be allowed the sum of six dollars & the other commissioners three dollars each for their services in dividing said land to be paid by the administrator of said Estate.

Ordered by the Court that the Overseer of the road be authorized to turn the road on the North side of the boiling fork of Elk River so that said road run between the bridge & the mill and under the bridge to the opposite side of the River & it shall be the duty of the Sheriff to notify said overseer of the order.

        Court adjourned untill tomorrow morning ten o'clock.
                         James Robinson
                         John Dougherty
                         Samuel Norwood.

Tuesday November the 24th one thousand eight hundred and thirty five Court met according to adjournment. Present four of the acting Justices of the peace for Franklin County.

A deed of conveyance from James Woods to John Handly for forty seven acres & eighty poles of land lying in Franklin County was duly acknowledged in open Court by the said James Woods to be his act and deed Whereupon it is ordered by the Court to be certified for registration. Let it be registered.

A deed of conveyance from William Ward & Leah his wife to Felix G. Ake for one tenth part of two hundred and sixty two acres of land lying in Bedford County was duly proven in open Court by the oaths of Jethro Goodman &Walter Miliham subscribing witnesses thereto to be the act and deed of the said William Ward & Leah his wife on the day that it bears date. Whereupon it is ordered by the Court to be certified for registration. Let it be registered.

(p-557)   This day Edmond Dyer brough into open Court one old wolf scalp and being examined on oath by the Court, the Court doth order that he have a certificate to the Treasury of Middle Tennessee for three dollars for the same. Isd.

Ordered by the Court that James Robinson, John Goodwin & Mark Hutchins be appointed commissioners to settle with Benjamin Decherd administrator of the Estate of Alexander S. Acklin deceased and that they make their report to the next Term of this Court.

Ordered by the Court that Willis Webb be appointed overseer of the Shelbyville road from Winchester to Elk River in room of Thomas Finch and that he keep the same in good repair according to law and that have the same hands that worked under the said Finch.

Ordered by the Court that Ann Floyd be appointed Guardian over the person and property of Mary Ann Floyd orphan of Alexander Floyd deceased by her coming into Court and entering into bond & security according to law during the present Term of this Court.

This day Peter Lenehan came into Open Court and resigned his appointment as school commissioner of the tract of school land near Mchergs ford which was received by the Court.

HENRY M. RUTLEDGE) Case
Against)
FELIX G. AKE) This day came the defendant into open Court and saith he cannot gainsay the plaintiffs action against him and confesses Judgment for the sum of ninety eight dollars damages Whereupon it is considered by the Court that the plaintiff recover against the defendant said sum of ninety eight dollars confessed as aforesaid and also his costs by him about said suit in this behalf expended and the said defendant in mercy &. and the plaintiff agrees to stay the execution untill the 1st of February next.

Ordered by the Court that William Simmons Esqr be appointed to give James Woods Overseer of the road a list of hands to work on the same.

Ordered by the Court that Lewis Harris be appointed overseer of the road from Esqr. Cunningham to Lackeys Gin in (p-558) room of Henry Gotcher and that he keep the same in good repair according to law and that he have the same hands that worked under the former overseer.

Ordered by the Court that the collector of the public taxes in Franklin County for the year 1835 refund to Squire B. Hawkins seventy five cents the tax on one black poll overcharged on the tax list for the year 1835 and that the Sheriff have a credit for the same on a settlement of his accounts with the county Trustee.

Ordered by the Court that Bledsoe Stewart be appointed overseer of the road from the forks of the road to a pond on the mountain and that he keep the same in good repair according to law and that James Kelly Esqr. give him a list of hands to work on said road and that he be permitted to purchase a sledge hammer crow bar & Matock for the use of said road and that he bring in his account for allowance at the next Term of this Court.

Ordered by the Court that George West be appointed overseer of the road from the State line to Adam S. Capertons Mill and that he keep the same in good repair according to law and that James Kelly Esqr. give him a list of hands to work on said road.

Ordered by the Court that Edwin Street be appointed Guardian over the persons and property of Leah, Jane, Mary A. Andrew Jackson & Charles H. Matlock orphans of William Matlock Deceased by his coming into Court and entering into bond & security according to law during the present Term of this Court.

This day William H. Matlock came into Open Court and chose John J. Hayter for his Guardian which is by the Court ordered accordingly by his coming into Court and entering into bond & security according to law during the present Term of this Court.

Ordered by the Court that Martha Raines be appointed Guardian over the person and property of Ann Mariah Raines who entered into bond with Henry A. Raines & Felix G. Ake her securities in the sum of fourteen hundred dollars according to law.

(p-559)   Ordered by the Court that the following persons be appointed Jurors to the next County Court, to wit, William Reeves1, James Logan 2, James A. Snowden 3, Robert Cowan 4, Daniel Keith 5, Wm. Thurmon 6, Thomas Muse 7, Absalom Guess 8, William Byrom 9, David Osborn 10, Lunsford L. Mathews 11, Joseph Franklin 12, Harmon Riddle 13, Hansford Arnett 14, Sandridge Arnett 15, Peter Helstan 16, William Bridges 17, Joseph Huddleston Jr. 18, Wm. P. Marten 19, Farlaigh B. Wade 20, Abner Adams 21 William Wallis 22 Squire B. Hawkins 23, William B. Knight 24, Thomas C. Duncan 25 & Edward Martin Jr. 26, and that William M. Cowan & John G. Brazelton be appointed constable to attend on said Court and that the Sheriff sum them to attend and make due return to the next Term of this Court.

Ordered by the Court that the following Justices of the peace be appointed to take a list of taxable property and polls in & for the County of Franklin for the year 1836 to wit, Samuel Norwood Esqr in captain Shooks Company, John Dougherty in Captain Nances Company James Robinson Esqr. in Captain Hines' Company, James F. Green Esqr. in Capt. Faris Company, William Simmons Esqr in Captain Wood's Old Company, John R. Patrick Esqr. in the Salem Company, William Larkins Esqr. in Captain Kavanaughs Company, David Bill Esqr. in Captain McClouds old Company Zachariah H. Murrell Esqr. in Captain Tipps Company, Asa D. Oakly Esqr. in Captain Brooks Old Company, Andrew Mann Esqr. in Captain Browns Company, James Byrom Esqr In Captain Majors Company Richmond P. Harris Esqr. in Captain D. B. Muses old Company, Thomas Wright Esqr. in Captain Stephens Company Jesse Jenkins Esqr. in Captain Burrows Company, John W. Camden Esqr. in Captain Deans, Company, James B. Stovall Esqr. in Captain Stamps Company George W. Thompson Esqr. in Captain Wilkinsons Company, John Jones Esqr. in Captain Sanders Old Company, Samuel Bradshaw Esqr. in Captain Gilliams Old Company, John Oliver Esqr. in Captain Millers Company, Jeremiah Blackard Esqr. in Captain Khights Company, James Robinson Esqr in Captain Martins Company, William Crownover Esqr in Captain Govers Company, Adam S. Caperton Esqr. in Captain Chiles Company and that they take in the same according to law and make due return to the next Term of this Court.

This day Benjamin Decherd Guardian for Edmond Russell came into Court and made his return upon oath which was received by the Court and ordered to be recorded.

(p-560)   Ordered by the Court that William K. Cowling Joseph Bratton, Joseph Coker, Rowland Lane & William Lane be appointed a Jury of view to view and turn the road leading through the land of James Greenlee, also on the north side of the river through the land of John J. Hayter to the Bridge across the river and that they view and turn the same having due regard to the convenience of travelers and as little as may be to the prejudice of Individuals and that they make their report to the next Term of this Court.

Ordered by the Court that Jesse Reynolds James B. Stovall & Samuel Bradshaw Esqrs. be appointed to examine the Bridge built across Elk River at Makerys ford and that they make their report at the next Term of this Court.

This day the inventory of the Estate of Wm. Hedger deceased was produced into Open Court was received by the Court and ordered to be recorded.

This day the amount of Sales of the Estate of Wm. Hedger decd was produced into Open Court was received by the Court and ordered to be recorded.

On petition of Polly Goin and the Court being Satisfied from the Statements of John Farris upon oath that she is the offspring of Aaron and Nacy Goin free people of color ordered that she have a certificate hereof from the Clerk of this Court.

This day came James Woods one of the Executors named in the last Will & Testament of Hannah Woods deceased and move the Court to prove said will, and it appearing to the satisfaction of the Court from the deposititions of Richard C. Arnett & Abigail Gibon the subscribing witnesses to said will taken in pursuance of an order made at the last term of this Court that it is the last Will & Testament of Hannah Woods deceased Whereupon it is ordered by the Court to be recorded Whereupon James Woods was qualified as Executor of said will came into Court and was qualified as executor of said will who entered into bond, with John handley his security in the sum of three thousand dollars according to law.

Court adjourned untill tomorrow morning ten o'clock
James Robinson
James Keith
John Dougherty

(p-561)   Wednesday November the twenty fifth one thousand eight hundred and thirty five Court met according to adjournment.
Present - James Robinson   ) Esquires
         James Keith &   )   Justices of the peace for Franklin County
         John Dougherty   )

The State of Tennessee
Proclamation being made the Sheriff of Franklin County made return of the States Writ of venire facias to the Court that he had summond the following persons being all good and lawful men of said County of Franklin County and being citzens of said County of Franklin to attend and serve

as Jurors at the present Term of this Court which persons so summoned
and returned as aforesaid had been nominated for that purpose by the
Justices of this said Court of Pleas and Quarter Sessions of said County
of Franklin at its last Session a list of whom was delivered to the Sheriff
of this said County by the Clerk of this said Court, to wit, Edwin M.
Tatum, James Taylor, James P. Keith, John K. Burton, William Francis,
Miles Francis, John D. Fennell, Willis Holder, Solomon Holder, Joab Short
Wiley Denson, David Robinson, Littleton Faris, Edward H. Wade, Absalom
Faris Senr. Joseph Bradford, John P. Davidson, John B. Wilkinson, John
Howard, William Taylor, John Frame, James V. Acklin, Edmond P. Lee,
Joseph Acklin, Hamilton Stewart, Bledsoe Stewart, and of whom the follow-
ing this day attended, to wit, Edwin Tatum, James Taylor, John K. Burton,
William Francis, Miles Francis John D. Fennell, Willis Holder, Solomon
Holder, Wiley Denson, David Robinson Littliton Faris, Edward H. Wade, A
Absalom Faris Senr. Joseph Bradford John P. Davidson, John Howard,
William Taylor, John Frame, James V. Acklin & Hamilton Stewart, and of
whom the following persons being good & lawful men of said county of
Franklin were elected empanneled sworn and charged to enquire for the
body of the County aforesaid, to wit, John Frame, Who was appointed
foreman Joseph Bradford, William Taylor, John K. Burton, John Howard,
John P. Davidson, Edward H. Wade, James V. Acklin, Solomon Holder,
David Robinson, Absalom Faris Senr, Wm. A. Francis & Littleton Faris
who after receiving their charge retired to consult of their present0
ments.

On moution of John Goodwin Esqr. it is ordered by the Court that
William H. Wisemen be appointed attorney General protem during the present
term of this Court Whereupon Wm. H. Wiesmen came into Court and was
qualified as atto. Genl. protem ~~during this term of the court~~

(p-562)   A power of Attorney from Mary E. Matlock to Edwin Street was
duly acknowledged in Open Court by the said Mary E. Matlock to be her
act and deed. Whereupon it is ordered by the Court to be certified.

Ordered by the Court that Joseph Acklin, Joab Short, John B. Wilkinson & Edwin M. Tatum be fined the sum of two dollars and fifty cents
each for their non attendance as Jurors summoned on the original pannel
and that a fi fa issure against them for the same.

LITTY WHITE   )
 Against   )
ZACHARIAH H. MURRELL ADMIN &   )
WINNING PHILIPS ADMIN OF THE   )
ESTATE OF JAS PHILIPS DECD   ) This day came the plaintiff by her
attorney and moved the Court to continue this cause untill the next term
of this Court on the affidavit of James Wiseman agent fer the said
plaintiff. Whereupon it is considered by the Court from the reasons set
forth in said affidavit that this cuase be continued for trial at the
next term of this court by the plaintiff paying the costs of the term.
Whereupon it is considered by the Court the defendant recover against
the plaintiff their costs about said suit at this Term expended and the
said Plaintiff in mercy &.

ANDREW W. CARENTON   )
 Against   )
William Ransom   ) This day came the Plaintiff by his attorney and

moved the Court for a commission to issure to any one Justice of the peace for the County of Carroll & State of Mississippi to take the deposition of Green W. Caperton to be read as evidence on the trial of the above cause on behalf of the plaintiff which is by the Court ordered accordingly by the Plaintiff giving the defendant thirty days notice of the time & place of taking said deposition.

JOHN OLIVER)   Case
 Against)
C. B. H. AKE) This day came the Plaintiff by this attorney and thereupon came a Jury to wit, John D. Fennell 1, Willis Holder 2, James Taylor 3, Hamilton Stewart 4, Wiley Denson 5, Joseph Campbell 6, Daniel Waggoner 7, Joseph Halpane 8, Archibald W. Nance 9, Daniel M. Roddy 10, Richard B. Moore 11, & Wm. Hendon 12, who being elected tried and sowrn well & truly to enquire of damages in this cause upon their oaths do say the plaintiff hath sustained damages by reason of the non performance of the assumptions in the Declaration mentioned to the amount of eighty dollars & seventy four cents (p-563) It is therefore considered by the Court that the plaintiff recover against the Defendant his damages aforesaid and also his costs by him about said suit in this behalf expended and the said defendant in mercy &.

MARK HUTCHINS ADMIN &)
MARTHA WALKER ADMINRX)
 VS)
JAMES ROBINSON)
WILLIAM DARDIS) This day came the parties by their attorney and by their mutual consent this cause is continued untill the next Term of this Court.

ROBERT GIBSON)
 Against)
GEORGE W. Thompson) This day came the plaintiff by his attorney and dismisses his suit and not further their prosecuting it is ordered that this suit be dismissed and the defendant assumes the costs. It is therefore considered by the Court that the plaintiff recover against the defendant his costs by him about said suit in this behalf expended and the said defendant in mercy &.

DANIEL WAGGONER JR &)   Case
DAVID WAGGONER EXECUTORS OF)
the last WILL & TESTAMENT OF)
DANIEL WAGGONER DEC'D)
 Against)
LUNSFORD L. MATHEWS) This day came the parties by their attorneys and thereupon came a Jury to wit, John D. Fennell 1, Willis Holder 2, Hamilton Stewart 3, Wiley Denson 4, Joseph Campbell 5, Miles Francis 6, Joseph Halpane 7, Archibald W. Nace 8, Daniel M. Roddy 9, Richard M. Moore 10, Wm. Hendon 11, & James Taylor 12 who being elected, tried and sworn the truth to speak upon the issue joined upon their oaths do say they find the issure in favor of the plaintiffs and assess their damages to one hundred dollars. It is Therefore considered by the Court that the Plaintiffs recover against the defendant their damages aforesaid assessed by the Jury aforesaid and also their costs by them about said suit in the behalf expended and the said defendant in Mercy &. from which Judgment the

defendant prayed an appeal to the next circuit Court to be held for this
County bond & security given & the appeal granted.

NANCY PRICE) Case
Against)
JOSEPH R. SHROPSHIRE) This day came the parties by thier attorneys and
thereupon came a Jury, to wit,- Joseph Bradford 1, Wm. Taylor 2,
John K. Burton 3, John Howard 4, John P. Davidson 5, Edward H. Wade 6,
James V. Acklin 7, Solomon Holder 8, David Robinson 9, Absalom Faris Ser.10
William A. Francis 11, (p-564)   and littleton Faris 12 who being elected
tried and sworn the truth to speak upon the issue joined upon their oath's
do say they find the issue in favor of the Plaintiff and assess her
damages to two hundred and ten dollars. It is therefore considered by
the Court that the Plaintiff recover against the defendant her damages
aforesaid assessed by the Jury aforesaid and also her costs by her about
said suit in this behalf expended for all of which Execution may issue &.

JOSEPH BICKLEY ADMR.)
 Against)
JOHN HAWS) On motion of the parties by their attorneys this
cause is continued untill the next term of the Court as on affidavit of
the said defendant.

EPHRAM H. FOSTER ASSEE & C) Debt
 Against)
JAMES R. SLATTER) This day came the parties by their
attorneys and thereupon came a Jury to wit,- Joseph Bradford 1, Wm. Taylor
2, John K. Burton 3, John Howard 4, John B. Davidson 5, Edward H. Wade 6
James V. Acklin 7, Solomon Holder 8, David Robinson 9, Absalom Faris Senr.
10, William A. Francis 11 & Littleton Faris 12, who being elected, tried
and sworn the truth to speak upon the issue joined upon their oaths do say
they find the issue in favor of the plaintiff and assess his damages to
ten dollars and twenty eight cents, It is therefore considered by the
Court that the plaintiff recover against the defendant two hundred and
fifty seven dollars the debt in the Delcaration mentioned together with
his damages aforesaid assessed by the Jury aforesaid and also his cost by
him about said suit in this behalf expended for all of which execution
may issue.

PETER & JOHN SIMMONS) Debt
 Against)
MARK VANZANT ADMIS OF)
THE ESTATE OF JACOB VANZANT DEC'D) This day came the parties by
their attorneys and thereupon came a Jury, to wit,- Joseph Bradford 1,
Wm. Taylor 2, John K. Burton 3, John Howard 4, John P. Davidson 5, Edward
H. Wade 6, James V. Acklin 7, Solomon Holder 8, David Robinson, 9, Absalom
Faris Senr. 10 Wm. A. Francis 11 & Littleton Faris 12 who being elected
tried, and sworn the truth to speak upon the issue joined upon their
oaths do say they find the issue in favor of the Plaintiffs and assess
their damages to nine dollars and thirty three cents. It is therefore
considered by the Court that the Plaintiff recover aginst the defendant
four hundred dollars the debt in the Declaration mentioned together with
their damages aforesaid assessed by (p-565) the Jury aforesaid and
also their costs by them about said suit in this behalf expended and the
said defendant in Mercy & to be levied of the goods & chattles rights
and credits of Jacob Vanzant deceased in the hands of said Administratrix
to be administered.

PETER & JOHN SIMMONS) Debt
  Against)
MARY VANZANT ADMINISTRATRIX)
OF THE ESTATE OF JACOB VANZANT DEC'd) This day came the parties by their
attorneys and thereupon came a Jury, to wit,- Joseph Bradford 1, Wm. Taylor
2, John K. Burton 3, John Howard 4, John P. Davidson 5, Edward H. Wade 6
James V. Acklin 7, Solomon Holder 8, David Robinson 8, Absalom Faris Senr
10, Wm. A. Francis 11 & Littleton Faris 12 who being elected tried and
sworn the truth to speak upon the issue joined upon their oaths do say
they find the issue in favor of the plaintiffs and assess their damages
to thirty four dollars. It is therefore considered by the Court that
the plaintiffs recover against the defendant thirteen hundred and
seventy two dollars and fifty two cents the debt in the Declaration
mentioned together with their damages aforesaid assessed by the Jury
aforesaid and also their costs by them about said suit in this behalf
expended and the said defendant in mercy & to be levid of the goods &
chattels rights & credits of Jacob Vanzant deceased in the hands of
said administratrix to be administered.

THOMAS L. ANTHONY) Debt
  Against)
JOHN D. MATLOCK) This day came the parties by their attorneys
and thereupon came a Jury to wit,- Joseph Bradford 1, Wm. Taylor 2,
John K. Burton 3, John Howard 4, John P. Davidson 5, Edward H. Wade 6
James V. Acklin 7, Solomon Holder 8, David Robinson 9, Absalom Faris
Senr. 10 Wm. A. Francis 11 & Littleton Faris 12 who being elected, tried
and sworn the truth to speak upon the issue joined upon their oaths do say
they find the issue in favor of the plaintiff and assess his damages
to ten dollars & seven cents besides costs. It is therefore considered
by the Court that the plaintiff recover against the defendant two hundred
and twenty six dollars & fifty cents the debt in the Declaration mentioned
together with his damages afroesaid assessed by the Jury aforesaid and
also his costs by him about said suit in this behalf expended for all
of which execution may issue.

    This day John J. Hayter who was heretofore on yesterday chosen by
Wm. H. Matlock as his Guardian came into Court and entered into bond
with Benjamin Decherd & James Robinson his securities in (p-566)
the sum of six thousand dollars according to law.

    This day Edwin Street who was heretofore on yesterday appointed
guardian over the person & property of Leah Jane, Mary A. Andrew J. &
Charles H. Matlock came into Court and entered into bond with William
Street & Charles Crisman his securities in the sum of twenty four
thousand dollars according to law.

CHARLES DARNELL)
  Against)
NOEL B. WARREN) This day came the plaintiff by his attorney and
moved the Court to discontinue this suit, it is therefore ordered by the
Court that this suit be discontinued, and it appearing to the satisfaction of the Court that the said plaintiff has failed to take out process
regularly, Whereupon it is considered by the Court that the Defendant
go hence without day and recover against the plaintiff his costs by him
about said suit in this behalf expended for all which execution may issue.

THOMAS L. GRAY &
WILLIAM CLARK ADMIN OF   )   Debt
THE ESTATE OF JAMES   )
ARMSTRONG DECEASED   )
  Against   )
MICAJAH L. GILLASPIE   )   This day came the parties by their
attorneys and thereupon came a Jury towit, Joseph Bradford &, Wm. Taylor2
John K. Burton 3, John Howard 4, John P. Davidson 5, Edward H. Wade 6
James V. Acklin 7, Solomon Holder 8, David Robinson 8, Absalom Faris Senr
10, Wm. A. Francis 11 & Littleton Faris 12, Who being elected tried
and sworn the truth to speak upon the issure joined upon their oaths do
say they find the issure in favor of the plaintiffs and assess their
damages to seven dollars and fifty cents. It is therefore considered
by the Court that the plaintiffs recover against the defendant two hundred
& sixty six dollars & sixty six & two third cents the debt in the
Declaration mentioned together with their damages aforesaid assessed
by the Jury aforesaid and also their costs by him about said suit in
this behalf expended for all which execution may issue.

JAMES ARMSTRONG   )
  Against   )
MICAJAH L. GILLASPIE   ) This day came the plaintiff Thos. L. Gray &
Wm. Clark by his attorney and it appearing to the Court that at the
last Term of this Court the plaintiff death was suggested which was
admitted by the defendant to be true and produced in Court here the letters
of administration from which it appears that the said Thomas L. Gray &
William Clark are authorized to administer on all and singular the goods
& chattels, (p-567)   rights and credits of the said James Armstrong
deceased & moved the Court to revive this suit in their names, whereupon
it is ordered by the Court that this suit be revived in their names as
administrators and that they be authorized to prosecute the same.

LITTLEPAGE & OTHERS   )
  Against   )
ELIZABETH GILLILAND   ) This day came the defendant by her attorney
and moved the Court to continue this cause upon the affidavit of the
said Defendant and from the reasons disclosed in said affidavit the
Court doth order that this suit be continued untill the next Term of this
Court upon condition that said give security for the costs of the Term
Whereupon came John Howard and acknowledged himself the defendants security for the costs of this suit at this Term expended. Whereupon it is
considered by the Court that the plaintiff recover against the said
defendant and John Howard the costs of this suit at this Term expended
for all of which execution may issue to which opinion of the Court the
Defendant by her attorney excepts and prays an appeal in the nature of a
writ of Error to the next circuit court to be held for this County.

DANIEL M. RODDY   )
  Against   )
SAUL CAMP   ) This day came the dependant by his attorney and
moved the Court to continue this cause untill the next Term of this Court
upon the affidavit of the said defendant and from the reasons disclosed
in said affidavit it is ordered by the Court that this suit be continued
and that the said defendant pay the costs of this suit at this term
expended. It istherefore considered by the Court that the plaintiff
recover against the defendant the the costs of this suit at this Term
expended and the said defendant in mercy &.

Wm. & John H. Knox)
 Aga'nst)
ISRAIL WILSON) This day came the defendant into open Court and took the oath prescribed by law for insolvent debtors, Whereupon it is considered by the Court that he be discharged out of custody.

        Court adjourned untill tomorrow morning nine o'clock.
                        John Dougherty
                        James Keith
                        James Robinson

(p-568)   Thursday November the twenty six one thousand eight hundred and thirty five Court met according to adjournment.
Present - James Robinson   ) Esquires
          James Keith &   )
          John Dougherty   ) Justices of the peace of Franklin County

        Ordered by the Court that the solicitor be permitted to fill a Bill of Indictment Exeficco against Edwin Eanes.
This day the grand Jury came into Open Court and returned a Bill of Indictment against Edwin Eanes for an assault & battery a True Bill.

        A deed of trust from Leroy D. Bean to Milton McQueen for the personal property therein named was duly acknowledged in Open Court by the said Leroy D. Bean to be his act and deed. Whereupon it is ordered by the Court to be certified for registration. Let it be registered.

        A Power of attorney from Chapman McDaniel & Polly his wife to Hiram Sanders and Thomas Poindexter was duly acknowledged in Open Court by the said Chapman McDaniel & Polly his wife to be their act and deed - and the said Polly McDaniel being privately examined by the Court separate and apart from her husband the said Chapman McDaniel acknowledged the execution of said Power of Attorney to have been done by her freely voluntarily and understandingly without compulsion or restrant from her said husband. Whereupon it is ordered by the Court to be certified.

CRUTCHEN & ALLISON   )   Case
   Against   )
HAYDEN ARNOLD &   )
JAMES L. BRYANT   ) This day the plaintiff by his attorney and thereupon came a Jury, to wit,- Miles Francis 1, John D. Fennell 2, Willis Holder 3, James Taylor 4, Hamilton Stewart 5, Wiley Denson 6, Aaron G. Griffith 7, James Faris 8, Christopher Acklin 9, Thomas Green 10 Phillips Williams 11 & William Corn 12 who being elected, tried and sworn well & truly to enquire of damages in this cause upon their oaths do say the Plaintiff hath sustained damages by reason of the non performance of the assumption in the Declaration mentioned to the amount of five hundred and twenty nine dollars and fifty cents. It is thereupon considered by the Court that the plaintiffs recover against the defendants their damages aforesaid assessed by the Jury aforesaid and also their costs by them about said suit in this behalf expended and the said debts in mercy &.

(p-569)   Ordered by the Court that Richard Charles be appointed Guardian over the person and property of Powhattan D. Littlepage orphan of Thomas Littlepage decd who entered into bond with John Charles his security in the sum of two thousand dollars according to law.

A deed of conveyance from James B. Drake to John R. Patrick for
two hundred two & one half acres of land lying in Franklin County was
duly proven in Open Court by the oath of Wm. C. Handley one of the subscribing witnesses thereto to be the act and deed of the said James B. Drake
on the day it bears date. It having been heretofore proven by the other
subscribing witnesses thereto. Whereupon it is ordered by the Court to
be certified for registration. Let it be registered.

THE STATE OF TENNESSEE) Indict for Malicious Mischief
  Against)
ANDREW H. MCCOLLUM) This day came the attorney General who
prosecutes for the State in this behalf as well as the defendant in his
proper person and the said defendant having heard said Indictment read
says he is thereof not guilty and puts himself upon the Country and the
attorney General doth the like and thereupon came a Jury, to wit, -
Miles Francis 1, Wilis Holder 2, James Taylor 3, Hamilton Stewart 4,
Wiley Denson 5, Aaron G. Griffeth 6, Christopher Acklin 7, Thomas Green 8
Philips Williams 9, William Corn 10 Garland Anderson 11 & Thomas C.
Duncan 12 who being elected, tried and sworn the truth of and upon the
premises to speak. Whereupon by the consent of the parties and with
the assent of the Court the Jury are permitted to disperse untill
tomorrow morning ten o'clock.

CRUTCHEN & ALLISON) Case
  Against)
LEROY S. CAMDEN)
STEWART COWAN &)
JOHN W. CAMDEN) This day came the parties by their attorneys
and thereupon cause a Jury, to wit,- Miles Frances 1, John D. Fennel 2
Willis Holder 3, James Taylor 4, Hamelton Stewart 5, Wiley Denson 6,
Aaron G. Griffeth 7, James Faris 8, Christopher Acklin 9, Thomas Green 10
Philips Williams 11 & William Corn 12 who being elected tried and sworn
the truth to speak upon the issues joined upon their oaths do say they
find the issues in favor of Leroy S. Camden one of the defendants and
upon their oaths aforesaid do say that they further find the issue between
the said Plaintiffs and Stewart Cowan & John W. Camden in favor of said
Plaintiffs and assess their damages to five hundred and thirty two
dollars & one half cents. It is thereupon considered by the Court that
the plaintiffs recover against the said Stewart Cowan & John W. Camden
two of the (p-570) Defendants their damages aforesaid assessed by
the Jury aforesaid and also their costs by them about said suit in this
behalf expended and the said defendants in mercy &.

ALFRED G. DAVIS & OTHERS) Issue to try Will
  Against)
ELIZABETH GILLILAND) This day their attorney came the parties
by their attorney and thereupon came a Jury, to wit,- Miles Francis 1
John D. Fennell 2, Willis Holder 3, James Taylor 4, Hamelton Stewart 5
Wiley Denson 6, Aaron G. Griffeth 7, James Faris 8, Christopher Acklin 9
Thomas Green 10, Philips Williams 11 & Wm. Corn 12 who being elected,
tried and sworn the truth to speak upon the issue joined upon their
oaths do say they find the issue in favor of the plaintiffs and that
the paper writing exhibited here in Court purporting to be the last
will and testament of Elizabeth E. Bowlin-deceased is the last will

and testament of Elizabeth E. ᴮowlin deceased, Whereupon it is ordered
by the Court that said last Will and testament be recorded. It is thereupon considered by the Court that the plaintiffs recover against the defendant their costs by them about said suit in this behalf expended for
all of which execution may issue. Whereupon by the consent of the parties
it is ordered by the Court that Richard Burton be appointed administrator
with the Will annexed of the estate of Elizabeth E. ᴮowlin deceased
who entered into bond with Richard Lawliss his security in the sum
of twenty thousand dollars according to law & was qualified accordingly.

Court adjourned untill tomorrow morning ten o'clock
John Dougherty
James Keith
, James Robinson

Friday November the twenty seventh one thousand eight hundred
and thirty five, Court met according to adjournment.
Present - John Doughtery   ) Esquires
         James Keith   )
         James Robinson   ) Justices of the peace for Franklin County

THE STATE OF TENNESSEE   ) Indict for malicious mischief.
 Against   )
ANDREW H. MCCOLLUM   ) This day came the parties by their attornies
and thereupon again came the same Jury who were on yesterday elected,
tried and sworn the truth of and upon the premises to speak and by the
consent of the parties and with the assent of the Court Miles Francis
one of the Jurors aforesaid is withdrawn and the rest of the Jury
from rendering their verdict are discharged and the cause continued for
trial at the next Term of this Court.

(p-571)   This day Andrew H. McCollum and Micah Taul came into Court
and acknowledged themselves to owe and stand justly indebted to the
State of Tennessee in the following sums, to wit,- the said Andrew H.
McCollum in the sum of two hundred and fifty dollars and Micah Taul
his security in the sum of one hundred and twenty five dollars to be
levied of their respective goods and chattels lands and tenements to
the use of said State but to be void on condition that Andrew H. McCollum
make his personal appearance before the Justices of our next Court of
Pleas & Quarter Sessions to be held for the County of Franklin at the
courthouse in Winchester on Thursday after the fourth Monday in February
next then and there to answer the State of Tennessee on a Bill of
Indictment found against him for malicious mischief and not depart the
same without leave first had and obtained.

THE STATE OF TENNESSEE   ) Indict for an Affray
  Against   )
JOSEPH R. SHROPSHIRE   ) This day came the Attorney General who
prosecutes for the State in this behalf and with the assent of the Court
enters a noleprosequi in this case.

THE STATE OF TENNESSEE   ) Indict for an assult & Battery
  Against   )
BENJAMIN F. JENKINS   ) This day came the Attorney General who
prosecutes for the State in this behalf as well as the defendant in his

proper person and the said defendant having heard said Indictment read says
he is thereof not guilty and puts himself upon the Country and the
Attorney General doth the like and thereupon came a Jury, to wit,-
Joseph Bradford 1, Wm. Taylor 2, John Howard 3, John P. Davidson 4,
Edward H. Wade 5, James V. Acklin 6, Solomon Holder 7, David Robinson 8
Absalom Faris Senr. 9, John Frame 10, William A. Francis 11 & Littleton
Faris 12, who being elected tried and sworn the truth of and upon the
premises to speak upon their oaths do say they find the defendant not
guilty in manner & form as charged in the Bill of Indictment. It is
therefore considered by the Court that the defendant go hence without
day. Whereupon on motion of the defendant by his attorney and it
appearing to the satisfaction of the Court that the Indictment in this
case is frivelous & malicious It is therefore ordered by the Court that
Daniel Marshall the prosecutor in this case be taxed with the costs of
this prosecution It is therefore considered by the Court that the State
recover against the said Daniel Marshall its cost about said suit in
this behalf expended for all of which Execution may issue.

(p-572)   On motion it is ordered by the Court that the fine heretofore
at this term assessed against Joseph Acklin be remitted by his paying
the costs of entering and remitting said fine.

THE STATE OF TENNESSEE   ) Indict for Malicious Mischief
    Against   )
CHARLES GURRANT   ) This day came the attorney General who prosecutes
for the State in this behalf and by & with the assent of the Court enters
a nole prosequi in this case and on motion ~~it is ordered by the court~~ and
it appearing to the satisfaction of the Court that the Indictment in this
case is frivilous and malicious. It is therefore ordered by the Court
that Daniel Marshall the prosecutor be taxed with the costs. It is
therefore considered by the Court that the State recover against the
said Daniel Marshall its costs about said suit in this behalf expended for
all of which execution may issue.

THE STATE OF TENNESSEE   ) Sci Fa
    Against   )
JAMES WILLIAMS   ) On motion of the defendant to be released
from the forfeiture in the Scire Facias mentioned and upon argument
thereupon had it is considered by the Court that he be released from
the payment of said penalty upon condition of his paying the costs of
this suit. It is therefore considered by the Court that the plaintiff
recover against the said defendant its costs about said suit in this
behalf expended for all of which execution may issue.

        This day the grand Jury came into Court and returned a Bill of
Indictment against Daniel Marshall for an assult & Batter a true Bill

        Court adjourned untill tomorrow morning ten o'clock
                                        James Keith
                                        John Doughtery
                                        James Robinson

        Saturday November the 28th one thousand eight hundred and thirty
five Court met according to adjournment.
Present - James Robinson   ) Esquires
          James Keith &   )
          John Doughtery   ) Justices of the peace for Franklin County

PETER & JOHN SIMMONS   )
   Against   )
MARY VANZANT ADMINISTRATRIX   )
OF THE ESTATE OF JACOB VANZANT DECD.) This day came the defendant by her
attorney and prayed prayed an appeal from the judgment of the Court heretofore at this term rendered against her to the next circuit Court to be
held for this county. Which is granted by the Court.

PETER & JOHN SIMMONS   )
   Against   )
MARY VANZANT ADMINISTRATRIX   )
OF JACOB VANZANT DECD   ) This day came the defendant by her
attorney and prayed an appeal from the judgment of the court heretofore
at this Term rendered against her to the next circuit court to be held
for this county which is granted by the court.

On motion it is ordered by the Court that the fine heretofore at
this Term assessed against Edwin M. Tatum for his non attendance as a
Juror be remitted by his paying the cost.

THE STATE OF TENNESSEE   )
   Against   )
EDWIN EANES   ) Indict for an assault & Battery
This day came the attorney General who prosecutes for the State in this
behalf as well as the defendant in his proper person and the said
dependant having heard said Indictment read says he is thereof guilty
and puts himself upon the grace and mercy of the Court.
Whereupon it is considered by the Court that the defendant for such his
offence be fined five dollars and pay the costs of this prosecution,
Whereupon Colwell P. Shipp came into Court and acknowledged himself
security for the fine & costs in this case. It is therefore considered
by the Court.that the plaintiff recover against the defendant and Colwell
P. Shipp the fine & costs in the above case for all of which Execution
may issue.

This day Thomas Finch came into Court and acknowledged himself to
owe and stand justly indebted to the State of Tennessee in the sum of
two hundred and fifty dollars to be levied of his proper goods &
chattels lands and tentements to the use of said State (p-573) but to
be void on condition that Martha Taylor make her personal appearance
before the Justices of our next Court of pleas and quarter sessions to
be held for the County of Franklin at the Courthouse in Winchester on
Thursday after the fourth Monday of February next then and there to
answer the State of Tennessee on a Presentment found against her for
retailing spiritious liquors and abide by and preform the judgment of
the court and not depart the same without leave first had & obtained.

DOUGLASS & WOOD   )   Debt
   Against   )
EDWIN EANES   )
JAMES OLIVER   )
HENRY RUNNELS &   )
HOPKINS L. TURNEY   ) This day came the defendants into open Court
and waive the necessity of an original writ and say he cannot gainsay the
plaintiffs action against them and confess judgment for five hundred
dollars debt together with the further sum of twenty five dollars interest

thereon at the rate of six percent peranum. It is therefore considered
by the Court that the plaintiffs recover against the defendants their
debt and Interest confessed as aforesaid and also their costs by them
about said suit in this behalf expended for all of which execution may
issue.

JOHN B. CARTER)   Debt
  Against   )
EDWIN EANES &   )
HENRY RUNNELS)   This day came the defendants into Open Court
and wavie the necessity of an original writ and say they cannot gainsay
the plaintiffs action against them and confess judgment for three hundred
dollars debt together with the further sum of eighteen dollars and
fifteen cents interest thereon at the rate of six percent peranum, It
is therefore considered by the Court that the plaintiff recover against
the said defendants his debt and interest confessed as aforesaid and also
his costs by him about said suit in this behalf expended and the said
defendants in mercy & the plaintiffs attorney agrees to stay the execution
untill the 25th of February next.

        Ordered by the Court that James Robinson be appointed Guardian
over the persons and property of Elizabeth Fidellia, Mary Emily &
Margaret Mathews orphans of John Mathews deceased who entered into bond
with William Street & James Taylor his securties in the sum of thirty
thousand dollars according to law.

CRUTCHER & AILISON)   Case
  Against   )
JAMES H. ARNOLD)   This day came the plaintiffs by their
attorney and having filed his Declaration and the defendant (p-574)
being solemnly called to appear and defend this suit came not but made
default, it is therefore considered by the Court that the plaintiff
recover against the defendant such damages as they have sustained by the
reason of the non performance of the assumptions in the Declaration
mentioned which damages are to be enquired of by a Jury at the next
Term of this Court.

JOHN HERRIFORD)   Debt
  Against   )
LEROY MAY   )   This day came the parties by their attorney
and the defendant having withdrew the pleas heretofore filed by him in
this cause and because he says nothing why judgment should not be rendered
against him wherefore it is considered by the Court that the plaintiff
recoveragainst the defendant two hundred dollars the debt in the Declaration mentioned togebher with the further sum of eleven dollars interest
thereon at the rate of six per cent peranum and also his costs by him
about said suit in this behalf expended for all of which execution may issue.

CRUTCHER & ALLISON)
  Against   )
LEROY S. CAMDEN &)
JAMES H. ARNOLD)
STEWART COWAN &)
JOHN W. CAMDEN   )   This day came the defendants by their attorney
and moved the Court for a new trial in this cause and on argument there-
upon had it is ordered by the Court that the virdict and judgment rendered
in this cause at this Term be set aside and that a new trial be granted
and on motion of the Plaintiff by his attorney a commission is awarded

him to take the deposition of Alpha Kingsly to be read as evidence on
the trial of the above cause in behalf of the said Plaintiffs by their
giving the defendants ten days notice of the time and place of taking the
same.

This day the grand jury came into Court and entered a Presentment
against Edwin Eanes, Dyer Moore & William McCoy for gaming a true Bill.

R. C. COLDWELL ASSEE & C)
FOR THE USE OF ROBERT & FLOYD)
  Against)
THOMAS KING SENR.)   This day came the parties by their
attornies and thereupon the matters of law arising from the Defendant
demures to the plaintiffs declaxtion being argued it seems to the Court
here that the law is for the defendant. It is thereupon considered
by the Court that (p-575) the demurer be sustained and that the
defendant go thereof without day and recover against the plaintiff
and Isaac H. Roberts and Joseph Floyd for whose use the suit was brought
his costs by him about his defence in this behalf expended for which
execution may issue.

    This day Daniel Marshall & Portland J. Curle came into Court and
acknowledged them to owe and stand justly indebted to the State of
Tennessee in the following sum to wit,- Daniel Marshell in the sum of
two hundred and fifty dollars and Portland J. Curle his security in the
sum of one hundred and twenty five dollars to be levied of their respective goods & chattels lands and tenements to the use of said State but to
be void on condition that Daniel Marshall make his personal appearance before the Justices of our Next Court of pleas and quarter sessions to be
held for the County of Franklin at the Courthouse in Winchester on the
Thursday after the fourth Monday in February next then and there to
answer the State on a bill of Indictment found against him for an assault
& Battery and abide by and perform the Judgment of the Court and not
depart the same without leave first had and obtained.

    Court adjourned untill Court in Course.

                        John Doughtery
                        James Robinson
                        James Keith

February Term 1836
(p-576)   State of Tennessee
     At a Court of Pleas and Quarter Sessions begun and held for
Franklin County on the Fourth Monday in February A. D. 1836 it being the
22nd day of said month and in the sixteenth year of the Independence of
the United States of America. Present thirteen of the acting Justices
of the peace for Franklin County.

     A deed of conveyance from Josephus R. Shropshere to Eli J. Capell
for 40 acres of land lying in Amite County Mississippi was duly acknowledged
in Open Court by the Said Josephus R. Shropshire to be his act and deed
whereupon it is ordered by the Court to be certified for registration.
Let it be registered.

     A deed of conveyance from Richrd Sharp to Henry Vamer for fifty
acres of land lying in Franklin County was duly acknowledged in Open
Court by the said Richrd Sharp to be his act and deed whereupon it is
ordered by the Court to be certified for registration. Let it be registered.

     A Bill of Sale from Samuel Corn to James Sharp for one negro boy
named Jack was duly acknowledged in Open Court by the said Samuel Corn
to be his act and deed whereupon it is ordered by the Court to be certified
for registration. Let it be registered.

     A deed of conveyance from Tucker Easley to Mathew Brown for one
hundred acres of land lying in County was duly acknowledged in Open Court
by the said Tucker Easley to be his act and deed and ordered to be
certified for registration. Let it be registered.

     A deed of conveyance from James Ewing to Joseph Willis for 540 acres
of land lying in Franklin County was duly acknowledged in Open Court by
the said James Ewing to be his act and deed Whereupon it is ordered by
the Court to be certified for registration. Let it be registered.

(p-577)   A deed of conveyance from George Caperton to William Wallace
for 50 acres of land lying in Franklin County was duly proven in Open
Court by the oaths of Ryan Caperton and Benj. F. Gibson subscribing
witnesses thereto to be the act and deed of the said George Caperton
whereupon it is ordered by the Court to be certified for registration.
let it be registered.

     A deed of conveyance from John Farror to William Stroud for 270
acres of land lying in Franklin County was duly proven in Open Court by
the Oaths of Jesse Reynolds and Robertson Nevills subscribing witnesses
thereto to be the act and deed of the said John Farror whereupon it is
ordered by the Court to be certified for registration. Let it be registered.

     A deed of conveyance from Anderson S. Goodman to Jethro Goodman
for 104 acres of land more or less lying in Franklin County was duly
acknowledged in Open Court by the said Anderson S. Goodman to be his
act and deed. Whereupon it is ordered by the Court to be certified for
registration. Let it be registered.

     A deed of conveyance from Thomas Bridges to William Baker for 157
acres of land lying in Franklin County was duly proven in open Court by
the oaths of John Handley and Arthur L. Campbell subscribing witnesses

thereto to be the act and deed of the said Thomas Bridges whereupon it is ordered by the Court to be certified for registration. Let it be registered.

A deed of conveyance from Granville Lipscomb to Wm. C. Lipscomb for 37 acres of land lying in Franklin County was duly acknowledged in Open Court by the said Granville Lipscomb to be his act and deed whereupon it is ordered by the Court to be certified for registration. Let it be registered.

A deed of conveyance from John Singleton to Alexander Suiter for 37 acres of land lying in Franklin County was duly acknowledged in Open Court by the said John Singleton to be his act and deed where upon it is ordered by the Court to be certified for registration. Let it be registered.

(p-578)   A deed of conveyance from Isaac W. Hanna to David W. Robertson for 40 acres of land lying in Franklin County was duly proven in Open Court by the oaths of Andrew Campbell and James F. Green subscribing witnesses thereto to be the act and deed of the said Isaac W. Hanna. Whereupon it is ordered by the Court to be certified for registration. Let it be registered.

A deed of conveyance from Isaac W. Hanna to David W. Robertson for 60 acres of land lying in Franklin County was duly proven in Open Court by the oaths of Andrew Campbell and James F. Green subscribing witnesses thereto to be the act and deed of the said Isaac U. Hanna Whereupon it is ordered by the Court to be certified for registration. Let it be registered.

A deed of conveyance from Patrick Smith, William Hodges, Gardner Smith, Henry Flippo, Thannon Flippo. Hubbard Hodges & Clark Smith to John A. Corn for 43½ acres of land lying in Franklin County was duly proven in open Court by the oaths of Samuel Corn & Jacob Mickler subscribing witnesses thereto to be the act and deed of the said bargainors, Whereupon it is ordered by the Court to be certified for registration. Let it be registered.

A deed of conveyance from John Mason to Peter C. Cartwright for 50 acres of land lying in Franklin County was duly proven in Open Court by the oaths of William Larkin and Jonathan Martin subscribing witnesses thereto to be the act and deed of the said John Mason Whereupon it is ordered by the Court to be certified for registration. Let it be registered.

Ordered by the Court that George P. Rowland be appointed overseer of the road of the 2nd class from the head of Spring Creek to Coffee County line, and that he keep the same in good repair according to law.

Ordered by the Court that Barnaley Burrow be appointed overseer of the upper road leading (p-579) to Jasper from Pelham to the County line and that he keep the same in good repair according to law and that he have the same hands that worked under former overseer.

Ordered by the Court that John O. Young be appointed overseer of the second class from Mannsford to William F. Longs Tan Yard in the place of David Weaver and that he keep the same in good repair according to law and that he have the same hands that worked under the former overseer.

Ordered by the Court that John K. Burton be appointed overseer of

the road from the mountain to the top of the hill opposite the corner of
David Docherd's fence this side of the Boiling Fork at Horton's Mill in
the room of Samuel Holland, and that he keep the same in good repair
according to law and that he have the same hands that worked under the
former overseer.

Ordered by the Court that Alexander E. Patton, John Jones, and
James Cunningham be appointed commissioners to settle with David Muckleroy
as executor of the Estate of Alexander Floyd decd. and that they make
this return to this term of this court.

Ordered by the Court that Elijah French be appointed overseer of
the road from the forks of the road near the Turnpike on the Sinking
cove road to a pond on the mountain near the narrows in the room of
Abner Adams and that he keep the same in good repair according to law and
that he have the same hands that worked under the former overseer.

Ordered by the Court that Abram Shook, James D. Keith Oliver D. Street
Capt. James Taylor, Wallis Estill Jr. Paschal Green & Willis Holder be
appointed a Jury of view to run the road from Winchester to the foot of
the mountain at James Keith's and that they make their return to the
next term of this Court.

Ordered by the Court that Meridith Catchings, Dennis Barnes,
Wm. D. Williams, Benjamin Walker & Nathan Prince be appointed a a Jury
to (p-580)   view and turn the road on Crow Creek on the land of Wallis
Estill and that they make their return to the next term of this Court.

This day an inventory of the Estate of William Hodges deceased
was produced in Open Court, was received by the Court and ordered to be
recorded.

This day a statement of the debts and credits belonging to the
Estate of Catharine Shropshire decd. which have come to the hands of the
Executor was produced in Open Court was received by the Court and ordered
to be recorded.

This day the amount of the sales of the negroes belonging to the
Estate of Robt. Hudspeth decd was produced in open Court, was received by
the Court and ordered ~~by the court~~ to be recorded.

Ordered by the Court that John G. Bostick, Barnaley Burrow &
Alexander E. Patton be appointed to settle with Susannah Sartain,
administratrix of the estate of Harrison Sartain deceased, and that they
make their return to the next term of this Court.

This day the Commissioners of the tract of school land near
George Rowlands, made their return in Open Court, which was received by
the Court and ordered to be recorded.

This day Elijah D. Robbins Corner of Franklin County ~~offered his~~
~~resignation~~ appeared in Open Court and offered his resignation as such
which was received by the Court.

Ordered by the Court that the overseer of the road that leads from Pelham by Hollingsworths be required to work to Spain's Bridge and that David G. Goodman work from there to the county line.

Ordered by the Court that William C. Handley be appointed overseer of the road of the first class from the creek at Bells to the County line in the place of William Johnson and that he keep the same in good repair according to law and that he have the same hands that worked under the former overseer.

(p-581)   Ordered by the Court that William H. Gillaspie be appointed overseer of the road from Dr. Bickleys to the boat yard in the room of Saunders Faris and that he keep the same in good repair according to law and that he have the same hands that worked under the former overseer.

Ordered by the Court that Charles Simmons be appointed overseer of the road from Bemas Creek to the Eight Mile Post in the room of John C. Deckey and that he keep the same in good repair according to law and that he have the same hands that worked under the former overseer.

Ordered by the Court that Jonathan Lasater be appointed overseer of the road from the Old Tanyard to the County line in the place of William ------- and that he keep the same in good repair according to law and that he have the same hands that worked under the former overseer.

This day Hugh Francis came into Court and took the necessary oaths of qualification as deputy Clerk of Franklin County Court.

Ordered by the Court that George Hudspeth be appointed to allot hands to work under Wm. C. Woods overseer of the road leading from Salem to the mountain.

This day Williamson S. Oldham came into open Court and took the necessary oaths of qualification as an attorney of this Court, Whereupon he is admitted as an attorney of this Court.

This day the valuation of the negroes, for the present year hire ×//×// in the possession of a Mary Vanzant Guardian of the infant children of Jacob Vanzant deceased, was produced in open Court, was received by the Court and ordered to be recorddd.

This day the last will and testament of Richard Holland deceased was produced in open Court by the executors therein named whereupon came Mitchell K. Jackson & Joseph Miller subscribing witnesses thereto, who being first duly sworn depose and say that the said Richard Holland assigned the same in their presence and at the time of signing the same he the said (p-582)   Richard Holland was of sound and disposing mind and memory and that they signed the same as witnesses thereto at his request Whereupon ×××× ××××// ×××/×××××××/ ×××××× ××× ××××××××× ×××××× ×××× it is ordered by the Court to be recorded Whereupon came Samuel and Granberry Holland the Executors therein named and were qualified as executors to execute said last will and testament and who entered into bond with Samuel Miller and Joseph Miller as their securities in the penal sum of eight thousand dollars according to law.

This day the last Will ans testament of Mary Wilson deceased was
produced in open Court by the Executor therein named whereupon came
Barnett Forsyth and George A. Brook subscribing witnesses thereto who
being first duly sworn depose and say that the said Mary Wilson signed the
same in their presence and at the time of signing the same she the said
Mary Wilson was of sound and disposing mind and memory, and that they
signed the same at her request Whereupon it is ordered by the court to be
recorded.

A paper writing purposing to be the last will ans testament of
Levi Shores deceased was produced in Open Court & proved by the oaths of
Richard C. Holder and George Hudspeth the subscribing witnesses thereto
and established as the nuncupative Will of said Decendant the said Will
not having been signed by the testator, who died shortly after said Will
was written which was done in strict conformity to his direction as proved
by said subscribing witnesses & it is ordered that said Will be recorded
& Solomon Sparks and Richard C. Holder the Executors named in said Will
came into Court in their proper persons and renounced the execution of
said Will.

This day Nathan Prince produced in open court one old wolf scalp
and from his statements upon oath the Court being satisfied thereupon
ordered that he have a certificate to the treasurer of the State for the
sum allowed him for the same by law.

(p-583)   On motion it is ordered by the Court that Anne Floyd be
appointed Guardian of the person and property of Mary Anne Floyd minor
orphan of Alexander Floyd deceased who entered into bond with David
Mackleroy and Thomas Finch her securities in the sum of two thousand
dollars as required by law.

On motion it is ordered by the Court that Isaac H. Roberts be
appointed guardian of Elizabeth Robbins who entered into bond with
John M. Marrow G. W. Sartin and David Muckleroy as his securities in
the sum of four hundred dollars according to law.

Ordered by the Court that John M. Morrow be appointed constable
for Franklin County in the bounds of Capt. Wilkinson's company for the
next ensueing two years who entered into bond with William M. Burton
and John G. Brazelton his securities according to law and was qualified
accordingly.

Ordered by the Court that John Byron be appointed constable for
Franklin County in the bounds of Capt. Majors Company for the next
ensueing two years who entered into bond with Dennis B. Muse and
John Roleman his securities according to law and was qualified accordingly

Ordered by the Court that John Roleman be appointed constable for
Franklin County in the bounds of Capt. Tipps Company for the next ensuing
two years who entered into bond with John Byron and Zachariah H. Murrell
his securities according to law and was qualified accordingly.

Ordered by the Court that George S. Miller be appointed coroner for
Franklin County for the next ensuing two years who entered into bond with

.Z.H.Murrell his security according to law and was qualified accordingly

Ordered by the Court Levi Byrom be appointed keeper of the Poor house for the ensuing year who entered into bond with John Roleman and John Byrom his securities in the sum of one thousand dollars according to law.

(p-584)   Ordered by the Court that David O. Anderson George Mosley and William McElvey be appointed comissioners of the tract of school land at the north of Boons Creek who entered into bond in the sum of one thousand dollars according to law.

Ordered by the Court that John Witt be appointed commissioner of the school land near Rowlands who entered into bond with James Stamps his security in the sum of one thousand dollars according to law.

It appearing to the satisfaction of the Court that Joseph Crownover late of this County died intestate and Jonathan Crownover having made application for letters testamentary to administer on the estate of said d ecedent It is therefore ordered by the Court that letters testamentary be granted to him who thereupon entered into bond with William Crownover h! is security in the sum of six hundred dollars and was qualified according to law.

Present,
John Dougherty
William Larkin
Samuel Norwood
George Gray
James B. Stovall
David Bell
Wm. Simmons
M. Catchings
James Keith
Z. H. Murrell
R. P. Harris
G. Hudspeth
Littleton G. Simpson

John Byrom
John James
Andrew Campbell
Andrew Mann
Asa D. Oakley
James Kellay
John W. Camden
Acting Justices of the peace for
     Franklin County

Ordered by the Court that Jane Woodard, a pauper be allowed the sum of fifty dollars a year for her support and Reubin Strambler have a certificate to the Treasurer of Franklin County for the same. Present -
John Dougherty, William Larkin, George Gray, James B. Stovall, David Bell
Wm. Simmons, M. Citchings, James Keith, Z. H. Murrell, R. P. Harris,
G. Hudspeth, Littleton G. Simpson, John Byrom, John Jones, A. Campbill,
Andrew Man, Asa D. Okley, James Kelley, John W. Camden Acting Justices
of the peace for Franklin Count.

(p-585)   Ordered by the Court that Jane Morgan be allowed the sum of forty dollars for her support for one year to be paid quarterly and that certificate to be issued by Antony Stewart on the Treasurer of Franklin County for the same. John Dougherty, William Larkin, Samuel Norwood
George Gray, James B. Stovall, David Bell, Wm. Simmons, M. Catchings,
James Keith, Z. H. Murrell, R. P. Harris, G. Hudspeth, Littleton G. Simpson

John Byrom, John Jones, Andrew Campbell, Andrew Man, Asa D. Oakly,
James Kelly, John W. Camdon, acting justices of the peace for Franklin
County.

Ordered by the Court that Becky Hill be allowed the sum of six
dollars per month for her support and that certificates be issued quarterly
to Joseph Miller on the Treasurer of Franklin County for the same, Present,
John Dougherty, William Larkin, Samuel Norwood, George Gray, James B.
Stovall, David Bell, Wm. Simmons, M. Citchings, James Keith, Z. H. Murrell
R. P. Harris, G. Hudspeth, Littleton G. Simpson, John Byrom, John Jones,
And rew Campbell, Andrew Man, Asa D. Oakly, James Kelly, John Norwood,
Acting Justices of the peace for Franklin County.

Ordered by the Court that R. Powel be allowed the sum of seven
dollars & a half for three days services as a County commissioner in
settling with the County Trustee & County Court Clerk for the year 1835,
and that John Hanly be allowed the sum of five dollars for two days
services for the same and certificates for the same. Isd to Handly
Present, John Dougherty, Wm. Larkin, Samuel Norwood, George Gray, James
B. Stovall, David Bell, Williams Simmons, M. Citchings, James Keith,
Z. H. Murrell, Richard P. Harris, George Hudspeth, Littleton G. Simpson
John Byrom, John Jones, Andrew Campbell, Andrew Mann, Asa D. Oakley, James
Kelly, John W. Camden Acting Justices of the peace for Franklin County.

Ordered by the Court that Hasting M. Seargeant be allowed the sum
of sixty dollars for rehinging door to the Jail of Franklin County and
that a certificate issue for the same. Present, John Dougherty,
William Larkin, Samuel Norwood, George Gray, James B. Stovall, David Bell
Williams Simmons, Meredith Catchings, James Keith, Z. H. Murrell,
Richard P. Harris, George Hudspeth, Littleton (p-586)   G. Simpson,
Jø×× James Byrom, John Jones, Andrew Campbell, Andrew Mann, Asa D. Oakley
James Kelly, John W. Camden, Acting Justices of Franklin County.

Ordered by the Court that George West be allowed the sum of nine
dollars and seventy eight cents for tools purchased by him for the use of
the public road and that a certificate issue for same.

Present, John Dougherty, William Larkin, Samuel Norwood, George Gray
James B. Stovall, David ----- Wm. Simmons Meredeth Citching, James Keith
Z. H. Murrell, R. P. Harris, George Hudspeth, Littleton P. Simpson,
James Byrom, John Jones, Andrew Campbell, Andrew Mann, Asa D. Okley,
James Kelley, John W. Camden, Acting Justices of the peace for Franklin
County.

Ordered by the Court that an additional allowance of ten dollars
be made to Lucinda Wilson a pauper and that a certificate issue for the
same.

This day the commissioners appointed to examine and receive the
Bridge across the Boiling fork on the stage road near Winchester made
their report in favor of the reception of the same. Whereupon, it is
ordered by the Court (a lawful number of acting majistrates being
present) that a certificate issue to the treasurer of Franklin County
for the sum of two hundred and fifty dollars to be applied to the

Dicharge of the sum heretofore appropriated to the building of said bridge.

Ordered by the Court that Martin Crabtree, James N. Chiles and William B. Wilkinson be appointed commissioners to lay off the dower of the Widow of Joseph Crownover deceased.

This day the Jury of view appointed at the last term of this court to view and turn the road leading through the land of James Greenlee and also on the North side of Elk River through the land of John J. Hayter to the bridge across the river made their report which was confirmed by the Court.

Ordered by the Court that Samuel Hollan, Samuel Miller, W. M. Cowan Wallace Estill Jr. John Cowan be appointed a Jury of view to view and turn the road leading by David Decherd and that they make their sector at this term of this Court.

(p-587) This day the Jury of view heretofore appointed at this term of this Court to view and turn the road leading by David Decherd made their report which was rec'd by the Court.

Ordered by the Court that Nathan Prince, Dennis Barry, M. Catchings Berry Walker and William B. Wilkinson be appointed a Jury of view to view and turn the road on the land of Wallis Estill Jr. on Crow Creek and that they make their report to this term of this Court. Error.

This Jury of view heretofore appointed at this term of this Court to view and turn the road leading through the land of Wallis Estill Jr. on Crow Creek made their report which was received by the Court.

At the request of Joseph Klepper & James Robinson Executors of the last Will testament of the late Adam Groose, I have run of and described one hundred acres of land for his son Isaac Groose. Beginning at two hickorys and post oak in the south boundry of Cunninghams land standing by George Jauny and runs south with Grooses old line forty one and half pose to a post oak standing by Daniel Lowes and William Lees well thence East crossing the old mill race at 108 poles and Norwoods Creek at 114 poles in all 274 poles to a stake in Mrs. Smitsh field in Hopkins west boundary being east boundary of said Adams old tract and with the same ninety-nine and one half poles to Nortons line & with the same west eighty poles to Cunninghams line and with the same south 58 poles to said Cunninghams South east corner and with his south boundary crossing Norwood's Creek in all 194 poles to the beginning said 100 acres is truly represented in the annexed plat of Adam Gross. 350¾ acres of which this is a part George Young   )   George Gray Surveyor
                    John Lee   ) C. C. Joseph Klepper, Marker

(p-588) This day appeared William H. Murray in open Court and moved the Court to be released from all further liability as security for Hugh Foster guardian of the heirs of John Boyd deceased and it appearing to the satisfaction of the Court that due notice had been served upon the

said Hugh Foster to appear at this Term of this Court and give other good
and sufficient counter security who failed to appear. It is therefore ordered by the Court the said Hugh Foster be removed as guardian aforesaid
and that he surrender the effects in his hands to the said William H.
Murry or appear and give other good and sufficient counter security.

This day the commissioners heretofore appointed at the last term of
this Court to settle with ~~the~~ Eliza Davidson Admx. of the estate of
Abner Davidson deceased, made their report which was received by the court
and ordered to be recorded.

This day the commissioners heretofore appointed at the last term of
this Court to settle with the administrator of the Estate of Wyatt Ballard
dec'd made their report which was received by the court ~~that~~ to be recorded.

This day an election came on for the election of a Quorum for this
term of this Court and upon counting out the votes it was found that John
Dougherty, James Keith and William Simmons were duly and constitutionaly
elected a Quorum to hold said Court.

Present, John Dougherty, William Larkin, Saml. Morwood, George Gray
James B. Stovall, David Bell, William Simmons, Meredith Catchings, James
Keith, Z. H. Murrell, R. P. Harris, George Hudspeth, Littleton G. Simpson,
James Byrom, John Jones, Andrew Campbell, Andrew Mann, Asa D. Oakly,
James Kelly, John W. Camden,

Ordered by the Court that the commissioners of the poor house be
allowed the sum of seventy five dollars and that a certificate issue for
the same, which allowance was uanimously made by said Court.   Isd. to
R. P. Harris.

(p-589)   Court adjourned until tomorrow morning 11 o'clock
                              John Dougherty
                              James Keith
                              David Bell.

Tuesday February the 23rd, 1836, Court met according to adjournment
Present, John Dougherty   ) Esquire Justices of the peace of
          James Keith   ) Franklin County.
          David Bell   )

A deed of conveyance from John Handly to Harmon Riddle for 204
acres of land lying in Franklin County was duly acknowledged in Open Court
by the said John Handly to be his act and deed whereupon it is ordered by
the Court to be certified for registration. Let it be registered.

A deed of trust from Harmon Riddle to John Staples for the benefit
of John Handly for 264 acres of land lying in Franklin County was duly
acknowledged in Open Court by the said Harmon Riddle and the said John
Staples to be their act and deed. Whereupon it is ordered by the Court
to be certified for registration. Let it be registered.

A deed of conveyance from John W. Camden to Barton B. Clements for

for one lot of land containing 66 poles was duly acknowledged in Open Court
by the said John W. Camden to be his act and deed, Whereupon it is ordered
by the Court to be certified for registration. Let it be registered.

Ordered by the Court that Wiley J. Hines be appointed overseer of
the road from where Samuel Holland stops to the house of Wallis Estill Jr.
in the place of Peter S. Deoherd and that he keep the same in good repair
according to law and that he have the same hands that worked under the
former overseer.

Ordered by the Court that Albert G. Black be appointed a school
commissioner of the school land on big harricane who entered into bond with
Joseph Smith his security according to law.

(p-590) Ordered by the Court that Daniel Keith and Robert Cowan be
appointed commissioners of the school land near Keiths who thereupon
entered into bond with William S. Oldham as their security in the sum
of one thousand dollars according to law.

This day the commissioners heretofore appointed at this term of
this Court to settle with David Muckleroy Admr. of Alexander Floyd
deceased made their return which was received by the Court and ordered
to be recorded.

Ordered by the Court that Richard P. Harris, John Pylant & Britton
Smith be appointed commissioner to settle with Joseph Smith Executor of
Martin Adams deceased and that they make their return to the next term of
this Court.

This day an inventory of the Estate of Jacob C; Isacks deceased
was produced in Open Court by the Administratrix was received by the
Court and ordered to be recorded.

This day Joseph Smith guardian of James Brasier made his return
on such an oath in Open Court which was received in open Court and
ordered to be recorded.

Ordered by the Court that Alexander E. Patton be appointed guardian
over the persons and property of Anne Jane, B. F. & Elizabeth Read minor
orphans of Benjamin A. Read deceased, Who thereupon entered into bond
with John Goodwin and John G Brazelton his securities in the sum of
six thousand dollars according to law.

Ordered by the Court that Alexander E. Patton be appointed Admr.
of the estate of Benjamin a Read deceased who thereupon entered into
bond with John Woodwin and John G. Brazelton his securities in the sum
of six thousand dollars and was qualified according to law.

Ordered by the Court that John S. Martin and John Staples be
appointed administrators of the Will annexed of Levi Shores, deceased who
there upon (p-591) entered into bond with John Hanly and Solmon Sparks
their securities in the sum of Seven thousand dollars and were qualified
according to law.

Ordered by the Court that William S. Mooney, Alex E. Patton and Barnaly Burrow be appointed commissioners to settle with Elijah & David Muckleroy executors of Isaac Muckleroy deceased and that they make their return to the next term of this Court.

Ordered by the Court that John Hanly and Benjamin Powell be appointed commissioners to settle with the county officers for this year.

This day Henry Myers produced in Open Court one old wolf scalp and from his statements on oath, the Court being satisfied thereof. It is ordered that he have a certificate to the Treasurer of this State for the sum allowed him by law for the same. Isd.

Ordered by the Court that A. E. Patton and Wm. L. Mooney and David Muckleroy be appointed commissioners to settle with the administrator of Henry Burrow, dec'd.

Ordered by the Court that Robert Hill be appointed overseer of the road leading to Coldwells Bridge from the Boiling fork to   in the room of John D. Fennell and that he keep the same in good repair according to law and that he have the same hands that worked under the former overseer, - and that the hands that work on the State road from the forks at Knights towards Winchester unite with the hands under said Hill and work one day on the Hill at the Bridge on the North side of the Boiling fork.

Ordered by the Court that Willie J. Hines be appointed overseer of the road from where Samuel Holland Stops to Wallis Estills house in room of Peter L. Decherd and that he keep the same in good repair according to law and that he have the same hands that worked under the former overseer.

(p-592)   Ordered by the Court that Thomas Finch sheriff of Franklin County and collection of public taxes have a credit for one hundred & eleven dollars & eighteen & three fourth cents on a settlement of his accounts with the County Trustee for delinquients and twice listed property on this tax lists for the year 1835. Isd.

Ordered by the Court that Thomas Finch Sheriff of Franklin County & Collector of public taxes be charged with two hundred and ninety seven dollars & seventy seven & one fourth cents that being the amount collected by him on property not listed for the year 1835. Isd.

Ordered by the Court that the County additional tax to pay Jurors & poor tax for the year 1836 be the same as the tax laid for the year 1835 on all taxable property & polls.

On petition of Peter Lenehan for a licence to keep an ordinary at his house in Franklin County. It is therefore ordered by the Court that he have License accordingly by entering into bond & security according to law.

This day Alexander E. Patton admr. de bonis non of the estate of B. A. Read, dec'd made his petition on oath to the Court praying an order empowering him to sell a certain negro man slave named Henry, belonging to said estate to enable him to make an equal division of the estate among the heirs of said Benjamin a. Read which was granted by the Court according to the prayer of said petitioners.

This day Benjamin Dechered Admr. and Martha Isacks Adms. of the estate of Jacob C. Isacks deceased, petitioned the Court on oath for an order empowering them to sell the slaves belonging to the estate or so many thereof as may necessary to enable them to dicharge the debts due and owing from said estate, which was granted by court according to the prayer of the said petiton And the Court being satisfied with the facts set forth in said petition whereupon it is ordered by the Court that the said administration proceed to sell all of said slaves or so many thereof as they may necessary to satisfy the debt due and oweing from said estate.

(p-593)   Court adjourned until tomorrow morning 10 o'clock.
                                    Williams Simmons
                                    James Keith
                                    John Dougherty

        Wednesday morning February 24th A. D. 1836 Court met according to adjournment.
Present. William Simmons   ) Esquires
          James Keith   ) Justices of the Peace for Franklin County
          John Dougherty   )

        State of Tennessee
        Proclamation being made the sheriff of Franklin County made return of the State writ of Venere facias to this Court that he had summoned the following persons being all good and lawful men of said County of Franklin County to attend and serve as Jurors at the present term of this Court which persons so summoned and returned as aforesaid had been nominated for the purpose by the Justices of this Court of Pleas and Quarter Sessions of said County of Franklin at its last session as list of whom was dddivered to the sheriff of this said County by the clerk of this said Court, to wit,- William Reeves, James Logan, James A. Snowder, Robert Cowan Daniel Keith, Wm. Thurman Thomas Muse, Absalom Guess, William Byrom, David Osborn, Lunsford L. Mathews, Joseph Franklin, Harmon Riddle, Hanceford Arnett, Sandridge Arnett, Peter Keiston, Wm. Bridges, Joseph Huddleston Jr. Wm. P. Martin, Farleigh B. Wade Abner Adams, William Wallis, Squire B. Hawkins, William B. Knight, Thomas C. Duncan, and Edward Martin Jr. of whom the following persons being good and lawful men of said County of Franklin were elected, empannelled sworn and charged to enquire for the body of the county aforesaid, to wit,- Robert Cowan, William Wallace, Joseph Franklin, James Logan Robert Cowan Abner Admas, Absalom Guess, Thomas C. Duncan, William H. Byrom, Hansford Arnett, William Thurman, William P. Martin, Lunsford L. Matthews, Daniel Keith who after receiving their charge retired to consult of their presentments.

        Ordered by the Court that John G. Brazelton be appointed constable to take charge of the grand Jury during the present term of this Court

(p-594)   Ordered by the Court that Williamson S. Oldham be appointed attorney General Pro. Tem. during the present term of this Court, Whereupon Williamson S. Oldham came into Court was qualified as Attorney General Pro. Tem.

Ordered by the Court that William Bridges, William Reeves and Thomas Muse who were summoned on the original Venire be released from serving as Jurors at this Term of this Court.

MARK HUTCHINS ADMR.
& MARTHAR WALKER ADMX.
   Vs
JAMES ROBINSON &
WILLIAM DARTIS   This day came the parties by their attorney and by their mutial consent this cause is continued until the next term of this Court.

VANZANT HARRIS & CO.
   Vs
E. P. BACON   This day came the parties by their attorneys and by their mutual consent this cause is continued until the next term of this Court.

ISAAC VANZANT SERVING
PARTNER & C
   Vs
E. P. BACON   This day came the parties by their attorneys and by their mutual consent this cause is continued until the next term of this Court.

BENJAMIN DECHERD
   Vs
EDMOND RUSSEIL   This day came the parties by their attorneys and by their mutal consent this cause is continued until the next term of this Court.

WHITE & WILSON
   Vs
B. F. MOORE   This day came the parties by their attorneys and thereupon came a Jury to wit,- Harmon Riddle, Edwin Martin Squire B. Hawkins, David Osborne, John D. Stovall, John Haws, Sandridge Arnett, Farleigh B. Wade, Joseph Huddleton, James P. Keith who being elected, tried and sworn the truth to speak upon the issue joined upon their oaths do say they find the issue in favor of the plaintiffs and assess their damages to thirty nine dollars. It is thereupon considered by the Court that the plaintiffs recover of the defendant the sum of fourteen hundred and thirty four dollars debt in their declaration mentioned together with the further sum of thirty nine (p-595) damage for its detention and also their costs by them about their suit in this behalf expended &.

WHITE & WILSON
   Vs
BENJAMIN F. MOORE   This day came the parties by their attorney and thereupon came a Jury, to wit,- Harmon Riddle 1, Edwin Martin 2, Sandridge Arnett 3, Farleigh B. Wade 4, Joseph Huddleston 5, Squire B. Hawkins 6,

David Osborne 7, James A. Snowdon 8, John D. Stovall 9, John J. Hayter 10
John Haws 11 & James P. Keith 12 who being elected tried and sworn ~~and~~
~~charged~~ well and truly to try the issue joined upon their oaths do say
they find for the plaintiffs and assess their damages to the sum of two
hundred and sixty one dollars & fifty cents the su. It is therefore
considered by the Court that the plaintiffs recover of the defendant their
damages aforesaid by the Jury aforesaid in form aforesaid assessed and
also their costs by them about their suit in this behalf expended &.

THOMAS WILSON ADMR. & C   )
        Vs   )
B. F. MOORE   )   This day came the parties by their
attorneys and thereupon came a Jury, to wit, Harmon Riddle 1, Edwin Martin 2
Sandridge Arnett 3, Farleigh B. Wade 4, Joseph Huddleston 5, Squire B.
Hawkins 6, David Osborne 7, James A. Snowder 8, John D. Stovall 9,
John J. Hayter 10, John Haws 11 & James P. Keith 12 who being elected
tried & sworn well and truly to try the issue joined upon their oaths do
say they find the issue in favor of the plaintiff and assess his damages
to the sum of seven dollars and twenty five cents. Whereupon it is
considered by the Court that the Plaintiff recover of the defendant the sum
of two hundred & thirty seven dollars & seventy five cents the debt in
the Declaration mentioned together with the damages aforesaid in form
aforesaid assessed and also his costs by him about his suit in
  this behalf expended &.

ANDREW CAPERTON   )
        Vs   )
WILLIAM RANSOM   ) This day came the parties by their attorneys and
by their mutual consent this cause is continued until the next term of
this Court.

(p-596) LITTIY WHITE   )
            Agt.   )
         ZACHARIAH H. MURRELL ADMR.   )
         & WINNY FHILIPS ADMS OF   )
         JameS PHILIPS DECEASED   )   This day came the parties by
their attorneys and thereupon came a Jury to wit,- Harmon Riddle 1,
Edwin Martin 2, Sandridge, Arnett 3, Farleigh B. Wade 4, Joseph Huddleston 5
Squire B. Hawkins 6, David Osborne 7, James A. Snowdon 8, John D. Stovall 9
John J. Hayter 10, John Haws 11, and James P. Keith 12 who being elected
tried and sworn well and truly to try the issue joined upon their oaths
do say we the Jury find the issue in favor of the defendant whereupon it
is considered by the Court that the said defendants recover of the plaintiffs
their costs by them about their defence in this behalf expended from which
Judgement the plaintiffs prayed an appeal to the next circuit court to be
held for this County who thereupon entered into bond with Thomas D. White
as her security and the appeal granted.

        This day the Grand Jury returned into Open Court and returned the
following Bills of indictment as true Bills to wit,- against Leroy H. Byrom
for an assualt and Battery, against Hugh Richardson for an assualt & Battery
and against John Reagan and William Reagan for an assault with unlawful
weapons.

WILLIAM H. FLOYD ADMR. OF)   Sci Fa
ELISHA FLOYD? DECEASED)
    Agt)
SAMUEL BRADSHAW) This day came the plaintiff by his attorney
and moved the Court that to recover the Judgement in the Sci facias mentioned
in his own name as administrator of Elisha Floyd against the said Samuel
Bradshaw and it appearing to the Court that at the May term of this Court
in the year 1824 by the consideration and judgement of said Court the
said Elisha Floyd recovered of Samuel Bradshaw three hundred and forty
nine dollars debt and also five dollars forty two & ½ cents his costs about
said suit expended and it also appearing to the satisfaction of the Court
that satisfaction of said Judgement yet remains to be had and that the said
Elisha Floyd sever the rendition of said Judgement has departed this life
intestate and that administration upon his estate has been granted to the
said plaintiff thereupon it is considered by the Court that the Judgement
aforesaid be revived in the name (P-597) of the said plaintiff admininstra-
tor as aforesaid and that execution issue thereon bearing interest from the
date of said Judgement.

WILLIAM P. CAMPBELL)   Motion
& GEORGE W. RICHARDSON)
    Agt.)
JOHN M. MORROW)
ISAAC H. ROBERTS &)
GEORGE W. THOMPSON) This day came the plaintiffs by their
attorney and moved the Court for a Judgement against the said John M. Morrow
as constable and the said Isaac H. Roberts and George W. Thompson his
securities for the failure of the said John M. Morrow to make due return
of an execution in favor of the said Plaintiffs against Andrew Cannon
Hayden Arnold, Joseph R. Drake & James H. Arnold issued by Jesse Jinkins one
of the acting Justices of the peace for said County for the sum of Sixty
five dollars Sixty one &½ cents debt and costs and thereupon the said
plaintiffs moved to amend their motion so as to insert the following words"
George W. Richardson and William P. Campbell merchants & partners trading
under the firm and by the name and style of Campbell & Richardson " and on
argument thereon had it is ordered by the Court that said amendment be
made and it appearing to the Court that the execution set forth and described
in said notice was regularly issued by said Jesse Jenkins and placed in the
hands of the said John M. Morrow constable as aforesaid to do execution
thereof and that the said John M. Morrow has failed to make due return of
said execution as he was by law bound to do wherefore it was considered by
the Court that the said plaintiff recover against the said John M. Morrow
constable as aforesaid and the said Isaac H. Roberts and George W. Thompson
his securities the sum of sixty five dollars sixty one & one half cents
being the amount of the debt and costs in said excution together with the
further sum of seven dollars and twenty cents interest thereon at the rate
of six per cent per annum and also their costs by them about their motion
in this behalf expended for all which execution may issure &. and from which
Judgement the said Defendant prayed an appeal to the next circuit Court to
be held for Franklin County at the Court house in Winchester on the
fourth Monday in April next who intered in to bond with Rush N. Wallace his
security according to law and the said appeal is therefore granted.

       Court adjourned untill tomorrow morning 10 o'clock.

(p-598)   DANIEL M. RODDY   )
                Agt.   )
           SAUL CAMP   ) This day came the parties by their
attornies and thereupon came a Jury, towit, Harmon Riddle 1, Edwin Martin 2,
Sandridge Arnett 3, Farleigh B. Made 4, Joseph Huddleston 5, Squire B.
Hawkins 6, David Osborn 7, James A. Snowdon 8, John D. Stovall 9,
John J. Hayter 10, John Haws 11 and James P. Keith 12 who being elected
tried and sworn well and truly to try the issure joined upon their oaths
do say they find the issure in favor of the Plaintiff and assess his
damages to the sum of eighty five dollars wherefore it is considered by
the Court that the plaintiff recover against the said defendant the said
sum of eighty five dollars the damages aforesaid by the Jury aforesaid
assessed and also his costs by him about his suit in this behalf expended
&.

            Court adjourned untill tomorrow morning 10 o'clock,
                                    John Dougherty
                                    James Keith
                                    William Simmons

            Thursday morning the 25th 1836 Court met according to adjournment.
Present - John Dougherty   ) Esquires
           James Keith   ) Justices of the Peace for Franklin County
           William Simmons)

CRUTCHER & ALLISON   )
     Vs   )
 LEROY S. CAMDEN J. H. ARNOLD   )
 STEWART COWAN & P. W. CAMDEN   ) This day came the parties by their
attorneys and by mutual consent this cause is continued until the next
term of this court.

GEORGE MILLER   )   Debt
      Against   )
JEREMIAH BLACKARD   ) This day came the plaintiff by his attorney and
having filed his declaration and the defendant being solemnly called to
appear and defend this suit came not but made default. It is therefore
considered by the Court that the plaintiff recover against the defendant
one hundred and nineteen dollars the balance of the debt in the Declaration
(p-599) mentioned to gether with further sum of twenty three dollars and
seventy five cents inter st thereon at the rate of six percent per annum
and also his costs by him about his suit in this behalf expended &.

GEORGE MILLER   )   Debt
      Against   )
JEREMIAH BLACKARD   ) This day came the plaintiff by his attorney
and having filed his declaration and the defendant being solemnly called
to appear and defend this suit came not but made default. It is therefore
considered by the Court that the plaintiff recover against the defendant
one hundred twenty five dollars the debt in the Declaration mentioned
together with the further sum of sixteen dollars and twenty five cents
interest thereon at the rate of six per cent per annum and also his costs

by him about said suit in the behalf expended &.

EDWARD SWANN JR.) Debt.
   Against)
JOHN B. TALLIAFERRO &)
WILLIAM W. DAVIS) This day came the plaintiff by his
attorney and having filed his Declaration and the defendants being solemnly
called to appear and defend this suit came not but made default. It is
therefore considered by the Court that the plaintiff recover against the
defendants two hundred and twenty six dollars the debt in the declaration
mentioned to gether with the further sum of two dollars and twenty six cents
Interest thereon at the rate of six per cent per annum and also his costs
by him about said suit in this behalf expended &.

HENRY W. RUTLEDGE) Debt
   Against)
DAVID G. GOODMAN) T his day came the plaintiff by his attorney and
having filed his declaration and the defendant being solemnly called to
 appear and defend this suit came not but made default. It is therefore
considered by the Court that the plaintiff recover against the defendant
one hundred and thirty three dollars & thirty three & one third cents the
debt in the Declaration mentioned together with the further sum of seven
dollars & ninety eight cents interest thereon at the rate of six per cent
per annum and also his costs by him about said suit in this behalf expended &.

(p-600) J. W. & A. L. Campbell & Co.) Debt.
    Against)
    SAMUEL BRANNON) This day came the plaintiffs
by their attorney and having filed their Declaration and the defendant being
solemnly called to appear and defend this suit came not but made default
It is therefore considered by the Court that the Plaintiffs recover against
the defendant three hundred twenty one dollars and fifty four cents the
debt in the Declaration mentioned together with the further sum of three
dollars and twenty one cents Interest thereon at the rate of six per cent
per annum and also their costs by them about said suit in this behalf
expended &.

WHITE & WILSON ASSEE & C)
   Against)
GEORGE ROBERTS) This day came the plaintiffs by their attorney
and having filed their Declaration and the defendant being solemnly called
to appear and defend this suit came not but made default. It is therefore
considered by the Court that the plaintiffs recover against the defendant
two hundred and seventy eight dollars & fifty cents the debt in the
Declaration mentioned together with the further sum of two dollars &
seventy eight cents. Interest thereon at the rate of six per cent per
annum and also their costs by them about said suit in this behalf expended &.

WILLIAM L. WATTERSON) Debt
TO THE USE OF P. J. CURIE)
   Against)
JOHN D. STOVALL &)
PATTON A STOVALL) This day came the plaintiff by his attorney

and having filed his Declaration and the defendant being Solemnly called
to appear and defend this suit came not but made default. It is therefore
considered by the Court that the plaintiff recover against the defendants
one hundred & seventy five dollars the debt in the Declaration mentioned
t'ogether with the further sum of one dollar & seventy five cents Interest
thereon at the rate of six per cent per annum and also his costs by him
about said suit in this behalf expended &.

CRUTCHER & ALLISON   )
   Against   )
JAMES H. ARNOLD & OTHERS   )   This day came the parties by their
attorneys and by their mutual consent this cause is continued untill the
next term of this Court.

   (p-601)   THE STATE OF TENNESSEE   )
               Against   )
            ANDREW H. MCCOLLUM   ) This day came the parties by their
attorneys and by their mutal consent this cause is continued untill the next
term of this Court.

THE STATE OF TENNESSEE   )   Indict for Selling Liquor
   Against   )
MARTHA TAYLOR   )   This day came the Attorney General who
prosecutes for the State in this behalf and with the assent of the Court
enters a Nolliprosequi in this case.

      This day Andrew H. McCollum, Edward Darnaby & Micajah L. Gillaspie
came into Court and acknowledged themselves to owe and stand justly indebted
to the State of Tennessee in the following sums to wit the said Andrew H.
McCollum in the sum of two hundred & fifty dollars and Edward Darnaby and
Micajah L. Gillaspie his securities in the sum of one hundred & twenty five
dollars each to be levied of their respective goods and chattels lands and
 tenements to the use of said State but to be void on condition that the
said Andrew H. McCollum make his personal appearance before the Justices of
our next Court of pleas and Quarter Sessions to be held for the County of
 Franklin at the Court house in the town of Winchester on Thursday after the
fourth Monday in May next then and there to answer the State of Tennessee
on a Bill of Indictment found against him for malicious mischief and abide
by and perform the Judgment of the Court and not depart the same without
leave first had and obtained.

THE STATE OF TENNESSEE)   A & B
   Vs   )
HUGH RICHARDSON   )   This day came the attorney general who prosecutes
for the State in this behalf and with the assent of the Court enters a
Nolli prosequi in this case as to Edwin Eanes and it appearing to the satis-
faction of the Court that Dyer Moorehad been regularly recognized by
Thomas Finch Sheriff of Franklin County with Richard B. Moore as (p-602)
security in the sum of two hundred and fifty dollars each to be levied of
their respective goods and chattels lands and tenements to be void on condition
that the said Dyer Moore should make his personal appearance here at the
Court and answer a present ment found against him for gaming. and the said
Dyer Moore being solemnly called to come into Court and answer as aforesaid
came not but made default and the said RichardB. Moore being also called to

come and bring with him the boyd of the said Dyer Moore according to his
undertaking came not but also made default. It is therefore considered by
the Court that the State of Tennessee recover of the said Dyer Moore and
Richard B. Moore his security the said sum of two hundred and fifty dollars
each the amount of their recognizante forfeited as aforesaid. Unless they
be and appear before this Court at the next term to be held on the fourth
Monday in May next and shew good cause if any they have or can why judgment
final shall not be entered against them in this behalf upon writs of
Sciri facios which is hereby awarded &. And it is also considered by the
Court that an alias Capios issue against the defendant William McCoy.

THE STATE OF TENNESSEE   )
  Against   )
DANIEL MARSHALL   ) For want of Counsel to prosecute for the State
in this behalf. It is considered by the Court that this cause be continued
until the next term of this Court.

THE STATE OF TENNESSEE
      Against   ) A & B
HUGH RICHARDSON

THE STATE OF TENNESSEE
    Against   ) A & B
LEORY H. BYROM

THE STATE OF TENNESSEE   ) It is ordered by the court court that
  AGT./   ASSAULT   ) Capios issue in each of the cases mentiod in
JOHN REAGAN AND   ) the margin
WILLIAM REAGAN

(p-603) JOSEPH BECKLEY ADMINISTRATOR)
         OF EDWIN BECKLEY DECEASED   )
              Agt.   )
              JOHN HAWS   ) This day came the parties by
their attornies and upon the affidavit of the plaintiff this cause is
continued untill the next of this Court upon his payment of the costs of
this term---

DAVID M. RODDY   )
  AGT.   )
SAUL CAMP   ) This day came the defendant by his attorney and the
said plaintiff being solemnly called to come into court and prosecute his
said suit in this behalf came, not but made default it is therefore
considered by the Court that the said plaintiff be nonsuited and that
the said defendant go hence and recover of the said plaintiff his costs
by him about his defence in this behalf expended &.

CROCKET & PARK   ) Debt
  Agt.   )
WILLIAM F. CAMPBELL) This day came the parties by their attorney
& GEORGE N. RICHARDSON and thereupon came a jury, to wit, Edwin Martin, Sandridge Arnett Farleigh
B. Made, Joseph Huddleston Squire B. Hawkins, James A. Snowdon Ersmus Tucker,
William Ranson David Osborn, Samuel Hudspeth, John Haws and John D. Matlock

who being elected sworn and charged well and truly to enquire and the truth
to speak upon the issure joined upon their oaths do say that they find th
issure in favor of the Plaintiffs and assess their damages to the sum of
eight hundred and seventy one dollars & sixty five cents damages. It is
therefore considered by the Court that the said Plaintiffs recover the sum
of five thousand six hundred and thirty two dollars & ninty four cents the
debt in the plaintiff declaration mentioned together with the damages aforesaid by the Juyyaforesaid assessed and also their costs by them about their
suit in the behalf expended for all which execution and issure &.

CROCKET & PARKS)
  Against)
CAMPBELL & RICHARDSON) This day came the parties by their attornies
and thereupon came a Jury, to wit, Edwin Martin, Sandridge Arnett,
Farleigh B. Wade, Joseph Huddleston Jr. Squire B. Hawkins, James A. Snowdon
Erasmus Tucker, William Ranson, David Osborn Samuel Hudspeth, John Haws
and John D. Matlock who being elected tried and sworn well and truly to
enquire and the truth to speak upon the (p-604) issure joined upon their
oaths do say that they find the issure in favor of the plaintiffs and assess
their damage to the sum of thirteen hundred and twenty one dollars & twenty
nine cents, Whereupon it is considered by the Court that the said Plaintiff
recover of the said defendants the damages aforesaid by the Jury aforesaid
assessed and also their costs by them about their suit in that behalf expended
&. for which execution may issure &.

CROCKET & PARK)
  Agt.)
WM. P.CAMPBELL)
GEO. M. RICHARDSON &)
LUDOLPHUS D. CAMPBELL) This day came the parties by their attornies
and thereupon came a Jury to wit, Edwin Martin, Sandridge Arnett,
Farleigh B. Wade, Joseph Huddleston, Squire B. Hawkins, James A. Snowdon,
David Osborn, Erasms Tucker, William Ransom, Samuel Hudspeth, John Haws
and John D. Matlock who being elected and sworn well and truly to enquire
and the truth to speak upon the issue joined upon their oaths do say they
find the issue in favor of the defendant Ludolphus D. Campbell whereupon
it is considered by the Court that said Ludolphus D. Campbell go hence
without day, And the said William P. Campbell and George W. Richardson
being solemnly called to come and defend this suit came not but made default
Whereupon it is considered by the Court that said plaintiff recover of the
against the said Wm. P. Campbell & George W. Richardson the sum of twenty
six hundred dollars the debt in the declaration mentioned together with
the further sum of four hundred and forty two dollars Interest thereon at
the rate of six per cent per annum and also their costs by them about their
suit in this behalf expended for all which execution may issue &.

DOUGLAS & WOOD)
Against)
EDWIN EANES WM. NORTH)
& EDWARD HOGUE) This day came the parties by their attornies
and thereupon came a Jury to wit,- Edwin Martin, Sandridge Arnett,
Farleigh B. Wade, Joseph Huddleton, Equire B. Hawkins, James A. Snowden,
David Osborne, Erasneus Tucker, William Tucker, William Ransom,
Samuel Hudspeth, John Haws and John D. Matlock who being elected, tried

and sworn well and truly to enquire and the truth to speak upon the issue
joined upon their oaths do say that they find (p-605)   the issue in
favor of the plaintiffs and assess their damages to nineteen dollars
and seventy one cents. Whereupon it is considered by the Court that the
said plaintiffs recover of the said defendant the sum of one hundred
and sixty two dollars and thirteen cents the debt in the declaration
mentioned together with the damages aforesaid by the Jury aforesaid
assessed and also their costs by them about their suit in this behalf
expended &. for all which execution may issue &.

HENRY M. RUTLEDGE   )
   Against   )
FELIX G. AKE   )   This day came the plaintiff by his attorney
and having filed his declaration and the defendant being solemnly called
to come and defend his suit came not but made default. Wherefore it is
considered by the Court that the said plaintiff recover of the said
defendant the sum of ninety eight dollars the balance of the debt in the
declaration mentioned together with the further sum of two dollars &
fifty cents Interest thereon at the rate of six per cent per annum and
also his cause by him about his suit in this behalf expended &. for all
which execution may issue &.

THE STATE OF TENNESSEE   )
   Against   )
CHARLES FARIS & JOSEPH KING   )   This day came the defendants by their
attorney and ~~the said State of Tennessee and~~ having solemnly called
Erwin P. Frierson the attorney General for the state of Tennessee being
solemnly called to come in and prosecute his suit came not but made default.
Wherefore it is considered by the Court that the said Defendant go hence
without day and recover against the said State of Tennessee their costs
by them about their defence in this behalf expended &.

       The commissioners appointed to settle with Susan Trigg administratrix
of the Estate of James S. McWhorter decd returned their report into Open
Court which was received by the Court and ordered to be recorded.

       This day Susan Trigg Guardian for William Trigg, Marshall Trigg
Alanson Trigg made her return in Open Court which was received by the
Court and ordered to be recorded.

(p-606)   WILLIAM D. MARCUM   )
           Against   )
           C. B. H. AKE   )   This day came the plaintiff by his
attorney and having filed his declaration and the defendant being solemnly called to come and defend his said suit came not but made default
Wherefore it is considered by the Court that the said plaintiff recover
against the said defendant the sum of thirty one dollars the debt in the
declaration mentioned together with his costs by him about his suit in
this behalf expended &. for all which execution may issue&.

MARK HUTCHINS   ) Sci fa
   Agt.   )
JOSEPH R. SHROPSHIRE ADMR.   )
OF CATHARINE SHROPSHIRE DE'CD   ) This day came the plaintiff by his

attorney & moved the Court to revive the Judgement in the said Scire facais
mentioned against the said Joseph R. Shropshire admr. of the said
Catharine for the sum of forty one dollars and eightyseven cents debt and
fifty cents costs before James Sharp /////// am acting Justice of the peace
for said County and that satisfaction of said Judgement yet remains to be
made, except the sum twenty four dollars & thirty nine cents which was paid
on the twenty fifth day of November A. D. 1830 and at the November Term
1834 of this Court letters of administration was granted to the said Joseph
R. Shropshire upon the estate of the said Catharine deceased and that the
said Scire facias has been duly made known to the said Joseph R. Shropshire
Wherefore it is considered by the Court that said Judgement be revised for r
the balance and thereon and that an execution issue therefore with interest
from the rendition thereof and that the said plaintiff recover of the said
defendant his costs by him about Scisi facias in this behalf expended &.

(p-607)   JACOB TALLY   )
              Against   )
           WILLIAM A. CALDWELL) This day came the plaintiff by his
attorney and having filed his declaration and the said defendant being
solemnly called to come into Court and defendant said suit came not but
made default wherefore it is considered by the Court that the plaintiff
recover of the defendants the sum of one hundred and ninety dollars the
balance of the debt in the declaration mentioned together with the further
sum of thireen dollars and thirty cents damage and also his costs by him
about his suit in this behalf expended &. for all which execution may Issue &

EDWARD SWANN JR.   )
  Against   )
JOHN B. TALIAFERRO   )
& WM. W. DAVIS   )   This day came the plaintiff by his attorney and
having filed his declaration and the said defendant being solemnly called
to come into Court and defend said suit came not but made default. Therefore
it is considered by the Court that the said plaintiff recover of the said
defendant the sum of two hundred and twenty six dollars the debt in the
Declaration mentioned together with the further sum of two dollars and
twenty six cents damage for its detention and also his costs by him about
his suit in this behalf expended &. for all which execution may issue. Error

     This day Richard Charles guardian of Powhattan Boling made his return
in open Court which was received by the Court and ordered to be recorded.

     Ordered by the Court that William B. Knight be appointed overseer of
the stage road from Dr. Turner's to the seven mile post in the place of
Edmund P. Lee and that he keep the same in good repair according to law
and that he have the same hands that worked under the former overseer.

     Court adjourned until tomorrow morning 10 o'clock.
                              John Dougherty
                              Williams Simmons
                              James Keith

(p-608)   Friday Morning February the 26th 1836 Court met according to
adjournment. Present - John Dougherty) Esquires
                        James Keith   )
                        William Simmons) Justices of the Peace for Franklin
                                             County

Court adjourned until tomorrow morning 12 o'clock.

John Dougherty
Williams Simmons
James Keith

Saturday Morning February the 27th 1836 Court met according to adjournment. Present - John Dougherty   ) Esquires acting justices of
                    William Simmons   () peace for Franklin County.

State of Tennessee
            On petition of George M. Hawkersmith for alicense to keep a tavern at his house in Franklin County. It is therefore ordered by the Court that he have license accordingly by entering into bond and security according to law. Isd.

This day George S. Miller coroner of Franklin County came into Court and offered his resignation as such which was received by the Court.

On motion of W. S. Oldham Esquire and it appearing to the satisfaction of the Court Hugh Francis is a man of honesty probity and good demeanor and that he is twenty one years of age and that he has been a resident citzen of Franklin County for the lasttwelve months. It is therefore ordered by the Court that the said Hugh Frances receive a certificate hereof of the clerk of this said Court.

Court adjourned until Court to course.

John Dougherty
James Keith
William Simmons.

209

(p-609) May Term 1836
        State of Tennessee
        At a Court Court begun and held for Franklin County on the first
Monday in May in the year of our Lord.

        State of Tennessee Franklin County est.
        Be it remembered that on Monday the second day of May 1836 at the
Court house in the town of Winchester being the day appointed by law for
holding the first County Court for the county of Franklin under the act
passed at the session of the General Assembly two commissions were produced
from his Excellancy Newton Cannon Governor of the State aforesaid bearing
date the 23rd day of March 1836 directed to James Robinson, Wallis Estill Jr.
Marshall W. Howell, Asa D. Okley Andrew Mann, George Hudspeth, Adam L. Hyder
Williams Larkins John R. Patrick, Jas. F. Green, Wesley Shores, William H.
Taylor, Zachariah H. Murrell, Samuel Corn, Richmond P. Harris, W. J. Wood,
Benjamin B. Knight, Manyard Gillam, John Nugent, Barnaby Burrough,
John Jones, Stewart Cowan, Isham Womack, Robert Larkin, James Wilkerson,
Samuel Miller, James S. Cowling, James Keith, James Bledsoe, Merredith
Catchings, William Crownover, Esquires appointing them justices of the peace
in & for the County of Franklin, Whereupon the oath of office, the oath
against Desslbing & the oaths to support the constttuion of the State of
 Tennessee & of the United States was administered to the said James
Robinson, Marshall W. Howell & James Keith Esquires by John Dougherty late
a justice of the peace of & for said county and the same othat were in like
manner administered to the remaining twenty eight justices by James
Robinson Esqr. one of the present & late justices of the peace in and for
said County.
The before named Justices being thus qualified took their seats & proceeded
to business.

        William Wilson Brazelton produced in Court a certified from John
Handley who was appointed to hold the elections for County officers,
agreeable to the provisions of the act of the last session of the General
Assembly certifying that he had been duly & constitutionally elected clerk
of this Court. Whereupon the said William Wl Brazelton took the oath to
support the constitution of the Unitdd States, the oath of office prescribed
by law & the oath against Duelling & entered into & acknowledged the
following bond, to wit,- know all men by these present that we William
W. Brazelton, Mark Hutchin, William Brazelton Sr. & Solomon Wagner all of
the County of Franklin State of Tennessee are held and firmly bound into
his Exccllency Newton Cannon Governor of said State and his successors in
office in the sum of five thousand dollars which payment well and truly to
be (p-610) made me bind ourselves our heirs executors administrations
jointly severally firmly by these presents sealed with our seals and dated
the 2nd day of May A. D. 183- . The condition of the above obligation is
such whereas it appears that at the general Elections held for said County
on the 5th day of March A. D. 1836 the above bound William W. Brazelton was
duly and contitutionally elected clerk of the County Court of said Franklin
County for the Term of Four years from this date, Now therefore if the said
William Wilson Brazelton Clerk as aforesaid shall well and truly keep and
preserve all the records of said Court and shall well and truly discharge
all the duties of his said office according to law then the above obligation
to be void else to be & remain in full force and virtue.
                                        W. W. Brazelton (Seal)

Mark Hutchins (Seal)
Wm. Brazelton (Seal)
Solomon Wagner (Seal)

Know all men by these presents that we William W. Brazelton Mark
Hutchens & William Brazelton Senr. all of the County of Franklin & State of
Tennessee are held and firmly bound into Newton Canan Governor of said
State and his successors in office in the sum of two thousand five hundred
dollars to which payment well and truly to be made we bind ourselves our
heirs administrators jointly severally and firmly by these presents sealed
with our seales this 2th day of May 1836. The condition of the above
obligation is such that Whereas it appears that at the General Election
held for Franklin County on the 5th day of March A. D. 1836 the above bound
William W. Brazelton was duly and constitutionally elected Clerk of the
County Court of Franklin County for the Term of four years from this day
Now therefore if the said William W. Brazelton doth well and truly pay over
all the money by him collected justly due the county or State as a tax to
the person or persons authorized to receive the same then the above obligation
to be void else to be and remain infull force and virtue.

W.W. Brazelton   (Seal)
Mark Hutchens   (Seal)
William Brazelton Senr. (Seal)

Thomas Finch produced in Open Court a certificate from John Handly
who was appointed to hold the election for county officers agreeably to
the provisions of the act of the last session of the General Assembly
certifying that he had ~~poppsy~~ been duly constitutionally elected sheriff
of this county Whereupon the said Thomas Finch took the oath to support
the constitution of the State of Tennessee and an oath to support the
constitution of the United States and the oaths of office prescribed by
law & the oath against duelling & entered into and acknowledged the
following bonds, to wit,- know all men by these presents that we Thomas Finch
(p-811) Thomas Howard, William Orear, James Sharp Sr. all of the county
of Franklin and State of Tennessee are held and firmly bound unto his
excellenct Newton Canon Governor in and over said State of Tennessee and
his successors in office in the penal sum of twelve thousand two hundred
dollars which payment well and truly to be made we bind ourselves, our
heirs executors and administrators jointly severally firmly by these presents
sealed with our seals and dated this 2nd day of may 1836 the condition
of the above obligation is such that Whereas it appears that at the general
election held for said County on the 5th day of March A. D. 1836. The above
bound Thomas Finch was duly and constitutionally elected Sheriff in and
for Franklin County for the ensuing two years from this date now therefore
if the above bound Thomas Finch shall well and truly execute and due return
make of process and precept to him directed and pay and satisfy all fees
and sums of money by him received or levied by Virtue of any process unto
the proper office by which the same by the tenor thereof ought to be paid
or to the person or persons to whom the same shall be due his her or their
executors administrators attorneys or agents and in all other things well
and truly and faithfully execute the said office of Sheriff during his
continuance therein then the above obligation to be void otherwise to remain
in full force and effect. Thomas Finch (Seal)
Test   Thomas Howard (Seal)

W. W. Brazelton   Wm. Orear (Seal)
     Clk.   Jas. Sharp (Seal)
Know all men by these presents that we Thomas Finch, James Sharp Senr.
Wm. Orear, Thomas Howard all of the County of Franklin and State of
Tennessee are held and firmly bound unto his Excellency Newton Canon
Governor of said State and his Successors in office in the sum of five
thousand dollars to which payment well and truly to be made we find
ourselves, our heirs executors administrators jointly severally firmly
by these presents sealed with our seals the 2nd day of May A. D. 1836. The
condition of the above obligation is such that whereas the above bound
Thomas Finch was duly and constitutionally appointed to collect the State
County poor and additional Taxes to pay Jurors for the year A. D. 1836
now therefore if the said Thomas Finch does well and truly collect and
pay over to the proper persons the aforesaid taxes for said year A. D. 1836
agreeably to the law then the above obligation to be void else to be and
remain in full force and virtue.   Thomas Finch (Seal)
Test   James Sharp Sr. (Seal)
W. W. Brazelton   Wm. Orear (Seal)
                                              Thomas Howard (Seal)

Know all men by these presents that we ~~all of the~~ Thomas Finch James Sharp
Thomas Howard & William Orear all of the county of Franklin and State of
Tennessee and held and firmly bound unto James Robinson Chaimen and
of the County Court of Franklin County for the time being & his successors
in office in the sum of five thousand dollars (p-612) to which payment
well and truly to be made we bind ourselves our heir executors and administrators jointly severally firmly by these presents sealed with ourselves
the 2nd day of May A. D. 1836. The condition of the above obligation is
such that whereas the above bound Thos Finch was duly and constitutionally
appointed to collect the County additional & poor tax for the year 1836
now therefore if the said Thomas Finch doth well and truly collect and
pay over to the proper person the County additional & poors tax for said
year 1836 agreeably to law then the above obligation to be void else to
be remain in full force and virtue.
     Test   Thomas Finch (Seal)
W.W. Brazelton Clerk   James Sharp)Seal)
                                              Thos. Howard (Seal)
                                              William Orear (Seal)

     Jessie F. Wallace produced in open Court a certificate from
John Handly who was appointed to hold the election for county officers
agreeably to the provisions of the act of the last session of the General
assembly certifying that he had been duly and constitutionally elected
register in and for Franklin County for the insuing four years.

     Whereupon the said Jessie F. Wallace took the oath to support the
constitution of the State of Tennessee the oath to support the constitution
of the United States the oath of office prescribed by law and and oath
against duelling and entered into bond ~~with of twelve thousand of~~ with
Mark Hutchins & George Grey his securities in the sum of twelve thousand
five hundred dollars conditioned according to law.

     James L. Bryant produced in Open Court a certificate from John
Handly who was appointed to hold the election for County officers agreeably

to the provision of the act of the last session of the General Assembly
certifying that he had been duly and constitutionally elected trustee for
the said County of Franklin for the insuing two years from this date.

Whereupon the said James L. Bryant took the oath to support the
constitution of the State of Tennessee the oath to support the constitution
of the United States the oath of office and the oath against duelling and
entered into bond with Petter S. Decherd & Benjamin Decherd his securities
in the sum of six thousand dollars conditioned as the law directs.

This day came on an election for ~~County Survey~~ the purpose of
electing a county surveyor for Franklin County and on countihg out the votes
it was found that George Gray was duly and constitutionally Survey for
Franklin County for the insuing four (p-613) years who thereupon came
into court and took the oath prescribed by law and entered into bond with
James Lewis John Francis & Jessie T. Wallace in the sum of ten thousand
dollars conditioned according to law.

This day came on an election for ~~coroner~~ the purpose of electing a
coroner for Franklin county and on counting out the votes its was found
that George S. Miller was duly and constitutionally elected coroner in
and for said county for the ensuing two years who thereupon came into court
and took the oaths prescribed by law and entered into bond with Jachariah
H. Murrel and Barnaby Burrow his securities in the sum of two thousand
five hundred dollars conditioned according to law.

This day came on an election for the purpose of electing Ranger for
Franklin County and on counting out the votes it was found that Robert
Dougan was duly and constitutionally elected Ranger in and for said County
for the insuing two years who thereupon came into Court and took the oaths
prescribed by law and entered into bond with Benjamin Decherd and John
Handly his securities in the sum of five Hundred dollars condition
according to law.

This day came on an election for the purpose of electing an entry
taker for Franklin County and on Counting out the votes it was found that
Frederick A. Loughmiller was duly and constitutionally elected Entry taker
in and for said County for the ensuing four years.

John G. Brazelton produced in Court a certificate from John Handly
who was appointed to hold the election for County officers agreeably to
the provision of the act of the last session of the General assembly
certifying that he had been duly and constitutionally elected constable
in and for said county in District No. 1 for the ensuing two years who
thereupon came into Court and took the oaths prescribed by law and entered
into bond with Benjamin Decherd and William Brazelton his securities in the
sum of one thousand dollars condition agreeably to law.

Sanders Faris produced in Court a certificate from John Handly who
was appointed to hold the Election for County officers agreeably to the
provisions of the act of the last session of the General assembly certifying
that he had been duly and constitutionally elected constable in and for
said county in District No. 1 for ensuing two years who thereupon came into
Court and took the oaths prescribed by law and entered into bond with

Henry Runnuls and T. J. Curle his securities in the sum of one thousand dollars condition agreeably to law.

(p-614)   William H. Gillaspie produced in Court a certificate from John Handly who was appointed to hold the election for County officers agreeably to the provisions of the act of the last session of the General Assembly certifying that he was duly and constitutionally elected constable in and for said county District No. 2 for the ensuing two years who thereupon came into Court and took the oaths prescribed by law and entered into bound with Nicholas W. Mathews and John Russell his securities in the sum of one thousand dollars greeably to law.

Present John Jones //// ////// George Hadspeth William Crownover Barnaby Burrow Wallis Estill Jr. James Keith James Robinson Adam L. Hydes Stewart Cowan Westly Shores John Nugent Samuel Miller Miniard Gillam Robert Lacky James Wilkinson James S. Cowling Andrew Mann Willian N. Taylor Richmond P. Harris John R. Patrick Samuel Corn James F. Green Asa D. Oakly William Larkin Esquires ordered by the Court that Thos. Finch Sheriff of Franklin County be allowed the sum of fifty dollars for Ex officio services for the year ending this Term of the Court. and that the clerk issue a certificate to the County Trustee to pay him the same which allowances was unanimously made by said Justices. Isued to Finch.

Present John Jones George Hadspeth William Crownover Barnaby Burrow Wallis Estill Jr. James Keith James Robinson Adam L. Hayder Stewart Cowan Westly Shores John Nugent Samuel Miller Miniard Gillam Robert Lacky James Wilkerson James S. Cowling Andrew Mann William N. Tayler Richmond P. Harris John R. Patrick Samuel Corn James F. Green Asa D. Oakley & William Larkin Esquires.

Ordered by the Court that Wiley B. Wagner the former Clerk of Franklin County Court be allowed for his Exofficio services for the last twelve months the sum of fifty dollars and that the clerk issue a certificate to the County Trustee to pay him the same which allowances was unanimously made said Justices "Isud".

Present John Jones George Hadspeth William Crownover Barnaby Burrows Wallis Estill Jr. James Keith James Robinson Adam L. Hyder Stewart Cowan Westly Shores John Nugent Samuel Miller Miniard Gillam Robert Lacky James Wilkinson James S. Cowling Andrew Mann William N. Tayler Richmond P. Harris John R. Patrick Samuel Corn James F. Green Asa D. Oakley William Larkin Esquires ordered by the Court that the following persons be allowed the following sums in the following cases in which Noli prosequis was entered in the circuit of Franklin County to writ in the case of the case of the State of Tennessee against Joseph R. Sopshire John Goodwin Clerk four dollars and (p-615)   Seventy five cents /////// //////// //////// /// /////// / ///// ///// Sheriff Finch two dollars, in the case of the State of Tennessee against George R. Kenerly John Goodwin Clerk five dollars & fifty cents /////// ////// /////// /// ///// / ///// ///// Sheriff Finch two dollars sixty six and half cents Benjamin Franklin a witness one dollar and fifty cents in the case of the State of Tennessee against James Bennet John Goodwin Clerk four dollars thirty seven and half cents /////// ////// /////// /// ////// / ///// ///// Sheriff Oliver one dollar thirty seven and a half cents. In the case of the State of Tennessee against Warren Rowe John Goodwin Clerk five dollars and fifty cents Attorney General ~~Truett Two Dollars & fifty cents~~ Sheriff Finch one dollar and that the Clerk issue a certificate to each of them to the County Trustee to pay the same which allowances was unanimously made said Justices Isd to Goodwin to Oliver to Finch to Franklin.

Joel Vanzant produced in Court a certificate from John Handly who was appointed to hold the elections for county officers agreeably to the provisions of the act of the last session of the General Assembly certifying that he had been duly and constitutionally elected constable in and for ~~District No 3~~ said county in District No 3 for the ensuing two years who thereupon came into Court and took the oaths prescribed by law and entered into bound with George Hadspeth & George Mosely his securities in the sum of one thousand dollars agreeably to law.

Clinton Hunt produced in Court a certificate from John Handly who was appointed to hold the election for County officers agreeably to the provisions of the act of the last session of the General Assembly certifying that he had been duly and constitutionally elected constable in and for the County in District no. 4 for the ensuing two years who thereupon came into Court and took the oaths prescribed by law and entered into bond with William Larkin & David W. Staples his securities in the sum of one thousand dollars agreeably to law.

Jesse Frazier produced in Court a certificate from John Handly who was appointed to hold the election for County officers agreeably to the provisions of the act of the last session of the General assembly certifying that he had been duly and constitutionally elected constable in and for said County in District no. 5 for the ensuing two years who thereupon came into Court and to the oaths prescribed by law and entered into bond with Andrew Mann & George Faris his securities in the sum of one thousand dollars agreeably to law.

(p-616) Wade Brown Produced a certificate from John Handly who was appointed to hold elections for county officers agreeably to the provisions of the act of the last session of the General assembly certifying that he had been duly and constitutionally elected constable in and for said county in District no. 6 for the ensuing two years who thereupon came into Court and took the oaths prescribed by law and entered into Bond with Jacob Awalt and J. W. Brown his securities in the sum of one thousand dollars agreeably to law.

John Byran produced a certificate from John Handly who was appointed to hold the elections for county officers agreeably to the provisions of the act of the last session of the General assembly certifying that he had been duly and constitutionally elected constable in and for said County in District no. 7 for the ensuing two years who thereupon came into Court and took the oaths prescribed by the law and entered into bond with James Byran and Willis Bert his securities in the sum of one thousand dollars agreeably to law.

John H. Duncan produced a certificate from John Handly who was appointed to hold the election for County officers agreeably to the

provisions of the act of the last session of the General Assembly cettifying
that he had been duly and constitutionally elected constable in and for said
County District No. 8 for the ensuing two years who thereupon came into
Court and took the oaths prescribed by law and entered into bond with
HHerendon Green and William Duncan his securities in the sum of one thousand
dollars agreeable to law.

Arman Gibson produced a certificate from John Handly who was appointed
to hold the election for County officers agreeable to the provisions of the
act of the last session of the General assembly cettifying that he had been
duly and constitutionally elected constable in and for said County District
No. 9 for the ensuing two years who thereupon came into Court and took the
Oaths prescribed by Law and entered into bond with Myniard Gillam John Anderson
his securities in the sum of one thousand dollars agreeable to law

George W. Partin produced in open Court a cettificate from John
Handly who was appointed to hold election of County officers agreeable to
the provisions of the act of the last General Assembly cettifying that he
had been duly and constitutionally elected constable in and for said County
District No. 10 for the ensuing two years who thereupon came into Court
and took the oaths prescribed by Law and entered into bond with David
Macleroy and Alexander E. Patton his securities in the sum of one thousand
dollars agreeable to law.

(p-617)   John M. Morrow produced in Open Court a certificate from John
Handly who was appointed to hold the election for County officers agreeable
to the provisions of an act of the last General Assembly cettifying that he
had been duly and constitutionally elected in and for said County in District
No. 11 for the next ensuing two years who thereupon came into Court and
entered into bond with John G. Bostick & David Macleroy his securities in
the sum of one thousand dollars the sum conditioned by law.

Wm. M. Cowan produced in open Court a cettificate from John Handly
who was appointed to hold the election for County officers agreeable to the
provisions of an act of the last session of the General Assembly cettifying
that he had been duly and constitutionally elected in and for said County
in District no. 13 for the next ensuing two years who thereupon came into
Court and entered into bond with John Handly and James T. Cowan his securities
in the sum of one thousand dollars the sum conditioned by law.

B. F. Gibson produced in open Court a cettificate from John Handly
who was appointed to hold the election for County officers agreeable to the
provisions of the act of the last General Assembly cettifying that he had
been duly and constitutionally elected in and for said County in District
No. 14 for the next ensuing two years who thereupon came into Court and took
the oath prescribed by law entered into bond with James F. Keith & John
Fitzpatrick his securities in the sum of one thousand dollars the sum conditioned by law.

John Anderson produced in open Court a cettificate from John Handly
who was apointed to hold the election for County officers agreeable to the
provisions of the act of the last General Assembly cettifying that he had
been duly and constitutionally elected in and for said County in District
15 for the next ensuing two years who thereupon came into Court and entered

into bond with Daniel Riggle and Reuben Ricordson his securities in the sum of prescribed by law.

This day James Roberson was duly and constitutionally appointed chairman of the County Court of Franklin until the first Monday in Jan. Next by unamimous vote.

This David O. Anderson and David Mackleroy came into Court and took the oaths prescribed by law to act as Deputy Sheriff of Franklin County.

This day G. W. Richardson, Hosea Stamps, Jesse Jenkins & Jesse Reynolds commissioners of the pond Spring School tract made a return (p-618) of their settlement with said tract which was recovered by the Court.

This day John G. Bostick, A. E. Patton & Barnoly Buxron who were appointed at Feby. Term 1836 to settle with Susannah Sartin Administratrix of the Estate of Harison Sartin Dec'd made their return which was received by the Court and ordered to be recorded.

This day Solomon Holder, Wilis Best & R. P. Harris were duly appointed commissioners of the Poor House of Franklin until first Jany and were qualified.

This day Richmond P. Harris was duly appointed treasure of the Poor house who intered into bond with A. D. Oakley his security in the sum of one thousand dollars.

This day the commissioners appointed at the last term of this Court to settle with Elijah & David Mackleroy ~~made their~~ Executors of Isaac Mackleroy Dec'd made their report to Court which was rec'd and ordered to be recorded.

It appearing to the satisfaction of the Court that William Thompson late of this County died intestate and letters of administration were applied for Wm. B. & Bryant B. Thompson sons of said Decedent and George W. Morris ~~applied for letters of administration~~ son in law on the Estate of said decedent wherefore it was ordered by the Court that letters of administration be granted to said Morris accordingly who entered into bond with Thos Knight & Benjamin Decherd his securities in the sum of four thousand dollars conditioned according to law and qualified accordingly. The Court upon an investagation of the matter gave the preference to Morris.

Ordered by the Court that the order making an allowance to James Moonard at the last Term of this Court be recinded and made void.

It appearing to the satisfaction of the Court the Ralph Crabb late of this County died intestate and Doctor Wallis Estill applied for letters of administration on the Estate of said Decedent Wherefore it was ordered by the Court that he have letters accordingly. Who entered into bond with Willie B. Wagner and Thos M. Pryor his securities in the sum of five thousand dollars condition according to law and was qualified accordingly.

It appearing to the satisfaction of the Court that cornelius N. Lewis late of this County died intestate and James Lewis applied for letters of administration on the Estate of said Decedent. Wherefore it was ordered by the Court that he have letters accordingly. Who entered into bond with George Gray his security in the sum of twelve hundred dollars condition according to law and was qualified accordingly.

(p-619)   This day the school commissioners in Tally Cove made their return to Court which was received by the Court in order to be recorded.

Ordered by the Court that Joseph Little be appointed Guardian over the person and property of William Wilder orphan of Nathaniel Wilder deceased who entered into bond with Berry Lynch and Alfred A. Loyd his securities in the sum of eight hundred dollars condition according to law.

It appearing to the satisfaction of the Court that Robert Frame hath departed this life intestate leaving a widow and several infant children and that his personal property is in this County therefore on the motion of the widow who declined administrating administratrix of said decedent estate is granted to James Morris. It was ordered by the Court that he have letters accordingly. Who entered into bond with John Frame and Lansford Mathews his securities in the sum of twelve thousand dollars condition according to law and was qualified accordingly.

On the petition of James Morris administrator of the Estate of Robert Frame Dec'd which was sworn to in Open Court setting forth that it would be to the interest of the distributor of said intestate to sell a negro man William belonging to said Estate and the Court being Satisfied of the truth of said petition and that said negro ought to be sold it is ordered by the Court that said administrator make sale of said negro man for the best price that can be obtained and accordnt therefar according to law, issued.

This day John Frame administrator with the will annexed of Ezekiel Philips deceased returned in open Court an inventory of said Estate which was received by the Court in order to be recorded.

This day the last Will and Testament of William Bostic deceased was produced in Open Court by John G. Bostick one of the securities therein named whereupon Sims Kelly one of the subscribing witnesses thereto named came into Open Court and being first only sworn desposeth and saith that William Bostick signed the same in his presence and at the time of signing the same he the said William Bostick was of sound and deposing mind and memory and that he signed the same as a witness thereto in his presence and at his request.

(p-620)   Present John Jones, George Hadspeth William Crownover, Barnaby Farrow Wallis Estill Jr. Jas. Keith, James Robinson, Adam L. Hayder, Stewart Cowan, Westly Shores, John Nugent Samuel Miller, Miniard Gilliam Robert Lacky, James Wilkinson J. G. Cowling, Andrew Mann William N. Tayler Richmond P. Harris J. R. Patrick, Samuel Corn, James F. Green, Ada D. Oakly William Larkin Esquires. Ordered by the Court that the following persons be allowed the following sums in the following cases in which Noleprosequise were entered in the County Court of Franklin County to wit, in the case of the State of Tennessee against Madison Goodman, Wiley B. Wagner Clerk two dollars sixty eight and three fourths cents. Sheriff Oliver two dollars.

sixity two and half cents in case of the State of Tennessee against
Reason Isom, Wiley B. Wagner Clerk one dollar and seventy five cents Sheriff
Finch one dollar and fifty cents. In the case of State of Tennessee against
Bryant B. Thompson & Richard F. McDoff, Wiley B. Wagner Clerk three dollars
and seventy five cents Sheriff Finch four dollars in the case of the State
of Tennessee against Merrel Emby Wiley B. Wagner Clerk four dollars eighty
seven and a half cents Sheriff Finch two dollars and seventy five cents in
the case of the State of Tennessee against Enock Hardcastle, Wiley B. Wagner
clerk three dollars and twenty five cents Sheriff Finch one dollar and
Fifty cents, in the case of the State of Tennessee Against Elias Oldham Jr.
Wiley B. Wagner Clerk two dollars twelve and a half cents Sheriff Finch one
Dollar and that the clerk of this Court issure a seperate certificate to
each of them to the County Trustee to pay the same which allowance was
unanmiously made by said justices issued to Wagner, to Oliver, to Finch.

Present John Jones, George Hudspeth, William Crownover, Barnaby Burrow
Wallis Estill Jr. James Keith Jas. Robinson Adam L. Hayden, Stewart Cowan
Westly Shores, John Nugent, Samuel Miller, Miniard Gilliam, Robert Lacky,
James Wilkinson, James S. Cowling, Andrew Mann, William N. Taylor
Richmond P. Harris, John R. Patrick Samuel Corn, James F. Green Asa D.
Oakley, William Larkin Esquires. Ordered by the Court that Wiley B. Wagner
be allowed the sum of eighteen dollars and seventy five cents for two record
books furnished for the circuit Clerks office of Franklin County and one for
the Registers office for said County and that the Clerk issure a certificate
to the County Trustee to pay him the same. Such allowances was unanimously
made by the said Justices. Isd.

(p-621)   Present, John Jones, William Crownover, Barnaby Burrows,
Wallis Estill, James Keith, James Robinson, Adam L. Hayden, Stewart Cowan
Westly Shores, J. Nugent, Samuel Miller, Mynard, Gilliam, Robert Lacky,
James Wilkerson, James S. Cawling, Andrew Mann, William N. Taylor,
R. P. Haris, J. R. Patrick, Saml. Corn. James F. Green, A. D. Oakly, William
Larkin, Z. H. Murrell, Esquires ordering the Court that John Handly be
allowed the sum of twelve dollars for holding the last election in the
differenct districts and thirty seven and one half cents postage on the
justices commissions and that the Clerk issue a certificate to the County
Trustee to pay the same this allowance was unanimously made by the above
Justices except James S. Cawling who voted in the negative. Issued Isued

Present John Jones, William Crownover, Barnaby Burrow, Wallis Estill Jr.
James Keith James Roberson, Adam L. Hayder Stewart Cowan, Wesly Shores,
John Nugent, Saml. Miller, Mynard Gilliam Robert Lacky James Wilkinson,
James S. Cawling Andrew Mann William N. Taylor R. P. Harris, J. R. Patrick
Samuel Corn, James F. Green A. D. Oakly William Larkin, Z. H. Murrell Esquires
Ordered by the Court that Thomas Finch be allowed the sum of three dollars
for furnishing two loads of wood and cutting same for the stoves at November
term 1835 & Feby Term 1836 of Franklin County Court and that the Clerk issue
a cettificate to the County Trustee to pay him the same which allowance was
unanimously made by said Justices. Isued to Finch.

Present John Jones, William Corwnover, Barnaby Burrow, Wallis Estill, Jr.
James Keith, James Robinson A. L. Hayden, Stewart Cowan, Wesly Shores,
John Nugent, Samuel Miller, M. Gillam R. Lacky, J. Wilkerson J. L. Cawling,
AndrewMann, W. N. Taylor, R. P. Haris, J. R. Patrick, Samuel Corn James F.

Green, A. D. Oakly Wm. Larkin Esquires ordered by the Court that Joseph Klepper, James sharp & James Roberson be allowed the sum of sixty six dollars & fifty cents for the completing the Bridge across the Boiling Fork of Elk river at Winchester and that the Clerk issue a certificate to the County Trustee to pay them the same which allowance was unanimously made by the above justices. Isd.

Ordered by the Court that William Simmons (p-622) Samuel Raseborre & John Turner be appointed commissioner to allot to Lucinda Frame the Widow of Robert Frame deceased one years support out of the estate of said decedent and that they make their report to the term of this Court.

Ordered by the Court that the following persons be appointed Jurors to the next circuit Court to be held for the County of Franklin at the Court House in Winchester on the 4th Monday in July Next Viz. Marshall W. Howell Ben Decherd, James Keith, William Brazelton, Meredeth Catchings, William Crownover William Capperton, David Hunt Sr. Alexander B. Patton Reuben Scrivner, Sanford W. Young John Stovall, Daniel Weaver, Wm. N. Taylor John Crocket Sr. James F. Green Robert C. Coldwell, Asa D. Oakly, Andrew Mann, Richmond P. Harris, James Bledsoe, Samuel Miller, James S. Cawling Mynard Gilliam Benjamin B. Knight, William G. Moore, and that the Sheriff summon them to attend said Court and make due return of the same and that John G. Brazelton & Sanders Faris be appointed constable to attend on said Court and that the Sheriff summon them to attend the same. Isd.

Ordered by the Court that the following persons be appointed commissioners in and for the County of Franklin to wit,- Marshall W. Howell in district No. 1 Andrew Mann in District No. 2 George Hudspeth District No.3
John R. Patrick in District No. 4
Westly Shore In district No. 5
William N. Taylor in District No. 6
Richmond P. Haris in District No. 7
Benjamin B. Knight In District No. 8
John Nugent in District No. 9
Barnaby Burrow in District No. 10
Stewart Cowan in District No. 11
Robert Lacky in District No. 12
Samuel Miller in District No. 13
James Bledsoe in District No. 14
Meredeth Kitchens in District No. 15 and that they make due return on or before the August Term 1836 of this Court.

Court adjourned untill tomorrow 10 o'clock.

James Robinson
M. W. Howell
B. B. Knight
Samuel Corn

Tuesday morning thirt May one thousand eight hundred and thirty six. Court meet pusuant to adjournment Present the following Justices James Roberson, B. Knight, B. Burrows, Samuel Corn, Wallis Estill Jr. Marshall W. Howell & Mynard Gilliam.

F. A. Langhmiller who was heretofore on yesterday elected Erty John

in and for Franklin County came into Court and took the oaths prescribed
by law and entered into bond with Jno. Decherd and Squire B. Hawkins his
securities in the sum of five hundred dollars.

(p-623)   Ordered by the Court that William Austill be appointed Guardian
over the persons and property of Eliza Ann, Betsy Ann Sally O. Austell,
Who entered into Bond of two thousand dollars with Samuel Austell and
Elijah Turner his securities according to law.

        Ordered by the Court that the following persons be appointed a Jury
of view Viz. Thomas S. Logan, P. L. Decherd, James Taylor, Edmond Dyer,
Alexander S. Porter, Thomas Garner & James Keith to view a road from
Winchester to the Chalebeate Springs on the Mountain and that they report
to the next Term of this Court.

        The following receipt was ordered to be entered upon record
Nashville Inn 4th November 1835. Received of W. B. Wagner clerk of
Franklin County Court one thousand dollars being the balance in full of
his return of taxes rec'd by him for the year ending the first day of Oct.
1835 which by law he is bound to account for agreeably to his return for
said year 1835.
$1000
                                        Thos. Crutcher
                                        Treasure

        This day Willis J. Hines Guardian of James Navod made his return as
Guardian for the year 1835 which was received by the Court and ordered to
be made apart of the record.

        This day Wm. B. Thompson & Bryant B. Thompson came into Open Court
& prayed an appeal to the next Circuit Court from the order made on
yesterday appointing G. W. Morris administrator of the Estate of William
Thompson Dec'd which is granted the said William B. Thompson & Bryant B.
Thompson they having executed Bond with Murry S. Emby and William Faris
securities in the penalty of $500 conditioned as the law directs.

        By the consent of William B. Thompson & Bryant B. Thompson George W.
Morris the parties contending for the administration of the estate of
William Thompson Deceased, Thomas Knight is appointed without security
to take charge of said intestate estate and make inventory of said estate
and return the same to the next court term & make Sale of all the personal
property (Slaves excepted) on a credit of twelve months taking bond and
good security from the purchasers and return an account thereof to the
next Court.

        It is further ordered that he hire out the slaves belonging to said
estate until the 25th day of December next taking Bond & Security for the
Hire & for the forth coming of taxes.

        Ordered by the Court that John Burris be appointed overseer of the
road from Pelham to the top of the Mountain near Elizabeth Jones in room
of Barnaby Burrow and that he keep the same in good repair according to
law and that he have the same hands that worked under the former overseer.

(p-624)   Ordered by the Court that Joseph Newman be appointed overseer of

the road leading from Winchester toward Nashville beginning at the forks
of the road by James Dardis and ending on the Hill by E. Turneys the
comencing in the Lane at Thos. Knights and that keep the same in good
repair and that he have knights hands, Mary Emley hands Hu Dickerson &
E. Turneys.

Ordered by the Court that John Miller be appointed overseer of the
road leading from Winchester to Jasper commencing at Duncans and work to
Holders and that he keep the same in good repair according to law and that
he have the same hands that worked under the former overseer.

This day Hugh Foster Guardian to George W. Francis Jr. and John
Boyd infant heirs of John Boyd deceased being required by a vote of the
Court at the Last Term at the instance of William Hillarry one of his
securities to appear here at this term and give counter security Whereupon
the said Hu Foster came into Court & entered into Bond with John G.
Frazelton & John Fitzpatrick his securities in the penal sum of five thous-
and Dollars conditioned according to law and to indemnify said Murry
in his security ship aforesaid & thereupon the rules aforesaid.

Ordered by the Court that William Stewart Thomas S. Logan and
William Buchanan be appointed commissioners to lay off to Maria Saxton the
widow of John Saxton deceased one years support out of said Intestates
Estate and that they report to the next term of this Court.

This day Edwin Eans returned into Open Court an additional sale of
the property belonging to the Estate of John Sarton Dec'd which was received
by the Court and ordered to be made apart of the record.

Ordered by the Court that Jesse T. Wallace be appointed keeper of
the Court house until the further order of this Court it shall be his duty
to keep the doors of said house locked except when it is wanted for public
service that he cause said house to be put in good order before the next
Court & to have the same kept in good order daily during the setting of
the several Courts. Isd.

Ordered by the Court that James Sherwood orphan be bound unto
Azarah R. Davis untill he be twenty one years old who entered into Bond
with James Roberson Chairman of said Court according to law.

(p-625)   Recd Winchesters 18th December 1835 of Willie B. Wagner Clerk
of the county Court of Franklin County twenty six dollars, the amount
of fines collected by him for the year ending first December 1835 as
per commissions report.
$26.00
                                    Benjamin Decherd
                                    County Trustee

    Court adjourned until Court on course.
                                    James Robinson
                                    W. Estill Jr.
                                    B. B. Knight
                                    Samuel Miller

June Term 1836
State of Tennessee

At a County Court began and held for Franklin County on the 6th day of said month being the first Monday of said month and the sixtieth year of the Independence of the United States of America. Present Twenty six of the acting justices of the peace for Franklin County.

This day A list of the sales of the property Estate of Levi Shores Dec'd was returned into Open Court and was received by the Court and ordered to be made apart of the record.

This day the last Will and Testament of William Bostick Deceased which was produced heretofore at the last Term of this Court by John G. Bostick one of the executors, mentioned and was proved by Sims Kelly one of the subscribing witnesses and ordered for further probate was proved by the oath William B. G. Muse this day in open Court.

This day a paper writing purporting to be the last will and testament of William Rawlins Deceased was produced in open Court having no subscribing witness thereto whereupon Benjamin Decherd, Andrew J. Brezelton & Willie B. Wagner were called into Court who being first duly sworn depose and say that they behlieve the writing thereof and the signature to be William Rawlins deceased Whereupon it is ordered to be recorded. Doctor Elisha Lewis Henry A. Rains & Jesse McGee the Executors mentioned in the will said Lewis and McGee refusing to act as executors. Whereupon Henry A. Rains executor above named came into Court and entered into bond with Adam Oehmig and Benjamin Decherd his securities in the sum of seven thousand dollars according to law.

(p-626)   Ordered by the Court that John B. Patrick and George Hudspeth Esquires be appointed to allot hands to William Holliday overseer of the road of the first Class from Benas Creek to Robinson Creek.

Ordered by the Court that the County Court Clerk request the former Justices who have in their possession Haywood and Cobbs Revisal to return them to his office so as that the Justices lately elected can be supplied.

This day Thomas Branch produced in Open Court certificate from Thomas Finch certifying that he was duly and constitutionally elected one of the constables in and for Franklin County in District No. 12 in the place of Burrell Pary removed who entered into bond with Willis Burt and Robert Lackey his securities in the sum of one thousand dollars conditioned according to law and was qualified.

Ordered by the Court that Noah McKelvy be appointed as overseer of the road from the rocky point on the Mohords ford road to the road leading to Coldwell Bridge and that he keep the same in good repair according to law and that James S. Cawling be appointed to allot to him hands to work on the same.

This day George Hudspeth Guardian over the property of Carter Hudspeth made his return which was received by the Court.

This day Willis B. Wagner was qualified deputy Clerk of the County

Court of Franklin County ~~and was qualified accordingly~~

Ordered by the Court that Hezekiah Keiton be appointed overseer of the road of the second class from a Hickory Tree above Buckners to Rowland Lanes in the room of Richard P. Holder and that he keep the same in good repair according to law and that he have the same hands that worked under the former overseer.

Ordered by the Court that Pleasant Nevells be appointed overseer of the road of the second Class from Joseph Millers to Bradley's creek in the room of Thomas Branch and that he keep the same in good repair according to law and that he have the same hands that worked under the former overseer.

Ordered by the Court that Dennis B. Muse be appointed overseer of the rock Creek road from the 14 miles post to the County line in the room of Abner Lasater and that he keep the same in good repair according to law and that he have the same hands that worked under the former overseer.

(p-627) Ordered by the Court that Wallis Estill Jr. M. W. Howell & R. P. Harris be appointed to enquire What the poor house can be said sold for & what a site for a new one can be had near Winchester and what the necessary buildings will costs and report to the next Court.

This day Thomas Night who was at the last term of this Court appointed administrator of the estate of William Thompson deceased produced in open Court and inventory of said decedents estate which was ordered to be made apart of the record.

This day the Jury of view heretofore appointed at the May Term of this Court ~~xxxx the~~ to view a road from Winchester to the Chalebeate Springs on Cumberland Mountain make their reports as follows that a road commencing at E. Petts on the Town of Winchester and running with the Street as reserved by John Turner adjoining the land of Luke Teorrass and others to near the Grave Yard thence by said Grave Yard and on the line of Mrs. Erving and William Reves as near as practible to a black oak tree marked by us thence nearly in a direct line to the mouth of Capt. James Taylors Lane thence with the Old Road to the section line thence the most direct way to the land of W. Adkins thence crossing dry creek at Atkins Spring Branch and runing on the West side thereof to the Old Ford thence across the same and up said Dry Creek and a cross Raschal Greens Spring Branch and from thence the most direct way to James Keith field & thence with the old road to the Chalebeate Springs which report was received by the Court.

Ordered by the Court that George Gray John Turner and William Brazelton be appointed a cometee to examine the road as laid out by Jury of view leading from Winchester to the Chalebeate Springs where it crosses Mrs. Ewings & Wm. Reeves Land and assess the damages thereof sustained and report to the next term of this Court. Error

Ordered by the Court that James Bledsoe, Davis Decherd and Robert

Cowan be appointed commissioners to examine into the turnpike road whereon Yereck keeps a turnpike.

Present James Robinson M. W. Howell, James Keith Asa D. Oakley, Wallis Estill Jr. George Hudspeth, Zachariah H. Murrell, Samuel Corn Adam L. Hyden, Andrew Mann, R. P. Harris, James Bledsoe, Meredith Catchings William Larkin Robert Lackey, James S. Cowling, Samuel Miller William N. Taylor, John R. Patrick, William J. Wood Mynard Gilliam Esquires

(p-628) Sixteen of whom voted the afirmative.

Ordered by the Court that the following allowances to made to Willie B. Wagner that he have seven dollars and seventy five cents for 2 record books furnished by him for the clerks office and that he have four dollars eighty seven & half cents as clerk in the case of the State agt. Garnum Scroggin in which nolleprosequin was entered and that the clerk of the Court issure certificate to the county trustee for the same. Issured.

Present James Robinson, Marshall W. Howell, James Keith, Asa D. Oakley Wallis Estille Jr. George Hudspeth Zachariah H. Murrell, Samuel Corn, Adam L. Hyden, Andrew Mann, R. P. Harris, James Bledsoe, Meredith Catchings, William Larkin, Robert Lackey, James S. Cawling Samuel Miller, William N. Taylor John R. Patrick, John Nugent, William J. Wood, Benjamin B. Night, Mynard Gilliam, Sixteen of whom voted in the affirmative.

Ordered by the Court that James L. Williamson be allowed for boad of Mathew Patton in the county Jail and for turn keys eleven dollars sixty two & half cents and that the clerk issure certificate to county trustee for the same. Issured.

This day Benjamin Decherd the county Trustee made his return upon oath of the monies received and paid out by him for the year 1835 ending the 2th day of June 1836 which was received by the Court and ordered to be recorded.

This day the commissioners heretofore appointed to settle with the County Trustee for Franklin County made there report to Court together with the vouchers exhibited to them by the trustee which report was received by the Court and ordered to be recorded. It is also ordered by the Court that the vouchers accompanying said report be carefully preserved by the clerk of this court.

Ordered by the Court that a road of the 2nd class leaving the mans ford road at John Morris and crossing Elks River near the mouth of big Hurican and runing up the creek so as to intersect the pond Spring road at the mouth of the Widow Young's land be established.

This day Dudly Johnson Guardian of Eshelbert C. George made his report of the disposition of said wards property for the year 1835 which was received by the Court.

This day the commissioners appointed to allot to Lucinda Frame widow of Robert Frame Deceased one year provissions out of said Decedents estate made their return which was received by the Court.

(p-629)   Present James Robinson Marshall W. Howell James Keith Asa D.
Oakley, Wallis Estill Jr. George Hudspeth, Z. H. Murrell, Samuel Corn,
A. L. Hyden Andrew Mann, R. P. Harris James Bledsoe, Meredith Catchings
William Larkin, Robert Lackey James S. Cawling; Samuel Miller William N.
Taylor John R. Patrick John Nugent Benjamin B. Knight Mynard Gilliam,
Wesly Shores, Isom Womie Bornaby Burrow Esquires Sixteen of whom voted in
the affirmative. Ordered by the Court that William Wilson be allowed the
sum of eighty seven dollars and fifty cents for completing a bridge across
Elk River near where he lives and that the clerk issue a certificate to
the county trustee for the same. Isd.

     This day the commissioners appointed at February Term of this Court
to settle with the administrators of Henry Burrow deceased made a report
of their settlement which was received by the court.

     Ordered by the Court that Thomas Green, A. J. Steel, John Fitzpatrick
Peter S. Decherd and James Cowan be appointed a Jury of view to turn the
road which leads to Capertons Cove from Winchester so as to run between
Green Brazeltons field and Thomas Green's and that they make their report
to the next term of this Court.

     Present James Robinson Marshall W. Howell, James Keith, Asa D. Oakley
Wallis Estill Jr. George Hudspeth Z. H. Murrell, Samuel Corn Adam L. Hyden
Andrew Mann, R. P. Harris, James Bledsoe, Meredith Citchings, William
Larkin, Robert Lackey, James L. Cowling Samuel Miller, William N. Taylor
John R. Patrick, John Nugent, Benajmin B. Knight, Mynard Gilliam
Wesly Shores, Isom Womic Barnaby Burrow, Esquires Sixteen of whom voted
in the affirmative. Ordered by the Court that John Handly be allowed the
sum of five dollars for two days settling with the County Trustee and
that the clerk of this court issue a certificate to the county trustee
for the same. Isd.

          Court adjourned untill Tuesday 11 o'clock
                              James Robinson
                              M. W. Howell,
                              W. Estill Jr.
                              M. Catchings

(p-630)   Tuesday morning eleven o'clock Court met according to
adjournment.

     Upon the application of Elizabeth Ewing and James Harris. It is
ordered by the Court that a writ of ad quod dommum issure to the sheriff
of Franklin. County requiring him to summon a Jury of good and lawful men
to view the premisis and assess the damages which they may sustain by the
road which was reported to this term of this Court leading from Winchester
to the Chalybeate Springs and to view and to turn said road having due
regard to the interest of the public and of individuals accordingly and that
they make their report to the next term of this Court.

     Ordered by the Court that James Sharp Jr. be appointed overseer of
the road of 2nd class leading from Winchester to Sharps Mill and that he

keep the same in good repair according to law and that he have the same
hands that worked under the former overseer.

This day Henry A. Rains Executor of William Rains deceased made a
report of the property belonging to said decedents estate and was qualified
to the same.

Ordered by the Court that Thomas Soleman be appointed overseer of
the road of the 2nd class from Sharps Mill to Soloman Holders in the room
of Thomas Muse and that he keep the same in good repair according to law
and that he have the same hands that worked under the former overseer.

Court adjourned untill Court in Course.
                                        M. Catchings
                                        James Robinson
                                        W. Estill Jr.

July Term 1836
State of Tennessee
        At a County Court began and held for Franklin County on the 4th
day of said month being the first Monday of said month and the 61st year
of the Independence of the United States of America. Present Eighteen of
the acting Justices of the peace for said County.

It appearing to the satisfaction of the Court that Lydia Wiggin late
of Maryland State departed this life (p-631) and having business to
settle in Tennessee Franklin County Henry J. Wiggin her relation applying
for letters of administration it is therefore ordered by the Court that
he have letters accordingly. Who entered into bond with Edd Tatum and
Henry a. Rains his securities in the sum of eighteen hundred dollars
according to law and was qualified.

Ordered by the Court that Joseph Klippin, Adam Oehmig, and William
Street be appointed a comitee to settle with Edwin Eans administrator
of the Estate of John Sarton Deceased and report to the next term of this
Court.

Ordered by the Court the Benjamin Decherd John Goodwin and Mark
Hutchens be appointed commissioners to lay off to the Widow Crabb consort
of Ralph Crabb decd. a years support out of sadd decedents Estate and
make their return at the next term of this Court.

Ordered by the Court the James Greenlee & George Powell be permitted to
put up a milk sick gate across the road leading from William Faris to the
Makerds ford.

Ordered by the Court that Mark Hutchins James Robinson, James A.
Snowden be appointed commissioners to settle with Benjamin Decherd
Guardian of Edmund Russell.

Ordered by the Court that John H. Morris, Allen Young, Daniel
Weaver, William N. Taylor, David Osborn, Jessie F. Brown, John Runnels
be appointed a Jury of view to lay off a road from John H. Morrises

Allen Young, Daniel Weaver, William N. Taylor, David Osborn, Jessie F. Brown, John Runnels be appointed a Jury of view to lay off a road from John H. Morrises Crossing Elk River near the mouth of Hurricane and up said creek to intersect the pond Spring road at the mouth of the Widow Youngs Lane.

This day James Wilkinson and Isaac Wilkinson Guardians of the minor heirs of John Wilkinson deceased made their return of the hire of said Decedents negroes which was received by the Court.

Ordered by the Court that Michael Williams be appointed overseer of that part of the milk sick fence over which William A. Francis was overseer and that he keep the same in good repair according to law and that he have his own hands Absalom Williams, Petter Williams, the Widow Williams hands, John Francis Bersefied Berry hill Sampson Thompson Bird Francis, William Thurman and his hands Oliver Can, Edmond Holder, William Lee, George Young (p-632) Stephen Law, James Lee David McGowan, Wiseman Adcook Jas. Posey, Edward H. Wade, Miles Francis, Madison Williams, Curtus Ridges Philip Williams, Jacob Williams, Warren Pasey, and Samiel Young to work on the same. The jury of view heretofore appointed at the last term of this Court to view a and turn the road leading to Capertons Cove from Winchester so as to run between Green Brazeltons filed and Thomas Green's field which report was received by the Court.

This day the Sheriff returned the writ of ad quad dum mata issued at the last Term of this Court authorizing him to summon a Jury of twelve good and lawful men to assess the damage sustained by the road running through Mrs. Ewings and James Harris land as he was required to do by the order which writ was by mutal consent of the parties defered by the court untill August Term.

Court adjourned untill tomorrow 10 o'clock.
W. Estille Jr.
James Robinson
M. W. Howell
Jas. Bledsoe

Tuesday the fifth day of July one thousand eight hundred and thirty six and sixty first of American Independence. This day James Robinson & Joseph Kleppen executors of the Adam Gross deceased made a return of a list of notes belonging to said estate which was received by the court and ordered to be recorded.

Ordered by the Court that James Robinson, James E. Harris and John Goodwin be appointed commissioners to settle with Marshall W. Howell one of the executors of the will of William Trigg deceased and with Susan Trigg administratrix of James McQuarter deceased estate and make their report to the next term of this Court.

Court adjourned untill Court in course.
James Robinson
W. Estill Jr.
M. W. Howell
Jas. Bledsoe

(p-633)   August Term 1836
            State of Tennessee
            At a County Court began and held for Franklin on the 1st day of
August one thousand eight hundred and thirty six and on the first Monday
of said month and the sixty first year of the Indenpendence of the United
States of America.

        Present twenty three of the Justices of the peace for Franklin
County.

        Ordered by the Court that John B. Kitchens be appointed overseer
of the road from the branch on this side at Shasteens to Timmes ford
on Elk River and that he keep the same in good repair according to law
and that he have the same hands that worked under the former Overseer.

        This day in Open Court the Widow Awalt Widow of Michael Awalt
was identified. And the said Widow acknowedged the power of attorney
annexed to the pension of Michael Awalt.

        This day Doctor Wallis Estill administrator of Ralph Crabb
deceased produced in Open Court an iventory of said decedent Estate which
was received by the Court and ordered to be recorded.

        On petition of Doctor Wallis Estill administrator of Ralph Crabb
deceased to sell a negro woman named Rhodas belonging to said decedents
estate and setting forth good reason it is ordered by the Court that
Doctor Wallis Estill have an order of sale to sell said negro woman
Rhoda upon eight months credit to the highest bider after giving thirty
day note by setting up written advertisements at the Court house in
Winchester.

        Ordered by the Court that Thomas Finch be appointed administrator
of the Estate of William Thompson deceased in campliance with the request
of the heirs at law, to wit, William B. Thompson, Bryant B. Thompson
and George W. Morris and Said Thomas Finch shall not be required to give
security.

        Ordered by the Court that William B. Sargent be appointed overseer
of the Huntsville road of the 1st class from Russells grocery to John
Staples in room of Wesley Shores and that he keep the same in good repair
according to law and that he have the same hands that worked under Shores.

        Ordered by the Court that William Hudson, Henry Wiggin, H. Green
Robert Turner & Nathan Martin be appointed a Jury of view to turn the
road at Milton McQueen or near his house so as to intersect the main
road at Wiggins Field and that they make their report to the next Term
of this Court.

(p-634)   Ordered by the Court that Richard Sharp senr. William Darwin,
William Hudson, Soloman Wagner & Madison Porter be appointed a Jury of
view to turn the road leading to Coldwells bridge where it runs between
Dardis & Turney so as to run on the line between them, and that they
report to the next therm of this Court.

Ordered by the Court that Willey J. Hines take care of the orphan children of Henry Wiggs and that he have them bound out by January 1839 or so many as he can and present an account of the expence to the Court.

Ordered by the Court that James P. Keith be appointed overseer of the road leading from Winchester to the Cholybeate Springs commencing at the section line near Capt. James Taylors and work the same to the Cholybeate Springs & that he keep the same in good repair according to law and that James Bledsoe and James Keith Esquires allot him hands to work on the same and that he keep said road in good repair according to law.

Ordered by the Court that the writ of ad qua dum un heretofore issued to the sheriff and returnable at the last term of this court be suspended until September Term.

Ordered by the Court that James Woods, William L. Sargent, John Russell, John Handley and Ed Burke be appointed a Jury of view to turn the Huntsville road around the pond at Russels Grocery and around the pond at Sargents old Grocery and report to this Court at the next Term.

Ordered by the Court that Ephraim Green be released from paying the Ranger for one half the price of the names which he posted belonging to Edward C. Harrican and that the clerk issure in order to the Ranger concerning the same. Isd.

Ordered by the Court that Thomas Finch Sheriff puchase 18 chairs for the use of the Court against November Term of the Circuit Court and present the account to the County Court.

Ordered by the Court that Afray Boss be appointed overseer of the road of the 2nd class called the Makerd road from the foot of the mountain to the creek at James P. Cowan and that he keep the same in good repair according to law and that Samuel Miller allot him hands.

Ordered by the Court that Colwell P. Shipp keep or boad the poor man that is up in the Court house and present his account to this Court charged at two dollars per week.

Ordered by the Court that Dudly Johnson & Wesley Shores be appointed commissioners to settle with Joseph R. Shropshire administrator of the estate of Catharine Shropshire decd and make return to this Court at the next Term.

(p-635) Ordered by the Court that James P. Cowan purchase a sledge for the use of the road and present the account to the court for pay thereof.

Present George Hudspeth, Adam L. Hyder, Wm. Howell, John Nugent James Bledsoe, Wallis Estill Jr. Jas. S. Cowling, William Larkin, Wm. N. Taylor, Medeth Catchings Benjamin B. Knight, Robert Lackey Andrew Mann, Samel Miller, Richmond P. Harris all of whom voting for the allowance. Ordered by the Court that the revenue commissioners individually be allowed the sum of ten dollars for their trouble in taking in their list of taxable property & polls liable to taxation for

the year 1836 and that the clerk of this Court issure a certificate to the
County Trustee for the same. Issured to Nugent, Miller, Bledsoe, to
W. Shores, Catchings Taylor to Knight to Howell, Mann, Hudspeth, Patrick
Burrow, to Robt. Lackey Jr. Cowan issured to Harris.

This day James Morris administrator of Robert Frame deceased returned
into Open Court and inventory of said decedents Estat which was received
by the Court and ordered to be recorded.

This day the commissioners heretofore appointed at the Feburary
Term of this Court to settle Joseph Smith Executor of the Estate of
Martin Adams, deceased made their return which was received by the Court.

Ordered by the Court that Allen Young be appointed overseer of the
road from John H. Morris to the river and that he keep the same in good
repair according to law and that William N. Taylor and Andrew Mann Esquires
allot him hands to work on the same.

Ordered by the Court that John Ander be appointed overseer of the
road from the river to the ford of the Creek at or above Black's Mill
and that he keep the same in good repair according to law and that
William N. Taylor & Andrew Mann allot him hands to work the same.

Ordered by the Court that John Runnels be appointed overseer of the
road from the ford of the creek at Blake Mill to the pond Spring road and
that he keep the same in good repair according to law and that William
N. Taylor & Andrew Mann Esqrs allot to him hands to work on same.

Ordered by the Court that Conrod Hice who oversees the Coffee Creek
road. have the following hands, to wit: E. Winkler E. M. Winkler,
Alen Cooble, Benjamin Baker, Daniel Baker, Jas. Wade & Walter Wade to
work on said road.

This day the last will and Testament of James Cunningham deceased
was duly proven in open Court by the oath of Thomas Cunningham one of
the witness and ordered by the Court to be received and kept for further
probate.

(p-636)   Ordered by the Court that Moses Merris, Benjamin Cherry
Thomas Sims, Maynard Gilliam & William Gilliam be appointed a Jury of
view to view a road from the baptist meeting house which is called mud
creek to run by Lawsan Rowe and intersect the Winchester road that passes
by Jacobe Sanders and that they report to this Court.

Ordered by the Court that a road be established commencing at
Wm. Adams in Capertons Cove and run on Willy J. Hines East boundry to the
school land thence with the School land west to intersect the road running
form Capertons Old place and with that road intersect the Maherds ford road.
and that William Wallis be appointed overseer on the same and that he keep
it in good repair and that Samuel Miller allot to him hands to work on the
same.

Ordered by the Court that James Campbell be appointed overseer of
the road of the 1st class from John Armstrongs to Callaways pond in room
of Samuel Taylor and that he keep the same in good repair according to

law and that he have the same hands that worked under the former overseer.

Ordered by the Court that Alexander Haflin be appointed overseer of the road of the 2nd class from Timmes ford to Limboughs in room of Nimrod Sandridge and that he keep the same in good repair according to law and that he have the same hands that worked under the former overseer.

This day the Jury of view heretofore appointed made their return as follows, commenceing at John H. Morris crossing Elk River near the mouth of Big Hurrican and up said creek to the pond Springs road athe mouth of Widow Youngs lane.

Ordered by the Court by Meredeth Catchings Esquire allot to Elijah French hands to work on the over which said French is overseer.

This day the return of Osborn D. Herender Guardian of the minor heirs of Pomperet Herender deceased was produced in Open Court and was received by the court and ordered to be recorded.

Ordered by the Court that William B. Thompson hands and John McCutchens hands be added to the number that work on the road leading from Winchester to Shelbyville from Winchester to Majors Sharps Mill.

(p-637) Present, James Robinson, James Keith, George Hudspeth, Adam L. Hayden, Marshall W. Howell, John Nugent Samuel Miller, A. Mann, James Bledsoe, Sam C. Corn, Richmond P. Harris, Wallis Estill Jr. James S. Cowling William Larkink Wesley Shores, James F. Green, Asa D. Oakley, Wm. N. Taylor Benjamin B. Knight, James Wilkinson, Robert Lackey Jr. & William J. Wood Esquires, Sixtten of whom voted for the allowance.

Ordered by the Court that Meredith Catchings be allowed the sum of five dollars for holding an inquest over the body of Joseph Wheler who was found dead and that the clerk of this Court issure a certificate to the County Trustee for the same. Isd.

Present the above Justices sixteen of whom voted for the allowance. Ordered by the Court that James Byron be allowed the sum of forty three dollars and thirty seven & half cents for keeping Hannah Arnold in the poor house for funeral expences and seventeen dollars & thirty five cents for keeping Joseph Royalty a pauper in the poor house and that the Clerk of this court issure a certificate to the County Trustee for the same issured to Byrom.

Ordered by the Court that the following persons be appointed Jurors for the circuit Court at November term 1836, to wit, Wallis Estill Jr. William Buchanan Porter Keith, Joseph Holder Senr. Peter Heastings, William Larkin George Hudspeth, Adma L. Ryder John B. Hawkins, Nelson Carter Samuel Rosebard, John Handley Willie Burt Spencer Rogers, John Nugent, John Oliver, Herender Green William Corn, Daniel Riggle, John Taylor, Thomas Garner, John S. Martin, James Wilinson, Robert Lackey Barnaby Burrow & John Jones. and it is further ordered the Joel Vansant & John H. Duncan constables be appointed to attend on the court and that the sheriff summon them with the Jurors accordingly.

Ordered by the Court that the Sheriff let out the well in the Court yard to Lowest bidder to have it filled up and the county will pay the cost thereof.

Court adjourned untill tomorrow 11 o'clock
> James Robinson
> M. W. Howell
> W. Estill Jr.

(p-638) Tuesday the second day of said month one thousand eight hundred and thirty six. Court met pusuant to adjournment present James Robinson Marshal W. Howell, Wallis Estill Jr.

On the petition of James Morris Administrator of the Estate of Robert Frame deceased which was sworn to in Open Court setting forth that it would be to the interest of the distribution of said Robert Frame Decd. to make sale of the remaining slaves belonging to said Estate in which the widow of said decddent concured and the Court being satisfied of the truth of said petition. It is ordered that said administrator make sale of the said Slaves on the public square in the town of Winchester on the first Monday in Spetember next to the highest bidder on a credit of twelve months taking bond and good security from the purchaser.

This day Thomas Finch who was heretofore appointed on yesterday. Administrator of the Estate of William Thompson Decd. was duly qualified as the law requires.

This day the commissioners heretofore appointed at the last Term of this Court to settle with Marshall W. Howell executor of the last will and testament of William Trigge deceased and with Susan Trigge administratrix of the estate of James McWharter Decd. made their return which was received by the Court and ordered to be recorded.

Ordered by the Court that the order heretofore made appointing James Robinson, James A. Snowden to Mark Hutchens, to settle with Benj. Decherd Guardian of Edward Russell, be revived and made returnable to the next term of this Court.
> James Robinson
> W. Estill Jr.
> M. W. Howell

(p-639) September Term 1836
State of Tennessee
At a County Court begun an held for the County of Franklin on the first Monday of September one thousand eight hundred and thirty six it being the fifth day of said month and the sixty first of the independence of the United States. Present nineteen of the acting Justices of the peace for the County of Franklin.

Ordered by the Court that Nathan R. Martin be appointed overseer of the road of the first Class from the mouth of Leroy D. Beans now Doctor Turners Lane to the fork of the road at William Knight place and that he keep the same in good repair according to law and that he have the same hands that worked under the former overseer.

This day William A. Breeden produced in open Court a certificate from Thomas Finch certifying that he was duly and constitutionally elected constable in district No. 2 in the stead of William R. Gillaspie resigned who entered into bond with Edward Darnaby and Andrew Mann his securities in the sum of one thousand dollars conditioned according to law and was qualified.

Ordered by the Court the Soloman Limbough be appointed overseer of the road of the 2nd class commincing at the Hollow at Isaac Vanzants plantation on the Elk River road and end at Cann Creek Hollow and that he keep the same in good repair according to law and that he have the following hands, to wit, William Marshall, Benjamin Franklin David Tipps, Franklin Tipps, John spencer, Thomas Breeden, William B. Breeden Alexander Heipler Harris Morgan & Samuel Church.

Ordered by the Court that John Armstrong be appointed overseer of the road of the first class from Elk river to where Wilkinsons Mill road crosses the same to Caldwells Bridge in the room of John W. D. Stamper and that he keep the same in good repair according to law and that he have the same hands that worked under the former overseer.

Ordered by the Court that John W. Jones be appointed overseer of the road leading from Winchester to the Bridge at Centerville commencing at Francis A. Oakley and work on to near halfway between Buckners and Faggs in the stead of Buckener and that he keep the same in good repair according to law and that he have the same hands that worked under the former overseer.

(p-640)   Ordered by the Court that Coldwell Sublitt be appointed overseer of the road leading from Burrows cove to Centerville commencing at Barnaby Burrows Old place and work to Centerville in the room of F. G. Akes on that he keeps the same in good repair and according to law and that Barnaby Burrow Esquire allot to him hands to work on the same.

Ordered by the Court that David O. Anderson, Peter Simmons & George Hudspeth be appointed commissioners to settle with Robert Taylor Administrator of the Estate of Joshua Hickman Decd. and that they make return to this Court.

Ordered by the Court that James Taylor be appointed overseer of the road from Winchester to the Chalybeate Springs commencing at the Square and work to adkins old place owned by Davidson and that he keep the same in good repair according to law and that James Keith and James Bledsoe Esquires allot to him hands to work on the same.

Ordered by the Court that James P. Keith only work from Adkins to the top of the mountain and that Jas. Keith and James Bledsoe Esquires allot to him hands to work on the same.

Ordered by the Court that the order heretofore issued appointing Joseph Klipper & Adam Oehmig and William Street commissioners to settle with Edwin Eans Administrator of the Estate of John Saxton decd be suspend untill next term agreeably to this request.

Ordered by the Court that the order heretofore issued to run a road through Mrs. Ewings land be recinded.

Ordered by the Court that John H. Lee be appointed overseer of the road from John Frances to Manns ford of Elk River in the room of Allen Young and that he have the same hands that worked under the former overseer and that he keep the same in good repair according to law.

This day Samuel Corh offered his resignation as Justice of the pleace which was received by the Court.

Ordered by the Court Bozeman May be appointed overseer of the Fayetteville road commencing at David Bells Blacksmith shop to the county line and that he keep the same in good repair and that according to law and that he have the same hands which worked on the road heretofore.

Ordered by the Court that Joseph Coker be appointed (p-641) overseer of the road from Mud Creek to Rolin Lanes on that he keep the same in good repair according to law and that he have the following hands to wit, Jacob Sander, Thomas Sander Saml. Bornan, Thos. Henly, William Henly, Saml. Snow, Martin Deal, Armon Coker, Jordan Morris, Benjamin Morris Rolen Morris, John B. Broman George Cherry, Melmuth Coker, Joseph Coker, Allen Gibson Nathl Dossett Lawson Row, 2 hands John Oliver John Gillium Saml Baker Robt. Branan Henry Portor Renely Owens, Thos Sims, William Sims Isaac Hensly Wm. Hill, Wm. Braman, Joseph Shaw G. Hawkersmith with William Gillum Charles Gillian, R. H. Gillum, E. G. Harris, W. B. York John Gibson, William Gibson George Powell to work on the same.

Ordered by the Court that Daniel Brazelton & John Mathews be appointed commissioners to lay off to Polly Downum Widow of Richard Downum decd. one years provision out of said decedents estate and that they make return to the court.

It appearing to the satisfaction of the Court that Josiah Muse late of this county died intestate and Richmond P. Harris applied for letters of administration on said decedents Estate. Whereupon it is ordered by the Court that he have letters accordingly who entered into bond with Thomas Finch his security in the sum of two thousand dollars according to law and was qualified accordingly.

Ordered by the Court that John Dougherty, George Gray & William Darwin be appointed commissioners to settle with James Lewis Administrator of James W. Lewis deceased and that they make return to this Court.

Ordered by the Court that the following receipts be recorded. Received Winchester 21st May 1836 of Thomas Finch Sheriff and collector of the County tax for Franklin for the year eighteen hundred and thirty five the sum of eighteen hundred and twenty one dollars 10$\frac{3}{4}$ being the amount of the tax laid for paying off Jurors county expendetures and the poor also on property not listed after deducting his commissions for the same. 1821.10\frac{3}{4}$

James L. Bryant Trustee

Nashville 7th May 1836   No Co

Received of Thomas Finch Nine hundred twenty three dollars and 66 cents audited to him by No 6 and due on account of State Tax Franklin County year 1835.
$923.66 Signed Duplicate

                                    Miller Francis
                                    Treasurer of Tennessee

Received of Thomas Finch Sheriff and collector of the public tax in and for the County of Franklin the sum of two hundred and four dollars and twenty six cents the amount of taxes (p-642) collected by him on school lands in Franklin County for the year 1835 after deducting his commission on the same May 1st 1836.
$204.26

                              Hugh Francis Clerk
                              And Treaniren of the bound of
                              Common School Commissioners for
                              Franklin County.

        This day the Jury of view heretofore appointed to view and turn the road as petitioned for by Milton McQueen made their report which is as follows in part the ground on which said Mcqueen proposes to turn the road is low and boggy and would be impossable in the winter consequently the road should not be turned which was received by the Court.

        This day the Jury of View heretofore appointed to turn the road leading from Winchester to Huntsville around the pond at Russells and at Sargents made their return which is as follows in part the road was viewed and marked round on the south saide of the ponds and intersect the main road.

        Ordered by the Court that County Tax be levied equal on all property to that of the State which is 5 cents on each hundred dollars and there be levied on each white poll 25 cents for county purposes.

        This day the last will and testament of Richard S. Easley deceased was produced in Open Court by Joseph Miller the Executor thereon named whereupon came Squire B. Hawkins, Hugh Montgomery and John Hopper subscribing witnesses thereto who being first duly sworn depose and say that the said Richard S. Easley declared and published this as his last will and testament and at the time of signing the same he the said Richard S. Easly was of sound and disposing mind and memery and that he acknowledged the same in their presence and they as witnesses signed the same at his request, whereupon it is ordered by the Court to be recorded. And it is further ordered by the Court that Joseph Miller the executor named in the will above mentioned have letters testamentory awarded him.

        On petition of David and Elijah Mackleroy executors of the will of Isaac Mackleroy deceased to sell a Negro man named Dick a woman named Nancy & girl named Jane to settle the debts of the Estate of Isaac Mackleroy Decd. It is therefore ordered by the Court that said Executors have an order of sale to sell said negroes either for cash or on a credit which (p-643) may appear most expedient to said executors after giving thirty days notice by setting up written advertisements at the Court house in Winchester.

Ordered by the Court that the following receipt be recorded
received of James B. Harris executor of the last will and testament of
James Harris deceased late of Franklin County & State of Tennessee two
hundred and eighty one dollars & twenty cents in full of my part of
said James Harris Decd Estate in right of my wife Sally late Sally Harris
May 6, 1836.

$208.20   Samuel A. Harris
John L. Keith   Sally Harris
Moses Keith

On motion it is ordered by the Court that Polly Hickman be
appointed Guardian over the persons & property of Sophia S. George
Y. William F. Francis A. Reuben A. Hickman Ophans of Joshua Hickman
deceased who entered into bond with William Larkin her security in the
sum of one hundred dollars according to law.

Received of James B. Harris executor of the last will and testament
of James Harris decd. late of Franklin County and State of Tennessee
two hundred dollars each in full of our part in the said James Harris
estate.

$400.00   September 5th day 1836
                                           her
                              Rebecca X Harris
                                          mark
                                           her
John L. Keith   Mary   X   Harris
Moses M. Keith   Mark

        Present Marshall W. Howell Jas. Keith Benjamin B. Knight
Wallis Estill, James Bledsoe, Asa D. Oakley R. P. Harris A. L. Hyder
Z. H. Murrell, Wm. N. Taylor Saml. Miller Andrew Mann, Wm. Larkin
J. R. Patrick, James S. Cawlin, William J. Wood, Medith Catchings, Jas.
Wilkerson Esquires fourteen of whom voted for the allowance.

        Ordered by the Court that Calwell P. Shipp be allowed the sum of
four dollar for keeping or boading a pauper 2 weeks and that the clerk
issure a certificate to the County Trustee for the same issured to Shipp.

        Present the above name Justices sixteen of whom voted for the allow-
ance ordered by the Court that Thomas Finch be allowed the sum of five
dollars for having the well in the Court house yard filled up and that
the clerk issure a certificate to the county Trustee for the same.
Issued to Finch.

        Present the above named Justices ordered by the Court G. W. D. Stamper
be refunded the sum of two dollars & twenty five cents a tax which he
paid in 1835 on property which he should not have listed and that the
clerk issure a certificate to the County Trustee for the same.

(p-644) Ordered by the Court that Lunceford Mathews be appointed overseer
of the road from his own house to John Frames in the stead of Edward
Morris and that he keep the same in good repair according to law and
that he have the hands that worked under the former overseer. Isd

Ordered by the Court that the Jail be repaired in the following manner, The two winders to be grated with iron bars the casing and facing be repaired so as to hold the steeples firm in the front door and that the Sheriff employ some person to do the work alone named.

Ordered by the Court that Jesse Rogers be appointed overseer of the road from Crow Creek from the State line to the 2 miles post and that he keep the same in good repair according to law and that Meredith Catchings Esquire allot him hands to work on the same.

Ordered by the Court that Fulden Wise be appointed overseer of the sinking cove road from the forks of the same to Capentors well and that he keep the same in good repair according to law and that he have the same hands which squire Catchings will allot to work on the same Court Adjourned untill 12 o'clock on Tuesday.

M. Catchings
M. W. Howell
W. Estill Jr.

Tuesday morning Court meet purisuant to adjournment.
Present Wallis Estill Jr. M. W. Howell Meredith Catchings Esqrs.

This day Henry A. Rains one of the executor of the last will and testament of Wm. Rawlins deceased produced in open Court an inventory of said Decedents estate and likewise a list of the amount of sales which was received by the Court and Ordered by the Court to be recorded.

Ordered by the Court that commissions issure from the clerk of this Court to James F. Green and James Bledsoe Esquires to take the privy examination of the wife of Paschal Green touching her assignment to a deed of conveyance from Paschal Green & his wife to John Holt for 14 acres of land in the State of Virginia and that they make return to the next Term of this Court.

(p-645) Ordered by the Court James Woods, Benjamin Deoherd, Mark Hutchens be appointed commissioners to lay off the Mrs. Crabb Widow of Ralph Crabb deceased one years provissions out of said Decedents Estate and that they make return to the Court.

Ordered by the Court that Z. H. Murrell, William N. Taylor and Andrew Mann be appointed commissioners to settle with Allen Young and Blanche Cook now Youngs wife Guardians of the heirs of Abram Cook Deceased and that they make return to this Court.

Ordered by the Court that James Roberson James Harris and William M. Brazelton be appointed commissions of the estate of William Trigg deceased to settle with M. W. Howell administrators executors of the estate of William Trigg decd. and Susan Trigg administratrix of James S. McWharten deceased in as much as there appears to be a mistake in the settlement made with them by James Roberson, James Harris and John Goodwin and they make return to the next term of this court.

Court adjournment untill Court in course

M. Catchings
M. W. Howell
W. Estill Jr.

State of Tennessee

At a County Court began and held for the County of Franklin /// on the 1st Monday of October A. D. 1836 it being the third day of said month and the sixty first year of the Independence of the United States of America. Present sixteen of the Justices for said County.

It appearing to the satisfaction of the Court that John McCloud late of this County died intestate and David Hunt applying for letters of administration and the estate of said deceased. Whereupon it is ordered by the Court that he have letters accordingly who entered into bond with William Larkin his security in the sum of one thousand dollars according to law and was qualified accordingly.

It appearing to the satisfaction of the Court that Elizabeth Thompson late of this County died intestate and John R. Patrick applied for letters of administration on the Estate (p-646) of said deceased Whereupon it is ordered by the Court that they have letters accordingly who entered into bond with William Larkin his security in the sum of five hundred dollars according to law and was qualified accordingly.

This day Jonathan Crownover Executor of the last will & testament of Joseph Crownover deceased returned into Open Court and amount of the sale of said deceased Estate which was received by the Court and ordered to be recorded.

Ordered by the Court that Thomas Wilson, Joseph Klipper and James Robinson be appointed commissioners to settle with Benjamin Decherd Guardian of the estate Edmund Russell and that they make return to this Court.

Ordered by the Court that James wood, Benjamin Decherd & James Robinson be appointed commissioner to lay off to Mrs. Crabb wife of Ralph Crabb deceased one years provisions out of said decedents estate.

Ordered by the Court that William McCowan, Thomas Green, & John B. Hawkins be appointed commissioners of the turnpike road leading from Winchester to Bellfonte from the foot of said mountain to where the Turnpike now stands and that they examine the road and see that it is kept in good repair.

Ordered by the Court that Panhattan D. Statum be appointed overseer of the road leading from Winchester to the boat yard commencing at Luceford Mathews and work to the boat yard and that he keep the same in good repair according to law and that he have the following hands, to wit, Young Roseboror, Saml. Rosebora, M. R. Mann, Nicholes W. Mathews John Mathews, Henry Hill, E. D. Robbins James Farris, Kiah Farris, Rich Farris Jesse Caroll 2 sons Wm. A. Preeden.

Ordered by the Court that William Freeman be appointed overseer

of the Bellfante road of the 2nd class from the wolf Pen to the State
line and that he keep the same in good repair according to law and that
he have the same hands that worked under Jonathan Martin.

Ordered by the Court that Edward Martin be appointed overseer of
the Nashville road commencing at Chitwoods the Ford of the river and
work to Spring Creek and that he keep the same in good repair according
to law and that he have the same hands that worked under the former overseer.

(p-647) Ordered by the Court that William Johnson & William Larkin be
appointed commissioners to lay off to Menerva McCloud wife of Jno.
McCloud deceased one years provissions out of said Decddents Estate.

This day James Faris administrator of the estate of G. M. Crawford
deceased produced in Open Court a note belonging to said estate on Isaac
Atkins for one hundred dollars which was received by the Court and ordered
to be put on record.

This day the last will and testament of William Bostick deceased which
was heretofore proved by the oaths of Sims Kelly & William G. G. Muse two
of the subscribing witnesses was produced in Open Court and thought to be
sufficiently authenticate to be recorded. Daniel McLanord a subscribing
witness being out of the State Whereupon it is ordered to be recorded.

Ordered by the Court that the Lustes Gap road continue along the
Hillsboro road a quarter of a mile further untill it passes Geo. Thompsons
house where he now lives.

Court adjourned untill tomorrow 11 o'clock
                    James Beldsoe
                    W. Estill Jr.
                    James Robinson.

This day Paschal Green came into Court and acknowledged a deed
make by said Paschal Green and his wife Phebe F. of Tennessee State
Franklin County, to be his act and deed to John Holt of Virginia State
Amded County for a tract of land contening 14 acres. Whereupon it is
ordered by the Court to be registered. Let it be registered.

This day William Hicks & Jeremiah Smith ~~Barnabas Johnson Jr.~~ came
into open Court and were examined in relation to the death of Barnabas
Johnson senr. deceased a pensianor who being duly qualifed depose and say
that they are acquainted with Barnabas Johnson Sr. above named and say
that he the said Barnabas Johnson departed this life the 2nd day of June
A. D. 1836. Barnabas Johnson Jr. also produced in Court a certificate
made by James Tally and Joseph Floyd certifying that Barnabas Johnson Sr.
was prevented untill the time of his death from making application to the
agent of tennessee at Nashville in consequence of the original certificate
of the original certificate being in the possession of Joseph Floyd.

(p-648) Court adjourned untill court incourse
                    James Robinson
                    W. Estill Jr.

State of Tennessee   ) In the County Court Setting
Franklin County   )
This Court certify that it appears to their satisfaction that William
Rowlins a pensioner of the United States died on the 2nd day of May 1836
leaving no widow and seven children now living viz Thomas Rowlins and
Sarah L. Rowlins (now Coleman) of Danville Virginia Samuel D. Rowlins
of Norfork Va. John A. Rowlins of Florida, Ann Rowlins, Nora McGee of
Kentuckey, Clarissa Rowlins (now Rains) and Elizabeth Rowlins now Sims
both of Franklin County Tenn. that it would be impracticable from the
small amount of the shares of each of the above children of the arrears
of pension of said William Rowlins decd. to obtain powers of attorney
from all of them and that Henry a Rains, Dr. Elisha Sims husbands of
said Clarissa and Elizabeth Rowlins are anxious to obtain the shares
of their wives. It is ordered that the Clerk of this Court affix the
seal of his office to the certificate according to the instructions of the
War Department so that the said Henry A. Rains & Dr. Elisha Sims may
obtain their shares of their wives of the arrears of pension of said
William Rowlins Dec.

                              James Robinson J.P.
                              W. Estill Jr. J. P.
                              James Pledsoe J. P.

        State of Tennessee
     At a County Court begun and held for the County of Franklin and on
the first Monday of November one thousand eight hundred and thirty six
and on the 7th day of said month it being the 61st year of the Independents
of the United States. Present 21 of the acting Justice for said County.

     Ordered by the Court that David Lynch be appointed overseer of the
road from Cross Creek to the mouth of Rush Creek in the room of John B.
Wilkinson and that he keep the same in good repair according to law and
that he have the same hands that worked under the forman overseer. Issured.

     Ordered by the Court that Benjamin Walker be appointed overseer of
the road over which John Anderson was, and that he keep the same in good
repair according to law and that he have the same that worked under Anderson.

     A Power of attorney from Ann Upton wife of Jno Upton Decd. to
Robert H. Burton Was duly acknowledged in open Court by said Ann Upton
to be done by her for the purpose there in express and ordered to be
certified.

(p-649) Ordered by the Court that Willie Brogen be appointed overseer
of the road of the 2nd class from Tims Ford to Limboughs in room of
Alexander Heiflin & that he keep the same in good repair according to
law and that he have the same hand that worked under the former overseer.Isd.

     Ordered by the Court that Hamilton Stewart be appointed overseer of
the road from the forks thereof to a pond on the mountain near the narrows
and that he keep the same in good repair according to law and that he
have the same hands that worked under the former overseer.

     Ordered by the Court that Moses Morris, Benjamin Cherry Thomas Sims

Mynord Gilliam William Gilliam, Robert Branan & George Hawkersmith be appointed a Jury of view to mark and lay off a road as much to the public good and as little to the projudice of individuals as possible from the Baptists meeting house which is called Mud Creek to run by Lawson Rowes and intersect the Winchester road that passes by John Sanders and that they make report to this Court.

Ordered by the Court that Alfred Walson be appointed overseer of the road of the 1st class from John Armstrongs to Callaways pond in the roor of James Campbell and that he keep the same in good repair according to law and that he have the same hands that worked under the former overseer.

Ordered by the Court that James Wade be appointed overseer of the road from William N. Taylor to the county line in the room & stead of Coonrod Hise and that he keep the same in good repair according to law & that he have the same hands that worked under the former overseer.

Ordered by the Court that James Roak be appointed overseer of the road of the 3rd class from Armon Coker in the room of Mynard Gilliam and that he keep the same in good repair according to law and that he have the same hands that worked under the former overseer. Isd.

Ordered by the Court that Camel Montgomery be appointed overseer of the road from the Boiling Fork of Elk River to the place where the said road crosses Rush Creek at the first place and that he keep the same in good repair according to law and that Samel Miller Esqurs allot him hands to work on the same Wallace Estill Jr. Will send 1 hand.

Ordered by the Court that Isaac Hines be appointed overseer of the road from John W. Halden's Esqr. to the Foot of the mountain in the room of _____ and that he keep the same in good repair according to law and that he have the same hands that worked under the former overseer.

This day Joseph Miller executor of the last will & Testament of Richard S. Easly decd returned in to open Court the amount of sales of the property belonging to said testator, which was received and (p-650) ordered to be recorded by the Court.

This day Thomas Finch Administrator of the Estate of William B. Thompson Decd returned into ppen Court a inventory of said decedents property which was received by the Court and ordered to be recorded.

This day the commissioners Viz Wm. N. Taylor, Z. H. Murrell & Andrew Mann heretofore appointed to settle with Allen Young and Blanch Cook Guardians of the minor heirs of Abram Cook Deceased made a return of the settlement which was received by the Court and ordered to be recorded.

This day the commissions to wit, Thomas Wilson, Joseph Klepper & James Robin Sr. heretofore appointed to settle with Benajmin Decherd Guardain of Edmund Russell made a report of the settlement which was received by the Court and ordered to be recorded.

This day James Byron who was elected to fill the vacancy of Saml. Corn Jr. resigned came into Court and qualified and produced a certificate from the G overnment commissioned one of the justice for Franklin County

A Power of Attorney from Mary Arnet to Hansford Arnett was duly acknowledged in open Court by said Mary Arnett and ordered to be certified by the clerk.

An Indenture or relinquestment from May Arnett to Joseph Milton was duly acknowledged in Open Court by May Arnett and ordered to be certified by the Clerk.

Ordered by the Court that James Robinson, Walace Estill Jr. & Samuel Milton Esqr. be appointed commissioners to examine the registers Book and see if any of them require transcribing and how many and report to the next term Court.

Ordered by the Court that John G. Brazelton be appointed special Guardian to XXXXXXX XXXXX over the minor heirs of Jacob Millers deceased and that he superintend receiving the corn for which the land rented, belonging to said heirs for the year 1836.

Ordered by the Court that John Frame and John, Morris Sr. be appointed commissioners to settle with Joshua Franklin administrator of the estate of John Conwell Decd.

Ordered by the Court that Benjamin Decherd & Willie B. Wagner be appointed commissions to settle with James Robinson & Joseph Klepper executors of the estate of Adam Gross deceased and that they make return to this next Court. Isd.

(p-651)   On motion it is ordered by the Court that Barnaby Burrows Esqr. be appointed Guardian over the person and property of Barnaby B. Burrows minor ophan of Henry Burrow Deceased who entered into bond of twenty four hundred dollars with Thomas Finch and John G. Bostick his securitors according to law.

Present Wallis Estill Jr. M W. Howell, James Bledsoe, Benjamin B. Knight, John Nugent & Mynord Gilliam, Samel Miller, M. Catchings George Hudspeth, Adam L. Hyden James F. Green, Andrew Mann Asa D. Oakly Wm. N. Taylor, Z. H. Murrell, James Byron, R. P. Harris Barnaby Burrow James S. Cowlin William J. Wood, Wesly Shores.

Ordered by the Court that William W. Brazelton clerk of this court be allowed the sum of seventy five dollars for recording the tax list and for making out a list for the tax collector as compensation for the year 1836 and that the clerk issure a certificate to the county trustee for the same nine of the magistrates voting for the allowance, issured

Present the above named justices twelve of whom voted for the allowance ordered by the Court that William N. Taylor Z. H. Murrell and James Byron, R. P. Harris Barnaby Burrow, James S. Cowlin William J. Wood Wesly Shores,

Ordered by the Court that William W. Brazelton clerk of this court be allowed the sum of seventy five dollars for recording the tax list and for making out a list for the tax collector as compensation for the

year 1836 and that the Clerk issure a certificate to the County Trustee
for the same nine of the magistrates voting for the allowance, issured.

Present the above named justices twelve of whom voted for the allowance ordered by the Court that William N. Taylor, Z. H. Murrell and Andrew
Mann be allowed the sum of six dollars each for three days by them spent
as commissioners settling with Allen Young and Blanchy Cook Guardians of
the minor ophans of Abram Cook deceased and that the Clerk issure certificate
to the County Trustee for the same.

Present the above Justices twelve of whom voted for the allowance
ordered by the Court that Bledsoe Stewart be allowed the sum of ten dollars
68¾ cents for tools which he purchased and payed for to use on the road
as overseer who brought in his account and swore to it and that a certificate issure to the County Trustee for the same from the Clerk. Issured.

Present the above Justices Sixtten of whom voted in the affirmative
Ordered by the Court that the Clerk of the chancery Court be allowed the
sum of thirty three dollars and fifty cents for 2 record books and one
a/c Book by him purchased for the chancery court and that a certificate
issure to the County Trustee for the same from the Clerk of this Court. Isd.

Present the above Justices twelve of whom voted for the allowance.
Ordered by the Court that James Williamson Jailor be allowed the sum of
one dollar for two turn keys and 37½ cents for one days boarding of a
negro man who was apprehended for stealing and a (p-652) certificate
issure from the clerk of this Court to the County Trustee for the same.
Issured. Isd.

Ordered by the Court that Thomas Finch be authorized to have the
windows of the Jail of this County repaired and return the accounts to this
Court.

Court adjourned untill 8 o'clock tomorrow.
James Robinson
W. Estill Jr.
M. W. Howell

Tuesday the 9th day of November 1836 Court meet according to adjournment. Present James Robinson, Wallis Estill Jr. John Nugent & M. W. Howell Esqr.

This day Thomas Wilson administrator of F. A. Moore deceased made and
additional return of said decedents Estate which was received by the Court
and ordered to be recorded.

Ordered by the Court that so much of the ordered as required James
Taylor to work from the public Square be recinded and that he only work
from the end of Ben Powell's lane.

Court adjourned untill Court in Course.
James Robinson
W. Estill Jr.
John Nugent & M. W. Howell

December Term 1836
State of Tennessee
        At a County Court began and held for the County of Franklin on the
first Monday of November one thousand eight hundred and thirty six and
the 5th day of said month it being the sixty first year of the Independence
of the United States Present twelve of the acting Justices of the peace for
said County.

        Ordered by the Court that the overseer of the road leading from
Winchester to Huntsville Straiten said road or that part of it between
Spykers and Benjamin Decherds.

        Ordered by the Court that Mury S. Embry be appointed overseer
of the road leading to Nashville from the one mile post to Wagnes's Creek
then from the line between Embry Sharp to the three mile post in the room
of Thomas Howard and that he keep the same in good repair according to law
and that he work the same hands that worked under the former overseer. Issured.

(p-653)   Ordered by the Court that John S. Martin & John R. Patrick be
appointed commissioners to settle with Mary Vanzant executrix of the last
will and testament of Jacob Vanzant deceased and that they make return
to the next term of this Court. Issured.

        Ordered by the Court that the order issued at the November Term
of this Court authorizing John Frame and John Morris Sr. to settle with
Joshua Franklin administrator of the Estate of John Conwell deceased be
renewed and made returnable to January Term of this Court.

        Ordered by the Court that the order be renewed appointing Benjamin
Decherd and Willie B. Wagner commissioner to settle with James Robinson
and Joseph Klepper executor of the last will and testament of Adam Gross
Decd. and be made returnable to the January Term of the County Court.

        Ordered by the Court that Benjamin Decherd be appointed overseer
of the road of the first class from Winchester to Enos C. England in the
room of said England and that he keep the same in good repair according
to law and that he have the same hands that worked under the former overseer.
issured. Ordered by the court that Jesse T. Wallace.

        James Robinson, Samuel Miller and Wallis Estill Jr. who was appointed
to examine the registers Books report as follows: to wit, That books E & F
require to be paged a new and an index made as amended so as to suit the
pages. Book J. Requires to be repaired as it is badly abused and several
leaves loose in it and we are of opinion by mending the back and carefully
fastening the leaves which are loose it will answer very well when paged
and indexed as E. & F.

        Ordered by the Court that Jess T. Wallace page Books E. & F. a new
and index them to suit the pages and fasten the leaves which are loose
in Book J. and present his account to this Court for pay. Isd.

        This day Alexander E. Patton administrator of the Estate of B. A.
Read deceased returned into Court an inventory of the property belonging
to said decedents estate and likewise a list of the sale of property

belonging to the estate of the above named Road deceased which was received by the Court and ordered to be recorded.

This day Martha Rains Guardian of Anas Rains minor orphans of William M. Rains Decd. returned into Court an account of the money which she the Guardian paid out for said minor orphan for the year 1836 which was received by the Court and ordered to be recorded.

(p-654)   Ordered by the Court that the following receipts be recorded, to wit,
$1123.57   Nashville October 1st 1836
                                        No. 104
Received of William M. Brazelton ¢/¢/¢ eleven hundred and twenty three dollars and 57 cents audited to him by No. 104 due on account of revenue by him collected as clerk of the County Court of Franklin County from 25th April to 1st September 1836.
Signed Duplicate   Willis Francis
                                        Treasure of Tennessee

$107.62½   Winchester No. 25th 1836
Received of William M. Brazelton one hundred and seventy dollars and sixty two & half cents due on account of revenue by him collected as clerk of the County Court of Franklin County from 25th April to the 1st September 1836 on retailers of spirits   James Sharp Sr.
                    Agent for School Fund Franklin Cty.

$563.15   Nashville 1st October 1836   No. 105
Received of W. B. Wagner five hundred and sixty three dollars and 15 cents audited to him by No. 105 and due on account of revenue collected by him as former clerk of Franklin County from 1st October 1835 to 25th April 1836
Signed Duplicate   Millis Francis
                    Treasurer of Tennessee.

On the Petition of Catharine Drake setting fourth that on the 1st day of December 1829 she conveyed by deed of gift to her Grand Children John D. Marshall, and William a Marshall infant children of Daniel Marshall and Nancy his wife, two negro boy slaves named Mark & Jack and that it is necessary to appoint a special Guardian to take care and preserve said property the said Daniel Marshall being present in Court and claiming the right to be appointed Whereupon the Court proceeded to hear and examine several witnesses in consideration whereof it is the opinion that the interest of said minors require some person other than their farther to be appointed and they do accordingly appoint Julias E. Sims & Catharine Drake guardian for said minors to take care and preserve said property according to the act of assembly in such cases made & provided whereupon the said Julias C. Sims and Catharine Drake entered into and acknowledged bond on the penalty of $3,000 conditioned according to law.

Ordered by the Court that the following persons be appointed Jurors for circuit Court of Franklin County to be holden for the County of Franklin on the fourth Monday in March 1836, to wit, Enos C. England Andrew Mann, William Duncan John Knight, Adam Oehmig M. W. Howell, James Kelly, James N. Chiles, James Byrom, Daniel Champion, William Brazelton Thomas Adkins, James Howar,d, James Keith, William N. Taylor, John Staples,

John S. Martin Eli B. Wedington, William Laster John Larkins, John L.
Keith, Joseph Miller, Zachariah H. Murrell Mynard Gilliam, Lawson Rowe and
Robert Lacky and Landers Faris and Mitchel Cowan constables to wait on the
Court and that the sheriff summon them to attend said Court. Isd

(p-655)   The noncupative will of Josiah Muse was this day produced in
Open Court by Richmond P. Harris and it appeared to the Court from the
Testimony of Richmond P. Harris and Dennis B. Muse that the widow did
not wish to contest said will but was anxious that the same should be
admited to record that said will was made from the testors last sickness
and on his own solitation and that said witnesses were specially requested
to bear witness thereto by the testator himself and that said testator was
of sound and disposing mind and memory at the time he made said noncupative
Will. Whereupon it is ordered by the Court that said noncupative will be
recorded.

        Ordered by the Court that the following persons be appointed revenue
commissioners for Franklin County for the year 183* to wit, Wallis Estill
Jr. District No. 1, A. D. Oakley No. 2, A. L. Hyder No. 3 William Larkin
No. 4, James F. Green No. 5, Zachariah H. Murrell No. 6, James Byran No. 7
William Wood No. 8 Mynord Gilliam No. 9 John Jones No. 10, John Womack
No. 11 James Wilkinson 12 James Cowlin No. 13 James Keith No. 14
Willian Crownover No. 15 Agreeable to the acts of 1835-6 in the case
made & provided.

        Present James Robinson, Wallis Estill Jr. M. W. Howell, B. B. Knight
Richmond P. Harris, James Byron Asa D. Oakly, William Crownover James F.
Green, Samuel Miller Isham Wammack, Wesly Shores Esqrs. a legal number of
whom voted for the allowance. Ordered by the Court that H. A. Rains
executor of the will of Wm. M. Raines decd be allowed the sum of Eleven
dollars 12½ cents on account of boarding Alex McCambridge in jail in the
life time of William M. Rains Decd. and that the clerk issure a certificate
to the county trustee for the same. Isd.

        Court adjourned untill tomorrow 10 o'clock.
                                        W. Estill Jr.
                                        M. W. Howell
                                        Z. H. Murrell

        Tuesday the 6th day of December A. D. 1836. Court met according
to adjournment Present Wallis Estill Jr.Zachariah Murrell, M. W. Howell
Esquires.

        Ordered by the Court that John Dougherty, George Grey, William
Darwin be appointed commissioners to settle with James Lewis administrator
of the estate of Cornelius Lewis deceased and that they make report to
the next Term of this Court.

(p-656)   Ordered by the Court that the order heretofore issured at the
November Term of this Court that Moses Morris, Benajmin Cherry Thomas Sims
Mynord Gilliam William Gilliam Robert Brown & George Hackersmith a Jury
of view to lay off a road, be made returnable to January Court 1837.

        Court adjourned untill Court in Course.
                                        W. Estill Jr.
                                        M. W. Howell
                                        A. H. Murrell

W. Estill Jr.
M. W. Howell
Z. H. Murrell

January Term 1837
State of Tennessee
At a County Court began and held for the County of Franklin at the Court House of Winchester on the first Monday of January eighteen hundred and thriby seven it being the 2nd day of said month and sixty first of American Independence of the United States of America Present Eleven of the Justice for said County.

Ordered by the Court that Henry Larkin, David Hunt, William Larkin William Freeman, Jonathan Martin, David Brown and Robert Taylor be appointed overseer a Jury of view to view and turn the road from the Cedar Springs to the State line as much to the public good and as little to the prejudice of individuals as practicable and that they report to the next term of this court. Isd.

Ordered by the Court that Andrew Martin be appointed overseer of the Veheids road from the bridge to the branch at the school land and that he keep the same in good repair according to law and that John Nugents and Mynard Gilliam Esqr allot to him hands to work on the same. Isd.

Ordered by the Court that Jery Arnold be appointed overseer of the road in the sinking Cove from the State line to the 2 miles post and that he keep the same in good repair according to law and that he have the same hands that worked under Jess Rogers.

Ordered by the Court that John R. Patrack Esqrs allot hands to Peter Heastors to work on the road over which he is overseer.

Ordered by the Court that William Larkin Esqr allott William Freeman hands to work on the road over which he is overseer. Isd.

Ordered by the Court that John G. Brazelton be appointed Special Guardian to rent out the land belonging to the estate of Jacob Miller Deceased and receive the proffits thereof for the use of the Legates.

(p-657)   This day the Jury of view heretofore appointed to view and lay off a road from Mud Creek meeting house to intersect the Winchester road, made their report which was received by the Court.

Ordered by the Court that Sansan Rowe be appointed to overseer the road from Mud Creek meeting House to where said road intersects the Winchester road and have the same out out and keep in good repair according to law and that Mynord Gilliam Esqrs allot him hands to out out the same and work on the same.

Ordered by the Court that John Frame, Joseph Franklin, John Morris, Ned Morris, Chapman McDaniel be appointed a Jury of view to lay off an be appointed a Jury of view to lay off and turn the road which leads to the boat yard commencing at Chapman McDaniel's Fence and to intersect the same at Beryhills Old house and that they report to the next term of this Court.

Ordered by the Court that Joshua Franklin Administrator of the Estate of John Conwell Deceased Allow John Frame and John Morris Sr. two dollars and fifty cents each for their trouble settling with said Franklin. out of said decedents estate.

Ordered by the Court that a power of attorney from William F. McDoff to his son Richard McDoff both of the State of Alabama and County of Jefferson be admited to registration. Let it be registered.

This day John Frame and John Morris Sr. who were heretofore appointed to settle with Joshua Franklin administrator of John Conwell deceased, made their return which was received by the court.

It appearing to the satisfaction of the Court that George Wagner Sr. late of this County died intestate and George Wagner Jr. Applied for letters of administration on said Decedents Estate. It is ordered by the Court that he have letters accordingly who entered into bond with C. P. Shipp and John Buckner his securities in the sum of one thousand dollars conditioned according to law and was qualified.

This day a paper writing purporting to be the last will and testament of William Street Deceased was produced in Court by the Executor therein named Whereupon came John Fitzpatrick and Thomas Adkins subscribing witness thereto who being first duly sworn depose and say that they were acquainted with the testator and that he was of sound and disposing mind and memory at the time of making the same and that they assigned the same as witnesses at the request (p-658) of said testator Whereupon it is ordered by the court to be recorded. Whereupon came William H. Street and Oliver D. Street who was qualified as executors to execute said will and entered into bond with Marshall W. Howell and James Robinson their securities in the sum of eight thousand dollars, conditioned according to law.

This day Thomas Finch Administrator of the Estate of William Thompson deceased returned into open Court an inventory of said decedents negroes which was received by the Court and ordered to be recorded.

On the petition of Thomas Finch administrator of the estate of William Thompson deceased to sell three negroes belonging to said Estate to wit, Sam, Scharlotte, Jeff and setting for the said pretition that it was necessary to sell them in order to make a distrabution among the Legatees and the Legatees being present to wit, George Morris William B. Thompson and William F. McDoff by his attorney Richard Mc Doff, Bryant B. Thompson one of the legatees being abset William B. Thompson his brother indeminified the said administrator by entering into a bond of a thousand dollars the afore mentioned Legatees who are present mutually agreeing and desiving the immediate sale of said negroes. And the Court being satisfied of the truth of said petition It is ordered by the Court that said Administrator proceed and seel said negroes before the Court House door and the 2nd day of Jany. to the hightest bidder an a credit untill the 23rd of may next 1837.

Ordered by the Court that Joseph Sherwood be bound to Robert Williamson as apprentice untill he arrives or attain the age of twenty one years of age said Williamson to give said apprentice a horse was the seventy five dollars saddle and bridle and suit of clothes and have him educated so as to Scipher through the single Rure of three at the expiration of his service.

Ordered by the Court that David Hunt be appointed Guardian over the person and property of John Lucy, Ann & Mary Jane McCloud Minors orphans of John McCloud deceased who entered into bond with William Larkin his security in the same of one thousand dollars conditioned as the law directs.

This day Joseph Little who was appointed guardian over the person and property of William Wilder minor orphan of Nathanial Wilder deceased presented his resignation as guardian which was received by the Court said little being qualified that none of said wards property had been delivered to him.

This day John Frame Admir of Ezekial Phillips Decd.'s Estate returned into open Court an inventory of the hire of said decedents negroes which was received by the Court and ordered to be recorded.

(p-659)   This day John Frame Administrator of the Estate of Ezekail Phillips Deceased returned into open Court an inventory of the hire of said Decedents slaves which was received by the Court and ordered to be recorded.

Present James Robinson, Marshall W. Howell Wallace Estill Jr. William Larkin, Andrew Mann, John Nugent Meredith Catchings, Asa D. Oakley M. Gilliam, William J. Wood, and Robert Lackey all of whom voted for the allowance. Ordered by the Court that the following persons be allowed the following sums on the following cases in which nolleprasiquies were entered in the circuit Court, to wit, Stat of Tennessee agt. Reuben Dixon Clerk Wagner $2.96¼, Attorney Freeman $250 Sheriff Oliver $125, John M. Morrow Witness for the State two days one dollar State of Tennessee agt. Reuben Dixon clerk Wagner $287½ Sheriff Jenkins for serving Sci fa $.62½ The State of Tennessee Agt. William D. Williams Clerk Wagner $4.43⅝ Sheriff Oliver for executing Capias & taking bonds summoning one witness $4.00 Sheriff Anderson for summoning one witness 25¢ attorney Whitesides $2.50 Moses Hill a witness 2 days $1.00 The state of Tennessee agt Elizabeth Machlerey Clerk Wagner $3.06½ Sheriff Machleory for executing Capias and taking bond $1.25 for summoning ten witnesses $16½ on these William Perters attendance five days $.83-1/3, 87½ Sheriff Finch for Jury Call, Saml Sutherland three days $.50 Anderson King 3 days $.50 Holt Lakey $.50 Attorney Whitesides $2.50 The State of Tennessee Agt. Reagins Clerk Wagner $4.28 attorney Whitesides $2.50 Sheriff Finch for executing Capias on the and taking 3 hands $3.75 and 2/3 fees for summoning seven witnesses $116-2/3 Addison Temple 2 days ; 66-2/3 cents *Nathaniel Anderson 2 days 66-2/3 cents and that certificate issure to the County Trustee from the clerk for the same is to John Oliver. Is to Wagner, to Finch to Mitchell Roberts, Hill, Witersider, Homan to wit; Present the above justices all of whom voted for the allowance. * Wesly Lambert 2 days $.66-2/3 cents

Ordered by the Court that James Estill be allowed the sum of seven dollars and fifteen cents for repair done the Fail by him and that the clerk issure a certificate to the county Trustee for the same. Is.

Present the above named Justices all of whom voted for the allowance
ordered by the Court that James Williamson be allowed the sum of four
dollars thirty seven and half cents for keeping George M. Rowan in Jail
and for 2 turn key and that the clerk issure certificate to the county
trustee for the same. Is.

Present the above Justices all of whom voted for the allowance
ordered by the Court that Thomas Finch be allowed the sum of twenty three
dollars and fifty cents for charis purchased for Court room funished and
cash paid by him to John McNabb for Palishing, White washing and laying
hearth and that the clerk issure certificate to the County Trustee for the
same. Isd.

(p-660)   This day John Byron presented to the court his resignation as
constable in District No. 7 Which was received by the Court.

Ordered by the Court that John G. Bostick, William S. Money and
David McGowan be appointed commissioners to settle with David Machleroy Exr.
of the Estate of Isaac Mackleroy deceased and deliver an account of the
distribution of said decedents estate to the court which belongs to
Fany McLeroy minor oprhan of Isaac McLeroy Decd.

Court adjourned untill tomorrow 11 o'clock.
                                        James Robinson
                                        M. W. Howell
                                        W. Estille Jr.

Tuesday the 3rd day of January A. D. 1837
    Court met presuent to adjournment. Present James Robinson, Wallis
EStill Jr. and Marshall W. Howell Esqrs for the county of Franklin
and State of Tennessee.

On petition of Ann Upton wife of John Upton deceased. It is
ordered by the court that Ann Upton above named be appointed Guardian over
the person and property of John E. Edword, T. William F. and Ann J. Upton
minor orphan of John Upton deceased who entered into bond with William
Reeves and Thomas S. Logan her securities in a bond of ten thousand dollars
conditioned as the law directs.

This day George Boyd, Francis Boyd and John Boyd minor orphans of
John Boyd deceased came into open Court and chose John G. Brazelton as
Guardian over their person and property who entered into bond with
William Brazelton and Daniel Keith his securities in the sum of Five
Thousand dollars conditioned as the law directs.

Court adjourned untill Court in Courte
                                        James Robinson
                                        M. W. Howell
                                        W. Estill Jr.

(p-661)

February Term 1837
State of Tennessee

At a County Court began and held for the County of Franklin on the first Monday of February and the 6th day of said month one thousand eight hundred and thirty seven and of the Independence of the United States 61.

Ordered by the Court that William Darwin be appointed overseer of the road leading to Caldwell Bridge from the Boiling Fork to ----- in the room of Robert Hill and that he keep the same in good repair according to law and that he have the same hands that worked under the former overseer. Is. Void

Ordered by the Court that George Simmons be appointed overseer of the road from Beens Creek to the eight miles post in the room of Charles Simmons and that he keep the same in good repair according to law and that he have the same hands that worked under the former overseer. Is.

Ordered by the Court that William McElvy be appointed overseer of the road from Elk River to Pattons land in room of Edward Swan and that he keep the same in Good repair according to law and that he have the same hands that worked under the former Overseer. Is.

Ordered by the Court that E. N. Stovall Campbells to where it strikes the stage road at Salem and that he keep the same in good repair according to law and that he have the same hand that worked under the former overseer.

Ordered by the Court that William L. Lasater be appointed overseer of the road from Esquire Majors to Widow Caldwells in room of William H. Byron and that he keep the same in good repair according to law and that he have the same hands that worked under the former overseer. Isd.

Ordered by the Court that a Jury of view be appointed to wit, John Larkin Terrell Gray, Wm. C. Handly Merrell D. Embery, Benjamin Higambatham, William Aklin George Dickey, to turn the road of the 3rd class which leads from Salem to Robert Campbells and that they make report to the next term of this Court. Isd.

Ordered by the Court that W. H. Brown, G. H. Brown, Abraham Bagget, Moses Ayres, Joseph Cooper, James Poe and Blake Bagget be appointed a Jury of view to view and turn the road that leads from Little Hurricain to Browns Gin, as much to the public good and as little to the prejudice of individuals as practicable and that the report to the next term of this Court Is.

(p-662)   This day John H. Duncan offered his resignation to the Court as constable in District No. 8 which was received by the Court and ordered to be spread on the minutes of the Court.

Ordered by the Court that John Keith Patrick Calaway G. Lipscomb William Laws Jno. Donaldson Amos Horton and Exerett Horton be appointed a Jury of view, to view and lay off a road from John Dotson to Simmons Mill as little to the pregudice of individuals as practicable and that they report to the next term of this Court. Is.

Ordered by the Court the Benjamin Decherd and William B. Wagner be appointed commissioners to settle with James Robinson and Joseph Klepper executors of the last will and testament of Adam Gross deceased and that they report to the next term of this Court.

Ordered by the Court that the School commissioners be allowed the sum of five per cent on all the moneys which they have heretofore or may hereafore collect as commissioners, or pay out, of the proceeds of rents or disbursments Provided this order shall not expend to the monesy transfered from coms. to this succession.

Ordered by the Court that Riley Daniel be appointed overseer of the Pond Springs road leading from said Spring to Lynch Burg and that he work to the County Line ih the room of John Waggner and that he keep the same in good repair according to law and that William N. Taylor Esqr. allot him hands to work on the same Is.

Ordered by the Court that Jonathan Runnels be appointed overseer of the road Murfreesboro road from the forks thereof to the county line ih the room of John Davenport and that he keep the same in good repair according to law and that he have the same hands that worked under Davenpprt. Is.

Ordered by the Court that John Haws work the road which leads from Salem to Bellefonte to the corner of Harris's fence and that Esqr. Larkin allot him hands. Isd.

Ordered by the Court that Henderson Badget be appointed overseer of the road from the mouth of Collins lane to Caxis in the room of William Woods and that he keep the same in good repair according to law and that William Larkin Esquire Allot him hands to work on the same. Is.

Ordered by the Court that the Order heretofore made at the last Term of this Court authorizing John G. Brazelton to rent out the land belonging to the Legatees of Jacob Miller deceased be recinded and that he be made void the obligation for which he rented said land.

Ordered by the Court that David Hunt, John Larkin David Brown James Neives, Robert Taylor William Larkin, William Freeman be appointed a Jury of view, to view and lay off a road from Blakely School House to the State line of the (p-683) 2nd class as much to the public good, and as little to the prejudice of individuals as practicable and that they report to the next term of this court. Isd.

This day Samuel Miller Esqr. returned to Court a certificate showing that Bryan Caperton William Wallis and abner adams were duly and constitutionally elected commissioners for the school tract of land in Caperton's Cove. Who came into Court and entered into bond with the Chariman of the Court in the sum of one thousand dollars with B. F. Gibson, John Fitzpatrick and William M. Cowan their securities and was qualified according to law.

This day James Byron Esqr returned to Court a certificate showing that James Byron Esqr returned to Court a certificate showing that James Byron, Soloman Holder and John S. Satphen were on the 1st Monday of Jany. 1837 duly and constitutionally electedsshool commissioners in the rock creek School tract who entered into bond payable to the chairman of the Court with William Blackwood and William B. Thompson their securities in the sum of one thousand dollars condition as the law directs and were qualified.

This day William Russell Squire B. Hawkins and John B. Hawkins who were duly and constitutionally elected School commissioners on the Tally Cove School tract as appears from J. S. Cowlin's certificate, came into Court with Joseph Huddleston Jr. and Jess Perkins their securities and entered into bond payable to the chariman of the Court for one thousand dollars, and were quallified.

This day John Nugent Esqr returned in Open Court a certificate certifying that William K. Cowlin, Benajmin Chery and Lawson Rowe were duly and constitutionally elected school commissioners in the 3rd section 9th range who came into Court and entered into bond with Alford A. Loyd and M. Gilliam their securities in the sum of one thousand dollars payable to the chariman of the Court and were qualified.

Benjamin B. Knight Esqr returned to Court a certificate showing that Benjamin B. Knight Samuel Corn Sr. and William Corn were duly and constitutionally elected school commissioners for one year on Rowlands Tract who came into Court and entered into bond payable to James Robinson Chairman of one thousand dollars with William Orear and William Faris their securities and were qualified.

This day James Robinson Esqr. returned to Court a certificate showing that P. S. Decherd Wallis Estill Jr. and F. A. Oakley were duly and constitutionally elected school commissioners in section 2nd and range 8 who entered into bond with James Estill, Thomas Knight (p-664) and a Shook in the sum of one thousand dollars payable to the Chariman of the Court and was qualified.

This day Adam L. Hyder returned to Court a certificate showing that George Hudspeth, William Lucas and William A. Crawford were on the 1st Monday of Jany. 1837 duly and constitutionally elected school commissioners on the School tract at the month of beens Creek for one year who entered into bond payable to the Chairman of the Court for one thousand dollars with David O. Anderson and A. L. Hyder their securities and were qualified.

This day James Keith Esqr returned to Court a certificate showing that William Thurman, Michael Williams and John K. Barton were on the 1st Monday of Jany. 1837 duly and constitutionally elected commissioners on Keiths tract for one year, who came into Court with Charles Woods Sr. and James Bledsoe their securities and entered into bond in the sum of one thousand dollars payable to the chariman of the County Court and were qualified.

This day James F. Green returned to the County Court a certificate showing that John Handly, John Staples and Reuben Scrivner were duly and constitutionally elected school commissioners on the George Town School tract for one year who came into court and entered into bond payable to the Charman of one thousand dollars with James F. Green their security and were qualified.

This day Doctor Wallis Estill administrator of the Estate of R. Crabb deceased returned into Court a Supplement of the estate of said decedent which return was received by the Court and ordered to be recorded.

This day the commissioners of the school tract at the mouth of Beens Creek made their return to the Court which was received by the Court and ordered to be recorded.

On motion it is ordered by the Court that Editha S. D. Hopkins bound as appointed bound to Thomas A. Coleman who entered into Indiredtures with James Robinson Chariman of the Court.

This day the Commissioners of Wagners Creek School Tract made their return which was received by the Court and ordered to be recorded.

This day the commissioners of the school tract in Capertowns Cove made their return which was received by the Court and ordered to be recorded.

(p-665) This day William N. Taylor returned to Court a certificate showing that Joseph Smith, J. M. Brown and Abraham Bagget were duly and constitu- tionally elected on the 1st Monday of January 1837 school commissioners on school Big Harrician Tract for one year who came into Court and entered into bond with Littleton G. Simpson and William N. Taylor in the sum of one thousand dollars and was qualified.

This day the Jury of view heretofore appointed at the last term of this Court to view and turn the road leading to the boat yard made their report which was received by the Court in addition to the report it is ordered that Mathews Shall Open said road agreeable to the report.

This day John R. Patrick administrator of the Estate of Elizabeth Thompson deceased offered his resignation as administrator aforesaid which was received by the Court. Whereupon Robert W. Thompson applied for letters of administration on said decedents estate which was granted who entered into bond with Thomas Robertson his security in the sum of Five Hundred dollars and was qualified accordingly.

The commissioners on Keiths School tract made their report in open Court this day which was received by the Court and ordered to be recorded.

This day James Robinson and Joseph Klepper executors of Adam Gross deceased made and additional return of notes etc which have come to their hands since their former return which was received by the Court and ordered to be recorded.

This day John Staples and John S. Martin returned into Court the value of the hire of the negroes belonging to the minor heirs of Jacob Vanzant deceased which was received by the Court.

This day the commissioners appointed heretofore to settle with Mary Vanzant executrix of Jacob Vanzant deceased made their report which was received by the Court and ordered to be recorded.

This day William Byron produced a certificate from the Sheriff showing that he was duly and constitutionally elected on the 21st day of Jany in District No. 7 one of the constables for said County to fill the vancy of John Byron resigned who entered into bond with John S. Sutphen and James Byron his securities in the sum of one thousand dollars conditional according to law and was quallified.

On the petition of MaryVanzant administratrix of the extate of Jacob Vanzant to the Court to confirm the sale of a negor woman which she sold belonging to said estate and which was not divided when the division of the property took place and the Court being satisfied of the truth of said petition and it appearing to the Court that said negro sold for a fair consideration. Ordered that said sale be received and confirmed.

(p-666). This day David Hunt administrator of the estate of John McCloud decd. returned into open Court a list of the sales of the property belonging to said decedents estate which was received by the Court and ordered to be recorded.

This day John R. Patrick administrator of the estate of Elizabeth Thompson deceased returned to Court an account of the sales belonging to the estate of said decedent which was received by the Court and ordered to be recorded.

It appearing to the satisfaction of the Court that Daniel Donathan late of this county died intestate and William Street applying for letters of administration on said decedents estate whereupon it is ordered by the Court that he have letters accordingly, who entered into bond with M. W. Howell Jr. James Robinson his securities in the sum of two hundred dollars conditioned as the law directs and was qualified.

Ordered by the Court that Isaac Wilkinson be appointed overseer of the road leading from Caldwells Bridge to the Hillsboro from Benjamin Novels to James Howards in the room of Jacob Kellian and that he keep the same in good repair according to law and that he have the same hands that worked under the former overseer.

This day Thomas Finch administrators of the estate of William Thompson deceased made a return of the sales of the negroes belonging to said decedents estate which received by the Court.

Ordered by the Court that Benjamin Powell and John Handley be appointed commissioners for the County to settle with the county officers for the year 1837.

This day the school commissioners of the school tract of land in Talley's Cove made their return as commissioners which was received by the Court and ordered by the Court to be recorded.

This day Thomas Branch offered his resignation as constable to the Court which received by the Court and ordered to be made a part of the record.

This day John M. Morrow offered his resignation as constable to the

Court which was received by the Court.

It is ordered by the Court that Thomas Knight Curator of the estate of William Thompson deceased be allowed the following sum to wit, to 3 days attendance taking an inventory of said Estate at $2 per day to paying John G. Brazelton $2.50 to paying Brazalton for Sanders Faris Clerking $1 and that it be paid out of said decedents estate.

(p-667) Rice Simpson one of the school commissioners on the Hurrican tract made a return of the amt. of the rents of said tract which was received by the Court.

This day Benjamin Decherd and Willie B. Wagner Commissioners to settle with Joseph Klepper and James Robinson executors of the last will and testament of Adam Gross deceased made their return which was received by the Court and ordered to be recorded.

Present M. W. Howell, James Keith Wallis Estill Jr. Samel Miller, J. S. Cawlin, James Bledsoe, James F. Green, M. Gilliam, J. Nugent, S. Cowan James Byron, R. P. Harris, Wm. N. Taylor Z. H. Murrell Wm. Larkin, G. Hudspeth B. B. Knight Esqrs. a legal number of voted for the allowance.

Ordered by the Court that William Rains deceased be allowed the sum of Ten dollars sixty two and an half cents for keeping William Dunaway in Jail of Franklin County from 22nd of April to the 15th of May and for Joining and turnkeys and that the clerk issure a certificate to the county trustee for the same.

Ordered by the Court that Andrew Mann Esqr. be allowed the sum of five dollars for holding an inquest over a dead body and that the clerk issure a certificate to the county Trustee for the same issuance of certificate suspended until papers returned. Isd.

A Power of Attorney from William B. Thompson to G. W. Morris was duly acknowledged in Open Court by the said William Thompson to be his act and deed. Whereupon it is ordered by the Court to be certified.

A power of attorney from Elisha Sims and Jess McGee to Henry A. Rains was duly acknowledged in Open Court by said Elisha Sims and Jess McGee to be their act and deed. Whereupon it is ordered by the Court to be certified by the clerk.

Court adjourned untill tomorrow 11 o'clock

W. Estill Jr.
Stewart Cowan
M. W. Howell

Tuesday the 17th Court met according to adjournment and after reading the minutes of the preceeding day.

Court adjourned until Court in course.

Stewart Cowan
W. Estill Jr.
M. W. Howell

March Term 1837
State of Tennessee
(p-668) At a Court began and held for the County of Franklin at the Court
House in the town of Winchester and being the first Monday and the sixth
day of said month and 61st year of the Indendence of United States.

This day George Wagner Jr. administrator of George Wagner Sr. returned
in open court and inventory of the estate of said decedent and also a list
of the sales of the property of said estate which was received by the Court
and ordered to be recorded.

This day William H. Street administrator of the estate of Daniel
Donathan deceased returned in open Court an inventory of said decedents
estate which was received by the Court and ordered to be recorded.

This day the school commissioners of the Pond Spring school tract of
land returned in Open Court a supplement to the return of 1836 which was
received by the Court and ordered to be recorded.

This day the school commissioners of the school tract of land know
as Rowlands tract made their return in open Court of the proceeds and
disbursements which was received by the Court and ordered to be recorded.

This day John Morrow Sr. produced in Court a certificate from the
Sheriff of Franklin County certifying that he was duly and constitutionally
elected one of the constables in and for said county in district No 11 on
the 25th day of February 1837 who entered into bond with John Morrow Jr.
and John Lefever his securities in the sum of one thousand dollars
conditioned as the law directs and was qualified.

This day George Miller produced in open Court a certificate from the
Sheriff of Franklin County certifying that he was duly & constitutionally
elected constable in and for said county in district No. 12 for the residue
of the two years for which his predecessor was elected, who entered into
bond with Robertson Nevels and John Lefever his securities in the sum of
one thousand dollars conditioned as the law directs and was qualified
accordingly.

This day on election came on for Ranger to fill the vacancy of
Robert Dougan deseased and upon counting out the votes it appeared that
William W. Corn was duly and constitutionally elected Ranger in and for
the county of Franklin untill the 1st Monday of May 1838. Who entered
into bond with Benjamin Decherd and William E. Venable his securities in
the sum of five hundred dollars conditioned as the law directs and was
qualified.

Ordered by the Court that Green B. Holland be appointed overseer of
the road from the mountain to the top of Hill opposite the corner of
(p-669) David Decherds field this side of the Boiling fork at Fitzpatricks
Mill in the room of John H. Burton and that he keep the same in good repair
according to law and that he have the same hands that worked under the
former overseer. Is.

Ordered by the Court that Thomas Adkins be appointed overseer of the road from Thomas Adkins to Goshen Meeting House in the room of James Bledsoe and that he keep the same in good repair according to law and that he have the same hands that worked under the former overseer. Isd.

Ordered by the Court that Andrew McCallum be appointed overseer of the road from John Frances to Manns ford of Elk River in the room of John Lee and that he keep the same in good repair according to law and that he have the same hands that worked under the former overseer. Is.

Ordered by the Court that Moses Gross be appointed overseer of the road from the Rocky Point on the Meherds Ford road to the road leading to Caldwells Bridge and that he keep the same in good repair according to law and that he have the same hands that worked under Noah McElvy. Isd.

Ordered by the Court that James Falkner be appointed overseer of the road of the 2nd class leading from Mansford to Lynchburg to intersect the fayetteville road near Brannans and that he keep the same in good repair according to law and that he have the same hands that worked under John Dewitt. Isd.

Ordered by the Court that William Corn be appointed overseer of the road of the 2nd class from Thomas Knights to Elk River in room of Banister Parton and that he keep the same in good repair and that he have the same hands that worked un der the former overseer.

Ordered by the Court that Ira Kinningham, P. S. Decherd W. J. Heines, Sol Wagner, Col James Lewis Benjamin F. Porter and Madison Porter be appointed a Jury of view to view and lay off a mill road from near Liberty Meeting house to David C. Lewis shop and that they report to the next Term of this Court.

This day William Crownover offered to the Court his resignation as magistrate which was received by the Court.

(p-670)   The Jury of view heretofore appointed at the last term of the County Court to lay off a road from Little Hurican to Brown's Gin made the following report to wit begining at the corner of James Poe's field on a beech tree on the fall Lick Branch down said Branch to intersect the road leading from Big Heurrican at Blacks Old Cribb.

This day the last will and testament of Robert Dougan was produced in Court whereupon came Wallis Estill M. D. and William W. Corn two of the subscribing witness thereto who being duly sworn depose and say that the testator was of sound and disposing mind and memory at the time of signing the same and that they assigned it as witnesses at his request where upon it is ordered to be recorded.

It appearing to the satisfaction of the Court that Zebediah Paine departed this life intestate and also being proved in Court that the relatives of the deceased declined administering and requested John Burrow who is very competent to administer whereupon said Burrows came into and entered into bond with David Burrows and James Jones his securities in a bond of one thousand dollars according to law and was qualified.

It appearing to the Court that Blake Bagget late of this County died intestate and upon application it is ordered by the Court that Abram Bagget have letters of administration who entered into bond with J. H. Brown and W. H. Brown his securities in the sum of one thousand dollars as the law directs and was qualified accordingly.

Ordered by the Court that James Taylor Thomas Wilson John Dougherty Ben Powell, John Handly George Gray and Madison Porter be appointed a Jury of view to lay off a road west of the Female Academy commencing at the Huntsville road running north west out to the lands of Capt. Turners as little to the prejudice of individuals as practicable and that they make return to the next term of this Court.

Ordered by the Court that road where Alexander Clyer has turned it which leads to Fayettville be established and continued thoughout his land Isd.

Ordered by the Court that Kindred H. Muse be appointed overseer of the road leading from Winchester to Shelbyville as far as Sharps Mill in the room of James Sharp Jr. and that he keep the same in good repair according to law and that he have the same hands that worked under the former overseer. Isd.

(p-671) This day Green Mosely produced in open Court a wolf scalp over six mouths old and from his statement an oath the Court was satisfied and ordered that the clerk give him a certificate to the Treasurer of the State for the compensation allowed him agreeable to the acts of assemebly passed 1811 chapter 51 sectionl five Justices Present. Isd.

This day Henry Garner brought into Open Court an old wolf scalp and from the evidence which was adduced it is ordered by the Court that the Clerk give him a certificate to the treasurer of the State that the treasurer may pay him the compensation allowed by the act of assembly passed 1811 chapter 51 section 1st five of the acting justices Present Isd.

Ordered by the Court that James Neaves be appointed overseer of the road of the 3rd class from the corner of Hunts Orchard to the road near William Larkin Esqr and that he keep the same in good repair according to law and that Esqr Larkin allot him hand to work on the same.

Ordered by the Court that William Fulliam be appointed overseer of the road of the 3rd class from Hunts fence where Neeves commences to Crabbs Old store house and that he keep the same in good repair according to law and that Esqr Larkin allot him hands to work on same. Isd.

Ordered by the Court that the keepers of the Poor house take a suitable vehicle and convey Becca Hill a pauper to the poor house. Provided she is willing to go.

Ordered by the Court that Elizabeth Phepps keep an orphan child which is with her untill the next term of this Court or untill she is notified to do otherwise, at the expense of the county.

Ordered by the Court that Harrisan Gilliam be appointed overseer of the road leading from Pelham to Battle Creek in the room of David Goodman and that he keep the same in good repair according to law and that he have the same hands that worked under the former overseer.

Ordered by the Court that John G. Bostick, William S. Mooney and Barney Burrows Esqr. be appointed commissioners to settle with General A.E. Patton administrator of the estate of B. A. Read deceased and that they make return to the next term of this Court and George W. Sarten in lieu of Wm. Mooney with the other two commissioners aforesaid value and divide the negroes among the Legatees of said Decedent. Isd.

(p-672)   Ordered by the Court that Everett Horton be appointed overseer of the road of the 2nd class from the sinking Hollow to Salem and that he keep the same in good repair according to law and that Esqr Heyder and Larkin Allot him hands to work on the same. Isd.

This day James Robinson chariman of the county court offered his resignation as chairman as chairman which was received by the Court.

This day an election came on for chariman an upon counting out the votes it was found that Wallis Estill Jr. was duly and constitutionally elected chariman of the county court of Franklin County untill the 1st Monday in January 1838.

Ordered by the Court the Doctor Elisha Sims, Julias C. Sims, William Corn and George McCutchen be appointed Trustees to view out and lay off a suitable site for a bridge across Elk River.

Present a Majority of all the justice of the peace for Franklin County Ordered by the Court that the tax for county purposes be the same as the State tax on all property which is 5 cents on each hundred dollars and that Poll tax be 25¢ cents for county purposes double the State Tax.

Present M. W. Howell, James Keith W. Estill Jr. James Bledsoe, A. Ss Heyden Asa D. Oakley, Isam Wamack, R. P. Harris M. Catchings, Wm. Larkin B. B. Knight J. Byron, William J. Wood, Jas. S. Cowlin, Saml Miller, Wm. N. Taylor B. Burrow, M. Gilliam, Andrew Mann, James F. Green Esqr. A legal number of whom voted for the allowance ordered by the Court that the county court clerk be allowed twenty nine dollars for two large record books by him purchased for the use of the county, out of any moneys not otherwise appropriated and that a certificate issure to the county trustee for the same.

Present the above justices a legal number of whom voted in the affirmative. Ordered by the Court that the following account be paid to R. P. Harris out of the County Treasury, to wit, 26 lb feathers furnished the poor house 9.75 bed tick 2 bolster 4.25, 3 blankets 10.50 6 yeads calico 2.25 funished. Hannah Arnold 4 yd flannel @ 2.25 making dress .50 amounting to twenty nine dollar and fifty cents and that the clerk of this court issue a certificate to the county trustee for the same. Isd.

Present the above Justices, Ordered by the Court that the commissioners of the poor house be allowed the following sum to wit one dollar per day for attending to the business of said poor house to wit, R. P. Harris 6 days Willis Burt 7 days, James Byran 5 days and Soloman Holder 2 days amounting in all to twenty dollars and that the clerk issure a certificate to the county trustee for the same. Isd to Harris for all.

(p-673) Present the before mentioned justices a legal number of whom voted for the allowance.

Ordered by the Court that James Byron Keeper of the poor house be allowed twenty nine dollars and seventy five cents for keeping Joseph Royalty a Pauper in the poor house from the 23rd of July 1836 to the 2nd of March 1837 at the rate of fifty dollars per year and that the clerk issure a certificate to the county trustee for the same. Isd.

Present the afore named justices a legal number of whom voted for the allowance. Ordered by the Court that the Revenue commissioners be allowed the sum of ten dollars each as a compensation for taking in a list of taxable property and polls liable to taxation in their respective districts for the year 1837 and that the clerk issure a certificate to the trustee of the county for the same. Isd to Cowlin, Oakly, Keith, Heyden Taylor, Byron, Wood, Gilliam, Larkin Estill Cornover, Green Jones, Womack Jas. Wilkinson.

Ordered by the Court that William M. Cowan be allowed the sum of one dollar and fifty cents to pay for a sledge which he bought for the use of the road that crosses the mountain by Montgomerys, and that the clerk issure a certificate to the county Trustee for the same.

Ordered by the Court that William Freeman purchase a sledge for the use of the road over which he is overseer which sledge shall decend to his successors for the use aforesaid and present his account to the Court. Isd.

Ordered by the Court that William Hudson be appointed overseer of the road leading to Caldwell's Bridge from the Boiling Fork to in the room of Robert Hill and that he keep the same in good repair according to law and that he have the same hands that worked under the former overseer.

Court adjourned untill tomorrow 10 o'clock.
                                        W. Estill
                                        M. W. Howell
                                        Asa D. Oakly

Tuedday the 7th day of March A. D. 1837
Court met according to adjournment Present Wallis Estill Jr. and
M. W. Howell Esqrs.
Court Adjourned untill tomorrow 10 o'clock
                                        W. Estill Jr.
                                        M. W. Howell
                                        Asa D. Oakley

(p-674)   Wednesday the 8th day of March A. D. 1837 pursuant to adjournment Present Wallis Estill M. W. Howell Asa D. Oakly Esqrs.

This day Doctor Wallis Estill administrator of the Estate of Ralph Crabb deceased returned into open Court an additional list of the sales of property belonging to said Estate which was received by the Court and ordered to be recorded.

Ordered by the Court that Thomas Finch Sheriff and Collector of the public for Franklin County has a credit of eight dollars eighty five cents ~~here by seven and half cents~~ pon a settlement of his account with the county treasure for delinquents or insolvents and twice listed property on the tax list per the year 1836.

Ordered by the Court that Thomas Finch Sheriff and Collector of the public Tax for Franklin County have credit of four dollars twelve and half cents an a settlement of his account with the treasure of the state for Delinquents and insolvent & twice listed property on the tax list for the year 1836. Isd.

Ordered by the Court that Thomas Finch Sheriff and collector of the public tax for Franklin County be charged with one hundred and twenty five dollars on a settlement of his accounts with the treasurer of the State for tax collected on Caperton's old turn pike gate for the year 1831 1832-1833-1834-1835 which one hundred and twenty five dollars was collected on the 12th of September 1838.

It appearing to the satisfaction of the Court that Moses Cook late of this county died intestate and John Dewitt applying for letters of administration on said decedents Estate. It is ordered by the Court that he have letters of administration who entered into bond with Moses Chambers his security in the sum of one thousand dollars conditioned as the law directs and was qualified.

Ordered by the Court that Willy Denson John Hardly and James F. Green be appointed commissioners to lay off to the widow Donathan wife of Daniel Donathan Decd. one years support out of said decedents estate.

This day Thomas Finch Sheriff and collector of the publick tax for Franklin County reported in Court a list of the land, Town lost, Slaves and white polls on which he has collected a double tax for the year 1836 which amounted to fifty two dollars and eighty one cents, which will be seen by reference to pages 2-3-4-5- of said report which was received by the Court and ordered that the clerk of this court render a copy thereof ot the treasurer and County Trustee also be reported to Court at lands, Town lots white polls for double taxes for (p-675)   the year 1836 which is not collected, which will be seen by refference to pages six and seven of said report and it is ordered by the Court that the Clerk render a copy of the above to the treasurer of the State and county trustee.

Court adjourned untill court in course.
                              W. Estill Jr.
                              Asa D. Oakly
                              M. W. Howell.

April Term 1837
State of Tennessee
At a County Court began and held for the County of Franklin and
state aforesaid at the court house in the Town of Winchester on the 1st
Monday of April one thousand eight hundred an thirty seven and on the 3rd
day of said month it being the 61st year of the Independence of the
United States. Present a legal number of the Justices.

Ordered that Molachi Simpson be appointed overseer of the
Mannsford road to the 12 miles post and that he keep the same in good
repair according to law and that he have the same hands that worked under
the former overseer.

This day Capt. John Turner came into open Court and made oath that
a certain cow which he had posted was dead to the best of his knowledge
it is therefore ordered by the Court that he be released from paying half
the appraisment money and that the clerk issure a certificate to the
Ranger. Is.

Ordered by the Court that all those persons who failed listing their
taxable property and polls liable to taxation by the 10th day of February
last past as the law requires but since has listed be exempted from paying
double tax.

This day Wallis Estill chariman of the Court on behalf of the Justices
entered into indentures with Thomas Muse and placed under him a certain
minor orphan child named Sarah E. Baxter about five or six years old, who
is to live with said Muse untill she arrives at full age or be sooner
married and said Muse is to give her a commer education such as to read
and write and a good bed and furniture.

Ordered by the Court that Thomas Muse take an inventory of the
property belonging to Sarah E. Baxter an orphan child who is bound to him
and present the same to the next term of this court.

Ordered by the Court that James Byron Esqr. allot hands to the
following overseer to work the road leading from Winchester (p-676)
to Shelbyville to work on their divisions to wit, to Dennis B. Muse,
Thomas Coleman, William Lasater, Jonathan Runnels and Stephen Lakey.

Ordered by the Court that Willis Young, Edmund Young, Edward Darnaly
Senr. Joseph Franklin, Geo Tipps, Joshua Franklin and William A. Breedin
be appointed a Jury of view to examine and turn the road leading from
Mann Ford to Winchester and that they report to the next term of this court.

Ordered by the Court that Amazine King David Hunt B. Higambotham
W. Acklin and M. D. Embery be appointed a Jury of view to view a road
from David Bell's black smith shop to his saw mill and that they report
to the next term of this court. This day the commissioners of the school
land on rock creek made their return which was received by the court and
ordered to be recorded.

This day O. D. Street and W. H. Street Executors of Wm. Street
deceased returned to Court an inventory of the estate of said decedent

which was received by the Court and ordered to be recorded.

This day R. P. Harris executor of Josiah Muse deceased returned to Open Court an inventory of said Decedents estate which was received by the Court and ordered to be recorded. Armon Gypson Constable in district No.9 offered his resignation as constable aforesaid to the Court which was received by the Court.

This day Susan Trigg returned in open Court by her agent J. R. Patrick Esqr. a statement of the amount for which the negroes hired that belongs to the Heirs of William Trigg deceased which was received by the Court and ordered to be recorded.

Ordered by the Court that the order heretofore made establishing the road where Alexander Colyer had turned it leading to Fayetteville be amended to read thus. Ordered by the Court that the road where Alexander Colyer has turned it which leads to Fayetteville be established and continue through out his land provided he said Colyer put the same in as good repair as the former road, and George Hudspeth & William Larkin Esqr will record it.

This day R. P. Harris executor of Josiah Muse Decd. returned to Court a list of the sale of the property belonging to said decedents estate which was received by the Court and ordered to be recorded.

This day John Burrows administrator of Zebediah Paine deceased returned to Court an inventory of the estate of said decedent which was received by the Court and ordered to be recorded.

(p-677)   This day Joseph Newman produced in Court a certificate from the Sheriff certifying that he was duly and constitutionally elected one of the constables in and for the said County in District No. 8 in room of John H. Duncan resigned to fill out the term for which said Duncan was elected who entered into bond of one thousand dollars with B. B. Knight and Thos Howard his securities conditioned as the law directs and was legally qualified.

Ordered by the Court that John C. Lipscomb be appointed overseer of the road Huntsville road from Beans Creek to where the Fayetteville road turns out, in the room of William Holliday and that he keep the same in good repair according to law and that he have the same hands that work under the former overseer. Isd.

Ordered by the Court that the order heretofore at the last Term of this Court appointing a Jury of view to lay off a certain road immediately west of the Female Academy be made returnable to the next term of this court in order that the jury of view may have time to make out their report. In as muchas the Sheriff had not time to summon the Jurors it is ordered by the Court that the order made at the last term of this court to a Jury of view to lay off a road from near liberty Meeting house to D. C. Lewis Blacksmith shop be made returnable to the next term of this Court.

Ordered by the Court that the following persons be appointed Jurors

to July Term of the circuit Court 1837 to wit, Richard Sharp Senr.
Benjamin Decherd Asa D. Oakly Dudly Johnson, George H. Britton
Samuel Rickett, David Arnet Joseph Rich, Joseph Baker, John Faris
Daniel Weaver, Rice Simpson George Rowland, R. P. Harris, Thomas Howard
Julias C. Sims William K. Cowlin, F. Hendrix, William S. Mooney, Jessie
Gotcher Reberson Nevels, Lewis Perkins James Cowan, James Bledsoe,
Saml. Norwood, Meredith Catching and John G. Brazelton and Sanders Faris
constable to attend and wait on said Court and that the sheriff summon all
the aforementioned persons to attend said Court.

This day Barnabus Johnson Jr. Jeremiah Smith and William Hicks came
into Open Court and made oath in due form of law that Barnabus Johnson
Senr. departed this Life on the 2nd of June 1836 and at that time was on
the roll list of Pensones.

(p-578)   Ordered by the Court that Alford A. Loyd be appointed overseer
of the Meherdford road of the 2nd Class from the Green Swamp Creek to the
widow Keetons and that he keep the same in good repair according to law
and that he have the same hands that worked under the former overseer.

Inconformity with an order made at March Term Willie Denson and
James F. Green proceeded to lay off to Delila Donathan Widow of James
Donathan Decd one years provisions out of said decedents estate and made
their return to the Court wjich was received by the court.

Ordered by the Court that the clerk of this Court draft Rules and
Regulations for the Government of this Court which shall be submitted to
the Court of their rejection or reception at the next term of this Court.

Court adjourned untill tomorrow 9 o'clock.
                                        W. Estill Jr.
                                        M. W. Howell
                                        James Bledsoe

Tuesday the 4th day of April in the year of our Lord one thousand
eight hundred and thirty seven Court met according to adjournment. Present
Esqrs. Estill Jr. James Bledsoe M. W. Howell and after reading the minutes
of the preceeding day and signing them.
                                        W. Estill Jr.
                                        M. W. Howell
                                        James Bledsoe

Court adjourned untill Court in course.

www.ingramcontent.com/pod-product-compliance
Lightning Source LLC
Chambersburg PA
CBHW051425290326
41932CB00048B/3157